Band 54: Fehlertolerierende Rechnersysteme. GI-Fachtagung, München, März 1982. Herausgegeben von E. Nett und H. Schwärtzel. VII, 322 Seiten. 1982.

Band 55: W. Kowalk, Verkehrsanalyse in endlichen Zeiträumen. VI, 181 Seiten. 1982.

Band 56: Simulationstechnik. Proceedings, 1982. Herausgegeben von M. Goller. VIII, 544 Seiten. 1982.

Band 57: GI-12. Jahrestagung. Proceedings, 1982. Herausgegeben von J. Nehmer. IX, 732 Seiten. 1982.

Band 58: GWAI-82. 6th German Workshop on Artificial Intelligence. Bad Honnef, September 1982. Edited by W. Wahlster. VI, 246 pages. 1982.

Band 59: Künstliche Intelligenz. Frühjahrsschule Teisendorf, März 1982. Herausgegeben von W. Bibel und J. H. Siekmann. XIII, 383 Seiten. 1982.

Band 60: Kommunikation in Verteilten Systemen. Anwendungen und Betrieb. Proceedings, 1983. Herausgegeben von Sigram Schindler und Otto Spaniol. IX, 738 Seiten. 1983.

Band 61: Messung, Modellierung und Bewertung von Rechensystemen. 2. GI/NTG-Fachtagung, Stuttgart, Februar 1983. Herausgegeben von P. J. Kühn und K. M. Schulz. VII, 421 Seiten. 1983.

Band 62: Ein inhaltsadressierbares Speichersystem zur Unterstützung zeitkritischer Prozesse der Informationswiedergewinnung in Datenbanksystemen. Michael Malms. XII, 228 Seiten. 1983.

Band 63: H. Bender, Korrekte Zugriffe zu Verteilten Daten. VIII, 203 Seiten. 1983.

Band 64: F. Hoßfeld, Parallele Algorithmen. VIII, 232 Seiten. 1983.

Band 65: Geometrisches Modellieren. Proceedings, 1982. Herausgegeben von H. Nowacki und R. Gnatz. VII, 399 Seiten. 1983.

Band 66: Applications and Theory of Petri Nets. Proceedings, 1982. Edited by G. Rozenberg. VI, 315 pages. 1983.

Band 67: Data Networks with Satellites. GI/NTG Working Conference, Cologne, September 1982. Edited by J. Majus and O. Spaniol. VI, 251 pages. 1983.

Band 68: B. Kutzler, F. Lichtenberger, Bibliography on Abstract Data Types. V, 194 Seiten. 1983.

Band 69: Betrieb von DN-Systemen in der Zukunft. GI-Fachgespräch, Tübingen, März 1983. Herausgegeben von M. A. Graef. VIII, 343 Seiten. 1983.

Band 70: W. E. Fischer, Datenbanksystem für CAD-Arbeitsplätze. VII, 222 Seiten. 1983.

Band 71: First European Simulation Congress ESC 83. Proceedings, 1983. Edited by W. Ameling. XII, 653 pages. 1983.

Band 72: Sprachen für Datenbanken. GI-Jahrestagung, Hamburg, Oktober 1983. Herausgegeben von J. W. Schmidt. VII, 237 Seiten. 1983.

Band 73: GI-13. Jahrestagung, Hamburg, Oktober 1983. Proceedings. Herausgegeben von J. Kupka. VIII, 502 Seiten. 1983.

Band 74: Requirements Engineering. Arbeitstagung der GI, 1983. Herausgegeben von G. Hommel und D. Krönig. VIII, 247 Seiten. 1983.

Band 75: K. R. Dittrich, Ein universelles Konzept zum flexiblen Informationsschutz in und mit Rechensystemen. VIII, 246 pages. 1983.

Band 76: GWAI-83. German Workshop on Artificial Intelligence. September 1983. Herausgegeben von B. Neumann. VI, 240 Seiten. 1983.

Band 77: Programmiersprachen und Programmentwicklung. 8. Fachtagung der GI, Zürich, März 1984. Herausgegeben von U. Ammann. VIII, 239 Seiten. 1984.

Band 78: Architektur und Betrieb von Rechensystemen. 8. GI-NTG-Fachtagung, Karlsruhe, März 1984. Herausgegeben von H. Wettstein. IX, 391 Seiten. 1984.

Band 79: Programmierumgebungen: Entwicklungswerkzeuge und Programmiersprachen. Herausgegeben von W. Sammer und W. Remmele. VIII, 236 Seiten. 1984.

Band 80: Neue Informationstechnologien und Verwaltung. Proceedings, 1983. Herausgegeben von R. Traunmüller, H. Fiedler, K. Grimmer und H. Reinermann. XI, 402 Seiten. 1984.

Band 81: Koordinaten von Informationen. Proceedings, 1983. Herausgegeben von R. Kuhlen. VI, 366 Seiten. 1984.

Band 82: A. Bode, Mikroarchitekturen und Mikroprogrammierung: Formale Beschreibung und Optimierung, 6, 7-227 Seiten. 1984.

Band 83: Software-Fehlertoleranz und -Zuverlässigkeit. Herausgegeben von F. Belli, S. Pfleger und M. Seifert. VII, 297 Seiten. 1984.

Band 84: Fehlertolerierende Rechensysteme. 2. GI/NTG/GMR-Fachtagung, Bonn 1984. Herausgegeben von K.-E. Großpietsch und M. Dal Cin. X, 433 Seiten. 1984.

Band 85: Simulationstechnik. Proceedings, 1984. Herausgegeben von F. Breitenecker und W. Kleinert. XII, 676 Seiten. 1984.

Band 86: Prozeßrechner 1984. 4. GI/GMR/KfK-Fachtagung, Karlsruhe, September 1984. Herausgegeben von H. Trauboth und A. Jaeschke. XII, 710 Seiten. 1984.

Band 87: Musterkennung 1984. Proceedings, 1984. Herausgegeben von W. Kropatsch. IX, 351 Seiten. 1984.

Band 88: GI-14. Jahrestagung. Braunschweig. Oktober 1984. Proceedings. Herausgegeben von H.-D. Ehrich. IX, 451 Seiten. 1984.

Band 89: Fachgespräche auf der 14. GI-Jahrestagung. Braunschweig, Oktober 1984. Herausgegeben von H.-D. Ehrich. V, 267 Seiten. 1984.

Band 90: Informatik als Herausforderung an Schule und Ausbildung. GI-Fachtagung, Berlin, Oktober 1984. Herausgegeben von W. Arlt und K. Haefner. X, 416 Seiten. 1984.

Band 91: H. Stoyan, Maschinen-unabhängige Code-Erzeugung als semantikerhaltende beweisbare Programmtransformation. IV, 365 Seiten. 1984.

Band 92: Offene Multifunktionale Büroarbeitsplätze. Proceedings, 1984. Herausgegeben von F. Krückeberg, S. Schindler und O. Spaniol. VI, 335 Seiten. 1985.

Band 93: Künstliche Intelligenz. Frühjahrsschule Dassel, März 1984. Herausgegeben von C. Habel. VII, 320 Seiten. 1985.

Band 94: Datenbank-Systeme für Büro, Technik und Wirtschaft. Proceedings, 1985. Herausgegeben von A. Blaser und P. Pistor. X, 519 Seiten. 1985

Band 95: Kommunikation in Verteilten Systemen I. GI-NTG-Fachtagung, Karlsruhe, März 1985. Herausgegeben von D. Heger, G. Krüger, O. Spaniol und W. Zorn. IX, 691 Seiten. 1985.

Band 96: Organisation und Betrieb der Informationsverarbeitung. Proceedings, 1985. Herausgegeben von W. Dirlewanger. XI, 261 Seiten. 1985.

Band 97: H. Willmer, Systematische Software-Qualitätssicherung anhand von Qualitäts- und Produktmodellen. VII, 162 Seiten. 1985.

Informatik-Fachberichte 143

Herausgegeben von W. Brauer
im Auftrag der Gesellschaft für Informatik (GI)

R. R. Wagner R. Traunmüller
H. C. Mayr (Hrsg.)

Informationsbedarfsermittlung und -analyse für den Entwurf von Informationssystemen

Fachtagung EMISA
Linz, 2. und 3. Juli 1987

Proceedings

Springer-Verlag
Berlin Heidelberg New York
London Paris Tokyo

Herausgeber

R. R. Wagner
Abteilung für Informationssysteme
R. Traunmüller
Abteilung für Informatik in Wirtschaft,
Technik und Gesellschaft
Johannes Kepler Universität Linz
Altenbergerstr. 69, A-4040 Linz

H. C. Mayr
KMK Kreutz & Mayr Ges. für Datentechnik mbH
Karlstr. 97-99, D-7500 Karlsruhe 1

CR Subject Classifications (1987): H.1, H.4, K.6.1

ISBN-13: 978-3-540-18052-4   e-ISBN: 978-3-642-72821-1
DOI: 10.1007/978-3-642-72821-1

Repro- u. Druckarbeiten: Weihert-Druck GmbH, Darmstadt
Bindearbeiten: Druckhaus Beltz, Hemsbach/Bergstraße
2145/3140-543210

VORWORT

Die Fachgruppe EMISA der GI (Bonn) beschäftigt sich mit Methoden und Werkzeugen für den Entwurf von Informationssystemen. Dabei haben verschiedene Tagungen der Fachgruppe spezielle Phasen oder Probleme des Entwurfsvorganges detailliert untersucht. In der Linzer Fachtagung sollen vor allem jene Fragen angeschnitten werden, die am Beginn eines jeden Entwurfes von Informationssystemen stehen müssen.

Obwohl der Informationsbedarfsermittlung und -analyse im Lebenszyklus eines Informationssystems zentrale Bedeutung zukommt, wird sie bislang noch immer wesentlich weniger beherrscht als die nachfolgenden Entwicklungsschritte. Die Fachtagung soll daher ein Forum schaffen, mit dem Praktiker und Wissenschaftler die zur Lösung anstehenden Probleme identifizieren und existierende Ansätze diskutieren. Das Tagungsprogramm überdeckt daher die gesamte Bandbreite, ausgehend von Erfahrungen mit bereits in der Praxis eingesetzten Verfahren bis zur Präsentation des aktuellen Standes der Entwicklung neuer Methoden.

Die Tagung wird gemeinsam mit den drei Informatikgesellschaften des deutschen Sprachraumes (Gesellschaft für Informatik, Österreichische Gesellschaft für Informatik, Schweizer Gesellschaft für Informatik) in Zusammenarbeit mit dem Institut für Informatik der Johannes Kepler Universität durchgeführt. Dabei hat sich das Programmkomitee zum Ziel gesetzt, aus der großen Anzahl der eingegangenen Arbeiten eine Auswahl vorzunehmen, in der fachliche Strenge und Vielseitigkeit der Standpunkte ausgewogen sind.

Die Herausgeber des Tagungsbandes danken dem Programmkomitee herzlich für die umfangreiche Bewertung: H. Ehrich (Braunschweig), P.C. Lockemann (Karlsruhe), B. E. Meyer (Heilbronn), E. Neuhold (Darmstadt), E. R. Reichl (Linz), G. Richter (Birlinghoven), H. J. Schneider (Berlin), A. Schulz (Linz), H. Thoma (Basel), M. Vetter (Zürich).

Die Vorbereitung der Tagung wurde von Mitgliedern des Institutes für Informatik übernommen, denen für ihr Engagement herzlich gedankt sei. Es sind dies die Damen und Herren Ch. Bauer, Ch. Gierlinger, V. Kadlec, A. Petz, I. Prock. Besonders gedankt sei Frl. V. Kadlec, die das Tagungssekretariat und die Gestaltung des Tagungsbandes übernommen hat. Die schon gewohnte gute Zusammenarbeit mit dem Verlag Springer sei ebenfalls erwähnt.

Die Herausgeber des Tagungsbandes hoffen, daß mit vorliegendem Band ein bisher in der wissenschaftlichen Literatur wenig bearbeitetes Gebiet so dokumentiert ist, wie es seiner Bedeutung bei der Gestaltung von Informationssystemen entspricht.

R. R. Wagner
R. Traunmüller
H. C. Mayr

Linz und Karlsruhe, 21. April 1987

INHALTSVERZEICHNIS

EINGELADENE VORTRÄGE

A Methodology for Joint Data and Functional Analysis   1
  C. Batini, S. Ceri

Formalizing Requirements Systematically   44
  A. Finkelstein, C. Potts

METHODEN I

Three-Level-Specification of Databases using an
  extended Entity-Relationship Model   58
  U. Hohenstein, L. Neugebauer, G. Saake, H.-D. Ehrich

Induktive und deduktive Ermittlung des Informationsbedarfs   89
  J. Eder, R. Mittermeir, H. Wernhart

METHODEN II

A Comparative Analysis of View Integration Methodologies   119
  M. Schrefl

Der Einsatz der Modellierungssprache OBLOG zum Entwurf
  von Juristischen Expertensystemen im Wege des Prototyping
  am Beispiel eines Modells des Verfahrens der Eidesstattlichen
  Versicherung   137
  T.F. Gordon, G. Quirchmayr

WERKZEUGE

Prototyping zur Unterstützung des konzeptuellen Entwurfs
  interaktiver Informationssysteme   155
  F. Schönthaler, A. Oberweis, G. Lausen, W. Stucky

Eine Prototyp-Entwicklung auf der Basis eines relationalen
  DBMS   181
  W. Hesse

Werkzeuge zum Entwurf von verteilten Informationssystemen
im Büro   201
J. Niemeier, A. Ness, F. Reim

ERFAHRUNGEN

Informationsbedarfsermittlung für die Gestaltung eines
Bürgeramtes   227
H. Stuhlmann

Entwicklung eines Dokumentationssystems für
Diabetespatienten   244
R. Engelbrecht, I. Kunze, J. Schneider

A METHODOLOGY FOR JOINT DATA AND FUNCTIONAL ANALYSIS

C. BATINI

Dipartimento di Informatica e Sistemistica

Universita' di Roma "La Sapienza" Italy

S. CERI

Dipartimento di Matematica

Universita' di Modena - Italy

Abstract: In this paper we propose an integrated approach to the analysis of data and functions in informaion systems. We show how data and functions can be analyzed jointly, in terms of the models used for their representation, the strategies followed and the qualities that should be achieved. The proposed methodology is finally applied to a case study.

1. INTRODUCTION

The analysis phase is usually placed in the information systems life-cycle after requirement collection, and before the design phase. The main goal of the analysis activity is the production of a high level representation of the resources of the information system. Such resources belong to two main categories, data and functions: they are represented during the analysis activity in such a way to suppress all details concerning the target systems and languages, and highlight their abstract structure and properties.

The first methodologies for the analysis of information systems, developed in the sixties or seventies, were focused almost exclusively on functional analysis (see for example, [DE MARCO 1981], [GANE SARSON 1979], [ROSS 1977]; data were taken into consideration only after developing a complete description of functions. Recently, data have gained a greater importance and an autonomous role for information systems analysis. Many approaches, as for instance in [OLLE SOL VERIJIN STUART 1982], [OLLE SOL TULLY 1983], [LUNDBERG], [CERI 1983], [ALBANO DE ANTONELLIS DI LEVA 1985], emphasize the importance of an early, precise description of data. In fact, if we compare data and functions, we argue that data are more valuable for the designer than functions. Data are considered as a relatively stable, processing-independent resource of the enterprise; while functions are less stable and more influenced by the current situation of the enterprise.

In this paper, we propose an integrated approach to data and functional analysis. We show how data and functions can be jointly analyzed, in terms of the models used for their representation, the strategies followed in the refinement process, and the qualities that should be achieved. Sections 2 compares models, strategies and qualities, showing similarities and differences between the two types of analyses. Section 3 presents our joint approach to data and functional analysis. The method of Section 4 is finally applied in Section 5 to a large case study.

2. METHODOLOGIES FOR THE ANALYSIS ACTIVITY

In this section we introduce the main features of methodologies for data and functional analysis. They correspond to: (1) models used in representing the object of the analysis activity, i.e. the data and functional schemas; (2) strategies typically followed in producing them; (3) qualities that should be achieved by schemas, both separately and considered together.

2.1 MODELS FOR DATA AND FUNCTIONAL ANALYSIS

Data analysis is concerned with the modelling of an information system in terms of data classes and their properties. The result of data analysis is producing a data schema (D-schema in the following) which represents all data classes of interest for the application, and their main properties. Various models have been proposed in the last ten years for data analysis. The common aspect to most of
them is the use of various abstraction mechanisms to represent the properties of data, like classification, generalization, aggregation. In the paper we make use of one of the most popular data model, the Entity Relationship model, in which the above abstractions are represented (according to [CERI 1983] by means of the following concepts:

1. An Entity represents a class of objects of the real world having common properties.
2. A Relationship represents a class of facts of the real world, defined among entities.
3   An Attribute is an elementary property of an entity or a relationship.
4. A Subset and a Generalization among entities relate respectively one or a group of entities to an new entity that represents their generalization abstraction.

Functional analysis is concerned with the modelling of an information system in terms of working activities and information flows between them. Functional analysis concentrates on the understanding of how information is used by each function, and is exchanged among functions. The ultimate result of functional analysis is producing a functional schema (F-schema) which contains a representation of activities, information flows, and other features. The F-schema includes the representation of database applications and of the interactions between them. We can consider this representation as the "dynamic description of the database", opposed to the "static description of the database" offered by the D-schema.

Different models for functional analysis have been proposed, emphasizing different features; for instance, some models concentrate on data and flows exchanged between activities, while other models concentrate on the synchronization of activities. In this paper we have selected a very simple model, the model of Dataflow Diagrams (DFD), which is convenient for our purposes. The model supports the following concepts:

1. A Process represents an activity within the information system. In particular, a process can generate, use, manipulate, or destroy information.When a process does not generateor destroy information, it transforms the data in the incoming flows into the data in the outgoing flows.

2. A Data Flow is an exchange of information between processes. Data flows do not represent flows of control, such as the activation of processes. They indicate instead processes' inputs or outputs as movements of discrete packets of data.

3. A Data Store is a repository of information. An edge from a data store to a process indicates that data from the store is used by the process; an edge from a process to a data store means that the process changes the content of the store in some way.

4. An Interface is an external user of the information system, that may be originator and/or receiver of data flows.

DFDs can be considered the simplest and more abstract representation for processes and information flows. This simplicity is deliberate, and stems from the position that no aspect related to causal and time relationships between processes should be expressed during the analysis: these are considered as procedural aspects, typical of the design phases. Data in DFDs are either represented by information flows or by permanently stored information, thus stressing a dynamic exchange and a static repository.

A different point of view is adopted in SADT diagrams ([ROSS 1977]) and Petri Nets ([PETERSON 1979]). In SADT diagrams, four different roles are distinguished among flows; in particular control flows allow to express to a certain extent the procedurality among processes: concurrency of activities however is left unspecified. At the same time, in SADT there is no mention of stored data, whose representation is left outside the activity model. Pure Petri Nets allow giving a precise description of concurrency, because the model is based on a sound mathematical theory. At the same time, Petri Nets do not include concepts for describing "static" information, neither flows not stores.

2.2 STRATEGIES FOR DATA AND FUNCTIONAL ANALYSIS

The process of producing an overall schema (data or functional) of the enterprise is complex, and typically performed by means of iterative steps; we describe now the primitives to transform an input schema into an output schema, and then the strategies to generate progressively a complex schema, showing similarities and differences among data and functional analysis.

The analysis of a schema evolves by iterating several SCHEMA TRANSFORMATIONS, with the following features:

1. Each transformation has a STARTING SCHEMA and a RESULTING SCHEMA.

2. Each transformation maps NAMES of concepts in the starting schema into names of concepts in the resulting schema.

3. Concepts in the resulting schema must inherit all LOGICAL LINKS defined for concepts of the starting schema.

The simplest transformations are called PRIMITIVES; they can be classified as TOP-DOWN or BOTTOM-UP. Top-down primitives have a single concept as starting schema, and produce a richer description of that concept in the resulting schema. By contrast, bottom-up primitives introduce new concepts and properties that do not appear in previous versions of the schema. In fig 1 and fig 2 we show several possible top-down and and bottom-up primitives for data analysis and functional analysis.

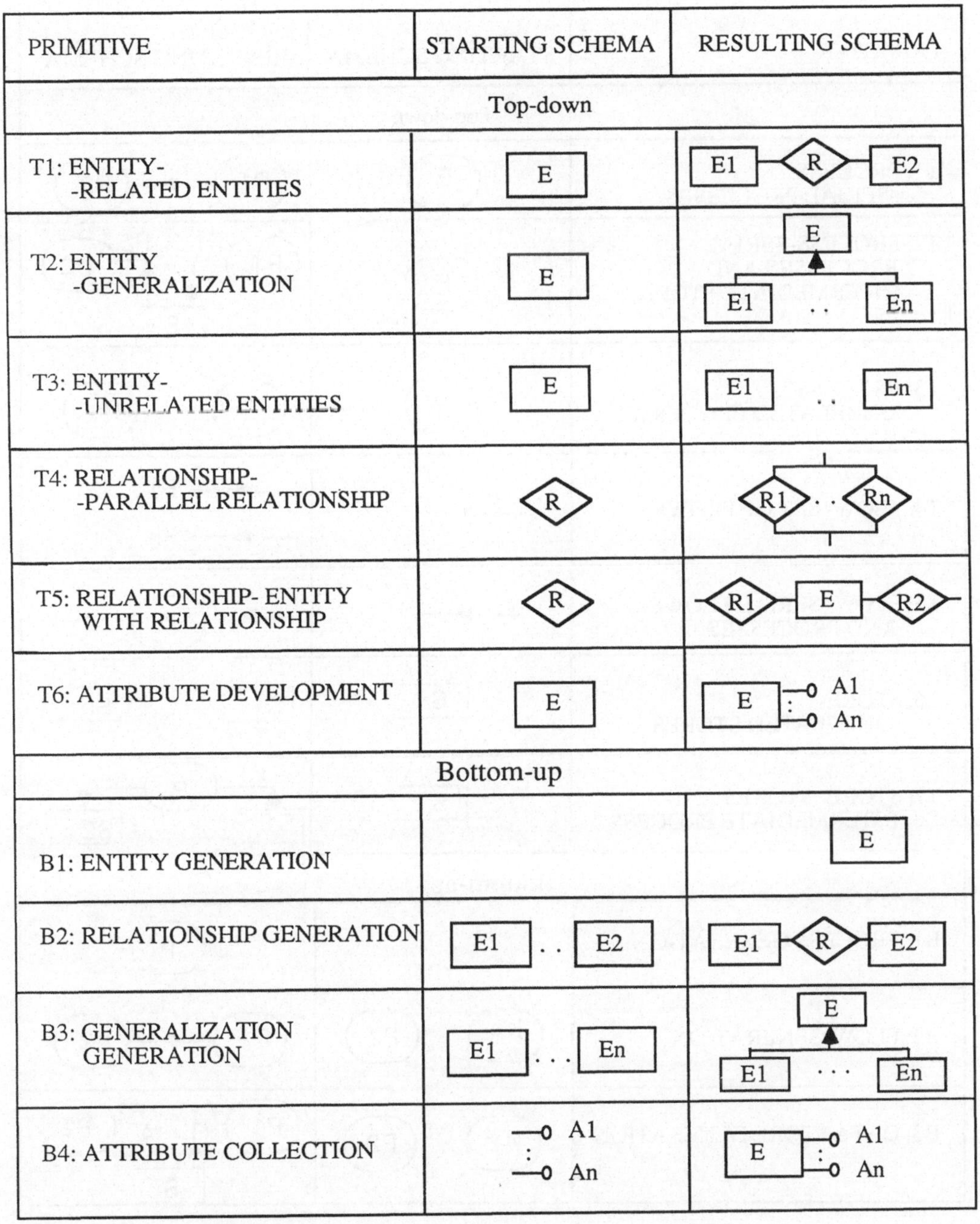

PRIMITIVE	STARTING SCHEMA	RESULTING SCHEMA
Top-down		
T1: ENTITY- -RELATED ENTITIES	E	E1 —◇R◇— E2
T2: ENTITY -GENERALIZATION	E	E ↑ E1 .. En
T3: ENTITY- -UNRELATED ENTITIES	E	E1 .. En
T4: RELATIONSHIP- -PARALLEL RELATIONSHIP	◇R◇	◇R1◇..◇Rn◇
T5: RELATIONSHIP- ENTITY WITH RELATIONSHIP	◇R◇	◇R1◇— E —◇R2◇
T6: ATTRIBUTE DEVELOPMENT	E	E —o A1 ⋮ —o An
Bottom-up		
B1: ENTITY GENERATION		E
B2: RELATIONSHIP GENERATION	E1 .. E2	E1 —◇R◇— E2
B3: GENERALIZATION GENERATION	E1 ... En	E ↑ E1 ⋯ En
B4: ATTRIBUTE COLLECTION	—o A1 ⋮ —o An	E —o A1 ⋮ —o An

Fig. 1   Top-down and bottom-up primitives for data analysis

PRIMITIVE	STARTING SCHEMA	RESULTING SCHEMA
Top-down		
T1: PROCESS- -SERIAL PROCESSES	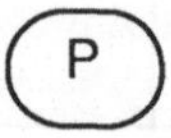	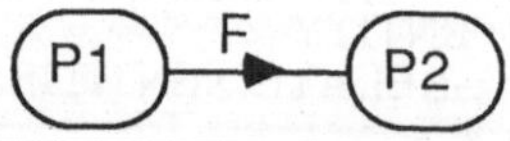
T2: PROCESS-SERIAL PROCESSES AND INTERMEDIATE STORE	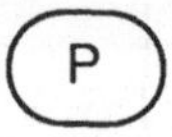	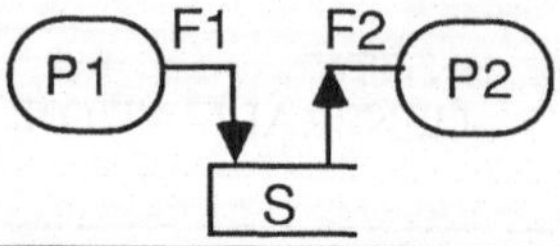
T3: PROCESS- -UNRELATED PROCESSES	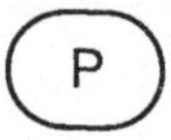	
T4: FLOW- SET OF FLOWS		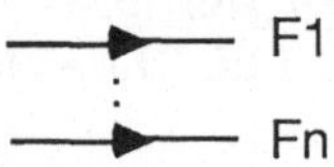
T5: FLOW- SERIAL FLOWS AND PROCESSES		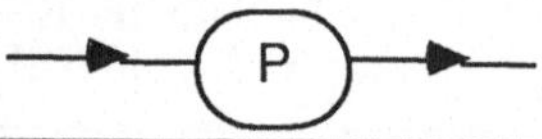
T6: STORE- -UNRELATED STORES	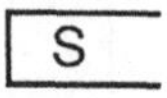	
T7: STORE- STORES AND INTERMEDIATE PROCESS		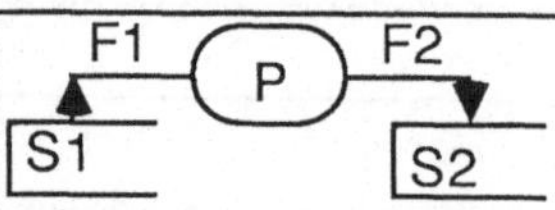
Bottom-up		
B1: PROCESS GENERATION		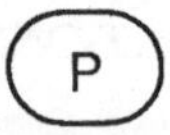
B2: FLOW GENERATION	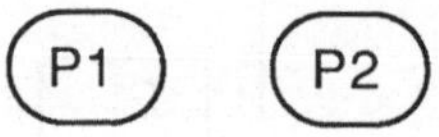	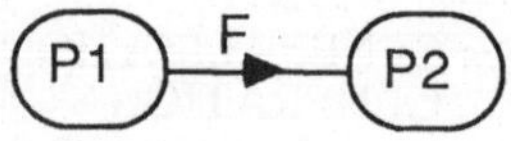
B3: DATA STORE GENERATION	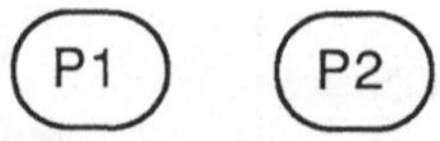	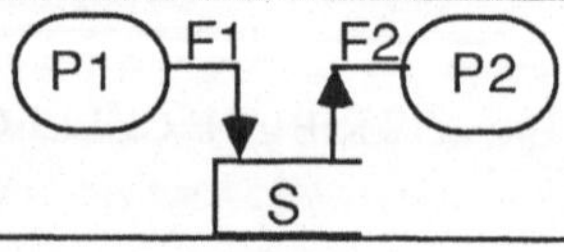

Fig. 2   Top-down and bottom-up primitives for functional analysis

In the attempt of isolating a Complete set of primitives, we find a difference between data analysis and functional analysis: while in the Entity Relationship model data abstractions are represented by a rich variety of concepts, in DFDs the concept of PROCESS is the only means of representing a variety of types of activities. For this reason, it is more difficult to isolate a complete set of primitives for functional analysis.

The above primitives can be composed in the analysis process according to several analysis strategies. We examine four of them: top-down, bottom-up, inside out, and mixed.

a. Top-down strategy

A top-down strategy consists in the application of "pure" top-down primitives, i.e. primitives such that each application produces the refinement of a single concept. In data analysis, pure top-down primitives correspond to applying the abstraction mechanisms as refinement mechanisms (see fig 1); in functional analysis, since the concept of process is the most important one, it is crucial to indicate how to perform the decomposition of a process into subprocesses. The most powerful criterium is called FUNCTIONAL INDEPENDENCE. The key idea is to decompose each process into well distinguished subprocesses, which are as much independent on each other as possible. In other words, each process should be clearly identifiable, and the connections among subprocesses should be weak. Primitives T1, T2, and T3 of fig 2 produce a top-down refinement of processes and should be largely used during the top-down analysis of a DFD.

b. Bottom-up strategy

With a bottom-up strategy, a schema is built by starting from a collection of elementary concepts and by building the connections between them. Requirements are decomposed, independently conceptualized and finally merged into a global schema. Note that the first step of the bottom-up approach is better defined in data analysis, as it produces the set of all attributes, which is clearly the most elementary data description. Here, instead, the concepts of DFDs are not easily comparable, and we can represent processes or flows or data stores rather arbitrarily.

c. Inside-out strategy

The inside-out strategy is a special case of the bottom-up strategy. Here, we first fix the most important or evident concepts, and then proceed by moving like an "oil stain", finding first of all the concepts that are conceptually close to the starting concepts, and then "navigating" toward the more distant ones.

The inside-out strategy can be applied naturally to functional analysis, as it corresponds to following the manipulations of information which is progrssively performed by processes. The most appropriate term for this strategy is perhaps "outside-inside", since the most natural application of this strategy starts from interfaces and determines progressively the processes which are involved in the production of flows exchanged with the interfaces. This process is performed "forward" if we start from interfaces that give some information in input to the system; it is performed "backward" if we start form interfaces that receive information in output from the system. A backward strategy is also called "output-oriented" and is typical of many methodologies for functional analysis.

d. Mixed strategy

The mixed strategy takes advantage of both top-down and bottom-up strategies, by allowing a "controlled" partitioning of resquirements. In other terms, when requirements are felt too complex to be managed together, the designer may split them, provided he produces first a skeleton schema, which includes the main concepts of the application. The skeleton schema acts as a frame for the most important concepts of the application domain, and embeds the links between partitions. The "overhead" skeleton schema allows an easier integration of the different schemas produced.

2.3 QUALITIES OF A SCHEMA

We distinguish two types of qualities, called respectively intra- and inter-schema qualities. Intra-schema qualities refer separately to the data and functional schema; inter-schema qualities refer to interrelationships among them.

Intra-schema qualities

Most of intra-schema properties apply to data schemas as well as functional schemas, with the only exception of functional independence, which is perhaps the most important one for functional analysis. We discuss now each of them.

1. *COMPLETENESS*. A Schema is complete when it represents all features of the application domain, at an "appropriate" level of detail (i.e., where sufficient details about it are specified, but no procedural feature is described).
2. *CORRECTNESS*. A schema is correct when it uses properly the concepts of the model to represent requirements.

3. *MINIMALITY*. A schema is minimal when every aspect of requirements appears only once in the schema. We can say alternaltively that a schema is minimal if no concept can be dropped by the schema, without changing its information content.

4. *READABILITY*. A schema is readable when it represents requirements in a natural way, and can be easily perceived without the need for further explanations.

5. *FUNCTIONAL INDEPENDENCE*. This property is achieved when each process is sufficiently autonomous, i.e., it can perform a substantial amount of work independent on other processes. We have already stressed that functional independence should drive the top-down refinement of processes. When functional independence is achieved, the resulting processes have additional properties of:

a. *SEPARABILITY*: each process can independently be analyzed in detail.

b. *INTEGRABILITY*: the DFD obtained as the refinement of one process should be easily integrable with the rest of the system.

c. *FLEXIBILTY*: each process should be able to adapt itself to the changes without creating the need of modifying other processes.

The above properties have practical relevance if the analysis is developed at stages, and therefore the specification and implementation of procedures corresponding to processes is performed at different times.

Inter-schema qualities

The main inter-schema quality is MUTUAL COMPLETENESS. We say that a D-schema is complete with respect to an F-schema if every concept implicitly expressed in data flows and data stores of the F-schema appears in the D-schema. The F-schema is COMPLETE with respect to the D-schema if every data retrieval or manipulation operation that has to be performed on data appears as one process of the F-schema.

We can be sure that the data and functional schemas are mutually complete only if we make a cross-comparison of their information content.

3. A METHODOLOGY FOR JOINT DATA AND FUNCTIONAL ANALYSIS

In the previous section, we have shown several similarities between data and functional analysis; these similarities suggest that data and functional analysis can be performed jointly. The main motivation for a joint analysis is that each analysis activity can support and integrate the other one: The process of analyzing an information system is performed through subsequent refinements, and these refinements are simplified if data and functions specifications are produced together. For instance, refinements of data schemas can suggest refinements of functional schemas, which in turn can suggest refinements of functional schemas, which in turn can suggest refinements on date definitions. This is similar to what is done by rock climbers, who typically alternate the movement of left and right limbs; each movement makes the next movement feasible.

A second reason in favour of an integrated approach is achieving MUTUAL COMPLETENESS. As we said, we can be sure that the data and functional schemas are mutually complete only if we make a cross-comparison of their information content. For instance, we verify that data stores within DFDs are represented in the D-schema, and likewise that data manipulation operations belong to some process. Mutual completeness is a property that should be achieved only on the final versions on the schema; however, it can be achieved more easily (and can actually drive the refinement process) if it is tested also on intermediate versions of the schemas.

As a consequence of the above arguments, in this section we propose a joint methodology for data and functional analysis; we will show how each of the two analysis activities can influence the other one in providing indications for schema refinement and coherence checking. The basic idea of the joint analysis methodology is to alternate refinements of the D-schema and of the F-schema; each refinement is influenced by both the previous versions of D and F Schemas. Eventually, a mutual consistency check ensures that the two specifications are consistent.

A methodology for joint data and functional analysis is shown in Fig. 3. The analysis activity is organized into the following phases:

1. Identify interfaces.

2. Identify input/output flows between interfaces and the system.

3. Identify a first skeleton data schema and a skeleton functional schema.

4. Repeat

4a. Refine the d-schema from the previous D-schema, looking also to the previous F-schema.	4b.Refine the F-schema from the previous F-schema, looking also to the previous D-schema.

In steps 4a. and 4b. make use of strategies described in section 2.2

4c.(optional step) Test the mutual consistency of D-schema and F-schema.

Until

All the concepts in requirements have been expressed in the schema.

5. Check the qualities of the D-schema and F-schema: self and mutual completeness, correctness, readability, minimality, functional independence (just for the F-schema).

Fig 3: A methodology for joint data and functional analysis

1. *INITIAL DESIGN* , i.e. determination of a skeleton D-schema and F-schema. In particular, the skeleton F-schema should concentrate on an input-output description of the system, by identifying interfaces and input-output flows.

2. *REFINEMENT* (conducted in parallel for D-schema and F-schema). For example, the process of identifying refinements of the D-schema is influenced both by the previous D-schema and by the previous F-schema. The strategies described in section 2.2 should be applied here.

3. *MUTUAL COMPLETENESS CHECK* (performed after one or more refinements): The two conditions for mutual completeness are to be checked whenever complex decisions have deeply modified previous analysis products

4. *FINAL ANALYSIS OF D-SCHEMA AND F-SCHEMA*, where the qualities of schemas are tested and achieved by means of schema restructuring.

Obviously, in the course of the analysis of a particular application, it is possible to emphasize data analysis or functional analysis; we say that the design is DATE-DRIVEN or FUNCTION-DRIVEN, respectively.

4. CASE STUDY

We apply the methodology described in the previous section to the analysis of the information system of the main office of a bus company. The main office is subdivided into two major areas: passenger management and service management. Passenger management deals with reservations of bus seats and with providing information to passengers and travel agencies about time-tables and fares. Service management organizes ordinary and special travels.

4.1 DESCRIPTION OF REQUIREMENTS

A. PASSENGER MANAGEMENT

Seat reservations are made directly by passengers or by travel agencies; they can be made on any bus service (both ordinary and special) and are free. The passengers can ask for a smoking or non-smoking area. Reservations can be made on part of the bus travel; thus, the same seat might, in principle, be made available to different persons on different parts of the same travel. The office holds the so called "travel description sheets", which are prepared about 4 weeks before the actual departure of the travel, and include the schedule of the travel, with the list of all intermediate stops, and spaces for each seat, where it is possible to write reservations.

Travel description sheets are prepared by the service management office and used by the "reservation office" to record the reservations. They are returned to the service management office at least 2 hours before the departure of the travel; thus, reservations cannot be taken immediately before the departure.

The main office has a reservation desk and some dedicated telephone lines for reservations. Fare information is given at a different desk, also with dedicated telephone lines. Fares are reported on a "fare description booklet", which is prepared monthly; fares are relatively stable. Office employees and operators at either of the lines cannot answer questions concerning the other office; at most, they can redirect clients to the other desk or switch telephone calls. Thus, we distinguish two separate activities of "reservations" and "fares".

Typically, passengers also request information about time-tables of travels. This information is prepared by the service management office, but it is much more variable; time-tables can be modified depending on road conditions or special events. Special travels can be organized for special events.

Thus, the collection of information about time-tables is centralized within a third activity, called "time-table", supporting the other two activities. Requests about time schedules from passengers can be answered directly at the reservation and fare offices, because the employees of these offices can use time-tables or travel description sheets. Modifications to the schedules of travels are communicated from service management to the "time-table" activity, which is responsible for updating the "travels description sheets" (and sometimes for notifying the change to the passengers holding reservations).

Passengers can enroll in a "frequent traveller" program; in this case, they can earn some bonus when they accumulate a given number of miles.

B. SERVICE MANAGEMENT

We distinguish four major activities, concerned with ordinary travels, special travels, bus management, and management of bus drivers.

The management of ordinary travels must prepare the "travel description sheets" and the "fare description booklet". Every season, ordinary travels are re-arranged to deal with different requirements of travellers. Officers of the "road condition service" and officers of the government give information that can be used to modify the travels.

Sometimes, based on external events (such as football games, elections, fairs, special holidays, etc...), the company decides to activate special travels; when this occurs, the "special travel management office" produces a "travel description sheet" for it. It then has the responsibility of communicating information on special travels to the "reservation" and "time-table" activities.

The "bus management" activity has the goal of organizing each individual travel. Specifically, it receives the "travel description sheets" with passengers reservations written on them, and adds the name of the bus driver, the make and the plate of the bus, and the total maximum number of passengers that can be accepted. Fares are also reported for each piece of the travel; thus, all the information which is necessary to the bus driver is recorded on the "travel description sheet".

The other activities of bus management include the mechanical revision of buses, their purchase and sell, the repair of damages, and so on. The office maintains buses" documents and a (paper) file on the buses, recording repairs, maintenance and usage of the bus.

The driver's management activity keeps a file on individual data of each driver. When a driver is sick, he communicates the absence to this office. Similarly, the driver communicates to this office all the mechanical problems that he discovers on his bus. In practice, this office provides assistance to drivers, and controls them.

4.2 PRODUCTION OF SKELETON SCHEMAS

Initially, we produce a skeleton F-schema. According to the methodology of Fig. 3, we first identify interfaces:

1. *CLIENTS* , i.e. PERSONS or AGENCIES, that need information or reservations.
2. *GOVERNMENT OFFICES* , that interact with the system by communicating road conditions and by requesting for special travels.
3. *DRIVERS* , who communicate to the system their availability and the state of the buses.

The result of this first analysis activity is the "black-box" schema of fig 4a. We then refine the F-schema by identifying the main processes of the system, and the flows between them. A first decomposition is immediately suggested by requirement descriptions, where the two main offices of PASSENGER MANAGEMENT and SERVICE MANAGEMENT are distinguished. Correspondingly, flows are refined as follows:

1. CLIENTS interact only with PASSENGER MANAGEMENT.
2. GOVERNMENT OFFICES and DRIVERS interact only with SERVICE MANAGEMENT.
3. Two flows, which are left unspecified, describe the exchange of information between PASSENGER MANAGEMENT and SERVICE MANAGEMENT.

In this way, the skeleton F-schema is completed (see fig 4b).

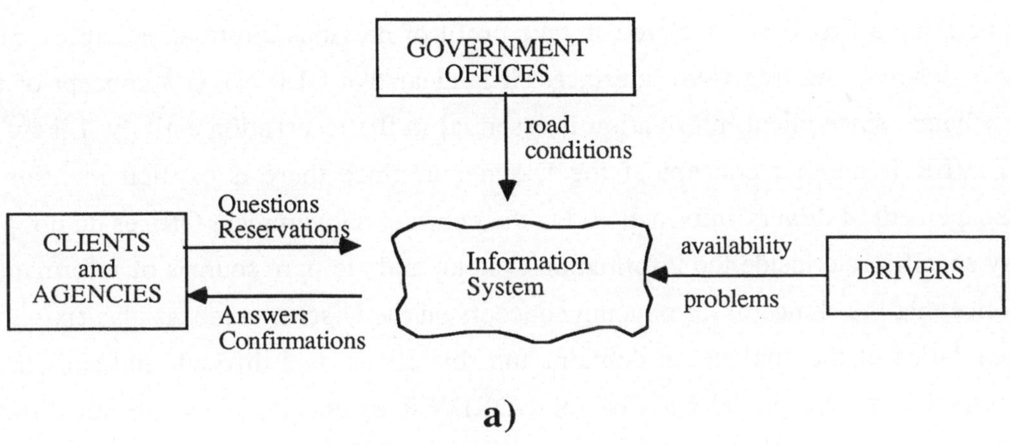

a)

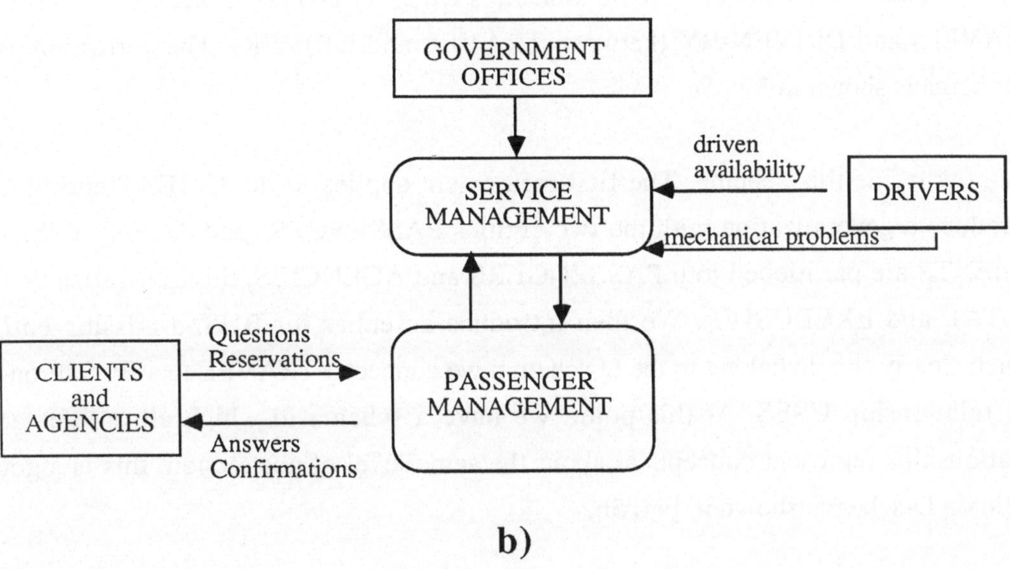

b)

Fig. 4   Skeleton F-schema

In deriving a first D-schema we can take profit of previous information expressed in the F-schema. Starting from interfaces, it is clear that CLIENT is a concept of the D-schema, since client information is essential in the reservation activity. Likewise, DRIVER is another concept of the D-schema, since there is explicit mention to management of drivers' information. On the contrary, Government Offices do not play any specific role inside the information system, and are pure sources of information. Notice that the choice of introducing concepts on the D-schema means also fixing the boundaries of the application domain, and this choice is a difficult and sometimes arbitrary one. We model CLIENT and DRIVER as entities; they are not directly connected, however they are both connected to the different concept TRAVEL, which is also modeled as an entity. Thus, a draft D-schema includes the entities CLIENT, DRIVER, and TRAVEL, and the relationships RELATED-TO (between CLIENT and TRAVEL) and DRIVEN-BY (between TRAVEL and DRIVER). The corresponding D-schema is shown in Fig. 5a.

We now refine this schema. The first refinement applies to the CLIENT entity; we introduce a generalization with the two entities PASSENGER and AGENCY. Since CLIENTS are partitioned into PASSENGERS and AGENCIES, this generalization is TOTAL and EXCLUSIVE. We then introduce an entity for BUS, a missing entity which clearly should belong to the D-schema; we connect a TRAVEL to a BUS through the relationship USES. At this point, we have a schema in which all entities and relationships represent concepts at about the same level of abstraction; this is a good skeleton D-schema, shown in Fig. 5b.

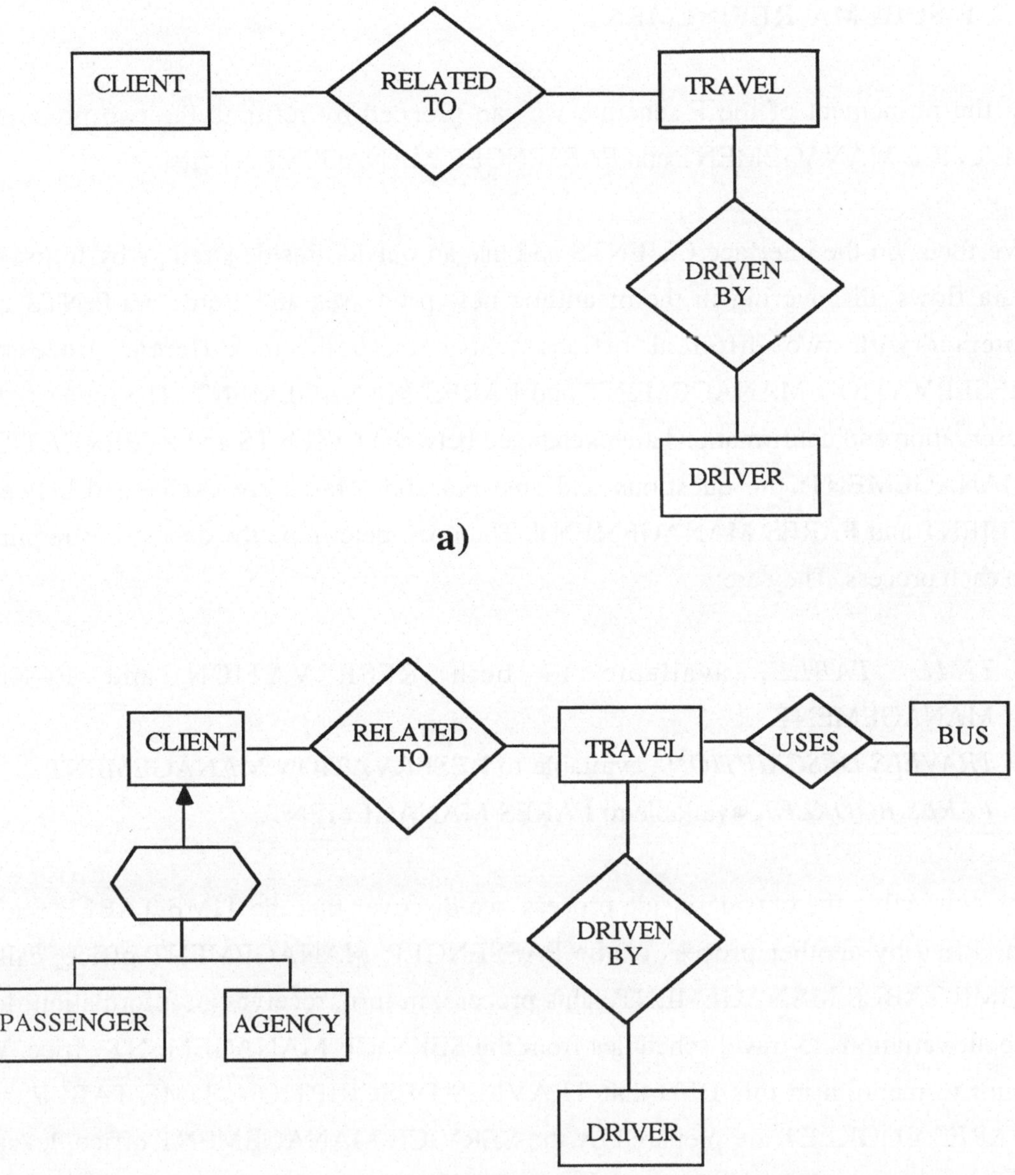

Fig. 5   Skeleton D-Schema

4.3 F-SCHEMA REFINEMENT

In the refinement of the F-schema, we can proceed by refining the two processes SERVICE MANAGEMENT and PASSENGER MANAGEMENT first.

We focus on the interface CLIENTS and use an outside-inside strategy by following data flows, discovering in the meantime new processes and stores. CLIENTS can interact with two different offices that correspond to different processes: RESERVATION MANAGEMENT and FARES MANAGEMENT. The requests for reservation and confirmations are exchanged between CLIENTS and RESERVATION MANAGEMENT; the questions and answers about fares are exchanged between CLIENT and FARES MANAGEMENT. Then, we determine the data stores required to each process. They are:

1. *TIME TABLE*, available to both RESERVATION and FARES MANAGEMENT.
2. *TRAVELS DESCRIPTION* , available to RESERVATION MANAGEMENT.
3. *FARES BOOKLET*, available to FARES MANAGEMENT.

By continuing the outside-inside process, we discover that the TIME TABLE can be modified by another process of the PASSENGER MANAGEMENT office, called TIME TABLE MANAGEMENT. This process, in turn, receives an information flow about variations to travel schedules from the SERVICE MANAGEMENT office. We omit to mention in this DFD that TRAVELS DESCRIPTION, TIME TABLE, and FARES BOOKLET are prepared by the SERVICE MANAGEMENT office, leaving this for future refinements. The corresponding F-schema is in Fig. 6a.

TRAVELS
DESCRIPTION
RESERVATION
MANAGEMENT
reservation
confirmation
CLIENT
TIME TABLE
TIME
TABLE
MANAGEMENT
questions
FARES
MANAGEMENT
answers
FARES
BOOKLET
variations
to time
table
SERVICE
MANAGEMENT

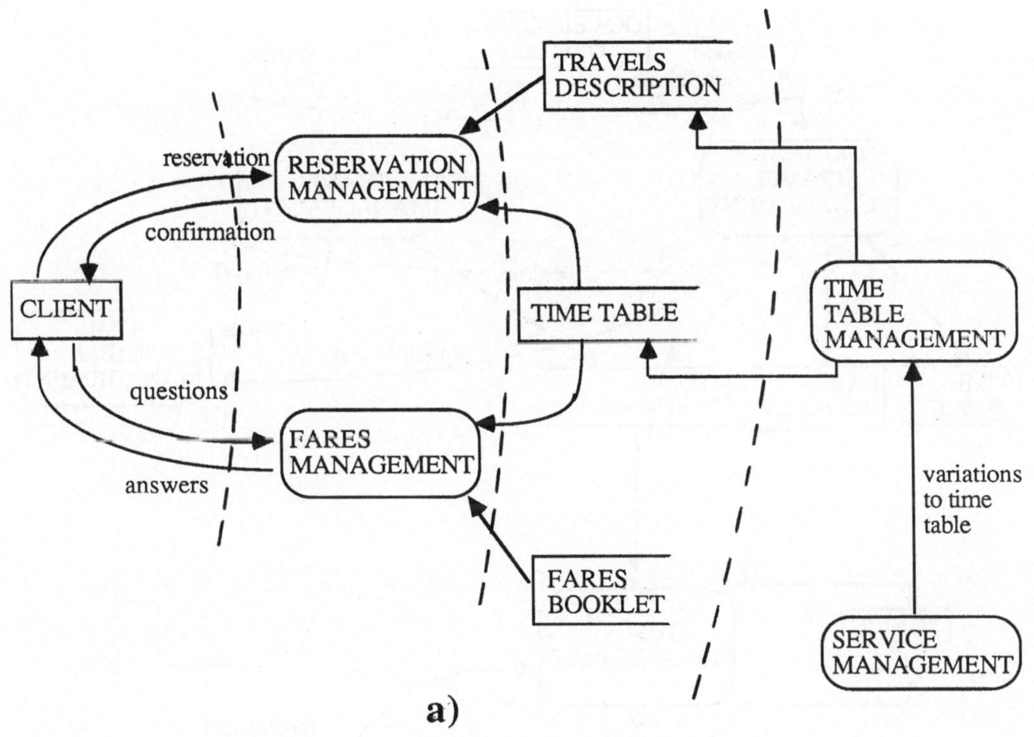

a)

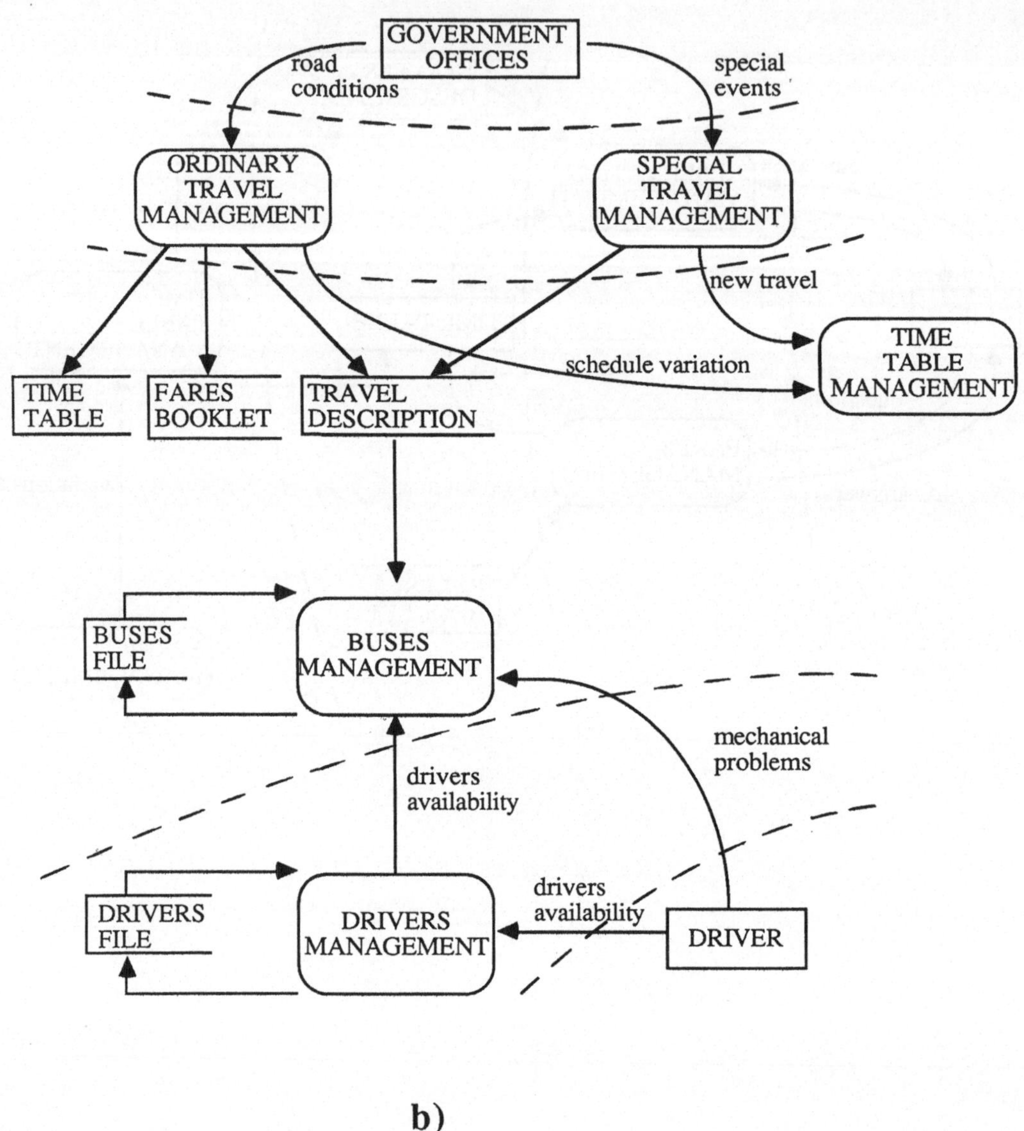

b)

Fig. 6   F-schema refinement

We then consider the SERVICE MANAGEMENT office. Again, we use an outside-inside strategy, starting from the interfaces. The GOVERNMENT OFFICES communicate road conditions, which affect ordinary travels, and special events, which can cause the creation of special travels. Thus, we determine two separate processes, called ORDINARY TRAVELS MANAGEMENT and SPECIAL TRAVELS MANAGEMENT. The former is responsible of creating the TIME TABLE, the FARES BOOKLET, and the TRAVEL DESCRIPTION; this latter data store is also created by the process SPECIAL TRAVELS MANAGEMENT for special travels. Finally, both ORDINARY and SPECIAL TRAVELS MANAGEMENT communicate with the TIME TABLE MANAGEMENT process; the former communicates variations to schedules of odinary travels, and the latter communicates the creation of a special travel.

If we concentrate instead on the DRIVER interface, we note that it exchanges with the SERVICE MANAGEMENT office two information flows. The former, DRIVER AVAILABILITY, is directed to a process the main purpose of which is to manage drivers, called DRIVERS MANAGEMENT. The latter, MECHANICAL PROBLEMS, is instead directed to a process, called BUSES MANAGEMENT, which is responsible for bus management and also for preparing travels by completing travel descriptions with the choice of the driver and of the bus. This is possible because the process has available information about buses (the data store BUSES FILE) and receives from the DRIVER MANAGEMENT process information about drivers' availability. The refined F-schema is shown in Fig. 6b.

4.4 D-SCHEMA REFINEMENT

Looking at the D-schema produced so far, it is evident that the entity TRAVEL and the relationship RELATED-TO express concept at a very high abstraction level; we proceed refining these concepts.

Consider the relationship RELATED-TO: from the previous F-schema, one can deduce that two connections exist between a client and a travel:

1. A client HOLDS a RESERVATION for one particular travel;
2. A client IS ON BOARD of a particular travel.

The corresponding top-down refinement is shown in Fig. 7a.

Consider the entity TRAVEL: we notice two directions of refinement for this entity.

1. We observe that each client holds a reservation or is on board on a specific, DAILY TRAVEL, while the concept of TRAVEL is a more general one; properties of TRAVEL include the route and schedule, while properties of a DAILY TRAVEL include its date, driver, and bus. It is assumed that each travel is operated at most daily.
2. We also observe that each client holds reservations or is on board just for one or more SECTIONs along the travel's route. Properties of SECTIONs include the departure and arrival city, the distance, and the price. Each travel has a variable number of sections, one for each intermediate stop. Passengers can hold reservations and be on board of multiple sections of the same travel.

If we apply both refinements given above, we end up with 4 entities: TRAVEL, DAILY TRAVEL, SECTION, DAILY SECTION.Each entity is required, because it corresponds to a different concept with its own properties. The four entities are represented in Fig. 7b.

We then analyze requirements in search for aspects which are not yet covered in the current D-schema. We notice that TRAVELS are partitioned into ORDINARY and SPECIAL TRAVELS, and we introduce a generalization hierarchy (see Fig. 7c). We also discover that the information flow on "road condition", in the F-schema, can affect the schedule of sections of travels on specific dates; thus, we introduce an entity (daily) SECTION WITH SCHEDULE VARIATION as a subset of DAILY SECTION to be able to represent variations to the schedule (see Fig. 7d).

Finally, we consider BUS and DRIVER data stores of the F-schema. In both cases, some detail information about BUS REPAIRS and DRIVER'S ABSENCE from work should be added to the schema; the corresponding refinement is shown in Fig. 7e. Figure 7f shows the refined D-schema.

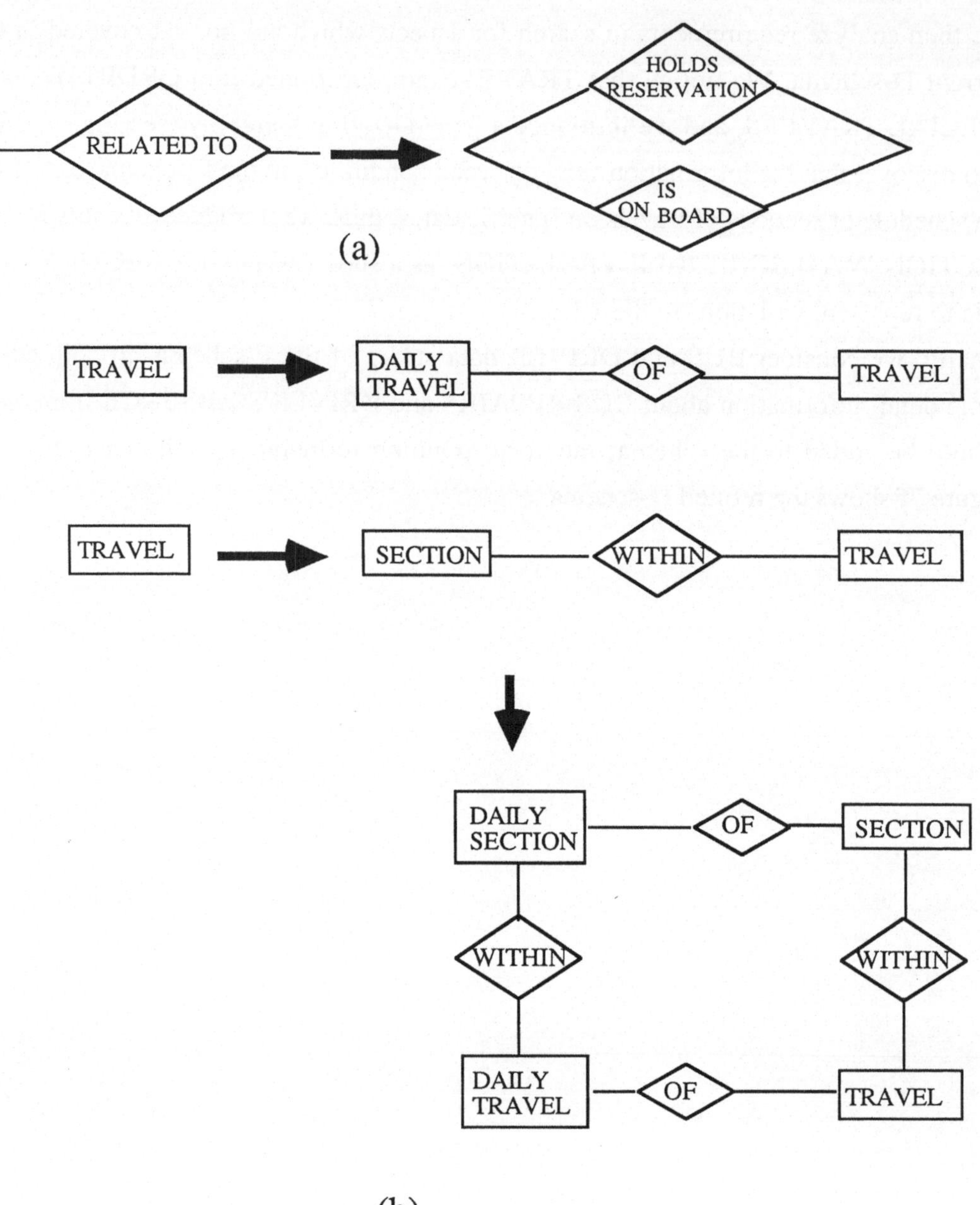

RELATED TO
HOLDS RESERVATION
IS ON BOARD
(a)
TRAVEL
DAILY TRAVEL
OF
TRAVEL
TRAVEL
SECTION
WITHIN
TRAVEL
DAILY SECTION
OF
SECTION
WITHIN
WITHIN
DAILY TRAVEL
OF
TRAVEL
(b)

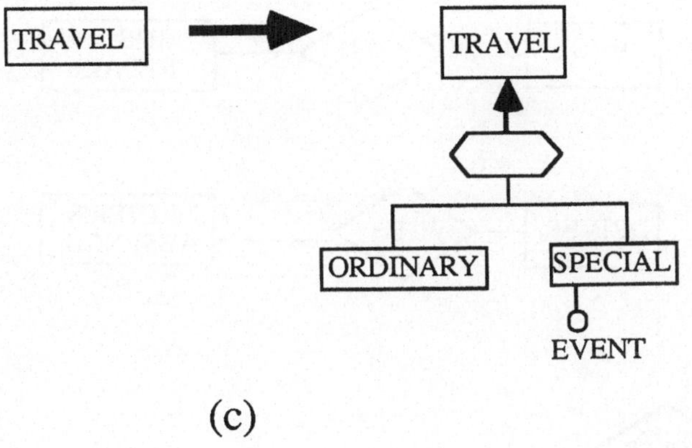

(c)

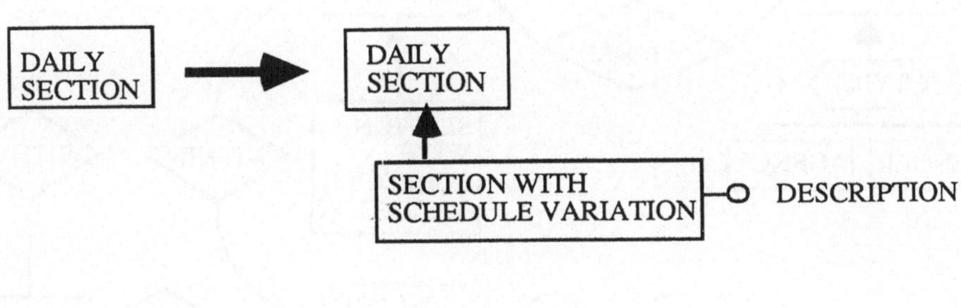

(d)

Fig. 7   (continued)

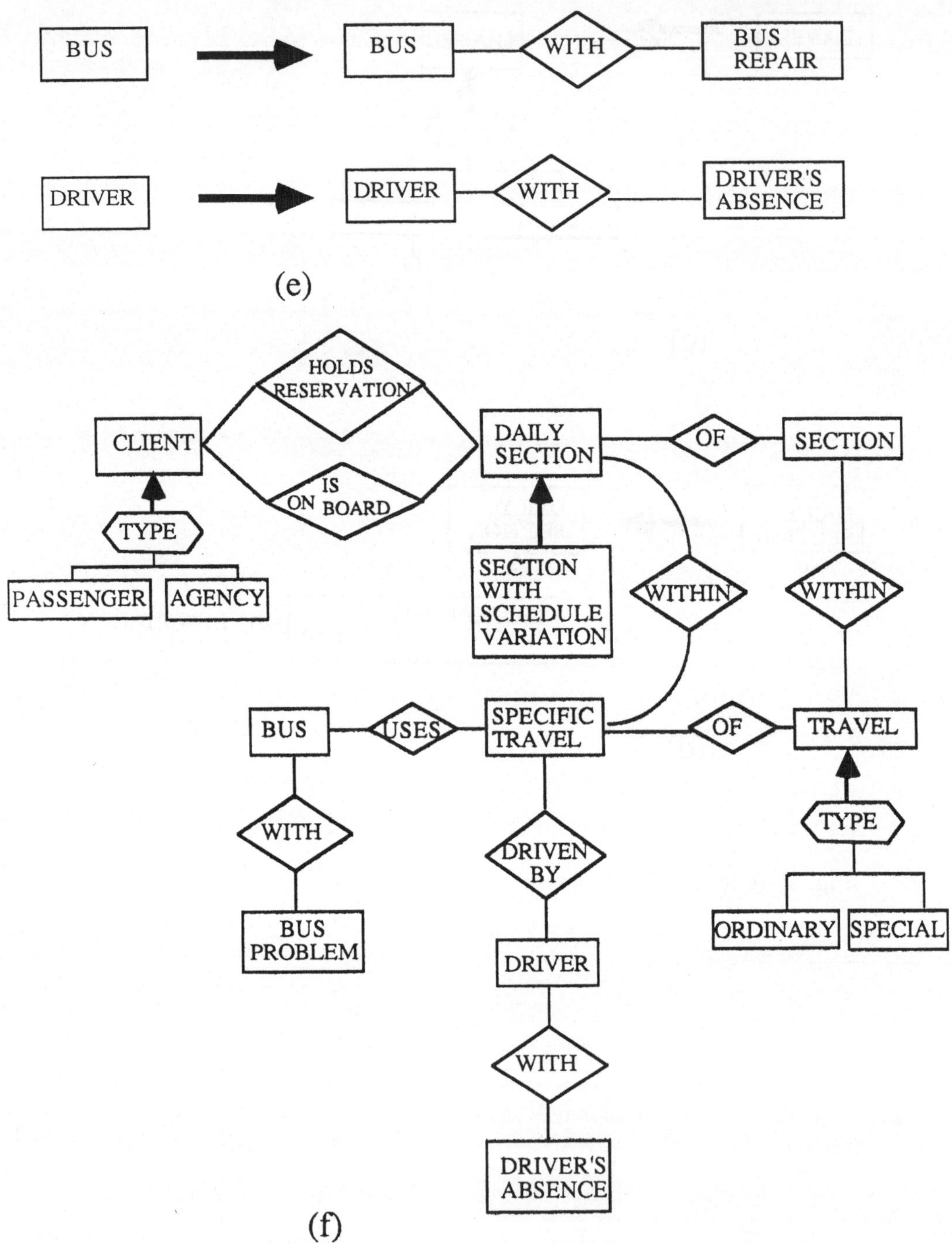

Fig. 7   D-schema refinement

4.5 F-SCHEMA COMPLETION

We complete the F-schema by refining some processes and then by integrating the F-schemas of PASSENGER MANAGEMENT and of SERVICE MANAGEMENT; refinements are introduced whenever a process can be decomposed into several processes which are functionally independent. All refinements refer to the SERVICE MANAGEMENT office (see fig 8).

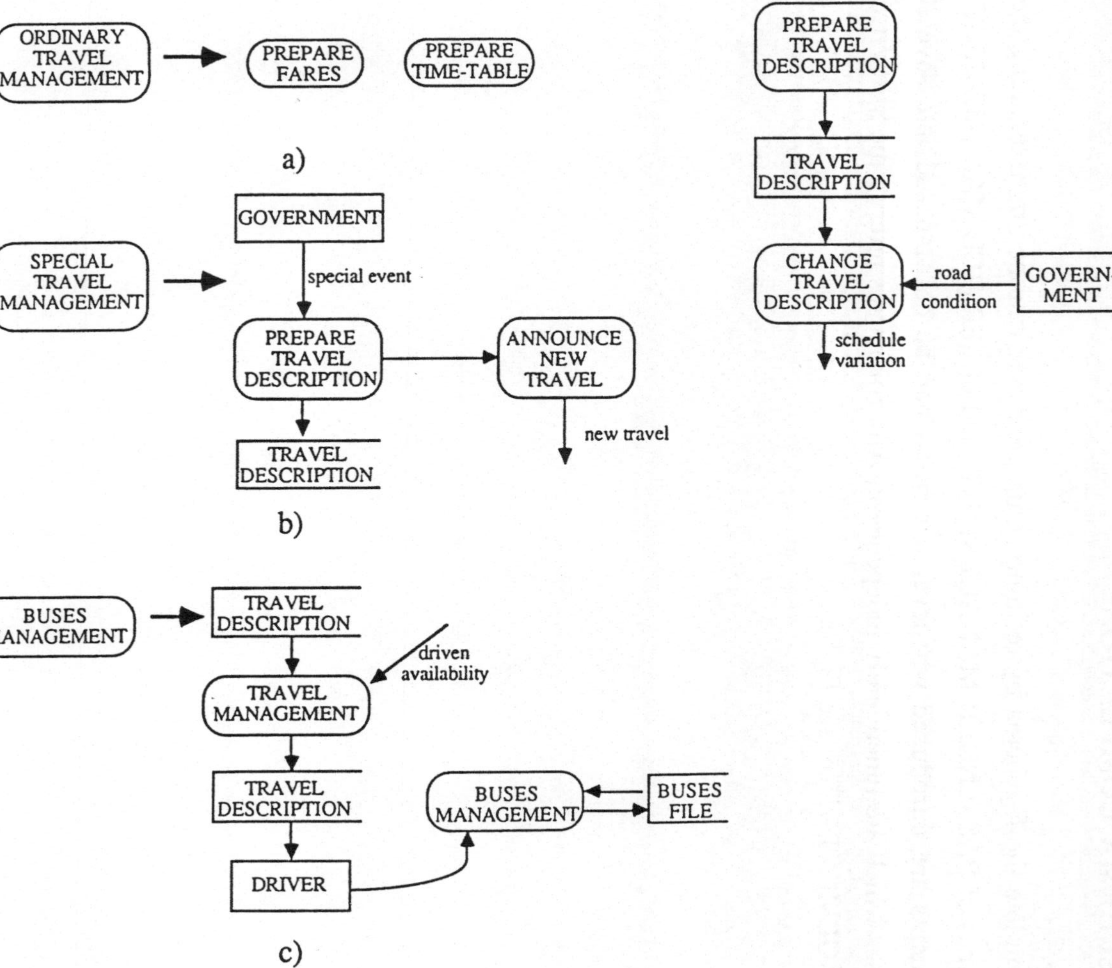

Fig. 8:   F-schema completion

Consider the process ORDINARY TRAVEL MANAGEMENT. We distinguish three independent groups of activities: PREPARE FARES, PREPARE TIME-TABLES, PREPARE TRAVEL DESCRIPTIONS. We also note that the process CHANGE TRAVEL DESCRIPTION is required in order to produce new schedules when ROAD CONDITIONS are bad. Similarly, we distinguish for the process SPECIAL TRAVEL MANAGEMENT two independent activities: PREPARE TRAVEL DESCRIPTION, and ANNOUNCE NEW TRAVEL. These refinements are shown in Fig. 8a und 8b.

Finally, we consider the process BUSES MANAGEMENT. We clearly distinguish in it two activities: TRAVEL MANAGEMENT, and BUSES MANAGEMENT. The former is responsible for arranging a specific travel, by associating to it a bus and a driver; the latter is responsible for managing buses, their purchase, repair, and sale.

The completion of the F-schema requires the integration of the two F-schemas of Fig. 6a and 6b (revised after the above refinements), guided by the skeleton F-schema. The connection between the PASSENGER MANAGEMENT office and the SERVICE MANAGEMENT office is given by the data stores FARE BOOKLET, TIME TABLE, and TRAVELS DESCRIPTION, which are used by the former and produced by the latter. Most information exchanged between the two offices is permanent, hence represented through data stores; however, the SERVICE MANAGEMENT office communicates schedule variations and new travels to the TIME TABLE MANAGEMENT activity, which in turns updates the TIME TABLES of the company and notifies CLIENTS about variations. The final F-schema resulting after integration is shown in Fig. 9. TRAVELS DESCRIPTION is in fact produced by both ORDINARY and SPECIAL TRAVELS management, then used by RESERVATION MANAGEMENT to add reservations to it, used by BUS MANAGEMENT to add final information about travels, and finally given to the driver. Thus, this document is of primary importance.

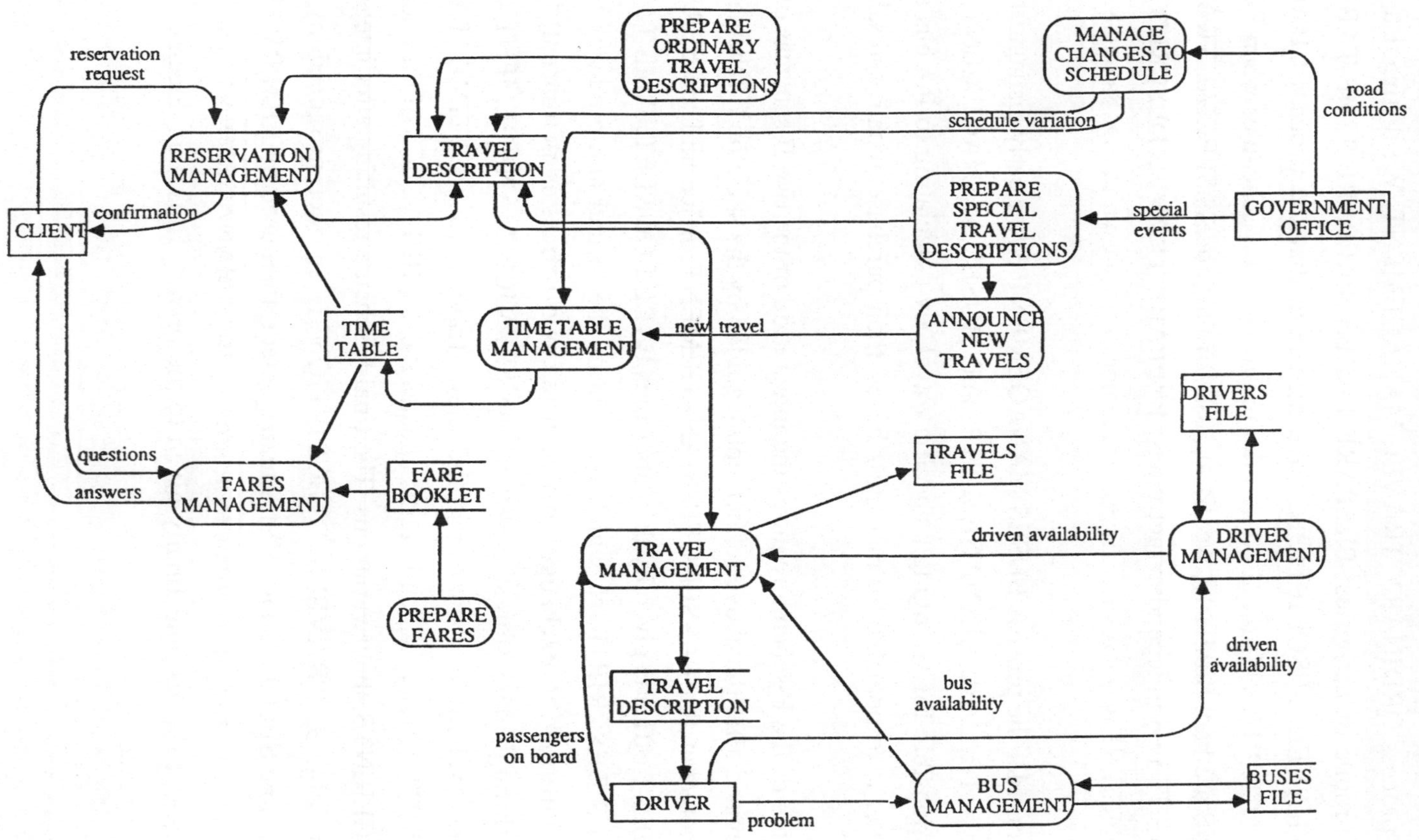

Fig. 9. Final F-Schema

4.6 D-SCHEMA COMPLETION

The D-schema of Fig. 7f does not need additional entities, relationships, or subsets; the completion of the D-schema consists in the specification of attributes, mapping cardinalities, identifiers, and optionalities.

Let us start with the entity CLIENT. We consider the pair NAME and TELEPHONE as the identifier of the CLIENT. Additionally, the boolean attribute FREQUENT TRAVELLER indicates the status of passengers; for "frequent travellers", the optional attribute MILEAGE gives the number of miles accumulated as yet (because passengers receive a bonus after a given number of miles earned). The two relationships HOLDS RESERVATION and IS ON BOARD have the same cardinalities; they are (0:m) since each CLIENT can hold zero or more reservations or be on board of multiple PORTIONS OF TRAVELs, and each PORTION OF TRAVEL can be reserved and have on board zero or more CLIENTS. HOLDS RESERVATIONS has two attributes: SMOKING OPTION, and SEAT NUMBER.

Consider now the cluster of entities: TRAVEL, DAILY TRAVEL, SECTION, DAILY SECTION.

1. TRAVEL is identified by the attribute TRAVEL-ID. The multivalue attribute WEEK DAYS indicates the days of the week in which the travel is operated. Other attributes are DEPARTURE CITY, ARRIVAL CITY, and the NUMBER OF PORTIONS in which the travel is decomposed.
2. DAILY TRAVEL is identified by the pair of attributes: TRAVEL-ID, DATE. This entity has no other attribute, however it is connected through the relationship USES to the BUS, and through the relationship DRIVEN BY to the entity DRIVER; it is assumed that a bus and a driver are assigned to an entire travel.
3. SECTION is identified by the pair of attributes: TRAVEL-ID, SECTION-ID; a SECTION-ID is a progressive number given to sections of travels. Attributes of SECTION include the DEPARTURE CITY and DEPARTURE TIME, the ARRIVAL CITY and ARRIVAL TIME, the PRICE, and the DISTANCE.

4. DAILY SECTION is identified by the triple of attributes: TRAVEL-ID, PORTION-ID, DATE. It has two other attributes, the NUMBER OF AVAILABLE SEATS and the NUMBER OF RESERVED SEATS.

The two instances of the relationship WITHIN have cardinalities (1:1) and (1:n), since each section belongs to exactly one travel, while each travel has one or more sections. Similarly, the two instances of the relaionship OF have cardinalities (1:1) and (1:n), since each daily travel corresponds exactly to one travel, while each travel corresponds to multiple daily travels.

We now consider the cluster of entities BUS and BUS PROBLEM and of relationships WITH and USES. The relationship USES has cardinalities (0:m) and (1:1), since each BUS is dynamically assigned to a DAILY TRAVEL but possibly is not assigned to any (for instance, when it is under repair), while each DAILY TRAVEL requires exactly one BUS. The entity BUS is identified by either the BUS-ID or the bus PLATE; it has the attributes MAKE, SEATS, CONDITIONS, and LAST CHECK DATE. The entity BUS PROBLEM is identified by the pair BUS-ID, DATE of the problem, and has the attribute DESCRIPTION. The relationship WITH is (0:m), (1:1), since each BUS can have zero or more BUS PROBLEMS, while each BUS PROBLEM relates exactly to one BUS.

Finally, we consider the cluster of entities DRIVER and DRIVER ABSENCE and of relationship DRIVEN-BY and WITH. Cardinalities of relationships are not discussed, but are similar to those of relationships USES and WITH discussed above. Each DRIVER is identified by the DRIVER-ID and has a NAME, ADDRESS, a LICENCE TYPE, and a driving RECORD. Each DRIVER ABSENCE is identified by the pair DRIVER-ID and DATE and has the attribute CAUSE.

The final D-schema is shown in Fig. 10.

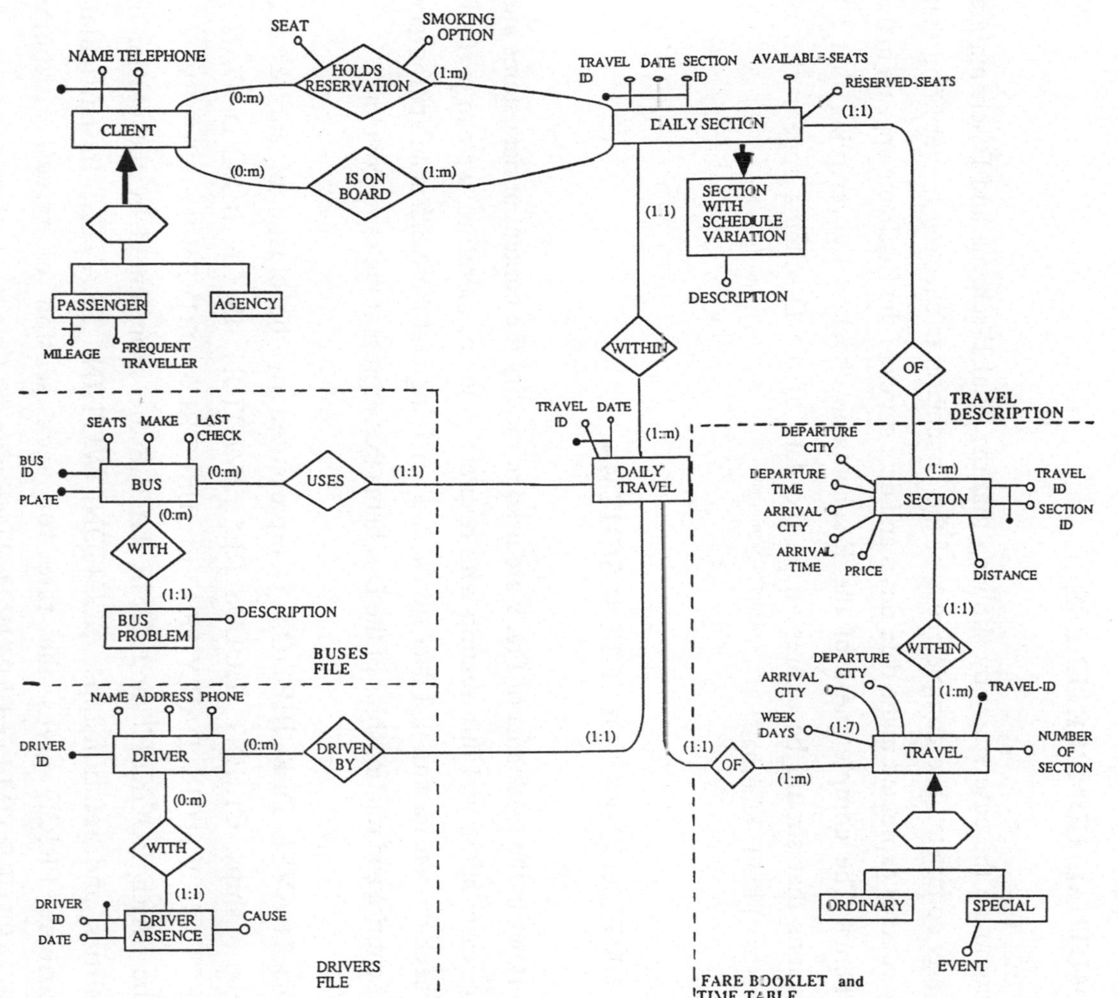

Fig. 10 :   Final D-Schema

4.7 MUTUAL COMPLETENESS

We complete the case study by showing that the final F-schema and D-schema are mutually complete. The completeness of the D-schema is checked by verifying that every concept expressed in the data flows and data stores of the F-schema appears in the D-schema. The completeness of the F-schema is checked by verifying that all operations that should be expressed on the data of the D-schema appear also as processes of the F-schema.

A. COMPLETENESS OF THE D-SCHEMA.

Data flows in the F-schema of Fig. 9 are used to modify the content of data stores and do not carry additional information with resprect to them; therefore, we can perform the check by considering just data stores, and verifying that there exists an appropriate set of entities and relationships of the D-schema that represent the same content.

1. The TRAVEL DESCRIPTION is represented by the cluster of entities and relationships: CLIENT, HOLDS RESERVATION, IS ON BOARD, DAILY SECTION, WITHIN, DAILY TRAVEL, USES BUS, DRIVEN-BY, DRIVER.
2. The FARE BOOKLET and TIME TABLE are represented by the cluster of entities and relationships: SECTION, WITHIN, TRAVEL. In particular, attribute PRICE gives the fare for each section of travel, attributes DEPARTURE TIME and ARRIVAL TIME give the time table information.
3. The BUSES FILE is represented by the cluster of entities and relationships: BUS, WITH, BUS PROBLEM.
4. The DRIVERS FILE is represented by the cluster of entities and relationships: DRIVER, WITH, DRIVER ABSENCE.

The correspondence between data stores and portions of the conceptual schema is represented in Fig 10.

4.8 COMPLETENESS OF THE F-SCHEMA

For each entity and relationship of the D-schema, we should verify that there exists at least one process responsible for its creation and usage.

1. The entities CLIENT and DAILY SECTION and relationships HOLDS RESERVATION and IS ON BOARD are created, retrieved, and modified by the process RESERVATIONS MANAGEMENT.
2. The entities DAILY TRAVEL and DAILY SECTION with the relationship WITHIN between them and both relationships OF are created by the two processes PREPARE ORDINARY TRAVEL DESCRIPTIONS and PREPARE SPECIAL TRAVEL DESCRIPTIONS, used by the processes RESERVATIONS MANAGEMENT and TRAVELS MANAGEMENT.
3. The entities TRAVEL and DAILY TRAVEL with the relationship WITHIN between them are created by the processes PREPARE FARES and TIME TABLE MANAGEMENT, used by the processes RESERVATIONS MANAGEMENT and FARES MANAGEMENT.
4. The entities BUS and BUS PROBLEM and relationships USES and WITH are created and used by the BUS MANAGEMENT process.
5. The entities DRIVER and DRIVER ABSENCE and relationships WITH are created and used by the DRIVER MANAGEMENT process; the relationship DRIVEN-BY is created and used by the BUS MANAGEMENT process.

4.9 CONCLUSIONS OF THE CASE STUDY

At the end of this case study, some considerations are appropriate. First, we have decided to describe the requirements "as they are", without introducing changes to them. Thus, requirements (particularly, the structure of processes) clearly reflect the work organization before the introduction of an automated information system. The new system will consist of a single, integrated database, instead of separate, partially automated data stores. This will certainly introduce innovations in the work organization. For instance, as an effect of the new system it will become possible to collect reservations also during the last 2 hours before departure; thus, one of the constraints of the present system is no longer true. Major innovations can involve the reorganization of processes, for instance by eliminating the need for the TIME TABLE MANAGEMENT process, since other processes can directly change the TIME TABLE on the computer. We consider organization problems as outside the scope of this paper.

Another consideration concerns the boundary of the information system. If one carefully considers requirements, he will discover that we have omitted considering some issues, like purchases or sales of buses, or damage repairs. This happens because, while modelling the information systems, its BOUNDARIES have become clearer. Hence, we have decided not to introduce in either of the D- or F-schemas the descriptions of those portions of the requirements which, at a given point of the analysis, have been considered outside this boundary.

Finally, by comparing the D-schema and F-schema at the end of the process, it is rather clear that the former is a much more "mature" document. The former gives the exact structure of the conceptual data schema; the latter identifies the processes of the information system, but is not at all specific on processes' procedurality. In fact, the distance between process identification and procedure specification is quite large, and the designer has to further investigate on requirements to complete his work.

5. CONCLUSIONS

In this paper we have presented a joint approach to data and functional analysis. We have shown by means of a detailed example the feasibility of our approach. Several problems in this area need to be investigated. Probably, the most important concerns the integration of categories used in data and functional models. A first proposal toward a model in which the same abstractions are homogeneously applied for data and functions appears in [BORGIDA GREENSPAN MYLOPOULOS 1985]. A second important problem concerns the integration of the formalisms and methods for data and functional analysis with the corresponding ones used for the analysis of the organizations.

ANNOTATED BIBLIOGRAPHY

A. ALBANO, V. DE ANTONELLIS, and A. DI LEVA - Computer aided database design: the DATAID project - North Holland 1985.

S. CERI ed. - Methodology and tools for data base design - North Holland, 1983.

A. BORGIDA, S. GREENSPAN, and J. MYLOPOULOS - A requirements modeling language and its logic - Proc. 4th Scandinavian Research Seminar on Information Modeling and Data Base Management, Ellivuori, Finland, 1985.

T. DE MARCO - Structured Analysis and System Specification - Prentice Hall Inc., Englewood Cliffs, N.J., 1982.

C. GANE and T. SARSON -- Structured System Analysis, Prentice Hall, Englewood Cliffs, N.J., 1979.

E. JOURDON and L. CONSTANTINE - Structured Design, Prentice-Hall, Englewood Cliffs, N.J. 1979.

M. LUNDBERG - The ISAC Approach to Specification of Information Systems and its Application to the Organization of an IFIP Working Conference, in Information Systems Design Methodologies: A Comparative Review, T. W. Olle, H. G. Sol, and A. A. Verrijin-Stuart eds., North Holland,1982.

T. W. OLLE, H.G. SOL, AND A. S. VERRIJIN-STUART eds., North Holland, 1982.

T. W. OLLE; H. G. SOL, AND C. J. TULLY eds. - Information Systems Design Methodologies: A Feature Analysis - , North Holland, 1983.

J. R. PETERSON - Petri Nets - Computing Surveys, 9:3, pp. 223-252.

D. ROSS - Structured Analysis: a Language for Communicating Ideas - IEEE Transactions for Software Engineering, Vol 3 N. 1, 1977.

Formalizing Requirements Systematically

Anthony Finkelstein & Colin Potts,
Imperial College of Science and Technology, London, UK

Abstract — ""Structured Common Sense" (SCS) is a method for eliciting requirements and formalizing them in modal action logic (MAL). SCS was developed using the methodology of focussing on MAL's principle concepts and abstract syntactic categories, and inventing or selecting techniques suitable for exactly those concepts. SCS is well suited to MAL because it is directly targeted on it.

We provide a brief review of MAL. The steps of SCS are outlined in more detail with illustrations from the specification of a simple system. The incorporation of temporal requirements, the structuring of larger specifications, iterative specification development and the role of tool support are discussed.

Index Terms — Requirements analysis. Formal specification. Modal logic. Temporal logic.

I. INTRODUCTION

A requirements specification method is a set of prescriptive heuristics for focusing attention on certain issues at some stages in the production and analysis of a specification and on other issues at other stages. Several systematic and prescriptive requirements analysis methods are in current use — e.g. SADT [1], SASD [2], and CORE [3]. All of these rely on informal diagrammatic and tabular media. By contrast, there are many approaches to the formal specification of systems — e.g. abstract data types [4], operational specifications [5], CSP [6]. These two traditions of research and practice do not overlap, despite the common interest in specifying systems. It is our belief that formal techniques will not be used in the specification of industrial scale systems until elicitation and formalization techniques are adopted that have equivalent communicative power to common informal requirements analysis methods.

In this paper we describe a requirements elicitation and formalization method that is targeted specifically on modal action logic [7]. For the purpose of this paper, it is necessary only to to understand the abstract syntax of the logic, which will be summarized below. For a detailed discussion of the formal system the reader is directed to the original paper and for a summary of the objectives of the project from which it arose to [8]. An account of an earlier version of the method is given in [9] and a more detailed account of the current version in [10].

A. Modal Action Logic

This summary of modal action logic (henceforth 'MAL') is deliberately oversimplified. Its sole purpose is to give the reader sufficient background to understand the the rationale for some of the the the decisions made in designing the elicitation and formalization method. Extracts from the formal specification of an embedded central heating system controller, selected for its conciseness, are given in the Appendix, an information systems example is give in [9]. We shall refer freely to this for illustrations.

MAL consists of several logical layers. The innermost is a many-sorted first-order logic with equality. It is assumed that the reader is familiar with such systems. On top of this is a modal component in which the modal operator [] denotes the performance of an action by an agent. Actions are defined in terms of relations between pre- and post-conditions (see Appendix, lines 36-38). Actions may also be composed using the combinators ';' (sequence), '‖' (parallel composition) and '+' (non-deterministic choice) (see Appendix, line 31).

The third layer is a deontic logic, which is used to specify the circumstances in which an agent is permitted or obliged to perform an action. Two operators are used to qualify actions accordingly; PER and OBL (see Appendix, lines 24-27).

B. Development of the method

Using a method in any branch of software engineering involves imposing some structure or constraints on the practitioner's existing skills. In requirements analysis, these skills are particularly diverse and non-specific. Because of this, we came to refer to the method we needed, half-jokingly, as 'Structured Common Sense' (SCS).

It would appear that existing requirements analysis and early design methods are not a wholly satisfactory basis for specifying systems in MAL [11]. We suspect this to be true in general of requirements methods and formal systems. They have evolved for different purposes, and very often their fundamental concepts are incompatible. This has lead us to reject the approach of welding existing methods and formal systems together. This is not to say that existing methods do not include many techniques, particularly notational techniques, that would be of use in producing formal specifications. In developing SCS, we have cannibalized several existing requirements methods for such techniques, but some techniques are novel (or at least reinvented).

Putting such techniques together into a coherent and prescriptive method targeted on a specific formal system requires a principled analysis of the abstract syntax of that formal system. If one considers an example formal specification in MAL (see Appendix) from the method developer's point of view, several questions spring to mind. Why are these agents selected? Do they cover the domain of discourse adequately? Would another set have lead to a better specification? How do we know that the agents perform precisely those actions? Wouldn't another set of actions have been selected that were equivalent? Why are the entity sorts the ones that are listed? Similarly for the predicates and functions: why specifically those? Where do the definitions of the functions, predicates and actions come from? How do we know which actions are obligatory? In general, when does one need to know the answer to each of these, and a number of similar questions? Which are the most critical to answer, in the sense that retracting such decisions may lead to a large amount of extra work in modifying the specification, and which can safely be deferred?

By answering these questions, a method can be built up step-by-step from the formalization stage backwards. The steps that comprise SCS and their relationship to the resulting MAL specification, will now be described.

C. Outline of the method

The next section describes the steps of the method in some detail. Each produces one or more formatted representation and an increment to an evolving formal specification. The formatted representations include a variety of diagrams, tables and highly constrained natural language descriptions. The representations, informal and formal have well-defined dependency relationships between them (see Figure 1).

Integral to SCS is the notion of *incremental formalization*. That is, the formal specification is built up incrementally during the steps rather than being written as a final step. The early steps amount to identifying the specification objects, rather than inter-relating them, that is, in formal terms, declaring them rather than writing axioms that include them. A large part of any MAL specification is in the form of declarations of objects and their signatures and in many cases these can — and should— be written early in the specification process. Having a nearly complete set of declarations forms a sound basis for the subsequent construction of axioms.

II. THE METHOD

A. Agents

In MAL, agents are the loci of responsibility. They perform actions, are permitted to perform actions or not and they incur obligations. This makes agent identification central to the writing of a MAL specification. Agents may be human users, affected individuals who do not directly use the system or organization, physical devices, other computer systems or functionally separate components of the system being specified. The agents and their interactions are treated as a closed world. Nothing that happens outside this closed world is considered as of any consequence.

Agent identification is based on the construction of viewpoint heirarchies in CORE [3] (see Figure 2). In basic SCS only agents, or viewpoints, at the lowest level are treated as agents from the standpoint of the formal specification. For simplicity we regard higher level agents as prompts and structuring aids for the agents below them. When dealing with specifications of very large systems, it is necessary to specify the system at several levels of the hierarchy.

In identifying agents, several heuristics may be used. Principally, the practitioner looks for job titles, organizational groups and non-standard or intelligent devices. Standard 'dumb' devices, such as printers, are disregarded as they arise out of implementation decisions. More sophisticated devices such as automatic bank tellers, or devices that are intrinsic to the application, such as sensors, should be considered to be agents as they perform actions that are of central importance to the successful understanding of the requirements.

The agents identified at this early stage will appear unchanged in the formal specification. It is possible, therefore, to write declarations of the agents in the skeletal formal specification (see Appendix, line 1).

Having simply identified the agents, the next step is to model their inter-relationships. Data flow analysis is used for this purpose (see Figure 3). It helps the practitioner identify agents' actions. Data flows are a natural way of understanding complex systems [2], and physical and logical data flow analyses are the traditional "first pass" techniques used in structured systems analysis. However, structured systems analysis is based on requirements analysis by top-down decomposition and there is a tendency to regard tangled or complex DFDs as a symptom of muddled thinking. Our DFDs only have one level , depicting communication between agents, and do not form the basis of a hierarchical analysis. It is important to appreciate the reason for this: requirements analysis is a process of discovery, and it is most unlikely that the first structuring of the problem will be a satisfactory starting point for further analysis (cf. [12]). If the DFD is really complicated and the agent hierarchy suggests an obvious structuring of the system then there is a case for structuring the specification hierarchically, but this is a decision made on the basis of the problem and is not dictated by the method.

The concept of 'data' flow is interpreted rather liberally. Sometimes the flow consists of physical objects rather than information (e.g. a blood sample in a patient monitoring system), or some signal that carries no information other than that it exists (e.g. a command).

Data flows are much used in later steps of the method and vestigial signs of the data flows identified at this stage can be detected in the formal specification, but there is no *direct* mapping from the data flow analysis to the skeletal formal specification.

B. Actions

To identify actions, it seems best to focus on the notion of *responsibility*; that is, to ask the question "what does this agent do?" The data flows serve as prompts. The result of this phase of analysis is an action table for each agent. Action tables are derived from CORE's tabular collection forms (see Figure 4). The columns of the action table represent; the sources of input data flows, the inputs themselves, the actions, the ouput data flows they produce, and the destinations of the outputs. The input and output data flows should correspond with those appearing in the data flow analysis for the agent.

An exception to the above rule happens when some information is retained by the agent. This takes the form of an internal data flow between actions (not necessarily different actions). Internal data flows do not appear in the preceding data flow analysis, in which only the external interfaces of agents are under consideration. Where possible, internal data flows should be avoided as they can be symptomatic of premature design or undue concern with the physical properties of the existing system. Internal data flows cannot always be avoided, for example where it is an intrinsic feature of an agent that it has a memory.

Action tabulation results in the identification of a set of actions for each agent. Declarations for these, but without parameters at this stage, may be added to the formal specification (see Appendix, lines 13-20).

When action and data flows are given meaningful names action tables capture much of the sense of the system being specified. A fuller natural language description of the actions is also necessary, however, at this stage. This action description serves several purposes; it informally documents what the actions do, and provides prompts in the subsequent identification of entities and the definition of the actions and their enabling conditions (see Table 1).

<u>CloseCValve</u> On receipt of a CCloseCmd, provided the circulation valve is open, it closes (making PhysCValvePos = Open).

<u>OpenCValve</u> On receipt of a COpenCmd, provided the circulation valve is closed, it opens (making PhysCValvePos = Closed).

Table 1: Action descriptions for agent CValve.

C. Entities

The purpose of the next part of SCS is to identify a set of entity sorts (i.e. types or classes), predicates and functions to be used in the formulae of the formal specification, and constants. Functions and predicates have *signatures* that is the sorts of the parameters they can take and, in the case of functions, return. These are defined at this stage. Parameterized actions also have signatures. As soon as the entity sorts have been identified, the action descriptions can be used to prepare action signatures.

Not all data flows carry significant information. Some, *signals*, merely carry the information that they exist. In simple systems many of the data flows are of this type and represent the issuing of commands. The other form of data flow, *information flows* carry real information. Using the action descriptions, all data flows should be categorized as either signals or information flows. Every information flow should be expanded into its constituent parts using data structure diagrams [13]. These have the power of regular expressions, which are sufficient for most purposes. That is an information flow is decomposed using *sequencing*, *selection* and *iteration*. (see Figure 5).

Entity-relationship-attribute (ERA) modelling captures the static structure of the system and provides the predicates, functions and sorts of entity (other than agents). ERA modelling is a conceptual, rather than notational technique, but it is invariably associated with the ERA diagram. The starting point for ERA analysis is a systematic examination of the agent hierarchy, data structures and action descriptions. Agents are of interest in ERA analysis, because as well as performing actions agents may have attributes that need to be referred to.

An *entity* is anything in the domain of discourse that performs or suffers actions, that has properties that change or are of interest, that enters into relationships with other entities that change or are of interest, or anything that is a named individual of some significance. These criteria are necessarily abstract and can only be fleshed out by knowledge of the problem domain.

Entities need not be physical objects in the real world. If it is sensible to treat forms as entities, then it is quite sensible to consider acknowledgements, warnings, notifications, bookings and the like as entities also. On the other hand, the full-blown approach of object-oriented design or specification by means of abstract data types would dictate that more abstract objects still should be considered as entities, such as sets of acknowledgements, the class of things that are either notifications or bookings, queues of warnings, etc. These may appear in the formal specification but are not treated as entities. The criterion is not how physically tangible the entity is, but how pertinent it is to the application domain.

Attributes are intrinsic properties of entities. Since attributes are tied to specific entities, it makes sense to concentrate first on the identification of entities, and only then on their attributes. Economy should be applied in identifying attributes. Often an entity may have a set of boolean attributes which, on further thought, are seen to be mutually exclusive. If this is the case then the situation is better modelled by just one (non-boolean) attribute that has the previous attribute names as its possible values. *Relationships* are the properties groups (generally pairs) of entities may have. They can be thought of as links between entities.

A sort is a kind, type or class of entity. Expanded information flows and the ERA analysis suggest the names of many sorts. Attributes may also need new sorts to be declared. In a central heating system the sort *switch position* may be necessary, even though by our criterion, it is not sufficiently concrete to be regarded as an entity in its own right. Similar or identical descriptions may appear in the data structures for different information flows. Rather than treat such similar things as different sorts, the analyst is encouraged to generalize them. Composite sorts are also usually needed.

Relationships and boolean attributes become predicates in the formal specification. Non-boolean attributes are formalized as functions. Entities not already included as agent sorts are declared as entity sorts (see Appendix, line 4).

Sort, constant, function and predicate descriptions are useful prompts when writing static axioms.

D. Causes

The actions performed by the system have been informally specified as part of the action tabulation and description activities. It has yet been determined, except perhaps indirectly in the definition of other actions, *when* each action occurs. This is considered now. To analyze the causal links between states and actions, three questions need to be asked separately. When does a particular action occur? when does it not occur? and what are the consequences when it does occur?

To answer the first two questions the practitioner should first try to identify the conditions under which each action may (PER) and must (OBL) occur and then the conditions under which it becomes the case that the action is not permissible. Conditions under which the action can, must or cannot occur are all described similarly, in English, in terms of an expanded form of the input data to the action on the action table (see Table 2).

The third question is anwered by describing the effects of each action under various circumstances. Hence an expanded form of the inputs to an action from the action table is linked with an expanded form of the output data. It may often be the case that an action has different effects under different circumstances (see Table 3).

<u>StopOilFlow</u> (1) If the Observed Flow Status is abnormal
(2) If the Observed Combustion Status is abnormal
(3) If the Room Temperature is hotter than the Temperature Setting + 2 degrees
(4) If the Observed Switch Position is Off

<u>StopMotor</u> (1) StopOilFlow was performed more than 5 seconds ago.

Table 2: Enabling Conditions for the StopOilFlow and StopMotor Actions

<u>OpenOilValve</u> Provided the Oil Valve Position was Closed, it becomes Open

<u>CloseOilValve</u> Provided the Oil Valve Position was Open, it becomes Closed and the Observed Flow and Combustion Statuses become Off.

Table 3: Informal Action Definition

An agent performing an action can only oblige an agent (possibly itself) to perform another action if there is a signal data flow between the two actions. Because of the importance of these interactions for real-time embedded systems, this is treated as a separate step, causal tabulation.

A causal table is a matrix with rows and columns labelled by the names of the actions. Each cell of the table represents a causal interaction. The matrix is always sparse and some cells are guaranteed to be empty by virtue of the absence of data flows between the actions in question. Instead of drawing up such a large and unwieldly table, a set of smaller tables is prepared, the actions of which are the actions of pairs of agents which, according to the data flow analysis, do communicate by data flows.

E. Formalization

We have stressed the notion of incremental formalization and have shown how formal declarations can be written at an early stage of the method. The action, relation and function descriptions produced at earlier stages are, of course, informal, but their format is constrained ins such a way that the transformation into MAL is straightforward (see Appendix, lines 24-38).

Not all axioms are produced quite as mechanically. Action definitions and behavioural axioms may include reference to specification objects that have not been encountered previously. These should not be invented on an ad hoc basis, but only within certain acceptable categories, such as termination predicates, functions of existing sorts, or new composite sorts. New objects have to be declared, and in certain cases defined in static axioms (see Appendix, lines 9, 21-22)

IV. TIME

Hitherto, our ontology of actions and states has been too simple. Actions have been treated as atomic transitions between (implicit) states. In real systems, however, actions and states endure and we need to specify requirements concerning relationships between their times of occurrence. For example, it is a common requirement that a particular action not start while another is happening, or for a timeout to be specified, that is for one action to be followed by a second action within an absolute interval or a third if that interval is exceeded. In the temporal extension to MAL [7], this is accomplished by the addition of a new primitive construct, the interval. Like states in basic MAL, but unlike the intervals of Allen [14], the intervals in MAL are *implicit*. That is, one refers directly to the relationships between the durations of actions or states rather than asserting that they endure over named intervals and then express relationships between those intervals.

Specifically, the extensions involve the qualified obligation and temporal operators. Obligations need to be qualified to express the requirement that the obligation be discharged before another action has finished executing or before a formula becomes false (see Appendix, lines 28, 29, 35).

The temporal operators include DURING, BEFORE, LAST-BEFORE and OVERLAPS. DURING and BEFORE have the obvious meanings. LAST-BEFORE(a, b) means that the interval during which a is true is the last before one during which b is true. The OVERLAPS(P, Q) means that P becomes true before Q starts and becomes false before Q ends. There is no MEETS operator, to provide exact abutment of intervals, as this would presuppose absolute precision.

As a syntactic shorthand we allow absolute intervals to be named. This obviates the need for an explicit calendar or clock agent that continually broadcasts ticks (see Appendix, lines 12, 28, 29, 35).

It is important to realize that this construct denotes a real-time interval, not its duration. If a requirement mentioned two five second intervals, two distinctly named intervals — 5secs1 and 5secs2 — would have to be declared.

Timing requirements have a surprisingly minor effect on the steps of SCS as a whole. Where timing requirements are articulated early they can be incorporated into the appropriate natural language action descriptions and thence into the formal action definitions. Indeed, for small systems, systems with relatively few timing requirements or those where the timing requirements appear to be precisely localized, it may be best to pretend initially that there are no timing requirements and then refine the simplified specification in a separate timing analysis pass.Where necessary simple diagrams showing intervals as blocks along a time line can be used to assist in visualisation of temporal requirements.

V. DISCUSSION

A. *Experience*

SCS has been continually revised as the result of its evaluation on case studies, but the version discussed in this paper and [10] is fairly stable. We are confident of the wide applicability and usefulness of SCS. It has been used on a broad class of case studies, for example the organization of IFIP working conferences, a holiday booking system, the central heating control system used to illustrate this paper, an elevator control and scheduling system, an intensive care unit patient monitoring system, and the control of road traffic lights. Although we have focused on embedded real-time systems, in which control is a more predominant issue than data processing, many of our case studies have been DP systems and there is every reason to believe that SCS could be used successfully for traditional DP applications.

As a disclaimer, however, we must emphasise that none of our case studies to date have been live industrial applications.

B. *Structure*

Large industrial formal specifications must be capable of being structured in some way. A large, complex flat specification would be impossibly difficult to understand. Furthermore, different parts of a well-structured specification can be given to different analysts to work on comparatively independently. Another pragmatic concern that suggests the need for structuring is reuse of specification components or instantiation of generic components.

We have performed experiments with two structuring mechanisms; top-down structuring using aggregation, and object-oriented structuring using inheritance [10].

In general, we contend that requirements analysis is not an activity that proceeds naturally in a top-down way. Structuring by aggregation, that is the composition of a specification out of sub-parts, is useful, however, where the problem legitimately suggests a hierarchical structuring. In SCS, this is naturally accomplished by multiple specifications at different levels of the agent hierarchy. The price paid is the redundancy and possible inconsistency of multiple specifications at different levels. Specifically, actions must be defined twice; in terms of the relations between pre- and post-conditions, and in terms of 'programs' of their component actions.

Object-oriented structuring, that is the use of specialization and generalization is a more formally tractable approach and has a potentially greater pay-off. However, it is often difficult to determine and exploit the commonalities between objects until a relatively late stage in requirements analysis. Incorporation of this form of structuring requires major changes to the specification language and some steps of SCS, particularly those addressing entities and their properties.

C. *Iteration*

In the preceding description of SCS, it may appear that a requirements analysis project is a neat sequence of steps. In practice, of course, this is not so. Changes to requirements are inevitable, and information elicited later on in the process may force a re-evaluation of information that was acquired earlier. Because of the strict dependencies between the products of the SCS steps (see Figure 1), change management is not difficult. It is greatly eased if the natural language descriptions are completed in a systematic and disciplined way. The descriptions can then be used for traceability.

D. *Tool Support*

Our work in the development of tool support is proceeding in two areas: general environmental support for specification management [15] and specific tools to support SCS and MAL. Specific tool support for SCS will take the form of consistency checking within and between the intermediate representation and graphics or form editing to construct these representations. Formal verification and validation tools (e.g. theorem proving for MAL) are being investigated, but are beyond the scope of this paper.

E. General Applicability

We have presented a new requirements analyis method for new formal system. Few modifications would be required to the existing version of SCS to re-target it onto GIST [16] as the primitive constructs of GIST, namely agents, actions and constraints, are closely related to those of MAL. In general, however, we are not confident of the ability to generalize SCS or any other method from one target to another. There seems to be a tradeoff here between suitability for a given target and general applicability; it is idle to aim for both.

Nevertheless, the goal-directed *methodology* we have adopted for the development of SCS seems to be of general applicability, regardless of the target formal system. The method developer should analyze the abstract syntactic categories of the target and their relative centrality to the conceptual core of the formal system, and then progress backward using, wherever possible, notational techniques and heuristics from other methods.

Acknowledgements

The research discussed in this paper was performed as part of the Alvey FOREST (Formal Specification Techniques) project with funding from the UK Science and Engineering Research Council and Department of Trade and Industry. The collaborators in FOREST are Imperial College of Science and Technology (London), GEC Avionics (Borehamwood), GEC Marconi Research Laboratory (Great Baddow) and AERE, Harwell. Particular thanks are due to Judy Booth (AERE) and Michael Aslett (GAv) for their significant contribution to the work reported.

REFERENCES

[1] Ross, D.T. & Shoman, K.E. 'Structured analysis for requirements definition' *IEEE Trans. Software Emg. SE-3:* 6-15, 1977

[2] De Marco, T. *Structured Analysis and System Specification* Yourdon, 1978

[3] Mullery, G. 'CORE — A method for controlled requirement specification' *Proc. 4th Int. Conf. Software Eng.* IEEE Comp. Soc. Press, 1976

[4] Guttag, J. & Horning, J.J. *Formal Specification as a Design Tool* Xerox Palo Alto Research Centre Report CSL-80-1, 1980

[5] Zave, P. 'The operational versus the conventional approach to software development' *Comm. ACM 27(2):* 104-118, 1984

[6] Hoare, C.A.R. *Communicating Sequential Processes* Prentice-Hall, 1985

[7] Maibaum, T.S.E. *A Logic for the Formal Requirements Specification of Real-Time/Embedded Systems* FOREST Report R3, GEC Research Laboratories, Marconi Research Centre, Great Baddow, Chelmsford, England, 1986

[8] Cunningham, R.J., Finkelstein, A.C.W., Goldsack, S.J., Maibaum, T.S.E. & Potts, C. 'Formal Requirements Specification — The FOREST Project' *Proc. 3rd Int. Workshop Software Specification & Design* IEEE Comp. Soc. Press, 1985

[9] Finkelstein, A.C.W. & Potts, C. 'Structured Common Sense: The elicitation and formalization of system requirements' in P.J. Brown and D.J. Barnes (Eds.) *Software Engineering '86* Peter Peregrinus, 1986

[10] Potts, C., Finkelstein, A.C.W., Aslett, M. & Booth, J. *A Requirements Elicitation and Formalization Method for Real-Time/Embedded Systems,* FOREST Report R2, GEC Research Laboratories, Marconi Research Centre, Great Baddow, Chelmsford, England, 1986

[11] Finkelstein, A.C.W. & Potts, C. *Evaluation of Existing Requirements Extraction Strategies* FOREST Report, R1, GEC Research Laboratories, Marconi Research Centre, Great Baddow, Chelmsford, England, 1985

[12] Jackson, M.A. 'Constructive methods of program design' *Lecture Notes in Computer Science, 44:* 236-262, Springer-Verlag, 1976

[13] Jackson, M.A. *Principles of Program Design* Academic Press, 1975

[14] Allen, J.F. 'Maintaining knowledge about temporal intervals' *Comm. ACM 26(11):* 832-843, 1983

[15] Jordan, D., Glensiter, S.M.D., Tavendale, R.D. & Gallacher, R. *Specification of a Support Environment for a Formal Requirements Specification Toolset* FOREST Report R8, GEC Research Laboratories, Marconi Research Centre, Great Baddow, Chelmsford, England, 1986

[16] Balzer, R., Cohen, D., Feather, M., Goldman, N., Swartout, W. & Wile, D. 'Operational specification as the basis for specification validation' in Ferrari, Boldognani & Goguen (Eds.) *Theory and Practice of Software Technology* North-Holland, 1983

APPENDIX

Extracts from a Specification of a Central Heating System Controller

<u>agent sorts</u>

1   MSwitch, CValve, Motor, Ignition, OilValve, FFI, OCS, Controller

<u>agent contstants</u> *Note overloading of names*

2   MSwitch   : MSwitch
...
3   Controller   : Controller

<u>entity sorts</u>

4   SwitchPos, ValvePos, Safety, Temperature, MotorSpeed

<u>entity constants</u>

Constant in all states

5   On, Off   : SwitchPos
...
6   Abn   : Safety   *Abnormality*

Constant within a state

7   PhysSwitchPos, ObsSwitchPos : SwitchPos
...
8   PhysCombStatus, ObsCombStatus,
        PhysFlowStatus, ObsFlowStatus : Safety

<u>functions</u>

9   Opposite   :SwitchPos -> SwitchPos

<u>predicates</u>

Regular predicates

10   Adequate   : MotorSpeed

Termination predicates

11   CCloseCommanded, COpenCommanded
      ...

<u>real time intervals</u>

12   5secs, 5mins

<u>actions</u>

*Notation is: Agent * Action : Arg1 * ... * Argn*

13   Controller * StartMotor
14   Controller * StartOilFlow
15   Controller * StartFurnace
16   Controller * StartCirculation
17   Controller * StopOilFlow
18   Controller * StopMotor
      ...
19   CValve * CloseCValve
20   CValve * OpenCValve

<u>static axioms</u>

21   Opposite (On) = Off
22   Opposite (Off) = On

23   Adequate (m) => m <> Stopped

<u>behavioural axioms</u>

Requirements on hardware components, including physical constraints (E.g. an open valve cannot be opened)

24   CCloseCommanded => OBL(Cvalve, CloseCValve)

25   PhysCValvePos = Closed =>
            ~PER(CValve, CloseCValve)

26   COpenCommanded => OBL(CValve, OpenCValve)

27   PhysCValvePos = Open =>
            ~PER(CValve, OpenCValve)

Requirements on the controller

If the observed switch position is on after more than five minutes have elapsed since the oil valve - last shut off the supply to the furnace, the controller should start the motor immediately. It is assumed that the criterion for furnace shut-off is the shutting off of the oil supply.

28   [OilValve,CloseOilValve](
      (ObsSwitchPos=On)=>
      DURING(5mins, ~PER(Controller,StartMotor)))

If the observed switch position is on during the five supply to the furnace, the controller should start the motor at the end of the five minutes.

29 [OilValve, CloseOilValve](
  [5mins] ObsSwitchPos = On =>
    OBL(Controller, StartMotor, 5mins))

30 ObsSwitchPos = Off =>
    ~PER(Controller, StartMotor)

When the motor speed is adequate, the controller must start the oil supply to the furnace and then ignite the furnace. While that is happening, it must stop the circulation of (cold) water

31 Adequate(MotorSpeed) =>
    OBL(Controller,
  (StartOilFlow; StartFurnace) || StopCirculation)

32 ~Adequate(MotorSpeed) =>
    ~PER(Controller, StartOilFlow) &
    ~PER(Controller, StartFurnace)

The furnace should be shut down whenever there is an abnormality in the oil flow or furnace behaviour, when the room is getting too warm, or when the master switch is switched off.

33 (ObsFlowAbn |
  ObsCombAbn |
  RoomTemp > TempSetting + 2 |
  ObsSwitchPos = Off) &
  OilValvePos = Open =>
    OBL(Controller, StopOilFlow)

34 OilValvePos = Closed =>
    ~PER(Controller, StopOilFlow)

The motor should be stopped (at least) five seconds after the oil valve has been closed.

35 DURING(5secs, OilValvePos = Closed) &
  DURING(5secs, MotorSpeed <> Stopped) =>
    OBL(Controller, StopMotor, 5secs)

  ... etc.

<u>action definitions</u>

37   [Controller, StartMotor] StartCommanded

38   [Controller, StopMotor] StopCommanded

  ... etc.

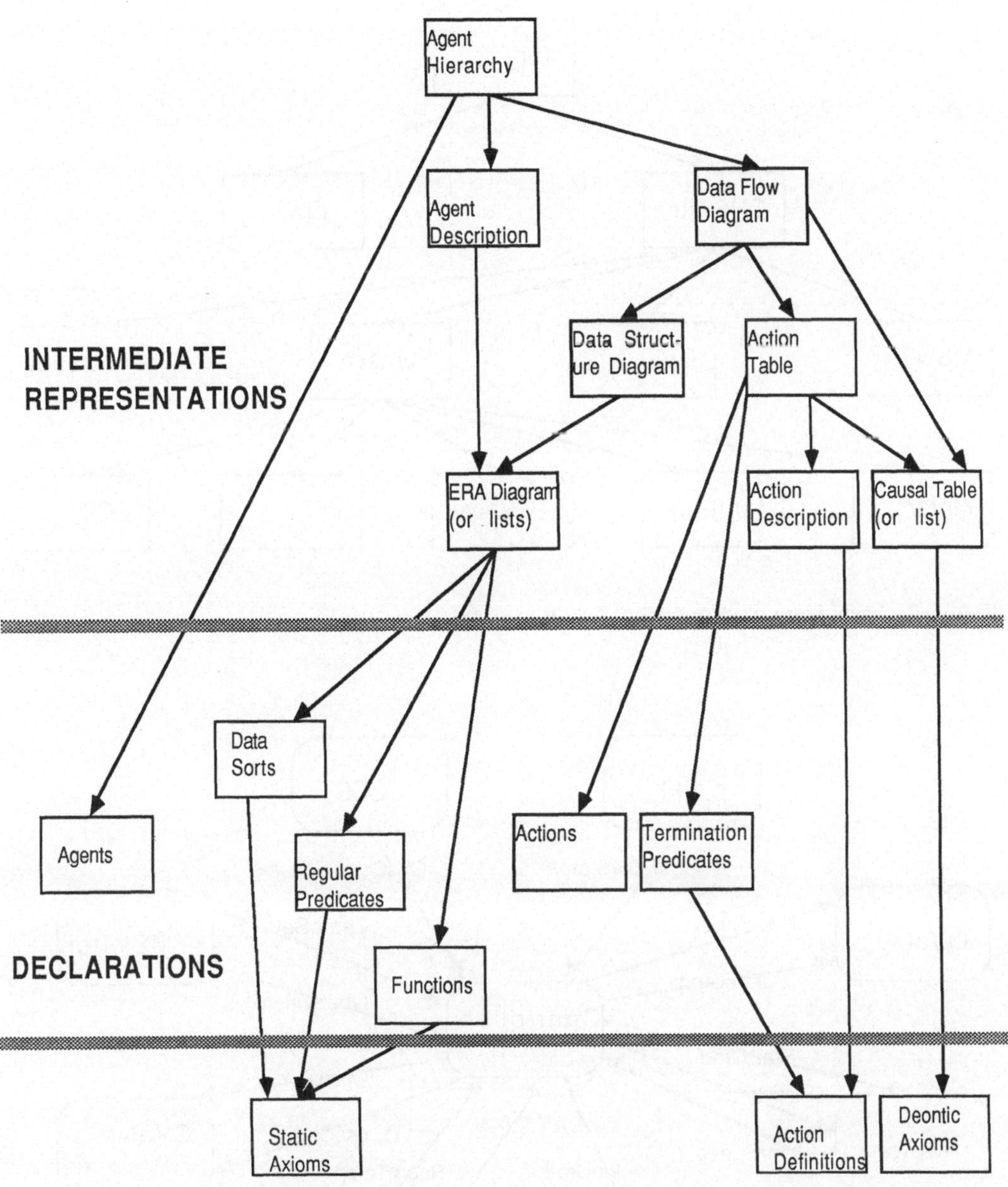

Figure 1: Dependencies between SCS intermediate representations and parts of a MAL specification.

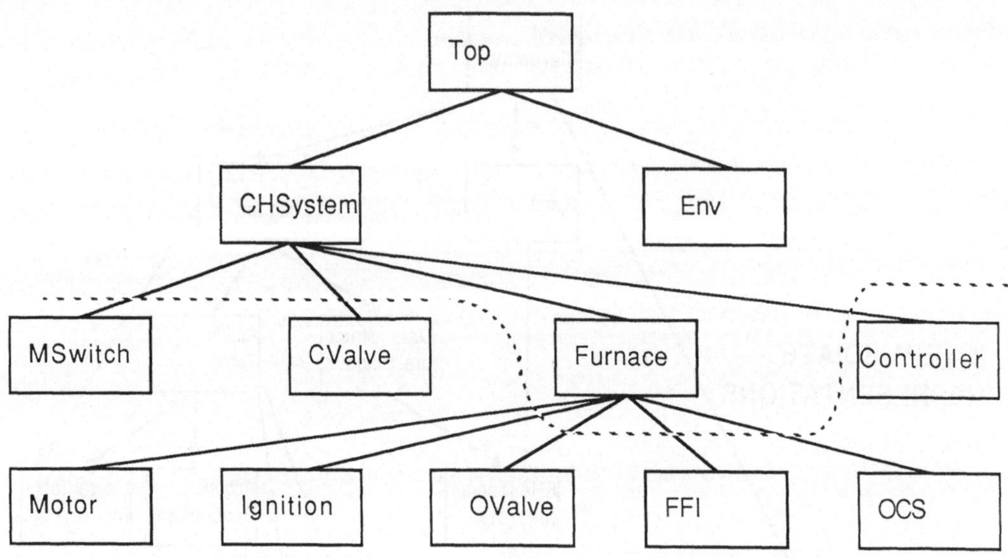

Figure 2: Agent hierarchy for central heating system

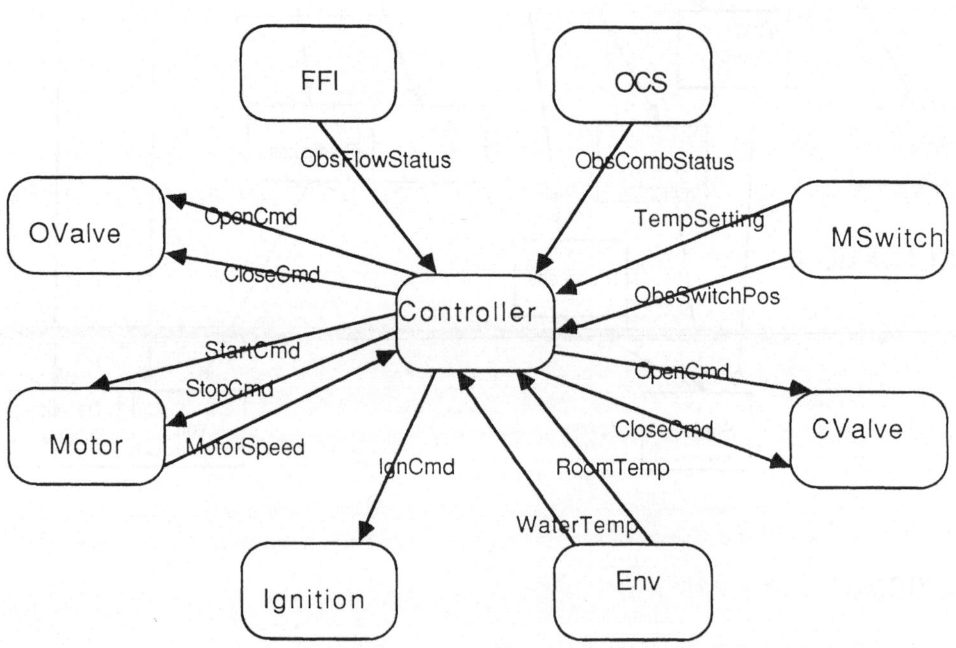

Figure 3: Data flow diagram for part of central heating system

CValve

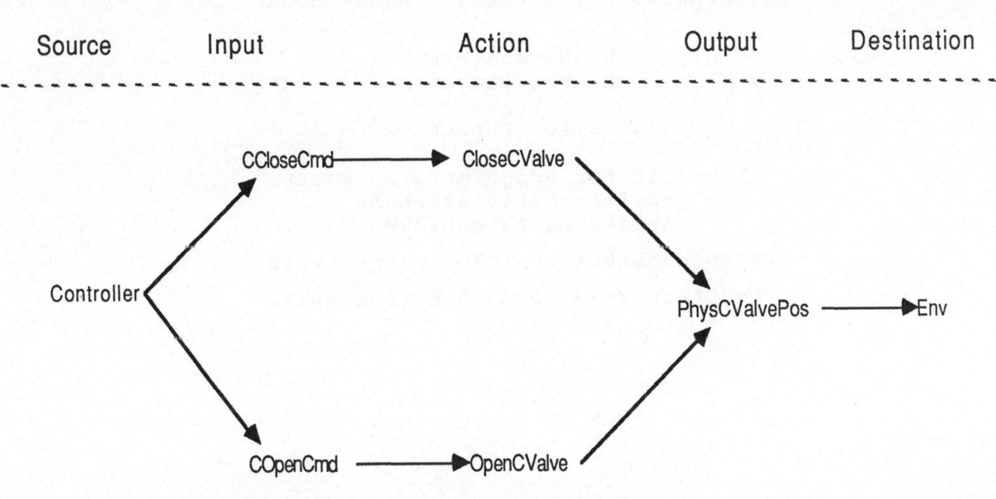

Figure 4: Action table for CValve agent in the central heating system.

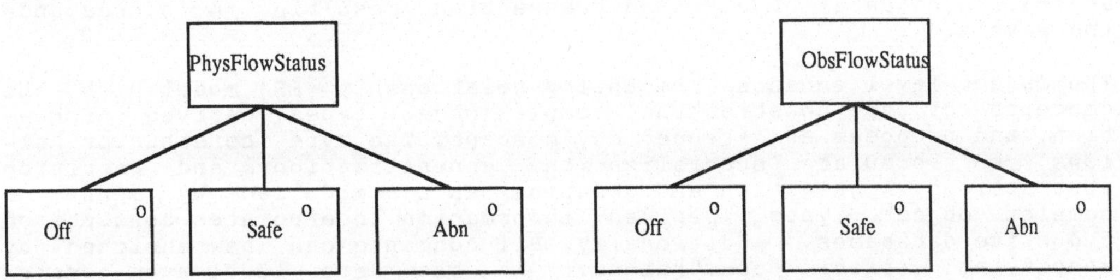

Figure 5: Data structure diagrams for two information flows in the central heating system.

THREE-LEVEL-SPECIFICATION OF DATABASES USING
AN EXTENDED ENTITY-RELATIONSHIP MODEL

U. Hohenstein
L. Neugebauer
G. Saake *
H.-D. Ehrich

Institut für Programmiersprachen
und Informationssysteme
Abteilung Datenbanken

Technische Universität Braunschweig

Postfach 3329, D-3300 Braunschweig

Abstract:

A great deal of (so-called) semantic data models has been proposed for the specification of conceptual schemas. Each of these offers many different, but semantically related constructs for modelling.

We, therefore, attempt to integrate all constructs into a few semantic constructs. The resulting data model emphasizes a clear conceptual separation of data, object, and transactions resulting in corresponding levels.

The object level enhances the Entity-Relationship (ER) model with the concepts of type construction, complex object types, derived information, and proposes an extended key concept. The type constructor allows to formulate specialization, generalization, and partition abstractions. Aggregation and grouping can be modelled by means of complex object types. Derived information incorporates concepts of deductive databases. Additionally, all concepts can be enriched by specifying explicit constraints. At the data level even complex domains of attributes can be specified by means of user-defined abstract data types. The transaction level allows the specification of arbitrary transactions.

*) G. Saake's work was supported by the Deutsche Forschungsgemeinschaft (DFG) under grant Eh75/6-1.

1. INTRODUCTION

In this paper we present (yet) another version of an extended Entity-Relationship (ER) model. As there already exist various versions of extended ER models, we feel that it needs some justification why we add one more model to the admittedly great number of existing ones. There are two main reasons why we decided to design a new model:

At first, this model shall form the basis for several database and information system design tools, as there are the translation from ER notation to relational schemas [HNS86], a graphical editor for input, test data generation [NN85], and some consistency and integrity checking components which are under development now. In the more distant future they might form an integrated DB design support system. For these tools we want a basis that is optimally tailored to our needs and has a straightforward semantic foundation.

The second point is that we want this extended ER model and the design support tools to be suited for the design of standard and non-standard applications as well, i.e. commercial databases <u>and</u> non-standard applications like CAD databases, geo-scientific databases [RNLE85], software engineering support databases, or VLSI design support databases. Design support systems that cover one of these applications are presented in [ADD85, BDRZ84, BH86, DKM85]. To be suitable for various of these applications our EER model integrates different concepts from other well-known semantic data models [Ch76, EHW85, Ne83, SS77].

Our semantic data model is divided into three levels, the data level, the object level, and the transaction level as proposed in [Eh85, EDG86].

On the data level basic data types like 'integer' and 'boolean' are provided. Further, more structured data types e.g., sets, lists, and Pascal-like records, may be specified by the user by means of abstract data types. The description of the data types consists of two parts, the specification part which gives the structure of the data types and the effects of the operations allowed on these data types, and the implementation that gives detailed implementation instructions.

The object level consists of an ER model [Ch76] enriched by concepts for generalization/specialization [SS77], complex objects like those defined in [RNLE85], and derived information. These concepts seem essential to us to support non-standard database design in an effective way, because a lot of non-standard databases which are under development nowadays rely on these or similar concepts, e.g., see [DKM85] for VLSI design, or [RNLE85] for geoscientific database design.

The transaction level offers the possibility to specify transactions that respect all integrity constraints inherent to the object model and constraints specified by the user on the object level. Similar to the data level a specification on the transaction level is given in two parts. At first, a specification of the effect of transactions is given by means of pre- and postconditions. In the implementation part the user describes the realization of the transaction by composing it from system-offered 'elementary operations' that respect all integrity constraints inherent to the data model.

Within the presentation of our model we describe our own new ideas beside well-known concepts because they are difficult to separate from each other. Furthermore, we hope the presentation of all concepts integrated into our model will have a certain tutorial effect for readers less familiar with ER models. For expository purposes we mainly use standard examples because examples on non-standard applications soon grow very complex.

The next three chapters of this paper describe the three levels, data, object, and transaction level. In the conclusions, open questions with regard to our data model are discussed.

2. DATA LEVEL

Data and object level together specify the structure of the information stored in a database, whereas the transaction level describes possible 'updating' of this information. At the object level, all things about which information is to be stored are modelled in an abstract manner, whereas the data level describes the data really stored. All directly visible information about objects stored in a database is only presented by the values of attributes of the objects. So, an important property of attribute values is a simple 'printable' structure allowing a well-readable output.

We propose **abstract data types** for describing attribute domains and operations on them. An introduction to algebraic specification of abstract data types is given in [EM85]. [Eh85] propose the use of abstract data types in conceptual database design and [RNLE85] introduce special data types for geoscientific databases.

We define an abstract data type by a specification module and an implementation module following the ideas of modular programming. The specification module contains the signature of the specified data type i.e., the sorts and operations of the data type. This module can also be extended by an equational specification of its behaviour to enable the verification of its implementation. In an early design step a prototype of this specification – using term-rewriting or logic programming as proposed in [DE84] – enables early analysis of the behaviour of the data type. However, we suppose that only a concrete implementation of the data types enables a valid prototyping of the entire database under acceptable circumstances.

The syntax of a specification module may be illustrated by the following examples:

```
data specification module date;
  import int, bool;
  sorts  date;
  operations create: int x int x int --> date,
             day:                date --> int,
             month:              date --> int,
             year:               date --> int,
             less:       date x date --> bool;
end module date.


data specification module p_status;
  import bool;
  sorts  p_status;
  operations single:              --> p_status,
             married:             --> p_status,
             divorced:            --> p_status,
             widowed:             --> p_status,
             not_married: p_status --> bool;
  equations
             not_married (single)   = true,
             not_married (divorced) = true,
             not_married (widowed)  = true,
             not_married (married)  = false;
end module p_status.
```

Each data type specified in this way is implemented by an **implementation module** using already defined data types. The standard data types 'integer', 'boolean', 'character' and 'text' are predefined. The set of standard data types can be enriched by geometric data types like 'point' or 'line'. Since data types are used for attribute domains, we only allow type definition schemas producing types with fixed storage requirements. This restriction does not seem to be too hard, because the object level offers set- and list-valued attributes. Moreover, most of the complex structures modelled in a database are typically 'updatable' (i.e. their properties may change in time) and are specified on the object level.

The implementation of a data type is done in terms of type definition mechanisms known from PASCAL-like programming languages: enumeration types, domain restrictions, arrays of fixed length and records. As an example the data types 'p-status' and 'date' specified above are implemented by following implementation modules:

```
data implementation module date;
  import int, bool;
  type  date = record
                 d,m,y : int;
               end;

  function create (a,b,c: int): date;
    begin
       if a in { 1 .. 31 } and
          b in { 1 .. 12 } and
          c in { 1850 .. 1999 }
       then create := (a,b,c)
       else create := (0,0,0)
       fi
    end;

  function day (x: date): int;
    begin day := x.d; end;

  function month (x: date): int;
    begin month := x.m; end;

  function year (x: date): int;
    begin year := x.y; end;

  function less (a,b: date): bool;
    var i,j : int;
    begin
       i := a.d + 100 * a.m + 10000 * a.y ;
       j := b.d + 100 * b.m + 10000 * b.y ;
       less := (i < j);
    end;

end module date.
```

The data type 'date' is underspecified : only the signature is specified in the specification module 'date'. This enables a flexible
error-handling in the function 'create', that is difficult to specify
by equations. The implementation of the function 'create' can be refined to detect impossible values of 'date' like '30 February 1989'
without changing the specification module.

```
    data implementation module p_status;
      import bool;
      type    p_status = (sing, marr, divo, wido);
      const   single   = sing,
              married  = marr,
              divorced = divo,
              widowed  = wido ;
      function not_married (x: p_status): bool;
         begin
           not_married := not (x = marr);
         end;
    end module p_status.
```

Now, we mention several useful software tools for database design support based on the data type modules. The design of the data level can
be supported by software tools known from modular programming and
abstract data type specification. These tools monitor the correct
hierarchic module structure and guarantee a consistent data level
specification after data type modifications. An equational specification of the data type may also be used to verify the given implementation or for prototyping of the data type.

Other software tools support the consistent design of the entire database schema. The signature of the data types defined in the specification module is used to check the syntax of the integrity constraints, the derived attributes and the transaction specifications
described in the next two chapters. This allows a valid specification
of the object and transaction levels even with unimplemented data
types. For prototyping on a relational database system the design
support system also has to generate an automatic translation of data
type values into the attribute domains which are used by the underlying relational database system.

3. OBJECT LEVEL

The object level is directly set upon the data level. Our approach starts from Chen's Entity-Relationship (ER) model [Ch76], since it is well-tried and widely accepted. It supports a natural modelling of the application environment that does not depend on later implementation, but can easily be mapped into implemented data models, especially the relational one [Ce83, HNS86]. We extend this model by concepts for describing structured objects similar to [RNLE85, LN86], generalizations [SS77], derivation, and propose a generalized key concept. Besides, attributes can even take values from complex data types specified at the data level.

When developing the object level we have attempted to integrate all important semantic constructs of recent semantic data models into a few concepts. Therefore, we provide three basic concepts, namely objects, relationships, and type construction to be modelled in corresponding schemas. Additionally, explicit constraints can be added to the schemas.

In the following, the syntax and semantics of the object, relationship, and type construction schemas are outlined by means of examples, and a graphic representation is given.

3.1 OBJECT SCHEMA

As in the ER model the universe of discourse modelled at the object level consists of entities and relationships among them. Objects represent abstract entities of interest. Properties of an entity are specified as attributes describing the object. Entities with common properties are classified into object classes (originally called entity types). The object schema now consists of all defined object classes modelling the considered application. A class is graphically represented by a rectangle, associated attributes and their corresponding data types are denoted as ovals. For instance, consider figure 3.1, where an object class PERSON with attributes 'name', 'address', etc. is shown.

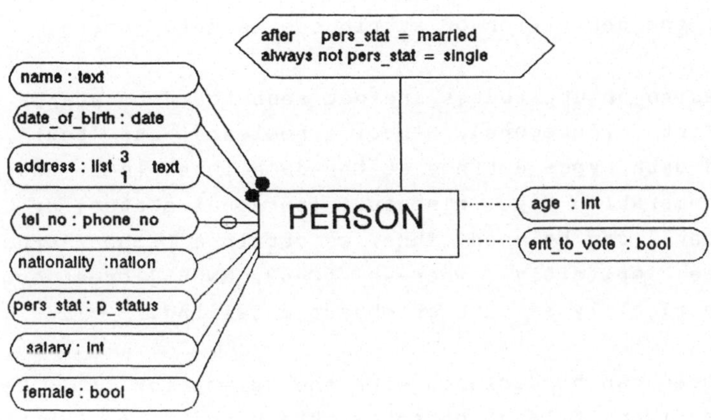

<u>figure</u> 3.1: Object class PERSON

The syntactical definition of PERSON in an object schema is given as
follows:

```
class PERSON
    attributes name:            text,
               date_of_birth:   date,
               address:         list of text  card (1,3),
               tel_no:          phone_no optional,
               salary:          int,
               nationality:     nation,
               pers_stat:       p_status,
               female:          bool,
               age:             int,
               ent_to_vote:     bool;
    key name,
        date_of_birth;
    derived age             as year (today) - year (date_of_birth),
            ent_to_vote as nationality = 'german' and
                            age          > 18;
    constraints after       pers_stat = married
                always not pers_stat = single;
    end PERSON.
```

In contrast to the ER model originally defined in [Ch76] we support
several extensions.

At first, the definition of attributes is more general.

- The domains of attributes are not restricted to standard data types like 'int' (integers), 'bool' (boolean), and 'text', but all **user defined data types** defined at the data level (see chapter 2) like the enumeration type 'p_status' (personal status) or the structured type 'date' can be used. Thus, we obtain a richer structure of attributes implicitly, whereas [Ce83, EWH85] treat composite attributes explicitly as part of object modelling.

- Attributes can be declared with the <u>key</u>-option. All **key** attributes together identify each object in the class, i.e., there must not exist two different persons (of class PERSON) having the same 'name' and 'date_of_birth' values.
Key attributes are marked by a broad dot in the graphical representation.

- Non-key attributes can be defined to be <u>optional</u> and/or multivalued (<u>list</u> <u>of</u> / <u>set</u> <u>of</u>). For **optional** attributes the null-value '-' is allowed, indicating that, e.g., a person need not have a telephone. Optional attributes are graphically marked by a circle on the connecting line. **Multivalued** attributes can be defined by means of <u>list</u> <u>of</u> (for enumerated multisets) or <u>set</u> <u>of</u> (for normal sets), both possibly constrained by **cardinalities** <u>card</u> (min, max), min $\in \mathbb{N}_0$ and max $\in \mathbb{N} \cup \{*\}$, where '*' denotes 'infinite'. In our example, a person must have at least one address (since it is not optional) and may have up to three addresses enumerated by first, second, and third domicile. If no cardinality is specified <u>card</u> (0,*) is assumed.

- **Derived** attributes are attributes that are not explicitly stored but computed from other attributes. The derivation rule is specified in the <u>derived</u>-clause. Thus, the age of a person is computed as the difference between the actual date (today) and the date of birth of that person, supposing a function 'today', which, at any time, yields the actual date. Furthermore, a person is entitled to vote if (s)he is at least 18 years old and has the german citizenship. In the graphical representation derived attributes are marked by a dotted line.
Derived attributes open the door to model concepts of deductive databases.

To restrict possible database instances to "consistent" ones, the object schema can be completed by **integrity constraints**. We do not only allow the definition of "static" constraints, i.e. criteria for admissible database states, but also **"dynamic"** constraints specifying admissible state sequences, using the proposals of [ELG84, LEG85] to incorporate temporal logic.

Constraints are graphically represented by hexagonal "integrity boxes". Since a derivation rule can be considered as a special kind of constraint supervising the computation of the derived attribute, the rule is also graphically put in an integrity box. For simplicity, we omit the derivation rules in our figures. Indeed, this can be done by means of the intended graphical editor.

Let us now examine some more features of the object schema. Therefore, consider the following example.

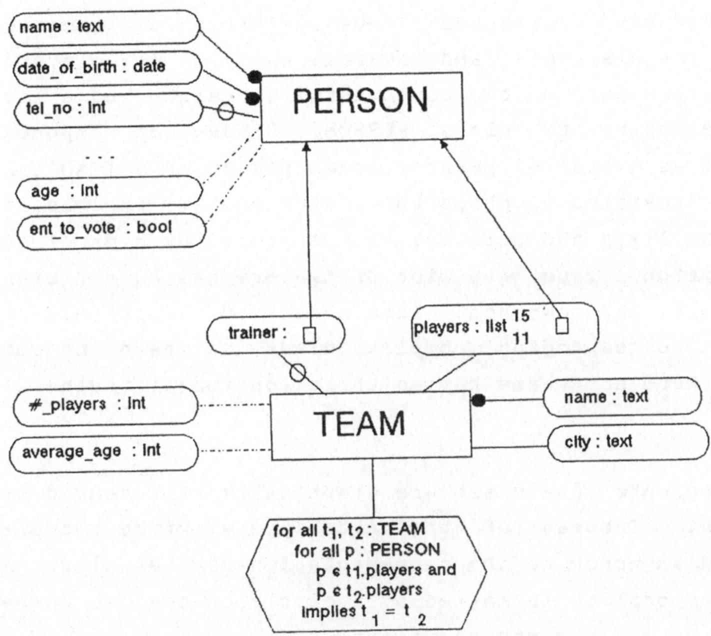

figure 3.2: Complex object class TEAM

```
class TEAM

    attributes name:          text,
               city:          text,
               #_players:     int,
               average_age:   real;

    components trainer: PERSON   optional,
               players: list of  PERSON   card (11,15);

    key name;

    derived #_players    as count (players),
            average_age  as sum (players.age) / #_players;

    constraints for all t , t  : TEAM
                             1    2
                    for all p : PERSON

                        p ∊ t .players and p ∊ t .players
                             1                      2
                        implies t  = t ;
                                 1    2
end TEAM.
```

By means of components it is possible to describe **complex objects** that
are composed of other objects. Each object of the defined complex
class TEAM has attributes 'name', 'city' of location, number of
players ('#_players'), and 'average_age' (of all players) and it additionally consists of two components, a trainer and a list of players,
both belonging to class PERSON. Since the component 'players' is
modelled as a list of persons, each player of a TEAM can be referenced
by the position (perhaps the player number) in this list. As for attributes, lists and sets may be restricted by a **cardinality** card (min,
max) option. Thus, the list of players has to contain between 11 and
15 persons. Any component class specified as **optional** allows objects
of the corresponding complex class to have no component for it.
Hence, there are teams having their (optional) trainer fired at the
moment.

The components of a class are graphically represented similar to attributes. Instead of the data type we write the class name in the
oval and an arrow to the representation of that class. As for attributes optionality is marked by a circle on the arc connecting the complex class and the component oval.

Again, we have **derived attributes** '#_players' and 'average_age' defined in the derived-clause, and a **constraint** requiring every player
to be member of exactly one team.

The semantics of components is very close to that of attributes. Let
$|E|$ denote the instances (objects) of class E, $|A|$ the domain (data
type) of attribute A, $P(V)$ the power set of V, and V^* a list of ele-
ments of V where V is either $|E|$ or $|A|$. Then, attributes A and com-
ponents E' are interpreted as total functions which become partial in
case of optional attributes or components.

$$A \; : \; |E| \; \longrightarrow \; |A| \qquad \text{for} \qquad A$$
$$|E| \; \longrightarrow \; |A|^* \qquad \text{for } \underline{\text{list of}} \text{ A}$$
$$|E| \; \longrightarrow \; P(\,|A|\,) \qquad \text{for } \underline{\text{set}} \; \underline{\text{of}} \text{ A}$$

$$E' \; : \; |E| \; \longrightarrow \; |E'| \qquad \text{for} \qquad E'$$
$$|E| \; \longrightarrow \; |E'|^* \qquad \text{for } \underline{\text{list}} \; \underline{\text{of}} \text{ E'}$$
$$|E| \; \longrightarrow \; P(\,|E'|\,) \qquad \text{for } \underline{\text{set}} \; \underline{\text{of}} \text{ E'}$$

Compared to other semantic data models we can express **aggregation**, as
defined in [SS77] and for SHM$^+$ ([BR84]), **grouping** from SDM ([HM81]),
and **association** ([BR84]) by means of complex objects. Aggregation is
a form of data abstraction which considers a relationship between components as a higher level aggregate (composite) object. This is the
'part of' relationship and is simply achieved by a complex object
without $\underline{\text{list}}/\underline{\text{set}} \; \underline{\text{of}}$ components. Grouping or association models the
'member of' relationship. Hence, every instance of the associate ob-
ject stands for a set of instances of the member object. This is
modelled by a complex object 'associate object' having one component
'$\underline{\text{set}} \; \underline{\text{of}}$ member'. Finally, we remark that every component class can
also be complex.

3.2 RELATIONSHIP SCHEMA

Another basic concept of the ER model we adapt is the concept of relationships among object classes. First, we should mention that, in contrast to [Ne83, DKML85], n-ary relationships are allowed. The semantics of an n-ary relationship R between (not necessarily distinct)
classes $E_1,\ldots,E_n$ can be understood as a predicate over the sets
of instances $|E_1|, \ldots, |E_n|$. It follows that there may exist in-
stances of the classes E_i not being part of any instance of the relationship R. We say that those participants are **partial**, otherwise they
are **total**.

We now extend our example by introducing two relationships where we
assume two additional, later defined classes DEPTMT (department) and
MANAGER.

```
relation works_in
  participants PERSON,
              DEPTMT;

  attributes  position: text;
end works_in.


relation manages
  participants MANAGER  card (1,*),
              DEPTMT;

  function DEPTMT to MANAGER;

  constraints for all m : MANAGER
               for all d : DEPTMT  manages (m,d) implies
                                   works_in (PERSON(m),d);
end manages.
```

Figure 3.3 shows the relationships graphically represented as dia-
monds.

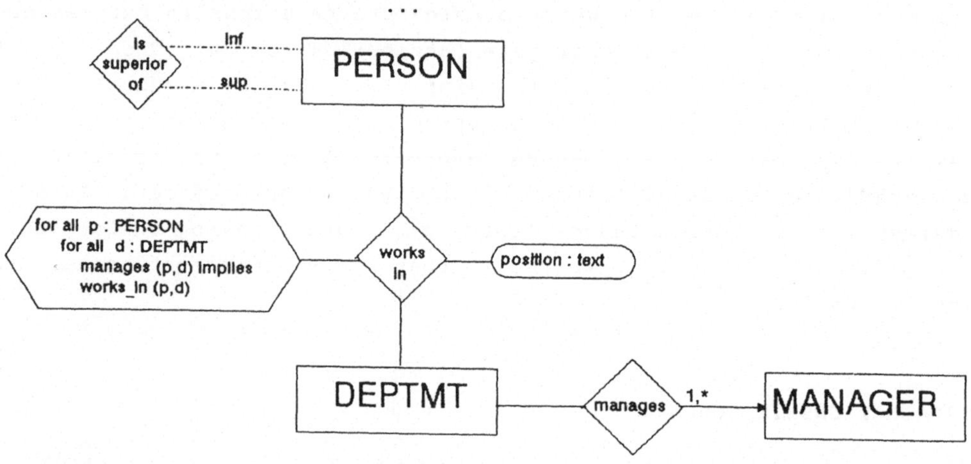

figure 3.3:   Relationships

We have extended the concept of relationship with some structural properties that may also be expressed by means of constraints.

First, a relationship can be declared as **functional**. For instance, the
relationship 'manages' is a function from DEPTMT to MANAGER indicated
by 'function DEPTMT to MANAGER'. Hence, for every instance in DEPTMT
participating in a relationship instance of 'manages' there is exactly
one instance of MANAGER in 'manages', i.e., every department must be
managed by exactly one manager whereas any manager may manage several
departments.

Functional relationships are represented by arrows denoting the mathematical direction of the function.

The participation of an object class can be enriched by two **cardinality numbers** specified in c̲a̲r̲d̲ (min, max), meaning that every object of that class participates in at least 'min' and at most 'max' relationship instances. While there may be persons not working in a department and departments having no employees, we can require every every manager to manage at least one (indeed between 1 and infinite) departments. If no cardinalities are specified c̲a̲r̲d̲ (0,*) is assumed. Cardinalities are written in the graphical representation on the arc connecting the corresponding class and the relationship symbol.

Like objects, relationships may have attributes. The attribute 'position' of 'works_in' specifies, whether the person working in a department is an engineer, a manager, or anything else. All features available for attributes of object classes can be applied here, except the k̲e̲y̲-clause. The semantics of an attribute A of a. relationship R between the classes $E_1, \ldots, E_n$ is then given by a function
$A : |R| \dashrightarrow |A|$, where $|R| = \{r \subseteq |E_1| \times \ldots \times |E_n| \mid R(r)\}$.

Additional **constraints** can be specified in a c̲o̲n̲s̲t̲r̲a̲i̲n̲t̲s̲-clause. In our example, we require any person managing a department to work also in that department, where we assume that every manager is a specialized person (see section 3.3). Thus, we can refer to the underlying person of a manager m by PERSON(m) and in the same way a managing person p by MANAGER(p).

Influenced by [EWH85] we introduce the notion of **derived relationships**. We define a relationship 'is_superior_of' that is computed from the relationships 'works_in' and 'manages'.

```
    relation is_superior_of is derived

    participants inf: PERSON,
                 sup: PERSON;

    derived is_superior_of (i,s) as  exists d : DEPTMT
                                     works_in (i,d) and
                                     manages  (MANAGER(s),d);
    end is_superior_of.
```

We see that it is possible to define a relationship where an object class participates more than once. To distinguish the different roles these classes play in the relationship, each occurence of such a participating class is identified by a **rolename**. Thus, 'sup' denotes the superior and 'inf' the inferior person in the 'is_superior_of' relationship. This relationship holds between two persons 'sup' and 'inf', if and only if there is at least one department that employs 'inf' and that is managed by 'sup' (direct authority).

The concept of derived relationships can easily be extended to compute the closure of a relation (-ship), e.g. the closure of 'is_superior_of' (i.e. is direct or indirect superior of). To avoid problems about consistency derived relationships must neither be specified to be functional nor have cardinalities. These structural properties are derived from the underlying relationships. Thus, 'is_superior_of' becomes a many-to-many relationship with both participants partial because 'works_in' is many-to-many and both participants of 'works_in' are partial. Derived relationships, like derived attributes, are graphically marked by dotted lines associating the participating object classes, as shown in figure 3.3.

Now we are able to present our extended key concept. Therefore, consider the following example belonging to figure 3.3.

```
class SOCIETY

    attributes name:      text;

    components chairman: PERSON,
               members:  set of PERSON;
    key name,
        chairman;

end SOCIETY;


class DEPTMT

    attributes dept_no: int,
               ...
    key dept_no;

end;
```

At first, we allow components to appear in the key-clause. As for attributes only singlevalued and non-optional components may be keys. In case of SOCIETY we consider a society identified by its name and its chairman (that is a person). Furthermore, we could have additionally specified in the key-clause of DEPTMT the 'function manages'. In this case we obtain the following semantics of such a key-function [Eh86, EDG86]: Every department is uniquely identified by its number (dept_no) and its managing person, i.e., there may exist a lot of departments (of different companies) having the same number but different managers.

Only binary and functional relationships having their domain total may be part of the key-clause because a relationship instance cannot identify an object that is not involved by this instance.

3.3 CONSTRUCTION SCHEMA

Up to now we have extended the basic concepts, i.e., objects and relationships (both with attributes), of the ER model. Using these concepts aggregation [SS77] can be modelled, but no modelling primitives
for generalization [SS77] are provided yet. Therefore, we introduce
the concept of **type construction** to support this important data semantics. Type construction may be regarded as an order on the object
classes. Starting with already defined classes new classes are constructed by a new classification of their objects. Consider figure 3.4
where we present the graphical representation of the general form of
type construction.

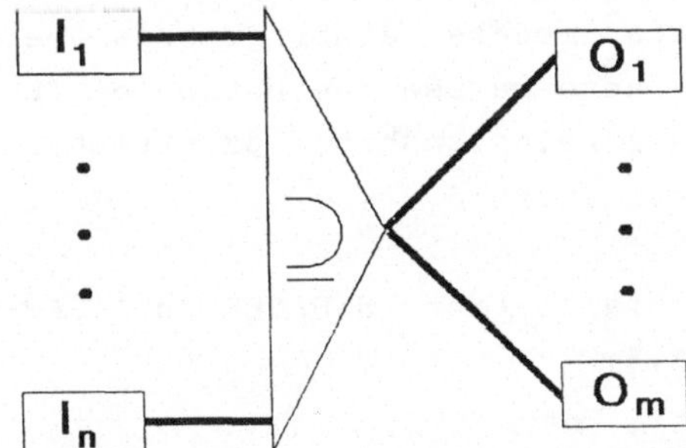

<u>figure</u> 3.4:   General form of type construction

At the base line of the triangle there are the already defined object
classes $I_1,...,I_n$, called <u>input classes</u>. The classes $O_1,...,O_m$ connected with the opposite point of the triangle are the constructed
<u>output classes</u>. Between the objects of the input and output classes
the following conditions must hold:

$$(1) \quad \bigcup_{j=1}^{n} |I_j| \supseteq \bigcup_{i=1}^{m} |O_i|$$

$$(2) \quad \text{for all } O_s, O_t, s \neq t, \quad |O_s| \cap |O_t| = \{\}$$

where $|E|$ denotes the set of instances of class E, 'U' the union, '$\cap$'
the intersection, and {} the empty set.

(1) requires that all instances of output classes are also instances
of input classes, but not all instances of input classes have to be
instances of output classes. However, sometimes it is significant to
demand explicitly this fact. Then we write the symbol '=' into the
triangle which restricts the semantics to

$$(1')\quad \bigcup_{j=1}^{n} |I_j| \;=\; \bigcup_{i=1}^{m} |O_i|\ .$$

(2) restricts further the output classes to be disjoint, i.e., each object of each input class appears at most in one of the output classes. On the other hand, input classes need not be disjoint.

Note that the direction of type construction, given by the triangle, is important for the (later discussed) attribute inheritance mechanism.

Given the above short description of the semantics of type construction, we now show the modelling of the generalization abstractions. Continued research in data models distinguishes between different types of generalization. Here we use the notion of [LN86], where **specialization** (subclass, is-a relationship), **partition**, and **generalization** (superclass) are distinguished.

At first, a simple specialization MANAGER of PERSON is defined corresponding to figure 3.5.

```
construct from PERSON

    MANAGER: attributes name:            text,
                        date_of_birth:   date,
                        salary:          int,
                        official_car:    bool;

        derived name              as PERSON.name,
                date_of_birth     as PERSON.date_of_birth,
                salary            as PERSON.salary;

        constraints salary > 600000 implies
                    official_car = true;
    end.
```

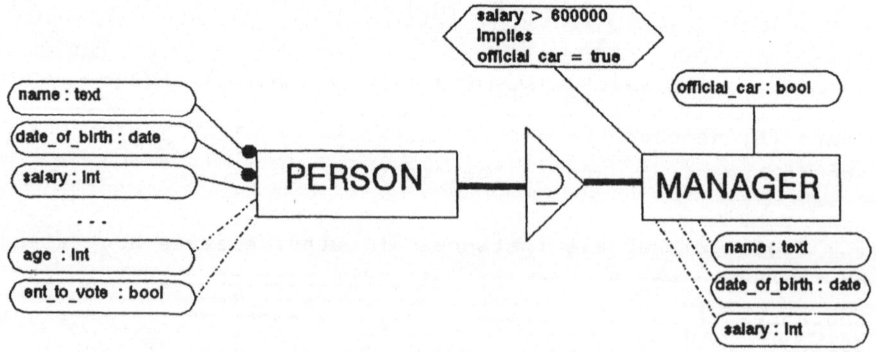

figure 3.5: Specialization

We say that MANAGER is a **specialization** (or <u>subclass</u>) of PERSON, because a manager is treated as a special person. By restriction (1) we have | PERSON | $\supseteq$ | MANAGER | , i.e., every manager is a person but not every person needs to participate in the construction of MANAGER.

We will now state some general remarks on type construction.

- While we require that "normal" non-constructed object classes must be disjoint, constructed classes accomplish the only way to see a single object in several different classes. Indeed, a constructed type forms a new object class but the instances of this class are not "new", because they are taken from the input classes. Consequently, constructed types cannot have key attributes since they are already identified by the sources. For the same reason constructed types cannot have new components except derived components from the input classes. Thus, we have a restricted form of complex object classes for constructed types.

- However, it is possible to define new attributes for constructed classes <u>not</u> inherited to the sources, such as 'official_car' for MANAGER. Attributes from the sources that are significant for the constructed classes can be explicitly taken up by means of **derivation**. 'name', 'salary', and 'date_of_birth' of MANAGER are examples where attributes are derived from the source PERSON. In contrast to [HM81, BR84, EWH84] and others we do not support an implicit attribute inheritance mechanism, because the explicit derivation provides the full power of derived attributes.

- Besides, constructed classes are handled as non-constructed ones, i.e., they may participate in relationships and may be used to build complex object classes. They can also be sources for new constructions. Nevertheless, there are two conditions that must hold:

  (i) A constructed class has to be the result of exactly one construction.
  (ii) Every constructed class must not, directly or indirectly, be input class for its own construction, i.e., the directed graph consisting of all classes as nodes and constructions as edges has to be acyclic.

We now turn back to another generalization abstraction, the partition.
Figure 3.6 presents a **partition** of PERSON into the classes WOMAN and
MAN defined as follows:

```
construct totally from PERSON
   MAN: attributes name:      text,
                   military:  bool;
            derived     name as PERSON.name;
   WOMAN: attributes name:      text,
                   #_children: int;
            derived     name as PERSON.name;

   derived  MAN    as PERSON.female = false,
            WOMAN  as PERSON.female = true;
end.
```

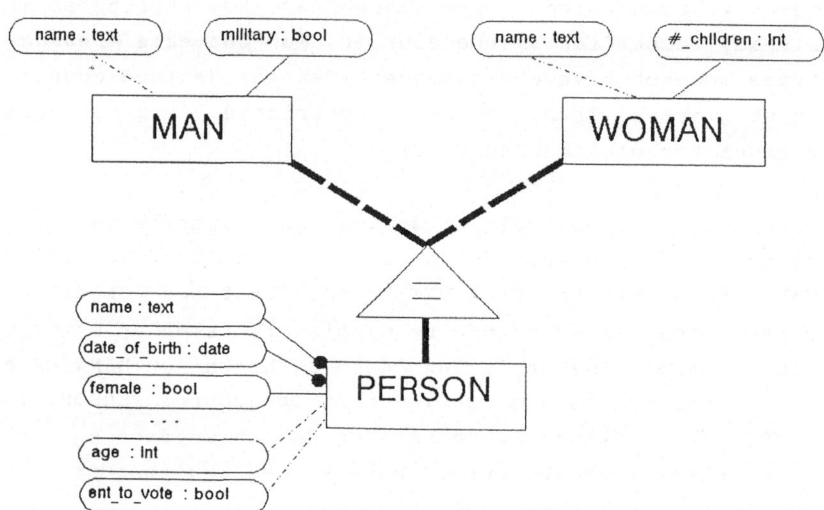

figure 3.6:   Partition

Since the construction is defined as totally the conditions (1') is
valid requiring every person to be a man or a woman. By restriction
(2) of our type construction, the constructed classes MAN and WOMAN
are disjoint (a non-disjoint partition could be achieved by two spe-
cializations, MAN ⊆ PERSON and WOMAN ⊆ PERSON). Again the name is inherited from PERSON by MAN and WOMAN. Both constructed classes also
have special attributes 'military' (true if military service is done)
and '#_children' (number of children) resp., once more not inherited
by PERSON in the inverse direction. The derived-clause specifies the
output classes to be **derived**, meaning that every newly inserted PERSON
automatically becomes a WOMAN for 'female' = true and a MAN for 'female' = false (i.e. male).

The derivation is indicated in figure 3.6 by dotted lines to the output classes.

Finally, we define a **generalization** CROWD of TEAM and SOCIETY presented in figure 3.7.

```
construct totally from TEAM, SOCIETY
    CROWD: attributes name:      text;
           components members:   set of PERSON;

           derived name       as case TEAM:     name;
                                      SOCIETY: name;
                              end;

                  members    as case TEAM: set of players U
                                           set of trainer;
                                      SOCIETY: members U
                                               set of chairman;
end.                          end;
```

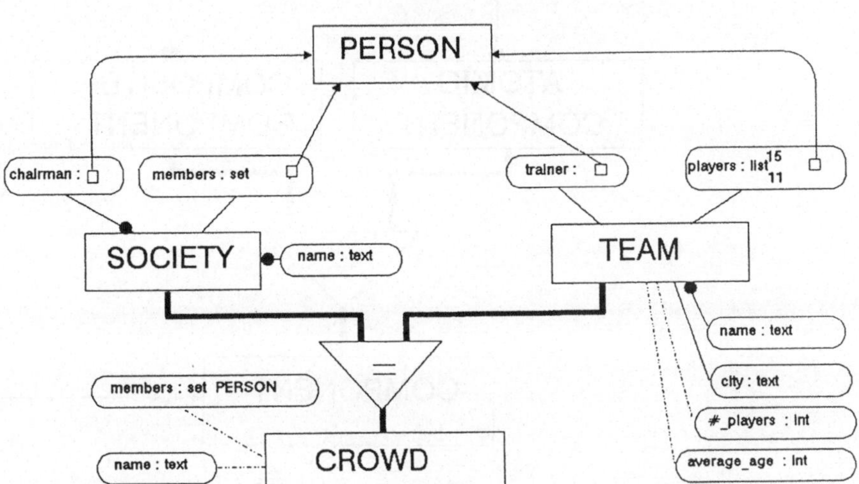

figure 3.7:   Generalization

Recalling again restriction (1'), we have the following condition on instances: | TEAM | U | SOCIETY | = |CROWD | , showing that we model every crowd to be a team or a society and vice versa.

Although constructed classes cannot have newly defined components, it is allowed to derive components from the sources. Thus, we have a component 'members' of CROWD, that either in case of a TEAM consists of the union of the list of players (by 'set of' coerced to a set) and the trainer (by 'set of' converted to a singleton), or that in case of a SOCIETY contains its members and its chairman.

Up to now we have examined the special cases
   (1) one   source , one   constructed type ,
   (2) one   source , several constructed types, and
   (3) several sources, one   constructed type .
We feel that the general case
   (4) several sources, several constructed types,
is not significant, because here several data abstractions are put together. Consequently, this case should be splitted into several constructions using (2) or (3), to make the abstractions more visible.
For reasons of unique semantics we yet allow the general construction.

Finally, we present an example combining the concepts of complex objects and type construction to illustrate the power of our data model.
Figure 3.8 presents a recursively defined object class COMPONENT.

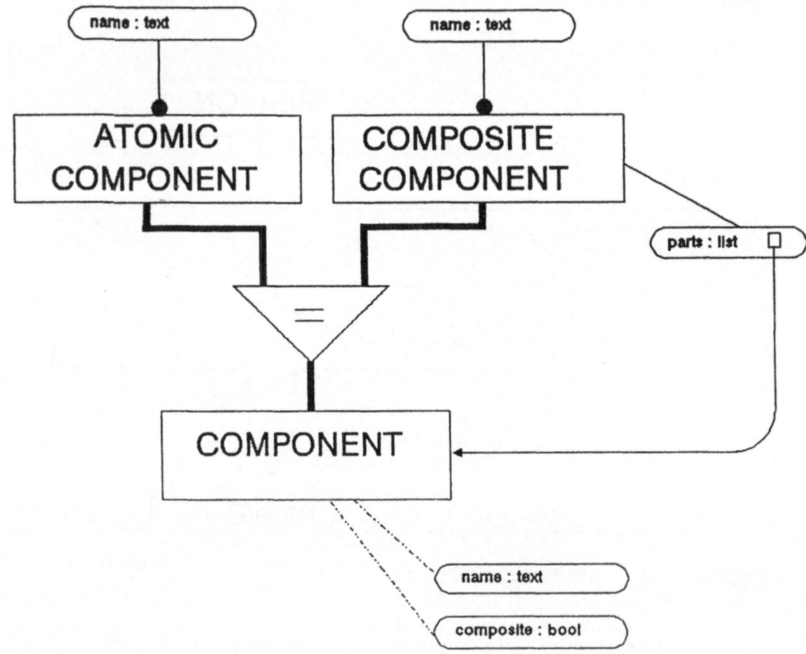

figure 3.8: Recursive object

Every COMPONENT is either a BASIC COMPONENT or a COMPOSITE COMPONENT
consisting of a list of components, being again basic or composite.
As far as we know there does not exist any other semantic data model
that supports a comparably elegant modelling of such recursions. However, proposals are made in [BB84] with the notion of molecular objects.

4.TRANSACTION LEVEL

A database transaction is a transformation of a database state into
another database state having the properties of atomicity and durabil-
ity. Up to now, database transactions are specified and implemented
when the database schema is already implemented. Because of this
method, the schema does often not consider all transaction requirements and, as a consequence, redesigning is becomes necessary. Our aim
is to enable prototyping of arbitrary transactions as early as possible in order to avoid this effect. For early specifications of transactions and their verification against integrity constraints we propose a descriptive specification methodology. To support an early prototyping a procedural transaction language based on the conceptual
schema is provided. A high level query language and a set of elementary update operations are necessary to write arbitrary transactions.

All transactions have to transform 'legal' database states (i.e.,
states satisfying all constraints) into other 'legal' states. We incorporate two methods which guarantee this property. One method is to
control it by a global integrity monitor as mentioned in [LS87, SL87].
Such a monitor only allows correct transactions. But incorrect transactions (i.e., transactions violating some constraints) are not
detected before execution is finished. This would cause an undoing of
all changes initiated by these transactions. To avoid this, transaction specifications can be transformed into integrity respecting
transaction specifications as mentioned in [Li85, Li86]. We propose a
combination of both methods depending on the frequency of use of the
transactions.

For all transactions changing the database contents a set of so-called
elementary (or primitive) operations i.e., insert, update, and delete,
is provided. These operations are to be used for changes of single instances by substituting their formal parameters by actual ones. They
will be generated and provided automatically by the system, respecting
all constraints inherent to the object model. These elementary operations form the only way to change the contents of the database, so
consistency in regard to object model inherent constraints will always
be guaranteed, since any transaction may be merely combined of these
elementary operations.

As the operations should fulfill all model inherent constraints, operations looking elementary to the user may not be elementary to the system. For instance, the insertion of a new 'works_in' relationship between an existing person and an existing department is elementary to the user and to the system as well, but the change of a manager's salary will change the corresponding person's salary (that is in fact the same person), too. Here, the user does not see the second changing and need not even know of the existence of the corresponding person.

But there are cases, when the user needs to have some knowledge about the overall schema structure. If, for instance, a new person shall be inserted, the insertion of a man or woman is enforced. Here, the only effect seen by the user is the requirement of an additional attribute which is 'military' or '#_children' resp. because these attributes are obligatory for MAN/WOMAN.

In complex database schemas the number of parameters for primitive operations can increase rapidly (see the second example below). Thus, we propose a flexible parameter notation in the operation calls allowing the definition of default values. Such cases are null values e.g., 'military' does not apply to women, or default values as they are supported by the programming language Ada (see [GH83]) e.g., '#_children' is set to zero in the case of no explicit description, because this is the most frequent case.

For arbitrary transactions we offer descriptive specifications with pre- and postconditions. This enables an early formulation of complex transactions during the design process. Descriptive transaction specifications can be refined into adequate transaction specifications respecting all database constraints as suggested in [Li85, Li86].

In a second design step transactions are expressed in a procedural transaction language. This transaction language offers control structures like loops and conditions (as they are well-known from "normal" programming languages) to connect the system-offered elementary operations and already specified transactions to complex transactions. These complex transactions are executable by the prototype system.

Since the elementary operations are automatically derived from the schema (by the system itself) and have a fixed formal semantics (similar to assignments in programming languages), frequent transactions can be verified against their specification (pre-/postcondition language) and against the database constraints as suggested in [GM79]. Ad hoc update transactions that are not verified against their specification (because this is a cumbersome process) are controlled by the integrity monitor [LS87] which will be part of the prototype system.

To illustrate what the two different specification levels are and how database consistency is ensured, we give two examples which belong to a part of our global example schema given in the appendix.

The first transaction 'increase_salary_manager()' is specified as follows in the pre-/postcondition notation:

```
transaction specification increase_salary_manager() :

    var M   : MANAGER,
        sal : int;

    pre  : M.salary = sal;
    post : (sal        < 1000000 implies M.salary = sal * 1.1)   and
           (M.salary > 600000  implies M.official_car = true);

end increase_salary_manager.
```

This (parameter-free) specification describes the effect of the transaction. The maintaining of an integrity constraint 'managers who earn more than 600000 are assigned an official car' is fulfilled. A correct implementation of this transaction written by the user in the procedural transaction language is the following:

```
transaction implementation increase_salary_manager() :

  begin

    update MANAGER
       set salary := salary * 1.1
     where salary < 1000000;

    update MANAGER
       set official_car := true
     where salary > 600000;

  end increase_salary_manager.
```

The side effect to preserve integrity i.e., the increasing of the corresponding person's salary, is initiated by the elementary operation 'update MANAGER' all alone and not visible to the user.

To show the full power of our transaction specification tools, we give a second more complex example. Here, the hiring of a new manager from the outside world is realized. The pre-/postcondition specification is the following one:

```
transaction specification hire_manager
      (M_PERSON : PERSON, M_official_car : bool, M_dept_no : int) :

   pre : exists DEPTMT where (dept_no = M_dept_no)   and
       not exists PERSON where (PERSON = M_PERSON)
          /* the manager does not exist, not even as a person */
   post : exists MANAGER M where (PERSON = M_PERSON and
                  official_car = M_official_car            and
                  exists DEPTMT D where (manages (M, D) and
                                 dept_no = M_dept_no) )
   end hire_manager.
```

Here, it is obvious that the transaction cannot be specified and processed unless the user knows that a MANAGER is also a PERSON and a MAN or a WOMAN. The user does not need to know these connections, but (s)he has to know that some additional attributes, say parameters, are required and what the key attributes are. (It would be different, if the manager had already existed in the database as a PERSON. Maybe anyone who should become a manager of a department should be hired first as a "simple" person.)

Now we show the procedural specification that fulfills the pre-/postconditions:

```
transaction specification hire_manager
                (M_name            : text, M_date_of_birth : date,
                 M_salary          : int,  M_female        : bool,
                 M_official_car : bool, M_military          : bool,
                 M_#_children   : bool, M_dept_no           : int )
   var M : MANAGER
       P : PERSON
       D : DEPTMT

   begin
   if (M_salary < 600000)   or
      (exists P where (P.name = m_name    and
                       P.date_of_birth = M_date_of_birth))
       then "reject"
       else insert MANAGER (M_name, M_date_of_birth, M_salary,
                            M_female, M_official_car,
                            M_military, M_#_children);
            M := select MANAGER where (name = M_name    and
                              date_of_birth = M_date_of_birth);
            D := select DEPTMT  where (dept_no = M_dept_no);
            delete manages (*, D);
            insert manages (M, D);
   fi
   end hire_manager.
```

Here, sequence and conditions are the only used control structures. But the procedural language also offers structures for choice and repetition and the use of constants, variables, and operations on user-defined data types.

We assume that the parameter list of 'insert MANAGER' is variable because in case of the existence of the corresponding person only the key attributes 'M_name' and 'M_date_of_birth' and the manager specific attribute 'M_official_car' are needed. Otherwise, if the corresponding person does not exist up to now, the full parameter list is required as in the example above.

There are several points at which this transaction may fail (and be rolled back). The first two points are clear to the programmer, he has written these error exits himself to ensure consistency: any manager has to earn more than 600000 otherwise he cannot be a manager and the new manager has not worked for this enterprise up to now.
Another one is hidden in 'insert MANAGER' and will be raised automatically: if the department denoted by 'M_dept_no' does not exist, the whole transaction will be rejected.

There are several actions that will be triggered automatically without an explicit statement. Mainly, the insertion of the manager that looks elementary to the user causes two subsequent insertions: The insertion of the corresponding person and the automatic classification of that person into man or woman. The additional parameters of 'insert MANAGER' are the only hints that these insertions will take place.

Secondly, as there exists an integrity constraint 'anyone who manages a department has to work in this department', (the formal expression is 'manages (M, D) implies (works_in (PERSON(M), D)') then the 'insert manages' operation could have been replaced (at another place) by a transaction that causes a second insertion of a relationship, the insertion of 'works_in (PERSON(M), M_dept_no)'.
This insertion is neither initiated nor seen by the user but transformed by the system to ensure consistency.

All together these additional effects either specified by the user at different places or automatically raised by the system make this transaction an "integrity respecting transaction" [Li85, Li86], because it avoids any changes that violate consistency.

5. CONCLUSIONS AND FUTURE WORK

Before the design tools mentioned in the introduction are ready to be
implemented, some refinements and precisions of several concepts are
to be made.

The possibilities of versioning and modelling alternatives have to be
added (for a definition see [Ne83, KCB86, Mi85]). We suggest a versioning concept at a separate level rather independent of the object
level specifications. The user may specify for which objects versions
and alternatives are possible and which attributes may be affected.
The versioning should be supervised by the system. The user is given
several operations for creating, deleting, etc. versions and alternatives.

In a next step a formal semantics for the specification language, i.e.
for specifying the data, object, and transaction level shall be esta-
blished. For the object and transaction level we suppose an axiomatic
semantics based upon a modified temporal logic similar to [GMS83,
FS86]. Furthermore, a query language has to be designed.

At this point the implementation of the graphical editor, the transla-
tor from graphic symbols into the specification language and the
integrity monitor may start. In [HNS86] we have already given the
transformation of our EER model into the relational one. The salient
features of the integrity monitor are the processing of static constraints and dynamic constraints that are formulated in a temporal
logic. For more details see [LS87].

For the distant future further design tools are planned to integrate
the above described tools into a complete DB design support system. As
such advanced design tools we intend components to generate automatically elementary operations from the schema description and to verify
transactions against their descriptive specifications and against integrity constraints automatically. As another useful tool there
should be some component checking the consistency of explicit integrity constraints.

REFERENCES

[ADD85]   Albano, A. / DeAntonellis, V. / DiLeva, A. (eds.):
            Computer-Aided Database Design : The DATAID Project.
            North-Holland, Amsterdam 1985.

[BB84]   Batory,D.S. / Buchmann,A.P.:
            Molecular Objects, Abstract Data Types, and Data Models.
            Proc. 10th VLDB, Singapur 1984 (pp.172-194).

[BDRZ84]   Brägger, R. / Dudler, A. / Rebsamen, J. / Zehnder, C.A.:
            Gambit - An Interactive Database Design Tool for Structures,
            Integrity Constraints, and Transactions.
            Proc. IEEE Int. Conf. on Software Engineering,
            Los Angeles, April 1984 (pp.399-407).

[BH86]   Bryce, D. / Hull, R.:
            SNAP : A Graphics-based Schema Manager.
            Proc. Int. Conf. on Data Engineering, Los Angeles 1986 (pp.
            151-164).

[BR84]   Brodie, M. / Ridjanovic, D.:
            Fundamental Concepts for Semantic Modelling of Objects.
            Computer Corporation of America, Technical Report, April
            1984.

[Ce83]   Ceri, S. (ed.):
            Methodology and Tools for Data Base Design.
            North-Holland, Amsterdam 1983.

[Ch76]   Chen, P.P.:
            The Entity-Relationship-Model - Towards a Unified View of
            Data.
            ACM ToDS Vol. 1, No. 1, 1976 (pp. 9-36).

[DE84]   Drosten, K. / Ehrich, H.-D.:
            Translating Algebraic Specifications to Prolog Programs.
            Informatik-Bericht Nr. 84-08, TU Braunschweig 1984.

[DKM85]   Dittrich, K.R. / Kotz, A.M. / Mülle, J.A.:
            DAMASCUS - ein Datenhaltungssystem für den VLSI-Entwurf.
            GI-Fachtagung Datenbanksysteme für Büro, Technik und Wissen-
            schaft (Blaser, A. / Pistor, P., eds.)
            Karlsruhe 1985, Informatik-Fachberichte 94 (pp. 70-72)
            Springer, Berlin 1985.

[EDG86]   Ehrich, H.-D. / Drosten, K. / Gogolla, M.:
            Towards an Algebraic Semantics for Database Specification.
            IFIP TC2 Working Conference on Knowledge & Data,
            Aldeia das Acoteias (Portugal) Nov. 1986.

[Eh84]   Ehrich, H.-D.:
            Algebraic (?) Specification of Conceptual Database Schemata
            (Extended Abstract).
            Proc. 3rd Workshop on Theory and Application of Abstract
            Data Types (H.-J. Kreowski, ed.),
            Informatik-Fachbericht Bd.116, Springer, Berlin 1984.

[Eh85]   Ehrich, H.-D.:
           Spezifikation konzeptioneller Schemata mit abstrakten Daten-
           typen und Versionen.
           GI-Fachgespräch 'Entwurf von Informationssystemen - Methoden
           und Modelle' (Mayr, H.C. / Meyer, B.E. eds.)

[Eh86]   Ehrich, H.-D.:
           Key Extensions of Abstract Data Types, Final Algebras, and
           Database Semantics.
           Informatik-Bericht Nr. 86-01, TU Braunschweig 1986.

[ELG84]   Ehrich, H.-D. / Lipeck, U.W., Gogolla, M.:
           Specification, Semantics and Enforcement of Dynamic Database
           Behaviour.
           Proc. 10th VLDB, Singapur 1984 (pp. 301-308).

[EM85]   Ehrig, H. / Mahr, B.:
           Fundamentals of Algebraic Specification I.
           Springer, Berlin 1985.

[EWH85]   Elmasri, R. / Weeldreyer, J. / Hevner, A.:
           The Category Concept : An Extension to the Entity-
           Relationship Model.
           Data & Knowledge Engineering Vol. 1, 1985 (pp.75-116).

[FS86]   Fiadeiro, J. / Sernadas, A.: The INFOLOG Linear Tense Propo-
           sitional Logic of Events and Transactions.
           Information Systems, Vol. 11, No. 1, (pp. 61-85), 1986

[GH83]   Goos, G. / Hartmanis, J.:
           The Programming Language Ada, Reference Manual.
           American National Standards Institute, Inc. ANSI-MIL-STD-
           1815A-1983,
           Springer, Berlin 1983.

[GM79]   Gardarin, G. / Melkanoff, M.:
           Proving Consistency of Database Transactions.
           Proc. 5th VLDB, Rio de Janeiro 1979.

[GMS83]   Golshani, F. / Maibaum, T. / Sadler, M.:
           A Modal System of Algebras for Database Specification and
           Query/Update Language Support.
           Proc. 9th. VLDB, Florence 1983 (pp. 331-339).

[HM81]   Hammer, M. / McLeod, D.:
           Database Description with SDM : A Semantic Database Model.
           ACM ToDS, Vol. 6, No. 3, 1981 (pp. 351-386).

[HNS86]   Hohenstein, U. / Neugebauer, L. / Saake, G.:
           An Extended Entity-Relationship Model for Non-Standard Data-
           bases.
           Proc. "Workshop über Relationale Datenbanken"
           Lessach (Austria), June 1986.
           TU Clausthal-Zellerfeld (ed. A. Heuer).

[KCB86]   Katz, R.H. / Chang, E. / Bhateja, R.:
           Version Modelling Concepts for Computer-Aided Design Data-
           bases.
           Proc. of ACM SIGMOD Conf. on Management of Data,
           Washington D.C. 1986 (pp. 379-386).

[LEG85]   Lipeck, U.W. / Ehrich, H.-D. / Gogolla, M.:
           Specifying Admissibility of Dynamic Database Behaviour Using
           Temporal Logic.
           Proc. IFIP Work. Conf. on Theoretical and Formal Aspects
           of Information Systems, (Sernadas, A. et al., eds.),
           North-Holland, Amsterdam 1985.

[Li85]   Lipeck, U.W.:
           Schrittweise Spezifikation des dynamischen Verhaltens von
           Datenbanken.
           GI-Fachgespräch 'Entwurf von Informationssystemen - Methoden
           und Modelle' (Mayr, H.C. / Meyer, B.E. eds.) 1985.

[Li86]   Lipeck, U.W.:
           Stepwise Specification of Dynamic Database Behaviour.
           Proc. Int. ACM SIGMOD Conf. on Management of Data,
           Washington D.C. 1986 (pp. 387-397).

[LN86]   Lipeck, U.W. / Neumann, K.:
           Modelling and Manipulating Objects in Geoscientific Data-
           bases.
           Proc. 5th. Int. Conf. on the ER-Approach, Dijon 1986.

[LS87]   Lipeck, U.W. / Saake, G.:
           Monitoring Dynamic Integrity Constraints Based on Temporal
           Logic.
           To appear in: Information Systems, Vol. 12, No. 3, 1987

[Ma83]   Maier, D.: The Theory of Databases.
           Computer Science Press, Rockville MD 1983

[Mi85]   Mitschang, B.:
           Charakteristiken des Komplex-Objekt-Begriffs und deren Real-
           isierung.
           GI-Fachtagung Datenbanksysteme für Büro, Technik und Wissen-
           schaft (Blaser, A. / Pistor, P., eds.),
           Karlsruhe 1985, Informatik-Fachberichte 94 (pp. 382-400),
           Springer, Berlin 1985.

[Ne83]   Neumann, T.:
           Konzepte zur Erweiterung von Datenbanksystemen für die
           Unterstützung von CAD/CAM-Anwendungen.
           Dissertation, TH Darmstadt, 1983.

[NN85]   Neugebauer, L. / Neumann, K.:
           Schemagesteuerte Testdatenerzeugung für relationale Daten-
           banken.
           Informatik-Bericht Nr.85-02, TU Braunschweig 1985.

[RNLE85]   Ramm, I. / Neumann, K. / Lipeck, U.W. / Ehrich, H.-D.:
           Eine Benutzerschnittstelle für geowissenschaftliche Daten-
           banken.
           Informatik-Bericht Nr.85-08, TU Braunschweig 1985.

[SL87]   Saake, G. / Lipeck, U.W.:
           Foundations of Temporal Integrity Monitoring.
           To appear in: Proc. IFIP WG 8.1 Conf. on "Temporal Aspects
           of Information Systems", Sophia-Antipolis, 1987

[SS77]   Smith,J.M. / Smith, D.C.P.:
           Database Abstractions: Aggregation and Generalization.
           ACM ToDS Vol. 2, No. 2, 1977 (pp. 105-173).

APPENDIX

name : text
military : bool
name : text
#_children : int
MAN
WOMAN
name : text
date_of_birth : date
address : list 1 3 text
tel_no : phone_no
salary : int
nationality : nation
pers_stat : p_status
female : bool
age : int
ent_to_vote : bool
official_car : bool
PERSON
MANAGER
name : text
date_of_birth : date
salary : int
inf
sup
works in
is superior of
position : text
1,*
DEPTMT
manages
dept_no : int
chairman :
members : set
trainer :
players : list 15 11
SOCIETY
name : text
TEAM
name : text
city : text
#_players : int
average_age : int
members : set PERSON
name : text
CROWD

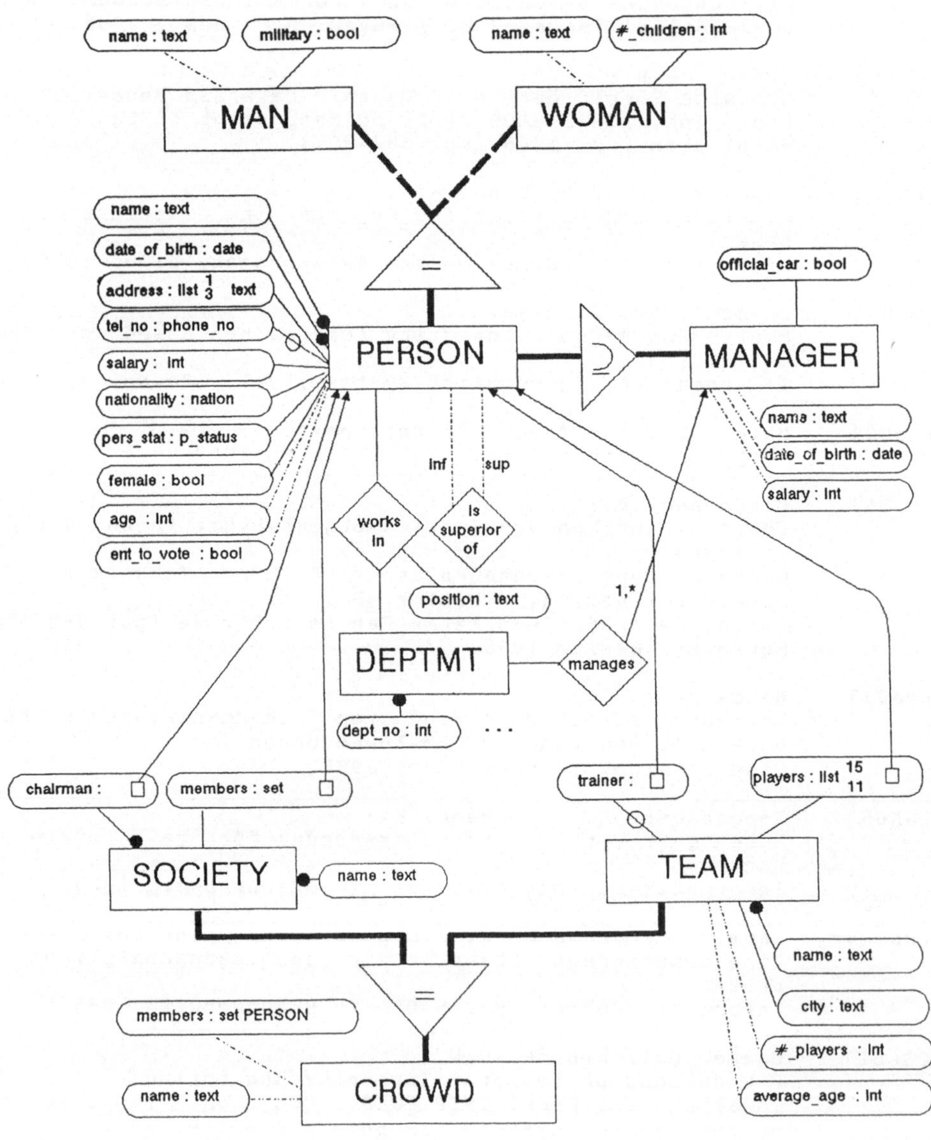

<u>INDUKTIVE UND DEDUKTIVE ERMITTLUNG</u>

<u>DES INFORMATIONSBEDARFS</u>

J. Eder, R. Mittermeir u. H. Wernhart

Institut für Informatik
Universität Klagenfurt *)

Universitätsstr.67
A-9020 Klagenfurt

<u>A B S T R A C T</u>

Diese Arbeit beschreibt einen Ansatz der Informationsbedarfsanalyse, bei dem aus einem Vergleich des an jedem einzelnen Arbeitsplatz erhobenen Informationsbedarfs mit den aus einem globalen Informationssystem-Entwurf abgeleiteten Bedürfnissen Informationsdefizite festgestellt werden können. Die Lösung dieser Unstimmigkeiten verbleibt als Kernaufgabe dem Designer des Informationssystems vorbehalten.

Als Werkzeug zur Beschreibung der Individualsichten wird HIBOL-2 verwendet, das Unternehmensmodell wird mittels BIER dargestellt.

____

*) Die in dieser Arbeit verwendeten Forschungsergebnisse wurden vom österreichischen Fonds zur Förderung der Wissenschaftlichen Forschung unter der Projektnummer P5341 gefördert.

1. EINLEITUNG

Informationsbedarfsanalyse kann sowohl als wichtiges Element der Organisationsentwicklung als auch als eine Fragestellung im Vorfeld der Gestaltung EDV-gestützter Informationssysteme angesehen werden. Die Grenzen zwischen diesen Bereichen sind zweifellos fließend, sodaß Methoden wie etwa BSP (/ZACH 82/) für beide Zwecke wesentliche Grundlageninformation liefern können. Allerdings sind vor Gestaltungsmaßnahmen im organisatorischen wie im sozio-technischen Bereich noch feinere Methoden anzuwenden.

Innerhalb dieses Spektrums konzentriert sich diese Arbeit auf Informationsbedarfsanalyse als Bestandteil der Anforderungsanalyse an ein Informationssystem auf der operativen Büroebene. Es wird versucht, Formularflüsse zu analysieren und aus dem Vergleich eines induktiv gewonnenen Verständnisses (etwa über den Istzustand) und einem deduktiv abgeleiteten Verständnis (des Sollzustands) Defizite der Infrastruktur bestehender (oder auch geplanter) Informationskanäle festzustellen.

Nach Darstellung der spezifischen Probleme, die sich bei einer Informationsbedarfsanalyse in Büro-Umgebungen stellen, versucht das folgende Kapitel einen Lösungsweg aufzuzeigen, der in der Verbindung von Individualsichten zu einem Informationsfluß-Netz besteht, welches einer deduktiv aufgebauten Unternehmenssicht über die Informationsbedürfnisse der einzelnen Stellen im Unternehmen gegenübergestellt wird. Aus dem Vergleich dieser beiden Sichtweisen läßt sich ein Informationsbedarfsmodell erarbeiten, das der realen Bedürfnislage besser entspricht als ein im klassischen Weg erarbeitetes Modell.

Entsprechend dieser Methodenkombination werden im Kapitel 3 die Methoden zur Erhebung von Individualbedürfnissen bzw. zu deren Integration in ein Globalmodell dargestellt. Kapitel 4 beschreibt den Übergang von Individualsichten zu einer daraus abgeleiteten Globalsicht. Der Vergleich zwischen dieser induktiven Gesamtsicht mit der deduktiven Gesamtsicht ist in Kapitel 5 beschrieben.

2. INFORMATIONSBEDARFSANALYSE IN BÜRO-UMGEBUNGEN

2.1 monistische Ansätze

Da Informationsbedarfsanalyse in dieser Arbeit als Bestandteil der Anforderungsanalyse bei der Neukonzeption bzw. bei der strukturellen Aktualisierung von Informationssystemen aufgefaßt wird, stehen im wesentlichen zwei methodische Zutrittswege zur Auswahl. Es sind dies formal-analytische Methoden einerseits und empirisch-experimentelle Methoden andererseits. Weiters ist zu beachten, daß bei Informationssystemen im weiteren Sinn, jedenfalls aber bei Büro-Kommunikations-Systemen, eine enge Verbindung von Datenbankproblemen und von prozeßorientierten Datenverarbeitungsproblemen besteht, die entsprechend methodisch unterstützt werden muß. Wir wollen im folgenden prüfen, wie weit klassische Ansätze die Erfordernisse einer derartigen Informationsbedarfsanalyse abdecken können.

Formal-analytische Methoden orientieren sich im allgemeinen an einer top-down getriebenen Vorgangsweise. Als klassischer Vertreter dieser Methodengruppe muß - obschon es nur als halbformal eingestuft werden kann - SADT (/ROSS 77/) angesehen werden. Freilich unterstützt dieses im wesentlichen lediglich entweder die Prozeß- oder die Datensicht. Die Beantwortung der Frage nach den Informationsbedürfnissen des einzelnen Sachbearbeiters verfehlt diese Methode jedenfalls insofern, als dieser lediglich als "Mechanismus" bzw. als "Prozessor" in ein Diagramm eingefügt werden könnte, der Entwurf jedoch ausschließlich von globalen Systembedürfnissen ausgehen würde. Die Bedürfnisse des "Prozessors", eines "Blattknotens der Hierarchie" werden jedoch keineswegs als eigenständig erkannt.

Dies ist insofern eine Umkehr der Tatsachen, als gerade der einzelne Sachbearbeiter - unbeschadet seiner hierarchischen Stellung innerhalb des Unternehmens - dazu neigt (oder bei entsprechend hoher intrinsischer Motivation jedenfalls dazu neigen sollte), seine Aufgabe als so zentral anzusehen, daß sich allein aus dieser Aufgabe ein reales und legitimes Informationsbedürfnis ergibt, das bei einer Neugestaltung des Systems zu beachten, ja zu erfüllen ist.

Es bleibt bei aktivitätszentrierten formalen Ansätzen somit eine Kluft zwischen einer steril durchentworfenen, aus übergeordneten Zielvorstellungen top-down abgeleiteten und formal minimalen "Ideallösung" und einer Fülle von sich gegenseitig überlappenden und möglicherweise widersprüchlichen Partikularlösungen. Aufgabe einer partizipativen Systementwicklung ist es, diese Kluft zu überbrücken (/MITT 83/); bleibt sie offen, entwickeln sich im Lauf der Zeit neben der formellen, EDV-unterstützten Organisation, informelle Nebenformen, die zu insgesamt suboptimaler Aufgabenerfüllung führen.

Datenbank-Entwurfsmethodiken scheinen in diesem Punkt weniger stringent vorzugehen. Nimmt man den Entity-Relationship-Approach als Archetyp einer Klasse semantischer Datenbank-Entwurfsmethodiken* (/CHEN 76/), so wird hier wenigstens nicht von einem einzigen hypothetischen Ausgangspunkt ausgegangen. Es bleibt jedoch die Gesamtproblematik, daß das Informationssystem auf der Basis des "corporate schema" entworfen wird, welches die Unternehmenssicht auf die den Daten zugrundeliegenden Entitäten (Objekte) und Beziehungen bietet. Diese Objekte können unter Umständen jedoch schon in deutlicher konzeptueller Distanz zu den Formalobjekten liegen, die der einzelne Sachbearbeiter manipuliert.

Verläßt man aufgrund dieser teils emotionalen Probleme den Pfad des durchentworfenen Gesamtkonzeptes, in dem sich auch ein adäquater "view" für den Einzelnen befinden sollte, drängt sich der empirisch-experimentelle Ansatz auf.

Doch auch empirisch-experimentelle Ansätze haben deutliche Schwächen. Zum einen reichen rapid-protoptyping Methoden sehr oft nicht über den einzelnen Arbeitsplatz hinaus, da sonst die Organisations- und Abstimmungskosten diesen im Prinzip sehr fruchtbaren Ansatz zum Fall bringen würden (/MITT 85b/). Zum anderen sind self-serving-Ansätze, wie etwa der Information-Center Approach (/HAMM 82/) keineswegs geeignet, der Planung von Informationsflüssen für Standardsituationen zu dienen. Ihre Hauptaufgabe ist es ja gerade, Stabsstelle für ungeplante ad-hoc Fragestellungen zu sein.

Bei formalen bottom-up Ansätzen (/MITT 82a/) werden diese Probleme zwar vermieden, es treten jedoch bei der Integration der erhobenen Sachverhalte zu einem Gesamtmodell Synonym-/ Homonym-Probleme auf, die erhebliche Schwierigkeiten bereiten. Diese werden jedoch noch von jenen Integrationsproblemen übertroffen, die sich daraus ergeben, daß einzelne Informanten aus unterschiedlichen Bezugsrahmen (frame of reference) argumentieren. Der Ansatz einer Lösung dieses Problems kann in einer möglichst gegenstandsbezogenen, objektorientierten Vorgangsweise gefunden werden.

2.2 Kombinierte Strategie

Dieser Ansatz geht von der Forderung aus, bei der Modellierung der Individualsichten möglichst wenig Anforderungen an das Abstraktionsvermögen eines Sachbearbeiters zu stellen und auch die Fähigkeit zur Darstellung von Gesamtzusammenhängen nicht zu hoch einzuschätzen. Aus dieser Forderung entstand der Wunsch, Formulare bzw. Formularflüsse als Modellierungsobjekte der ersten Stufe zu betrachten.

Wir gehen davon aus, daß Formularflüsse im wesentlichen Objektflüsse der physischen (oder kontraktuell-abstrakten) Ebene oder Zustandsveränderungen an physischen (kontraktuell-abstrakten) Objekten innerhalb eines manuell geführten Informationssystems nachvollziehen. Somit erlaubt uns die Interpretation eines Formulars als Objekt folgende dreistufige Objekt-Interpretation:

- reales Objekt: Gegenstand über den Information vorliegt,
  etwa physisches Objekt;

- konzeptuelles Objekt: Abstraktion über die informations-
  relevanten Attribute eines realen Objektes, Gegenstand
  der Datenmodellierung;

- formales Objekt: Formular, das Daten über reale Objekte
  enthält, bzw. formatierte Sicht auf eine Datenbank.

Diese Entkopplung soll nicht nur eine klare Trennung - und somit saubere Übersetzungsmöglichkeit - zwischen der Sprache des Informatikers und der Sprache des Sachbearbeiters ermöglichen, sondern auch die Modellierung von Formularflüssen höherer Ordnung, also von Formularflüssen, deren Gegenstandsbereich nicht physische Objekte sondern andere Formulare sind. (Diese Arbeit beschäftigt sich allerdings lediglich mit Formularflüssen einheitlicher Ordnung.)

Neben dem Objektbezug bietet der Einstieg in die Modellierung über Formularflüsse auch den Vorteil, daß hierbei die Datensicht und die Prozeßsicht einfach harmonisch verbunden werden können. Dies stellen unter anderem Programmiersprachen unter Beweis, die, wie HIBOL (/MITT 85a/), auf dem Formularparadigma beruhen. Aber auch BIER, eine Erweiterung des Entity-Relationship-Approaches um Aspekte der dynamischen Modellierung, hat die Modellierung von Formularflüssen als eine wesentliche Anwendungskomponente (/EDER 86b/). Weiters bieten sich Formularflüsse zur Verbindung von Individualsichten - mit all ihren perspektivischen Verzerrungen - zu induktiv erhobenen Globalsicht(en) an. Diese wird einer deduktiv - also im klassischen Stil der konzeptuellen Datenmodellierung - gewonnenen Globalsicht gegenübergestellt, sodaß aus der Analyse der Abweichungen methodisch gezielt eine möglichst bedarfskonforme Systemlösung erarbeitet werden kann.

Aus der Vielzahl objektorientierter Methoden zur Modellierung der Individualsichten (etwa CML (/MITT 82b/)) entschieden wir uns für HIBOL-2, da es als anwendungsbezogene Programmiersprache zur exekutierbaren Spezifikation wird. Somit können Unklarheiten des Benutzers bei Bedarf durch Prototyping erhellt werden (/MITT 82c/).

Die Verbindung von durch HIBOL-2 modellierten "Schreibtischen" führt zu Formularflußnetzen, die dazu benutzt werden können, wenigstens am Typ-Niveau jene Vorbedingungen festzustellen, die gegeben sein müssen, damit ein Sachbearbeiter seinen Aufgaben nachkommen kann. Somit wird für den einzelnen Sachbearbeiter eine Sichtweise unterstützt, in der er Endpunkt in einem möglicherweise sehr langen Informationsfluß ist. Als solcher ist er jedoch auch Produzent neuer Informationen, die er in ausgefüllten Formularen weitergibt. Für Sachbearbeiter, die auf der Arbeit des eben betrachteten Kollegen aufbauen, ist er somit lediglich ein Glied in der Kette der Vorbedingungen. Daher müssem im Modell lediglich die unmittelbaren Informationslieferanten und die unmittelbaren Informationskonsumenten eines Sachbearbeiters bekannt sein.

Aus der Flußsicht ergibt sich nun, daß Formulare nicht nur zwischen Schreibtischen zirkulieren, sondern dabei auch unterschiedliche Zustände durchwandern. Diese Formularzustände (Zustände formaler Objekte) stehen in Beziehung zu Zuständen jener realen Objekte, die durch diese Formulare beschrieben werden. Da wir die realen Objekte nicht EDV-mäßig erfassen können, ordnen wir diese Zustandsübergänge den entsprechenden konzeptuellen Objekten zu (vgl. level-0 und level-1 entities in (/JACK 82/)).

Wesentlich für die Modellierung von Informationssystemen ist nun, festzustellen, wie weit der Formularfluß bzw. die Zustandsänderungen der formalen Objekte den Zustandsänderungen der konzeptuellen Objekte entspricht. Diese Analysen werden in BIER durchgeführt.

3. WERKZEUGE DER MODELLIERUNG

Im folgenden wird ein kurzer Abriß über die hier verwendeten Werkzeuge, BIER und HIBOL-2, gegeben.

3.1 BIER

Das Modell BIER (Behaviour Integrated Entity Relationship Approach) bietet eine Methodologie für den Entwurf von Informationssystemen. Es ermöglicht sowohl statische als auch dynamische Aspekte des betrachteten Ausschnitts der realen Welt zu modellieren. Das Modell BIER wurde in /EDER 86a/ vorgestellt. In /EDER 86b/ wurde gezeigt, wie dieser Ansatz für den Entwurf von Formularflußsystemen verwendet werden kann. In /EDER 87/ wurde die Anwendung dieser Methode auf den Entwurf von Informationssystemen beschrieben.

Das Modell besteht aus drei Komponenten:
- die statischen Konzepte
- die dynamischen Konzepte
- die Abbildung der statischen und dynamischen Konzepte in
  ein erweitertes relationales Modell.

a) statische Konzepte

Die statischen Konzepte des Systems werden durch ein erweitertes Entity - Relationship Modell (/CHEN 76/) dargestellt. Die Erweierungen beziehen sich auf die Verwendung von Surrogatschlüsseln, die Einführung der Zeitdimension und der Generalisationshierarchie. Insbesondere wird das Generalisationskonzept verwendet, um die verschiedenen Zustände eines Entity-Sets bezüglich eines Kategorieattributes zu repräsentieren. Dabei werden die Zustände als Sub-Entity-Sets (kurz für Subordinate-Entity-Set) des entsprechenden Superordinate-Entity-Sets modelliert. Um den Lebensweg von Entities rekonstruieren zu können, enthält jedes dieser Sub-Entity-Sets alle Instanzen des Superordinate-Entity-Sets, die jemals in dem entsprechenden Zustand gewesen sind. Um den aktuellen Zustand von Entities darzustellen, wird jedem der Zustands - Entity-Sets ein weiteres Sub-Entity-Set angefügt, das alle Entities enthält, die sich zum aktuellen Zeitpunkt in diesem Zustand befinden. Zustandsänderungen eines Entities werden also durch Löschen und Einfügen in den aktuellen Zuständen dieser zweiten Ebene der Generalisationshierarchie modelliert.

b) dynamische Konzepte

Die dynamischen Konzepte des Modells werden in drei Komponenten unterteilt:
  - elementare Aktivitäten
  - elementare Prozesse
  - komplexe Aktivitäten

Zur Modellierung der dynamischen Konzepte wird eine graphische Notation verwendet, die auf Petri-Netzen basiert.

Jede elementare und komplexe Aktivität ist durch ihre Eingabedaten (Vorbedingungen) charakterisiert, die das Feuern ermöglichen. Feuern bedeutet insbesonders ein Update auf einem Kategorieattribut und die Erzeugung von Ausgabedaten (Nachbedingungen), die ihrerseits wieder nachfolgende Aktivitäten initiieren können. Eine Aktivität kann feuern, wenn alle Eingabedaten vorliegen. Die Stellen im Graph repräsentieren die aktuellen Zustände, die in der statischen Datenbeschreibung durch eine zweistufige Generalisationshierarchie modelliert wurden. Sie werden durch Sechsecke dargestellt. Die Transitionen stellen die Aktivitäten dar. Elementare Aktivitäten werden durch Balken symbolisiert, komplexe Aktivitäten durch Rauten.

Elementare Aktivitäten beschreiben Operationen, die Daten eines einzelnen konzeptuellen Objektes manipulieren. Jede elementare Aktivität bedingt den Übergang von einer Zustandsmenge des konzeptuellen Objektes in eine andere. Elementare Prozesse beschreiben ein Netz von aufeinanderfolgenden elementaren Aktivitäten, die dasselbe konzeptuelle Objekt betreffen.

Operationen, die mehrere konzeptuelle Objekte desselben Typs oder unterschiedlicher Typen manipulieren, werden als komplexe Aktivitäten modelliert. Eine komplexe Aktivität ist eine Schnittstelle zwischen mehreren elementaren Prozessen.

Je nach der Beziehung zwischen den beteiligten konzeptuellen Objekten werden vier verschiedene Typen von komplexen Aktivitäten unterschieden.

(1) Entstehung oder Manipulation von existenzabhängigen schwachen
    Entities.

Diese komplexe Aktivität hat als Eingangszustand ein konzeptuelles Objekt, das über ein mengenwertiges Attribut verfügt. Der Ausgangszustand repräsentiert die diesem Attribut entsprechenden existenzabhängigen schwachen Objekte.

(2) Group-by Aktivität

Bei einem schwachen Entity-Set hat die group-by Aktivität die Aufgabe alle schwachen Entities zu einem übergeordneten Entity zu aggregiern. Andererseits kann eine group-by Aktivität mehrere Entities zu einem Cover - Entity assoziieren.

(3) Entstehung und Manipulation von schwachen Relationship-Entities

Diese komplexe Aktivität repräsentiert die Entstehung oder Manipulation eines schwachen Entities, das direkt von einer Relationship abgeleitet werden kann. Dieses schwache Entity bezieht sich auf zwei oder mehrere Entities desselben oder verschiedener Entity-Sets.

(4) Triviale komplexe Aktivität

Die triviale komplexe Aktivität modelliert die Manipulation von Entities desselben Entity-Sets, die in verschiedenen elementaren Prozessen involviert sind (z.B. weil sie in verschiedenen Rollen auftreten).

Sowohl die statischen als auch die dynamischen Komponenten des Modells können in einem relationalen Modell mit teilweise relationenwertigen Attributen (NF^2-Modell: /SCHE 83/, /SCHE 86/) abgebildet werden.

Die graphische Darstellung des Modells verbindet die statischen und die dynamischen Komponenten in einem Netz, bei dem die Subtypen des statischen Modells (ER-Diagramm), die die aktuellen Zustände repräsentieren, gleichzeitig die Stellen des Petri-Netz basierten Zustandsänderungsdiagramms (B-Diagramm) darstellen. Die Integration der beiden Diagramme wird als BIER-Diagramm bezeichnet. Im Anhang ist ein Beispiel für ein BIER-Diagramm angegeben.

3.2. HIBOL-2

Im Konzept der Programmiersprache HIBOL-2 (/MITT 85, 86/) wird davon ausgegangen, daß eine abgeschlossene Aufgabe an einem Schreibtisch mit Hilfe von Formularen durchgeführt werden kann und somit ein Programm als ein Satz von Abbildungsregeln in Formularelemente selbst für Nichtprogrammierer einfach formulierbar ist.

Wie dem Sachbearbeiter steht auch dem HIBOL-2-Programmierer zur Erledigung der Arbeiten ein Schreibtisch (Desk) zur Verfügung, auf dem es Fächer (Slots) gibt, über welche Formulare einlangen, weitergereicht oder abgelegt werden können. Die Grobbeschreibung der Vorgänge am Schreibtisch wird durch eine Arbeitsanweisung (Work Rule) angegeben.

Es können folgende Arten von Fächern (Slots) unterschieden werden:

Input Slots: Über Input Slots gelangen Formulare auf den Desk.

Output Slots: Output Slots dienen zur Aus- bzw. Weitergabe von Formularen.

Update Slots: Durch ein Update Slot werden Formulare eines bestimmten Typs zur Verfügung gestellt. Durch entsprechende Befehle in der

Work Rule können neue Formulare hinzugefügt bzw. bereits vorhandene geändert oder gelöscht werden.

<u>Dialog Slots</u>: Dialog Slots sind für das interaktive Ausfüllen von Formularen vorgesehen.

Die den Slots zugeordneten Formulare werden dementsprechend Input, Output, Update bzw. Dialog Forms genannt. Temporary Forms sind solche, welche nur für Zwischenergebnisse vorgesehen und an keinen Slot gebunden sind.

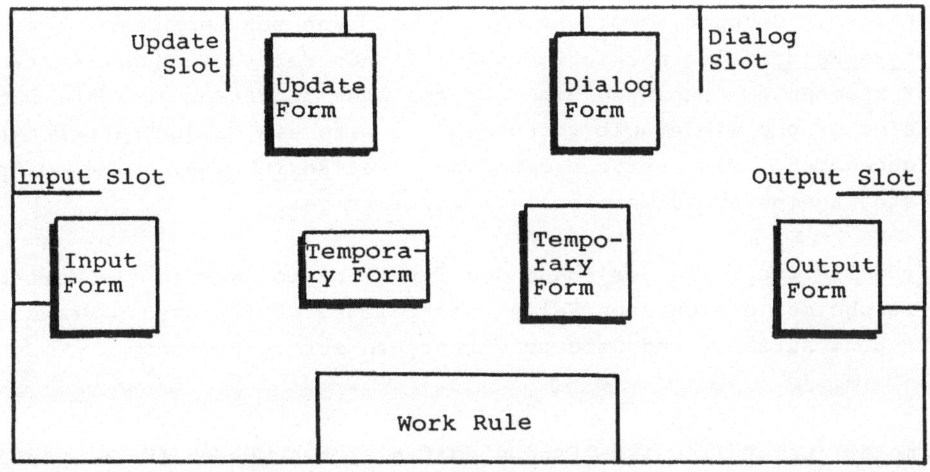

Schematische Darstellung eines Desks

Die Programmierung in HIBOL-2 besteht aus der Definition eines Desks und dem detaillierten Entwurf der benötigten Formulare. Zur Definition des Desks sind mehrere Schritte erforderlich:

a1) <u>Identifikation des Desks</u>: Hier wird dem Desk ein Name zugeordnet. Auch Version, Autor und Datum der Erstellung des Desks können angegeben werden.

<u>a2) Definition der Slots und Formulare</u>: Für alle benötigten Slots
werden Slot-Typ, Slot-Bezeichnung und zugeordnete Formulare
angegeben.

<u>a3) Definition der Work Rule</u>: Die Anweisungen der Work Rule legen die
Reihenfolge fest, in welcher einzelne Formulartypen oder Formu-
larexemplare auszufüllen sind.

Neben der Definition eines Desks sind alle angegebenen Formulare zu
entwerfen. Dazu sind vier Phasen vorgesehen:

<u>b1) Definition der Formularstruktur</u>: Hier wird das Aussehen des Formu-
lars festgelegt. Dazu können Texte, Kommentare und Strukturelemente verwendet werden. Als Strukturelemente stehen elementare
Felder, Gruppen, Kollektion und Matrizen zur Verfügung. <u>Elemen-
tare Felder</u> sind markierte auszufüllende Bereiche. Mehrere Strukturelemente können zu einer <u>Gruppe</u> zusammengefaßt werden. Soll
eine Gruppe wiederholt vorkommen, so wird ein Wiederholungsfaktor
angegeben. Man spricht dann von einer <u>Kollektion</u>. Eine <u>Matrix</u>
stellt eine zweidimensionale Kollektion dar.

<u>b2) Typdefinition</u>: In der Phase der Typdefinition werden die Wertebe-
reiche der elementaren Felder festgelegt. Dafür stehen Standard-
typen, Aufzähl- und Unterbereichstypen zur Verfügung.

<u>b3) Ergebnisdefinition</u>: In dieser Phase wird angegeben, wie das For-
mular auszufüllen ist. Ergebnisdefinitionen müssen für elementare
Felder, Kollektionen und Matrizen, können aber auch für Gruppen
angegeben werden.

<u>b4) Optimierungsdefinition</u>: Hier können Hinweise für eine effiziente
Abspeicherung der Formulare gegeben werden.

Das Weiterreichen von Formularen zwischen Desks kann dadurch erreicht
werden, daß ein Output Slot des einen Desks dem Input Slot eines
anderen entspricht.

Im Zusammenhang mit der hier verfolgten Informationsbedarfsanalyse
werden nur diese groben Konstrukte von HIBOL-2 benötigt. In Kapitel 4
wird das Hauptaugenmerk auf die unterschiedlichen Slots gerichtet
sein. Allerdings entfällt derzeit noch die Modellierung der Dialog

Slots, da diese wie der besetzte Sessel vor dem Schreibtisch des Sachbearbeiters aufgefaßt werden. Die Informationsquellen, aus denen der Sachbearbeiter seine Dialogeingaben bezieht, bleiben somit vorläufig unerfaßt.

Im Anhang werden Beispiele für die Definition von HIBOL-2-Formularen und von HIBOL-2-Desks angegeben.

4. Induktive statische und dynamische Objektbeschreibung

4.1 Ausgangsbedingungen

Die statische und dynamische Objektbeschreibung geht von der Definition der HIBOL-2 Desks aus. Dabei muß sichergestellt sein, daß die HIBOL-2 Desks in dem Sinne minimal sind, daß kein Desk zwei voneinander unabhängige Aufgaben (Tasks) erfüllt. Wenn ein Desk mehrere Tasks beschreibt, so muß er in mehrere Desks aufgespalten werden.

4.2 Beschreibung der statischen Struktur

Die statische Beschreibung der formalen Objekte (formale Datenbeschreibung) gibt eine Übersicht über die in den Desks verwendeten Formulare. Alle Informationen werden den Formulardefinitionen entnommen. Zur Beschreibung der Formulare wird das NF^2-Relationenmodell (/SCHE 83, 86/) verwendet, in dem die Struktur von Formularen leicht dargestellt werden kann (/KAPP 85/,/EDER 86b/).

Dabei gilt, daß jeder Formularname zum Namen einer Relation wird. Jeder Name eines elementaren Feldes wird Name eines einfachen Attributes. Der Name eines Feldes einer (einfachen) Gruppe wird mit dem Namen der Gruppe qualifiziert zum Namen eines einfachen Attributes. Jeder Name einer Kollektion wird zum Namen eines relationenwertigen Attributes. Jeder Name einer Matrix wird zum Namen eines relationenwertigen Attributes, das über 3 Attribute verfügt, nämlich "Zeile",

"Spalte" und "Wert". Jedem somit ermittelten Attribut der formalen Datenbeschreibung wird ein Wertebereich zugeordnet. Die Wertebereiche werden aus der Formularbeschreibung übernommen. Für relationenwertige Attribute, die Matrizen von HIBOL-2 Formularen darstellen, gilt, daß die Wertebereiche der Attribute Zeile und Spalte numerisch sind, und der Wertebereich des Attributes Wert gleich dem Wertebereich der Matrixelemente ist.

Die Relationen der formalen Datenbeschreibung sind Benutzersichten auf das konzeptuelle Datenmodell. Die Beschreibung des konzeptuellen Modells basiert auf einer Analyse der formalen Datenbeschreibung. Die konzeptuellen Objekte werden in Form eines Entity-Relationship-Diagrammes dargestellt (/CHEN 76/). Dabei ist festzuhalten, daß das auf diesem Wege gewonnene konzeptuelle Datenmodell von einem auf klassische deduktive Weise entworfenen abweichen kann. Im induktiv entwickkelten Modell wird man vor allem versuchen, die verschiedenen Formulare einfach zu integrieren, sodaß wenig Probleme bei der Ableitung der formalen Objekte aus den konzeptuellen Objekten zu erwarten sind. Es können daher in diesem Modell Redundanzen entstehen, die bei einem deduktiv entworfenen Modell eher vermieden werden. Vermeidet man diese Redundanzen und definiert z.B. formale Objekte, die aggregierte Informationen darstellen, als Sichten über Mengen von konzeptuellen Objekten, so werden Probleme bei der Beschreibung des dynamischen Verhaltens dieser formalen Objekte auftreten, da diese nicht mehr einfach identifiziert werden können.

4.3 Beschreibung der dynamischen Struktur

Bei der Beschreibung der dynamischen Struktur wird zwischen der Flußbeschreibung, das ist die Darstellung des Flusses der formalen Objekte, und der Beschreibung des dynamischen Verhaltens der konzeptuellen Objekte durch Zustandsänderungen unterschieden.

In einem solchen System verfügt ein Informationsbedarfsträger über einen oder mehrere Desks. Zur Befriedigung seines Informationsbedarfs müssen i.a. informationstragende Objekte (hier die HIBOL-2-Formulare) von anderen Desks zu seinen Desks weitergeleitet werden. Die Struktur dieses Systems kann daher als Netz beschrieben werden, bei dem zwi-

schen den Knoten, die die Desks darstellen, Kanten den Informationsfluß anzeigen.

4.4 Flußbeschreibung

Jeder Desk modifiziert die Formulare oder füllt neue Formulare aus,
die an andere Desks übermittelt werden. Die Flußbeschreibung gibt nun
an, wie und auf welche Weise Formulare von Desk zu Desk gesandt werden. Die Darstellung des Flusses erfolgt durch ein Petri-Netz-ähn-
liches Diagramm. Jeder HIBOL-2-Desk wird als Transition des Netzes
repräsentiert. Die Stellen des Netzes entsprechen den formalen Objekten und deren Zuständen.

Dabei gibt es folgende Möglichkeiten:

a) Verbindung Output - Input - Slot

   Wenn ein Formular in einem Output Slot eines Desks und in einem
   Input Slot gleichen Namens eines anderen Desks spezifiziert
   wurde, so wird der erste Desk als Vorgängertransition und der
   zweite Desk als Nachfolgetransition einer Stelle modelliert, die
   mit dem Namen des Formulars und mit einer fortlaufenden Nummer
   gekennzeichnet wird.

   Beispiel:

   wird dargestellt als

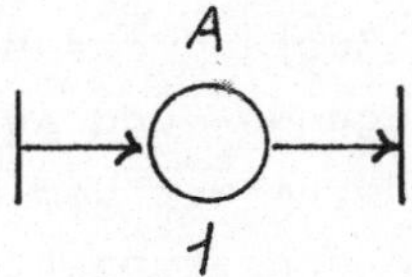

b) Allgemeine Verbindung Input - Output - Slots

Allgemein können mehrere Desks über Output Slots mit dem gleichen Namen verfügen und mit diesem Namen auch die Input Slots mehrerer Desks bezeichnet werden. Das formale Objekt und sein Zustand, der durch diese Slots charakterisiert wird, wird als eine Stelle modelliert, die mit dem Namen des formalen Objekts und einer fortlaufenden Nummer gekennzeichnet wird.

Beispiel:

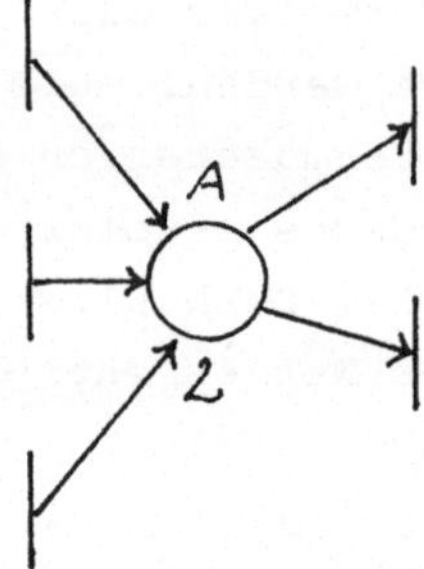

c) Formulare, die in Update Slots auftreten.

Die Operationen, die in Update Slots auftreten, werden in zustandsverändernde und zustandserhaltende eingeteilt. Dabei ist allerdings festzuhalten, daß diese Aufteilung im Gegensatz zu den in a) und b) beschriebenen Strukturen nicht aus der Syntax der Formular- und Slotdefinitionen abgeleitet werden kann. Die Feststellung, ob ein Desk für ein bestimmtes formales Objekt, das einem seiner Update Slots zugeordnet wurde, zustandserhaltend oder zustandsverändernd wirkt, kann erst nach Analyse der Work Rule und der Ergebnisdefinitionen des HIBOL-2-Desks getroffen werden. Bei der Modellierung kann diese Unterscheidung auch vorerst unterlassen werden und erst beim Vergleich der konzeptuellen Modelle (siehe Kapitel 5) berücksichtigt werden.

c1) Zustandserhaltende Desks

Die Stelle, die den Zustand des betreffenden formalen Objekts repräsentiert, ist Eingangs- und Ausgangsstelle der Transition. Die Stelle wird wiederum mit dem Namen des Objekts und einer fortlaufenden Nummer gekennzeichnet.

Beispiel:

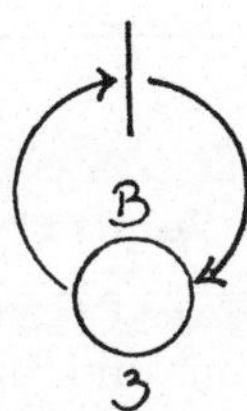

c2) Zustandsverändernde Desks

Wird der Zustand eines formalen Objektes in einem Desks verändert, so muß die Eingangsstelle von der Ausgangsstelle verschieden sein. Jede dieser Stellen wird mit dem Namen des Objektes und einer fortlaufenden Nummer gekennzeichnet.

Beispiel:

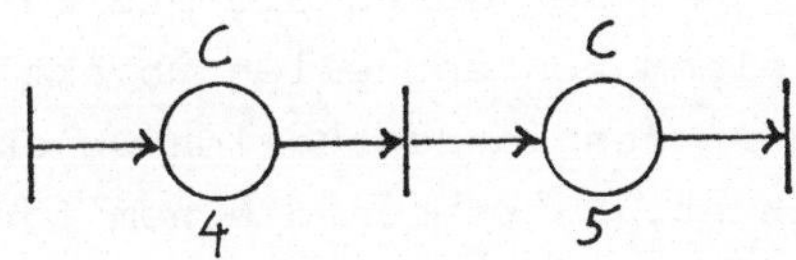

Die Stellen im Netz werden mit einer fortlaufenden Nummer versehen, um sie unterscheiden zu können, und mit dem Namen des entsprechenden formalen Objekts gekennzeichnet. Die Stellen beschreiben jeweils ein bestimmtes formales Objekt in einem bestimmten Zustand. Genauer: Wenn man wie im Kapitel 3 davon ausgeht, daß Zustände Spezialisierungen auf Objekte im Sinne einer Generalisationshierarchie definieren, so stehen die Stellen für die durch eine solche Spezialisierung entstandenen Subtypen der formalen Objekttypen.

Die Stellen haben die Bedeutung, daß Formulare, die sich in einer Stelle befinden, von den nachfolgenden Transitionen als Input verwendet werden können. Weitere Semantik wird den Stellen noch nicht zugeordnet. Eine semantische Beschreibung der Zustände erfolgt erst nach der Beschreibung des dynamischen Verhaltens der konzeptuellen Objekte.

Im Anhang ist ein Beispiel für die Flußbeschreibung der formalen Objekte aufgrund von HIBOL-2-Desks angegeben.

4.5 Beschreibung des dynamischen Verhaltens der konzeptuellen Objekte

Die Beschreibung des dynamischen Verhaltens der konzeptuellen Objekte
(konzeptuelle Zustandsübergangsbeschreibung) wird aus der formalen und
der konzeptuellen Datenbeschreibung und der formalen Flußbeschreibung
abgeleitet. Dabei gilt vorerst, daß jede Transition der formalen
Flußbeschreibung auch als Transition in der konzeptuellen Zustandsübergangsbeschreibung aufscheint. Die Stellen der formalen Flußbeschreibung entsprechen allerdings den formalen Objekten und deren
Zuständen, während sich die Stellen der konzeptuellen Zustandsübergangsbeschreibung auf die konzeptuellen Objekte und deren Zustände
beziehen. Da formale Objekte Sichten auf die konzeptuellen Objekte
sind, muß keine 1:1 Beziehung vorliegen. Für jede Stelle wird daher
wie folgt vorgegangen: Wenn der durch die Stelle repräsentierte formale Formulartyp genau einem konzeptuellen Objekt entspricht, so wird
die Stelle mit dem Namen des konzeptuellen Objekts und einer fortlaufenden Nummer bezeichnet. Entsprechen einem formalen Objekt mehrere
konzeptuelle Objekte, so wird die betreffende Stelle für jedes dieser
konzeptuellen Objekte angelegt und mit dem Namen des Objektes und
einer fortlaufenden Nummer gekennzeichnet.

Wenn einem konzeptuellen Objekt mehrere formale Objekte entsprechen,
so kann dies daraus ersehen werden, daß Stellen, die im formalen Netz
mit verschiedenen Objektnamen gekennzeichnet waren, nunmehr mit dem
selben konzeptuellen Objektnamen versehen sind. Die fortlaufende
Numerierung aller Stellen ist daher notwendig, um solche Stellen
unterscheiden zu können. Für n:m Beziehungen zwischen formalen und
konzeptuellen Objekten gilt Analoges. Durch die Vervielfältigung der
Stellen wurde jedes formale Objekt in die von ihm beschriebenen konzeptuellen Objekte aufgespaltet. Stellen, die verschiedenen formalen
Objekten zugeordnet wurden, aber mit dem selben konzeptuellen Objekt
gekennzeichnet wurden, werden als verschiedene Zustände eben dieses
konzeptuellen Objekts aufgefaßt.

Ein Sonderfall tritt ein, wenn ein formales Objekt keinem konzeptuellen Objekt entspricht aber eine Sicht auf eine Menge von konzeptuellen
Objekten beschreibt, wie dies bei aggregierten Informationen möglich
ist. In einem solchen Fall ist die Stelle für den späteren Vergleich
der Modelle zu kennzeichnen.

Die Transformation der formalen Flußbeschreibung in die konzeptuelle Flußbeschreibung liefert ein B-Diagramm. Die konzeptuelle Datenbeschreibung wird in Form von Generalisationshierarchien um die Zustände der konzeptuellen Objekte erweitert. Diese Zustände sind im Netz die mit dem jeweiligen Objektnamen gekennzeichneten Stellen. An einem Beispiel im Anhang wird gezeigt, wie aus der formalen Flußbeschreibung ein Zustandsübergangsdiagramm abgeleitet wird.

Die Transitionen werden nun in elementare und komplexe Aktivitäten eingeteilt. Dabei werden alle Stellen, mit denen die Transition direkt in Verbindung steht, betrachtet. Sind alle Stellen mit demselben Namen gekennzeichnet, so repräsentiert diese Transition eine elementare Aktivität, sonst eine komplexe Aktivität. Die Art der komplexen Aktivität (assoziative Aktivität, group-by Aktivität) wird durch die Beziehung der durch die benachbarten Stellen repräsentierten konzeptuellen Entities und die Work Rule der Desks erkannt.

5. Vergleich der Modelle

5.1 Ausgangsbasis

Nachdem die BIER-Diagramme auf induktive und deduktive Weise erstellt wurden, ist es die Aufgabe des Designers diese einander gegenüberzustellen. Dabei ist wesentlich, daß bei beiden Modellvarianten identische Ausgangsbasen gewählt wurden. Für eine Schwachstellenanalyse etwa müßten beide Modelle am Niveau einer Istanalyse aufsetzen, für Entwurfsüberlegungen sollten beide einem Sollkonzept entsprechen. Es ist auch denkbar, daß man eine Differenzbetrachtung (Ist versus Soll) vornimmt, doch ist insbesondere hier wichtig sicherzustellen, daß jeder der einzelnen Individualinformanten von identischen Prämissen ausging.

Beim Entwurf komplexer Informationssysteme ist anzunehmen, daß die beiden Modelle nicht identisch sind. Der Designer wird die Unterschiede betrachten und versuchen Fehler, die in einem der beiden Ansätze gemacht wurden, zu entdecken, den Entwurfsprozeß in den divergierenden Teilen wiederholen und so Entwurfsfehler sukzessive zu eliminieren. Dabei werden sowohl Fehler zutage treten, die auf Mängel bei der Erhebung der Informationen zurückzuführen sind, als auch solche, die während der Modellierung entstanden sind. Eine besondere Rolle werden dabei Fehler spielen, die aufgrund von Problemen mit Homonymen und Synonymen auftreten. Gerade diese Fehler können durch den Entwurf des Systems mit Hilfe der kombinierten Strategie leichter erkannt werden. Weitere Fehler können durch Übersehen von Objekten oder von Transaktionen entstanden sein, durch falsche Darstellung des Flusses, durch falsches Modellieren von Zuständen, etc.

Wenn der Designer diese Fehler, die bei der Erhebung oder bei der Modellierung entstanden sind, korrigiert hat, können noch immer Unterschiede in den Modellen verbleiben. Im folgenden werden mögliche Ursachen für diese Unterschiede untersucht.

5.2 Objektebene

Ein wichtiger Grund für verbleibende Differenzen liegt in unterschiedlichen Sichtweisen der Elemente des Informationssystems durch verschiedene Betrachter. Es kann etwa für einen Betrachter etwas ein Attribut sein, was für einen anderen ein eigenständiges Objekt ist; was für einen eine Beziehung zwischen Objekten ist, ist für einen anderen ein Objekt (vergl. /LEE 86/). Diese unterschiedlichen Betrachtungsweisen können selten in richtig oder falsch eingeteilt werden, da es sich um durchaus legitime Beschreibungen des betrachteten Systems handelt. Man muß vielmehr versuchen, sie in einfach oder kompliziert, aussagekräftig oder weniger aussagekräftig, für die Anwendungen mehr oder weniger passend, für alle Beteiligten akzeptierbar oder exzentrisch einzuteilen. Diese Abklärung der Betrachtungsweise ist eine zentrale Aufgabe beim Entwurf von Informationssystemen. Durch den Vergleich von induktivem und deduktivem Modell können diese unterschiedlichen Sichtweisen leichter erkannt werden. Sichtweisen, die in diesem Ausgleichsprozeß "unterlegen" sind, können durch View-Mechanismen für den Anwender jedoch weiterhin unterstützt werden.

Bei der vergleichenden Analyse von induktiv und deduktiv gewonnenem Modell können weiters Unterschiede bei den konzeptuellen Objekten festgestellt werden, die bei einer Transition einlangen. Hier muß

untersucht werden, ob bei der betreffenden Operation (beim betreffenden Sachbearbeiter) ein Informationsdefizit oder ein Überangebot an
Information vorliegt.

5.3 Zustandsebene

Unterschiede auf der Zustandsebene können die Existenz von Zuständen
oder Zustandsübergänge betreffen. Derartige Unterschiede können entweder auf die im Folgenden beschriebenen Problemsituationen hinweisen,
oder sie können dadurch entstehen, daß aus der "Implementierung" des
Formularflusses Abweichungen vom konzeptuellen Idealmodell entstanden.

Wenn die Zustände in den Modellen nicht übereinstimmen, müssen zwei
Fälle unterschieden werden. Zum einen kann ein Zustand im induktiven
Modell vorkommen, der im deduktiven Modell fehlt. Dieser Zustand kann
irrelevant sein und aus alten formalen Systemen übernommen worden
sein. In einem solchen Fall soll untersucht werden, ob Parallelisie-
rung von Transaktionen möglich ist. Ein solcher Zustand kann aber auch
auf ein Informationsüberangebot (auf formaler Ebene) hinweisen.

Zum anderen kann ein Zustand, der im deduktiven Modell aufscheint, im
induktiven Modell nicht vorhanden sein. Ein solcher Zustand kann
irrelevant sein oder auf ein Informationsdefizit (auf formaler Ebene)
hinweisen. Diese Situation kann auch auftreten, wenn ein Desk nicht in
dem in Kapitel 4 geforderten Sinne "minimal" ist, oder wenn Elemente
aus Informationsflüssen anderer Ordnung in die Modellierung eingeflos-
sen sind.

Divergierende Zustandsfolgen deuten in erster Linie auf Fehler hin,
die entweder bei der Modellierung entstanden sind oder aber im Formularfluß vorhanden sind. Aber auch unterschiedliche Bezugsrahmen oder
Sichtweisen können zu den Differenzen führen. Im Besonderen werden
unterschiedliche Zustandsfolgen auftreten, wenn Unterschiede auf der
Objektebene vorliegen. Unterschiede bei den Transitionen können darin
liegen, daß eine Folge von Transitionen in einem Modell einer Transition in einem anderen Modell entspricht, daß redundante oder über-
flüssige Transitionen modelliert wurden, oder daß Transitionen verges-
sen wurden.

6. Zusammenfassung und Ausblick

In dieser Arbeit wurde eine Strategie zum Entwurf von Informationssystemen vorgestellt, bei der die Informationsbedarfsanalyse deduktiv und induktiv erfolgt und zu zwei Modellen führt, die miteinander verglichen werden, um auf Probleme, Fehler, unterschiedliche Betrachtungsweisen oder Mängel hinzuweisen.

Ein wesentlicher Bereich, die Analyse von Informationsflüssen, die nicht auf formellen Kanälen fließen, wurde in dieser Arbeit noch ausgespart. Sie ließen sich in analoger Form modellieren, wenn man den HIBOL-2-Desk über die Ebene des Sachbearbeiters (Dialog Slot) spiegelt und so die lokalen Speicher oder informellen Kontakte einbezieht. Praktiker des Faches wissen jedoch, daß diesem Problem bloß durch die Angabe eines Formalismus nicht beizukommen ist.

A N H A N G

Ein Beispiel soll die Modellierung von Informationssystemen durch induktive und deduktive Analyse des Informationsbedarfs veranschaulichen. Dafür wurde eine vereinfachte Problemstellung aus dem Bereich des Prüfungswesens an Universitäten gewählt. Die zu modellierenden Aufgaben können wie folgt beschrieben werden:

Die Ergebnisse einer Prüfung in Form von Punktebewertungen vorliegen. Aus diesen werden in einem ersten Desk "Prüfungsbeurteilung" mit Hilfe eines Notenschlüssels die entsprechenden Noten ermittelt. Da die Studenten in der Notenliste nur mit ihrer Matrikelnummer vorkommen, benötigt der Desk "Zeugnisausstellung" zusätzlich Studentendaten, welche über ein Input Slot zur Verfügung gestellt werden. Die auf diesem Desk generierten Zeugnisse gehen, je nachdem, welcher Fakultät der Student angehört, an die Studienabteilung der technisch-naturwissenschaftlichen bzw. der sozial- und wirtschaftswissenschaftlichen Fakultät. Dort werden die Studentendaten um diese durch die Zeugnisse belegten Prüfungen erweitert. Auf den Desks der Studienabteilungen werden außerdem die Summen der insgesamt eingelangten Zeugnisse gebildet, welche an die Quästur weitergeleitet werden. Der Desk "Quästur" veranlaßt die Überweisungen der Prüfungstaxen. Die Abbildung A-1 skizziert diese Vorgänge als Formularflüsse zwischen HIBOL-2-Desks.

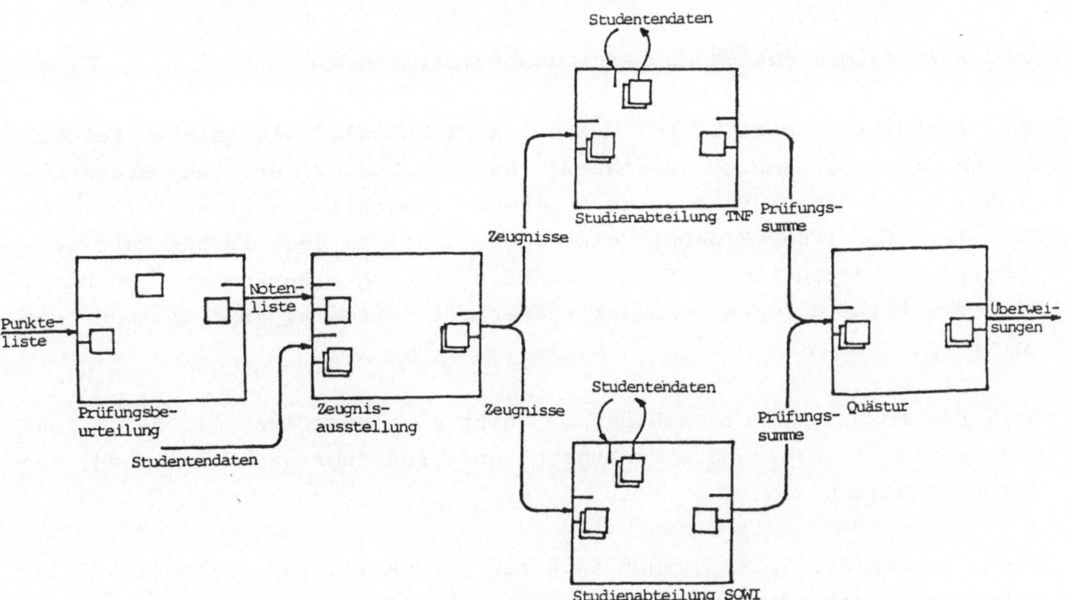

Abb. A-1: Beispiel für Formularflüsse zwischen HIBOL-2-Desks.

Betrachten wir nun beispielsweise den Desk "Prüfungsbeurteilung" näher: Auf diesem kommen drei Formulare vor. Das Input Form "Punkteliste" gelangt über das Input Slot "Fach-Punkteliste" auf den Desk. Das Output Form "Notenliste" benötigt zur Ermittlung der Noten aus den erreichten Punkten das Temporary Form "Notenschlüssel" und wird über das Output Slot "Fach-Notenliste" weitergegeben. Die Work Rule dieses Desks enthält lediglich zwei Befehle, welche bedeuten, daß zuerst das Formular "Punkteliste" geholt und dann das Formular "Notenliste" geschaffen wird. Der Aufbau des Desks ist in Abbildung A-2 dargestellt.

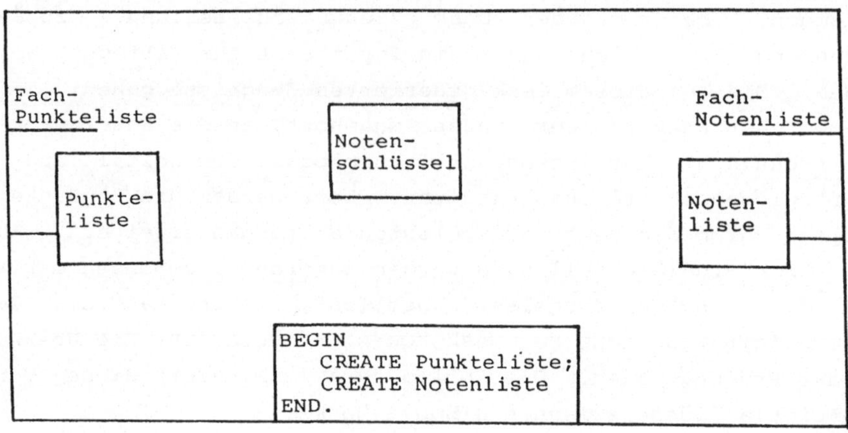

Abb. A-2: Aufbau des Desks "Prüfungsbeurteilung".

Das Formular "Punkteliste" (Abb. A-3) enthält elementare Felder, welche die Bezeichnung, die Nummer und den Leiter der Lehrveranstaltung, sowie das Prüfungsdatum angeben. Zusätzlich gibt es auf diesem Formular für jedes Ergebnis eine Zeile, welche jeweils die Matrikelnummer des geprüften Studenten und die erreichte Punktezahl enthält. Da diese Zeile auf dem Formular wiederholt vorkommt, spricht man von einer Kollektion.

Auf dem Formular "Notenschlüssel" gibt es elementare Felder, welche die maximal erreichbare Punktezahl und Punktegrenzen zwischen den Noten enthalten.

Die "Notenliste" ist symmetrisch zur "Punkteliste" aufgebaut. Die Ergebnisdefinitionen von "Notenliste" beziehen sich sowohl auf die "Punkteliste" wie auch auf den "Notenschlüssel".

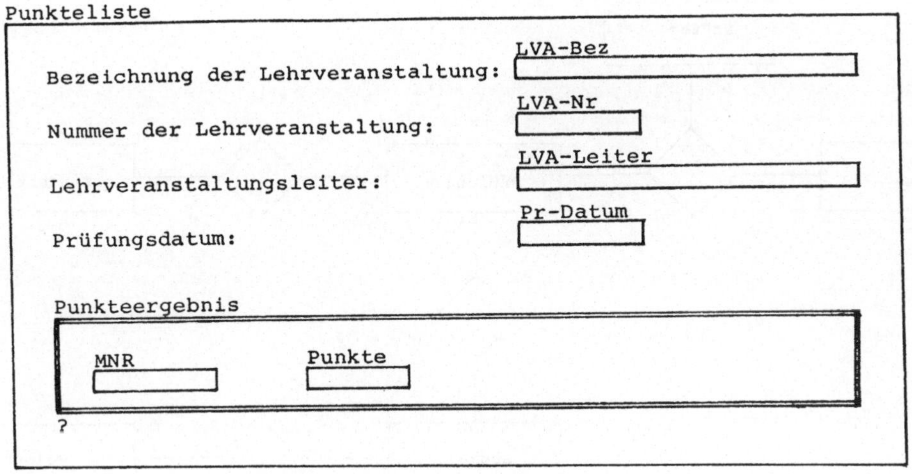

Punkteliste

Bezeichnung der Lehrveranstaltung: LVA-Bez

Nummer der Lehrveranstaltung: LVA-Nr

Lehrveranstaltungsleiter: LVA-Leiter

Prüfungsdatum: Pr-Datum

Punkteergebnis

MNR   Punkte

?

Abb. A-3: Aufbau des Formulars "Punkteliste".

Aus der Analyse der Formulare wird ein konzeptuelles Datenmodell entwickelt, das in Form eines Entity-Relationship-Diagrammes in Abb. A-4 dargestellt ist. Dabei wurden die Formulare sehr unmittelbar in konzeptuelle Objekte übergeführt, was z.B. beim konzeptuellen Objekt Prüfungssumme dazu führt, daß dieses Objekt auch als eine Sicht auf die Objektmenge Prüfungen angesehen werden kann. Die in diesem konzeptuellen Modell enthaltene Redundanz kann bei Implementierung in einem Datenbanksystem zu Problemen führen. Aus dem Vergleich des durch Abstraktion formaler Objekte erreichten konzeptuellen Modells mit dem durch deduktive Analyse entwickelten Modells können solche problematischen Konstruktionen leichter erkannt werden.

Abb. A-5 zeigt die Beschreibung der formalen Flußstruktur, die aus der Beschreibung der HIBOL-2-Desks abgeleitet wird. Wenn die Verbindungen zwischen HIBOL-2-Desks bereits wie in Abb. A-1 skizziert wurde, bringt diese Flußbeschreibung nur eine etwas knappere Darstellung, aber kaum neue Information. Eine Flußskizze ist allerdings nicht immer vorgesehen, da ein HIBOL-2-Desk nur seine unmittelbaren Vorgänger und Nachfolger kennen muß.

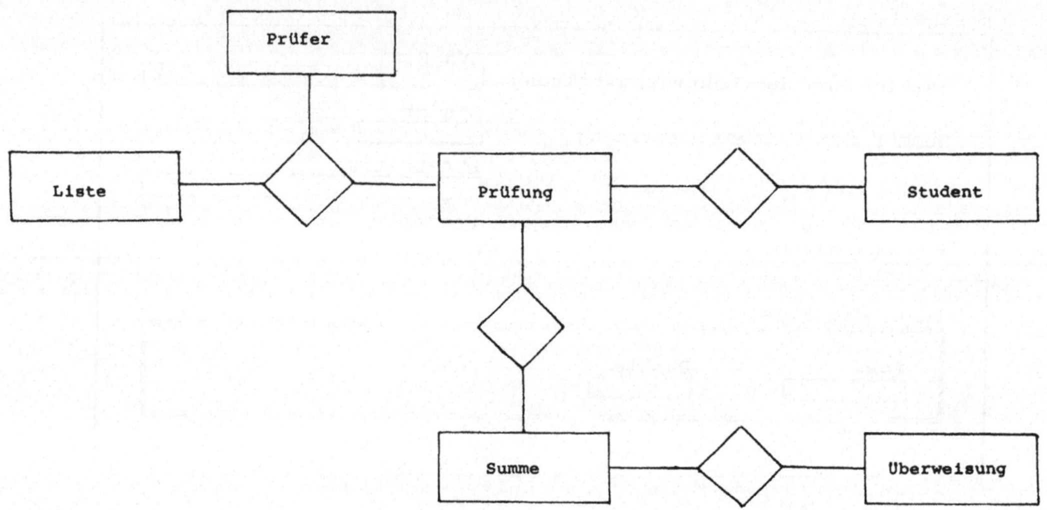

Abb. A-4: E-R-Diagramm der aus den formalen Objekten abgeleiteten konzeptuellen Objekte.

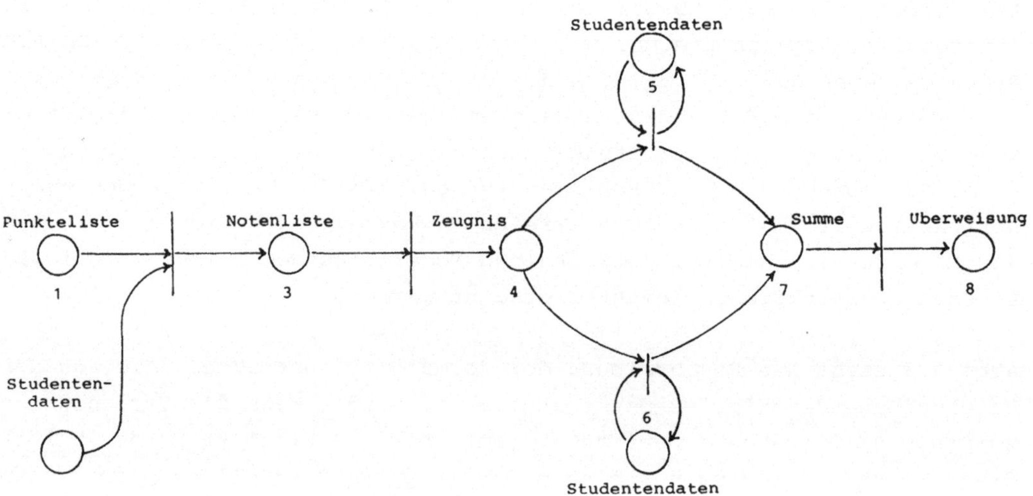

Abb. A-5: Flußbeschreibung der formalen Objekte.

Abb. A-6 beschreibt die induktiv gewonnenen Zustandsübergänge der
konzeptuellen Objekte. Gegenüber der Flußbeschreibung der formalen
Objekte fällt insbesonders auf, daß die Studentendaten in diesem
Diagramm fehlen. Dies ist deshalb möglich, weil die konzeptuellen
Objekte vom Typ Studenten in diesem Teil der betrachteten Realität
keine Zustandsübergänge erfahren und die relevanten Daten durch die
Objekte "Termin" bzw. "Prüfung" hinreichend identifiziert werden kön-
nen. Die Objekte "Punkteliste" und "Notenliste" sind zwei verschieden
Formen desselben konzeptuellen Objektes "Liste". Es mußten weiters
zwei neue Zustände des Objektes Prüfung eingeführt werden, weil die
Desks nicht minimal waren, d.h. die Überprüfung eines Zeugnisses und
das Zählen der Zeugnisse wurden in einem Desk durchgeführt.

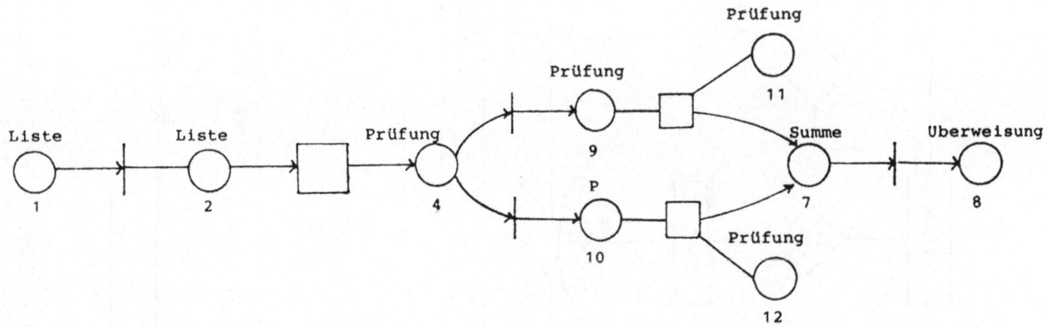

Abb. A-6: Induktiv entwickeltes B-Diagramm der konzeptuellen Objekte.

Das für dieses Problem deduktiv entwickelte BIER-Diagramm ist in Abb.
A-7 dargestellt. Im Bier-Diagramm sind folgende Aktivitäten angegeben:

t1   Berechnung der Noten
ct2   Austellen der Zeugnisse (komplexe Aktivität)
t3   Überprüfen der Zeugnisse TNF
t4   Überprüfen der Zeugnisse SOWI
ct5   Ermitteln der Prüfungstaxen (komplexe Aktivität)

Ein wichtiger Unterschied zwischen dem in Abb. A-7 gezeigten BIER-
Diagramm und dem B-Diagramm von Abb. A-6 ist der Zustand für das
Objekt Summe. Im deduktiven Modell fehlt dieser Objekttyp, weil er als
Sicht auf die Prüfungen ausreichend definiert ist (aggregierte Infor-
mationen). Deshalb sind auch die Zustandsfolgen unterschiedlich.

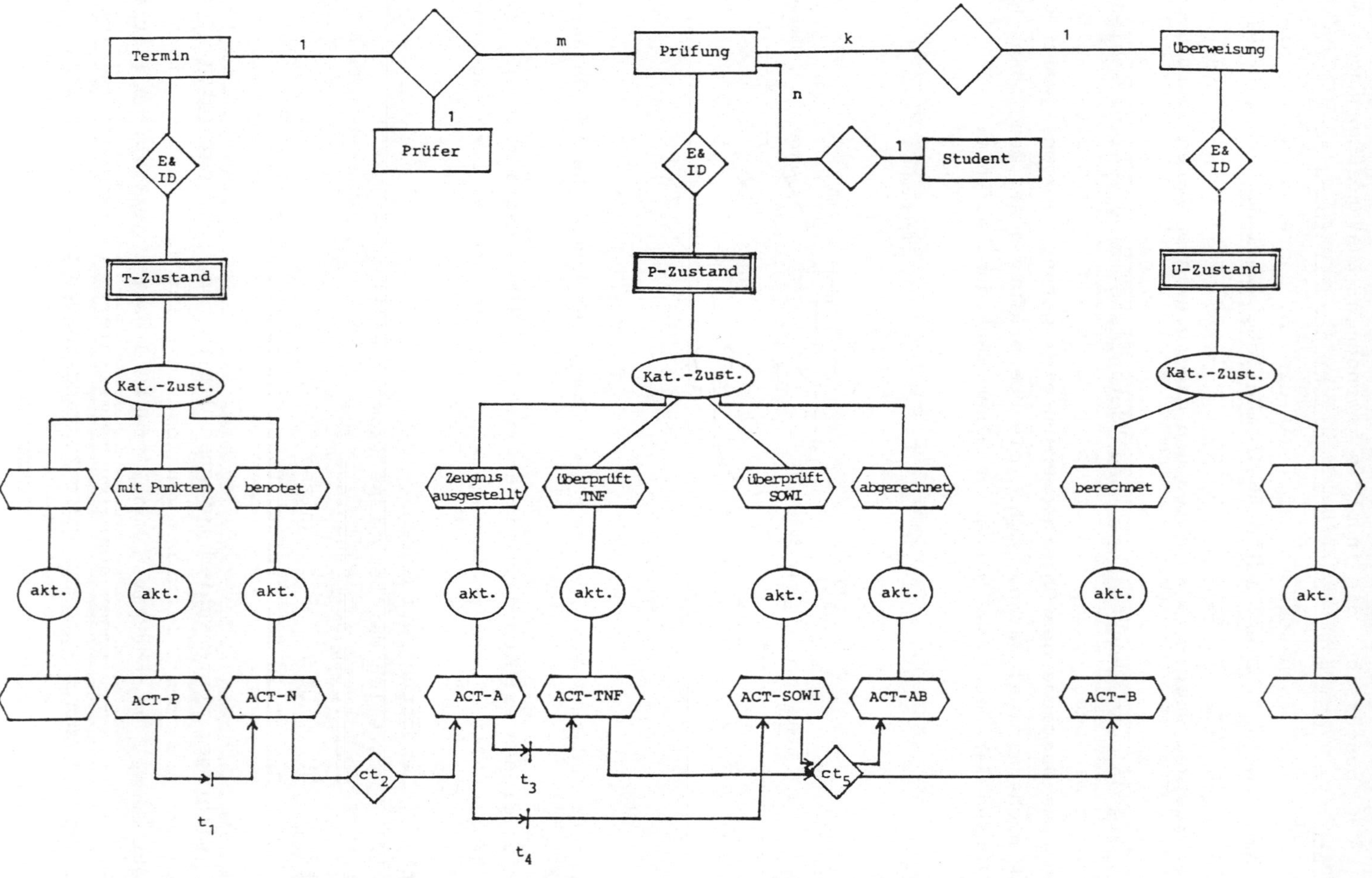

Abb. A-7: Deduktiv ermitteltes BIER-Diagramm

Literatur

/CHEN 76/   P.P.-S. CHEN: "The Entity-Relationship Model - Toward a Unified View of Data", ACM Trans. on Database Systems, Vol. 1/1, March 1976, pp. 9-36.

/EDER 86a/   J. EDER, G. KAPPEL, A M. TJOA, R.R. WAGNER: "BIER - A Behaviour Integrated Entity Relationsship Approach", 5th Int. Conference on the Entity Relationsship Approach 1986, North Holland (in print).

/EDER 86b/   J. EDER, G. KAPPEL, A M. TJOA, R.R. WAGNER: "A Behaviour Design Methodology for Form Flow Systems". Technischer Bericht, Universität Wien, Institut für Statistik und Informatik, 1986.

/EDER 87/   J. EDER, G. KAPPEL, A M. TJOA, R.R. WAGNER: "A Behaviour Design Methodology for Information Systems". Proc. 6th Phönix Conference on Computers and Communications, IEEE-CS Press, 1987.

/HAMM 82/   L.W. HAMMOND: "Management Considerations for an Information Center", IBM Systems Journal, Vol. 21/2, 1982, pp. 131-161.

/JACK 82/   M. A. JACKSON: "System Development", Prent. Hall, 1982.

/KAPP 85/   G. KAPPEL, A M. TJOA, R.R. WAGNER: "Form Flow Systems Based on NF^2-Relations", in: A Blaser, P. Pistor (Hrsg.): Datenbank-System für Büro, Technik und Wirtschaft, Springer-Verlag, 1985.

/LEE 86/   R.M. LEE: "Logic, Semantics and Data Modelling: an Ontology", in: Proceedings of the IFIP TC 2 Working Conference on Knowledge and Data (DS-2) 1986, North Holland (im Druck).

/MITT 82a/   R. T. MITTERMEIR: "Semantic Nets for Modelling the Requirements of Evolvable Systems - An Example", in: J. Hawgood (ed.): "Evolutionary Information Systems", North Holland Publ., 1982, pp. 193 - 216.

/MITT 82b/   R.T. MITTERMEIR: "CML-GRAPHS - A Notation for Systems Development", in: R. TRAPPL (ed.): "Cybernetics and Systems Research", Proc. 6th European Meeting on Cybernetics and Systems Research, Vienna, Apr. 1982, North Holland Publ., 1982, pp. 803 - 809.

/MITT 82c/   R.T. MITTERMEIR, P. HSIA, R.T. YEH: "Alternatives to Overcome The Communications Problem of Formal Requirements Analysis", in Ohno,Y.: Proceedings International Symposium on Current Issues of Requirements Engineering Environments, September 20-21, 1982, Kyoto, Japan. OHM & North-Holland, 1982, pp. 163-169.

/MITT 83/   R.T. MITTERMEIR und L. WENINGER: "Gestufte Formen von Partizipation in unternehmensweiten Projekten - Ein Erfahrungsbericht", Proc. 13. GI Jahrestagung, Informatik Fachberichte Hr 73, Springer 1983, pp. 461-469.

/MITT 85a/   R.T. MITTERMEIR: "HIBOL-BO - Objektorientierte Programmie-
              rung für kommerzielle Anwendungen", in: Notizen zu inter-
              aktiven Systemen, Heft 14, Mai 1985, pp. 63-72.

/MITT 85b/   R.T. MITTERMEIR: "Requirements Elicitation by Rapid Pro-
              totyping", Proc. Informatica 85, Nova Gorica, pp.
              105 - 108, 1985.

/MITT 86/   R. MITTERMEIR und H. WERNHART: "Benutzerhandbuch zur
              Programmiersprache HIBOL-2", Inst. f. Informatik, Univ.
              Klagenfurt, 1986.

/ROSS 77/   D.T. ROSS: "Structured Analysis (SA): A Language for Com-
              municating Ideas", IEEE Transactions on Software Enginee-
              ring, Vol. SE-3, No. 1, January 1977, pp. 16 - 34.

/SCHE 83/   H.J. SCHEK, M. SCHOLL: "Die NF^2-Relationenalgebra
              zur einheitlichen Manipulation externer, konzep-
              tueller und interner Datenstrukturen", in:
              Sprachen für Datenbanken, Informatik-Fachberichte, Nr. 72,
              Springer Verlag, 1983.

/SCHE 86/   H.J. SCHEK, M. SCHOLL: "The relational model with
              relation-valued attributes", Information Systems,
              Vol 11, No. 2, 1986.

/ZACH 82/   J.A. ZACHMANN: "Business System Planing and Business
              Information Control Study: A comparison", IBM Systems
              Journal, Vol 21/1 1982, pp. 31-53.

A COMPARATIVE ANALYSIS OF VIEW INTEGRATION METHODOLOGIES

M. Schrefl[1]

Institut fuer Angewandte Informatik und Systemanalyse
Abteilung fuer Verteilte Datenbanken und Expertensysteme
Technische Universitaet Wien

ABSTRACT

One of the most difficult tasks in logical database design is the analysis and the integration of the requirements different user groups have on the whole application. Once the requirements of each user group have been formally described by view database schemas, view integration methodologies are used to construct a conceptual database schema that can support all different user views.

Furthermore view integration methodologies are used in a domain which is similar to user view integration: in the design of multidatabase systems. There the problem is to define a single global view for several databases already in use.

Recently, several methodologies for user view integration and global view definition have been proposed in literature. The purpose of this paper is, first, to define comparison criteria for view integration methodologies and, secondly, to provide a comparative analysis of the features and main characteristics of the most important view integration methodologies with respect to the given criteria.

1. INTRODUCTION

View Integration is used in two different contexts, in logical database design for user view integration, and in multidatabase system design for global view definition.

In logical database design <u>user view integration</u> refers to the merging of separate views of data held by different user groups of a data base (<u>user views</u>) to form a single global schema of the entire database (<u>conceptual schema</u>). The main motivation for user view integration is to reduce redundancies and the size of the conceptual schema.

The main steps in user view integration are the view analysis step, the optimization step and the mapping step. During the <u>view analysis</u> step integration constraints, which capture time-invariable connections between several view data base schemas, are defined. During the <u>optimization</u> step the previously defined integration constraints are used to reduce the redundancy and size of the conceptual schema. During the <u>mapping</u> step the mapping between the conceptual schema and the user views are generated (Fig. 1a).

In a multidatabase system environment <u>global view definition</u> refers to the combination of the conceptual schemas of several existing databases into a single global schema (<u>global view</u>) which can then be used as an interface to the multidatabase system. The motivation for global view definition is to capture the meaning and similarities between the database schemas of different databases explicitly in a single global

---

[1] Current address: Institut fuer Integrierte Informations- und Publikationssysteme, Gesellschaft fuer Mathematik und Datenverarbeitung, Darmstadt

view. Contrary to user view integration, whose main motivation is to reduce redundancies, the process of global view definition may even involve the introduction of new abstractions to express hidden semantics, properties and constraints explicitly in the global view in order to gain further clarity and autoexplicativity of the global view (schema enrichment)[2].

The main steps in global view definition are the schema analysis step, the schema combination step and the mapping step. During the <u>schema analysis</u> step interschema relationships which capture the meaning and similarities between the data in different schemas are identified. During the <u>schema combination</u> step appropriate abstractions to represent interschema relationships are introduced. During the mapping step mappings between the global view and the database schemas are generated (see figure 1b)[3].

The purpose of this paper is to provide a comparative analysis of the features and main characteristics of the recently proposed methodologies for user view integration and global view definition. These methodologies are:

Batini, Lenzerini: "A Methodology of Data Schema Integration in the Entity-Relationship Model" /BAT84/

Navathe, Elmasri, Larson: "Integrating user views in Database Design" /NAV86/

Dayal, Hwang: "View Definition and Generalization for Database Integration in a Multidatabase System" /DAY84/

Yao, Waddle, Housel: " View Modeling and Integration Using the Functional Data Model" /YAO82/

Casanova, Vidal: "Towards a sound view integration methodology" /CAS83/

Biskup, Covent: "A Formal View Integration Method" /BIS86/

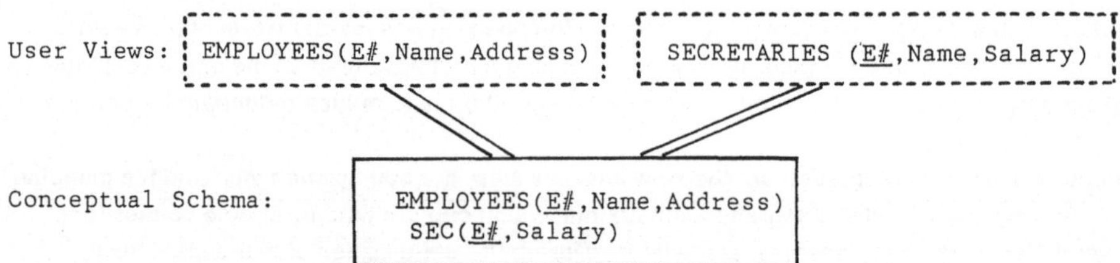

```
User Views:  ┌ ─ ─ ─ ─ ─ ─ ─ ─ ─ ─ ─ ─ ─ ─ ─ ─ ─ ┐   ┌ ─ ─ ─ ─ ─ ─ ─ ─ ─ ─ ─ ─ ─ ─ ─ ─ ─ ─ ┐
             │ EMPLOYEES(E#,Name,Address) │   │  SECRETARIES (E#,Name,Salary)  │
             └ ─ ─ ─ ─ ─ ─ ─ ─ ─ ─ ─ ─ ─ ─ ─ ─ ─ ┘   └ ─ ─ ─ ─ ─ ─ ─ ─ ─ ─ ─ ─ ─ ─ ─ ─ ─ ─ ┘


Conceptual Schema:        ┌──────────────────────────────┐
                          │  EMPLOYEES(E#,Name,Address)  │
                          │  SEC(E#,Salary)              │
                          └──────────────────────────────┘
```

(a) <u>view analysis</u>: SECRETARIES[E#] ⊆ EMPLOYEES[E#]
(b) <u>optimization</u>: Attribute Name can be dropped from Secretaries: SEC(E#,Salary)
(c) <u>mapping</u>:   SECRETARIES = (EMPLOYEES ⋈ SEC)[E#,Name,Salary]

<u>Figure 1a</u>: Steps of user view integration in logical database design

---

[2] Note: clarity is a subjective matter and different people may disagree upon whether a more complex schema which does express the semantics of the application environment is more desirable to a more simple schema which does not.

[3] Note: whereas in user view integration the integrated schema (conceptual schema) has stored instances and the component schemas (views) have virtual instances, in global view definition the integrated schema (global view) has virtual instances and the component schemas (local database schemas) have actual instances.

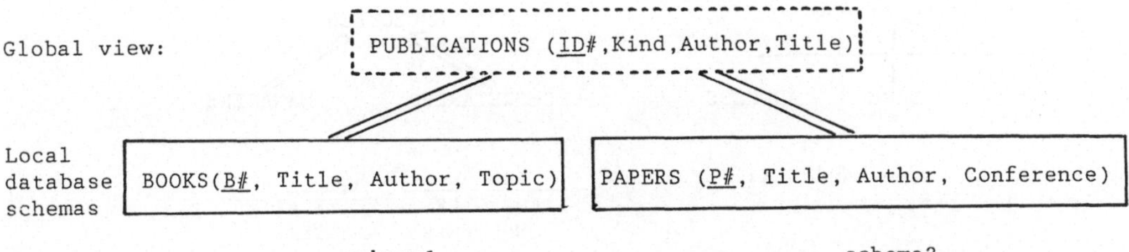

(a) <u>schema analysis</u>:   BOOKS, PAPERS are "kinds-of" publications
(b) <u>schema combination</u>: the generalization of BOOKS and PAPERS is introduced into
     the global view: PUBLICATIONS
(c) <u>mapping</u>: translate queries against PUBLICATIONS to queries against BOOKS in
     schema1 and PAPERS in schema2

<u>Figure 1b:</u> Steps of global view definition in multidatabase system integration

2. MODEL-INDEPENDENT DISCUSSION OF VIEW INTEGRATION

We will use the concepts and terminology of semantic data models to provide a model-independent discussion, comparison and evaluation of the different approaches used in view integration methodologies. In the following we will give short definitions of the terminology we will use.

<u>Model world - real world</u>: Model world objects represent real world entities. Attributes of model world objects represent properties of real world entities.

<u>Classification</u>: Objects which represent the <u>same</u> type of entity are collected to object-classes. The extension of an object-class is the set of all current instances of that object-class.

<u>Aggregation</u>: Aggregation /SMI77b/ is a form of abstraction in which a relationship between component objects forms a higher level composite object. The component objects can be perceived as attributes of the composite object. Attribute values are objects themselves.

<u>Generalization</u>: Generalization /SMI77/ is a form of abstraction in which objects are viewed as higher-level generic objects, suppressing the differences between the objects and emphasizing their common properties. Generalization establishes the "is-a relationship" between the subclass and the superclass. Attributes are inherited along the generalization hierarchy.

The modelling constructs of semantic data models will be depicted graphically by objectschemes /BRO84/ (Fig. 2). Notationally we will use relation schemes for the concept of aggregation and the UGI-catalogue relation of the RM/T-Model /COD79/ for the concept of generalization.[4]

Some of the investigated methodologies have been proposed for user view integration, some of them for global view definition, and some of them for both. In order to use a uniform terminology we will refer to the user view or the local database schema as the <u>component schema</u> and to the conceptual database schema or the global view as the <u>integrated schema</u>.

---

[4] For simplicity we will not distinguish - as it is done in the RM/T-Model - between unconditional and alternative generalization and we will normally not mention explicitly entity-relations and entity-surrogates, although we assume their presence.

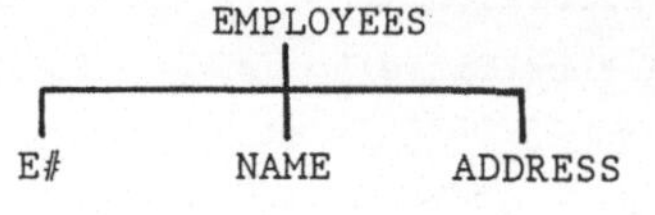
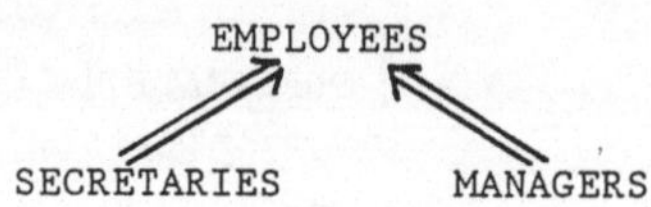

```
EMPLOYEES(E#, Name, Address)       UGI (    Sup         Sub    )
                                         EMPLOYEES   SECRETARIES
                                         EMPLOYEES   MANAGERS
```

<u>Figure 2:</u> Aggregation and Generalization

Generally all investigated view integration methodologies proceed as follows:
(a) In case a component schema is defined in another data model than that which is used for the integrated schema, the component schema must be mapped to an equivalent representation in the integrated schema's data model (use of a canonical data model).
(b) Representation problems, which occur when the same real world concept is modelled by a different modelling construct in different component schemas, are resolved.
(c) Timeinvariable connections between different component schemas, called "integration constraints", are used to remove redundancies (redundancy removal).
(d) Implicit semantic relationships between different component schemas, called "interschema relationships" are captured explicitly in the integrated schema (schema enrichment).
<u>Note</u>: Most user view integration methods address redundancy removal only and neglect schema enrichment, on the other hand global view definition methods are mainly interested in schema enrichment. Both, however, redundancy removal and schema enrichment, can contribute to user view integration as well as global view definition.

Given this generalized approach to view integration we have analyzed the view integration methodologies with respect to
(a) the canonical data model used,
(b) their approaches to attack various representation problems,
(c) the concepts used for redundancy removal
(d) the concepts used for schema enrichment.

2.1 Data Model

The Entity Relationship Model (ER-Model,/CHE76/), the Entity-Category-Relationship Model[5] (ECR-Model, /ELM85/), the Functional Data Model /SHI79/ and the Relational Model have been used as canonical models. For a comparative evaluation of the semantic data models the reader is referred to /URB86,SCH84/. In this paper we will draw the reader's attention only to the requirement that the canonical model should be closed with respect to aggregation and generalization, i.e. the canonical data model should support arbitrary many levels of aggregation and generalization. Methodologies using a canonical data model which is not closed with respect to aggregation - like the ER-Model[6] or the ECR-Model - will classify mergeable object-classes in different component schemas as "non-mergeable" (see below). Methodologies using a canonical data model which does not support generalization do not make any provisions for schema enrichment, because the process of schema enrichment relies heavily on the capability to define generic object-classes.

---

[5] The ECR-Model is basically an ER-Model extended with generalization

[6] The entity-relationship model has two levels of aggregation: (1) attributes are aggregated to entities, (2) entities are aggregated to relationships.

Under the heading "Data Model" (see: Table 1) we have also arranged the criteria, whether the investigated methodology has been presented rather informally or rather formally, whether the methodology has been proposed for user view integration or global view definition, whether the necessary schema mappings from the integrated schema to the component schema have been taken care of, and in particular, whether query modification - i.e. the task of mapping queries against the integrated schema to a set of subqueries to component schemas - has been addressed.

2.2 Representation Problems

Representation problems can be classified as naming differences, scaling differences and structural differences.

<u>Naming Differences</u> occur when the same term is used in different component schemas for different real world concepts (homonyms) or different terms are used in different component schemas for the same real world concept (synonyms). The approaches to overcome naming differences are either (a) to rename a homonym/synonym in the component schemas, (b) to give new names in the integrated schema and specify appropriate mappings to the corresponding names in the component schemas, or (c) to assume that names in different component schemas are only equal if this has been explicitly specified.

<u>Scaling differences</u> occur when different scales (e.g. miles, km) are used for the same measure. The approaches to handle different scales are (a) to use one global scale in the integrated schema and provide appropriate conversion functions from scales in the integrated schema to scales in the component schemas, (b) to have conversion functions between all different scales of the component schemas.

<u>Structural Differences</u> occur when the same real world concept is represented by different modelling constructs of the data model. Structural Differences may be classified as differences in aggregation, differences in generalization and differences in abstraction.

As an example for <u>differences in aggregation</u> consider the fact: "students enroll in courses" which may be modelled by either (a) a multivalued attribute Enrolled-Courses of the object-class STUDENT (Fig. 3a), or (b) a multivalued attribute Enrolled-Students of the object-class COURSE (Fig. 3b), or (c) by an object-class ENROLLMENT with the attributes Enrolled-Course and Enrolled-Student (Fig. 3c).

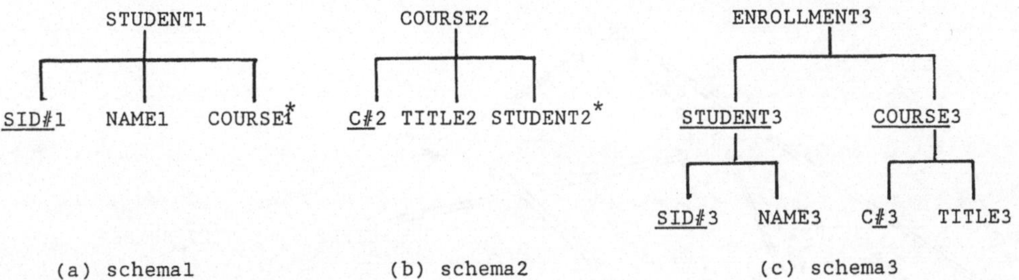

Note: "*" denotes a multivalued attribute,
      keys are underlined,
      names are postfixed with the component schema number

<u>Figure 3:</u> Representation Problems: differences in aggregation

The approaches to overcome differences in aggregation are (a) to transform the component schemas to a common representation (e.g.: transform schema1 and schema3 of Fig. 3 to schema1' and schema3' in Fig. 4), or (b) to provide compatible views of the component schemas (e.g.: define schema1' and schema3' in Fig. 4 as views on schema1 and schema3 in Fig. 3), or (c) to assume a common representation per se. Methodologies using the Relational Model /CAS83,BIS86/ as canonical model are restricted to a special class of component schemas in Boyce-Codd-Normal-Form (BCNF). Then each component schema corresponds to a set of object-classes identified by their keys. It has not been formally proved, but only implicitly assumed, that this requirement avoids the problem of differences in aggregation.

Figure 4: Approaches to overcome differences in aggregation

Differences in generalization occur when two component schemas differ in their generalization hierarchies. For example one schema may contain the object-class SHIPS1, another one may contain the object-classes US_SHIPS2 and SOVIET_SHIPS2 (Fig. 5). To overcome differences in generalization appropriate subclasses - in our example US_SHIPS1, SOVIET_SHIPS1 and OTHER_SHIPS1 - and appropriate superclasses - in our example SHIPS, US_SHIPS and SOVIET_SHIPS - must be defined in order to align the generalization hierarchies of the different component schemas (Fig. 6).

```
        SHIPS1                US_SHIPS2    SOVIET_SHIPS2

  (a) schema1                 (b) schema2
```

Figure 5: Representation Problems: differences in generalization

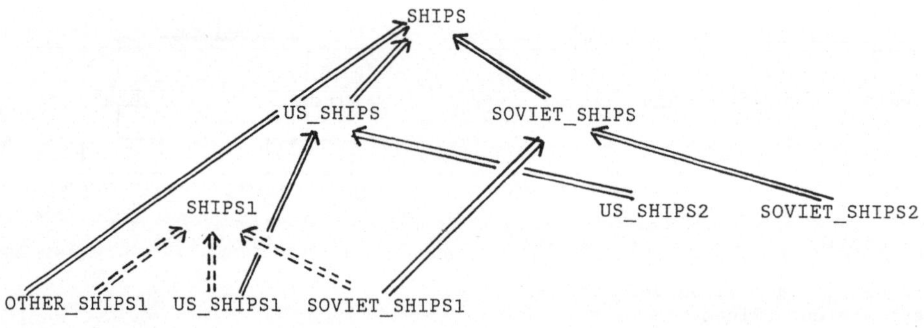

Figure 6: Approaches to overcome differences in generalization

<u>Differences in Abstraction</u> are due to the duality of specialization and decomposition /JAN85/. By stepwise decomposition of complex objects the aggregation hierarchy is generated, by stepwise specialization the generalization hierarchy is developed. In a sense specialization and decomposition are complementary: (a) specialization has the purpose to classify, whereas (b) decomposition has the purpose to assert properties. For example on one hand you can classify a person as student, on the other hand or you can assert that a person's profession is studying. Then one component schema will contain the object-classes PERSON and STUDENT, and the other one the object-class PERSON with the attribute Profession (Fig. 7). In this case students are those PERSONs where the value of the attribute Profession is "student".

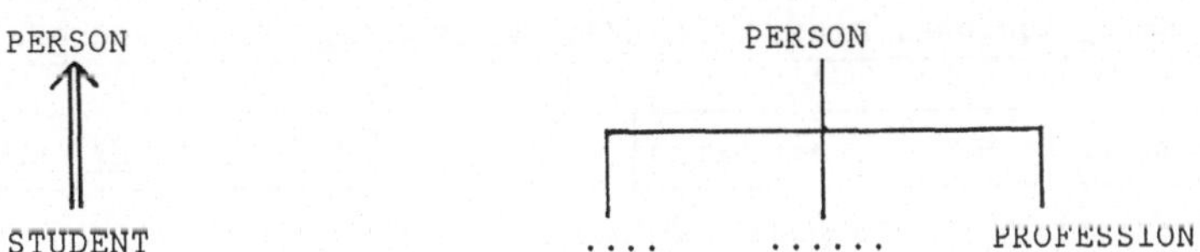

(a) persons classified as students   (b) asserted property "profession is studying"

<u>Figure 7</u>: Representation Problems: differences in abstraction

2.3 Integration constraints

<u>Integration constraints</u> describe time-invariable connections between different component schemas. In this analysis we have considered the following integration constraints: The <u>object-class identity constraint</u> states that the extensions of two object-classes are the same for all points of times (e.g. EMPLOYEES[E#] = SALARIES[E#], Fig. 8). The <u>attribute identity constraint</u> states that an attribute A1 of an object-class O1 is semantically equal to an attribute A2 of another object-class O2 (e.g. EMPLOYEES[Name] $\sim$ SALARIES[Name], Fig. 8). The values of two semantically equal attributes of two objects which represent the same real world entity must be the same. The <u>subclass constraint</u> states that the extension of an object-class B is contained in the extension of an object-class A. (e.g. MANAGERS[E#] $\subseteq$ EMPLOYEES[E#], Fig. 8). The <u>selection constraint</u> is a special form of the subclass constraint: the extension of B can be derived by a selection predicate over the attributes of A (e.g. MARKETING-EMPL:= ..., Fig.8). The <u>mutual exclusion constraint</u> states that two object-classes have mutually exclusive sets of actual instances. The <u>referential integrity constraint</u> between object-classes A and B states that for every instance of A the values of some property-attributes[7] of A or (exclusive) some identifying-attributes[8] of A are contained in the values of the identifying attributes of some instance of B (Fig. 12).

2.4 Redundancy removal

Integration constraints describe situations in which information is recorded redundantly[9] in different component schemas and can therefore be used to remove redundancies. <u>Redundant object-class removal</u> can be applied when (a) an object-class identity constraint or (b) a selection constraint holds. In case (a) the concerned object-classes are merged to one: the new object-class has as attributes the common key-attributes and the union of the non-key attributes of the concerned object-classes (e.g.: EMPLOYEES and SALARIES are replaced by EMPLOYEES', Figures 8,9). In case (b) the selected object-

---

[7] A property-attribute of A is an attribute which is not part of the   primary key of A.

[8] An identifying-attribute of A is part of the primary key of A.

[9] with the exception of the Exclusion Constraint

class can be dropped (e.g. MARKETING-EMPL is dropped, Fig. 8). <u>Redundant attribute removal</u> can be applied when (a) an attribute-identity constraint holds or (b) if an attribute can be derived from a composition of other attributes. In case (a) the redundant attribute is removed from the subclass (e.g. Name is dropped from MANAGERS, Figures 8,9). Case (b) may be determined by a heuristic redundancy check, which uses necessary conditions to determine if an attribute can be derived from a composition of other attributes (Fig. 10). Such heuristics are either based on the subset, the equality or the non-empty intersection of corresponding domain and ranges of attributes. For further detail see /YAO82/.

```
EMPLOYEES(E#, Name, Address, Div)        MARKETING-EMPL (E#, Name, Address)

      MANAGERS(E#,Name, Department)            SALARIES(E#, Name, Salary)
```

Component Schemas

<u>Integration constraints</u>:
```
object identity:        EMPLOYEES[E#] = SALARIES[E#]
subclass constraint:    MANAGERS[E#] ⊆ EMPLOYEES[E#]
selection constraint:   MARKETING-EMPL:= (Div="M")EMPLOYEES[E#,Name,Address]
attribute identity :    EMPLOYEES(Name) ~ MANAGERS(Name)
```

<u>Figure 8</u>: Integration constraints describe timeinvariable connections between different component schemas

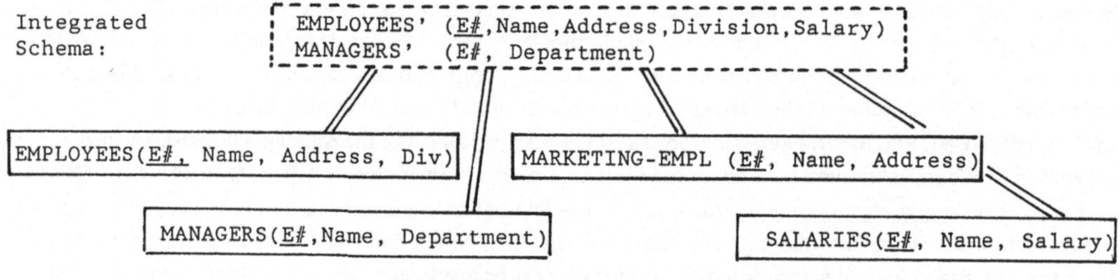

<u>Figure 9</u>: Integration constraints used for redundancy removal

```
STUDENT (SS#,Office,Prof,Courses*,Enrollments)
PROFESSOR (SS#, Office)
ENROLLMENT (E#, Student, Course, Grade)
```

Heuristic redundancy check to answer:
$$\text{STUDENT.Office} = \text{STUDENT.Prof.Office}^{10} \ ?$$
$$\text{STUDENT.Courses} = \text{STUDENT.Enrollments.Course} \ ?$$

<u>Figure 10</u>: Analysis of composition of attributes

---

[10] shorthand notation for: $\forall s \in SS\# : \pi_{Office}[\sigma_{SS\#=s}(\text{STUDENT})] = \pi_{Office}(\text{PROFESSOR} \bowtie (\pi_{Prof}\sigma_{SS\#=s}(\text{STUDENT})))$

Object-class merging is used to flatten the generalization hierarchy in the presence of a subclass constraint. Different object-classes in a generalization hierarchy are merged to one single object-class. A "separation attribute" is used to specify the original object-class membership (e.g.: object-classes EMPLOYEE and MANAGER are merged to EMPLOYEE'; "Position" is used as a "separation attribute" to distinguish among mangers and common employees, Fig. 11). Note: It is questionable whether the concept of object-class merging should be actually applied since it is contrary to the principle of schema enrichment (see below).

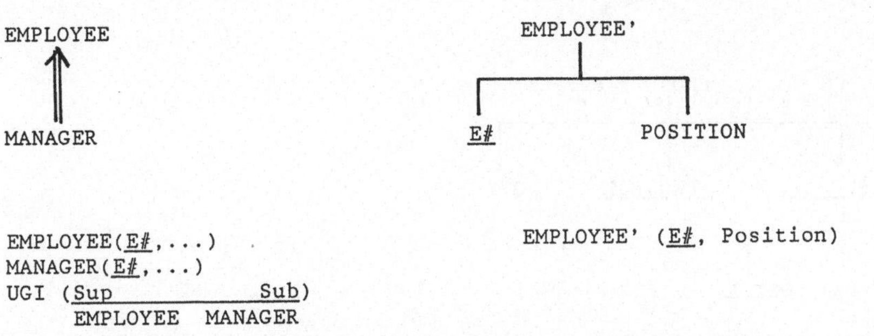

(a) generalization hierarchy   (b) flattened generalization hierarchy

<u>Figure 11</u>: Flattening of the generalization hierarchy

Referential Integrity Constraints can be expressed directly in the integrated schema if the canonical data model is closed with respect to aggregation (Fig. 12). Modelled in the ER-Model the relationships PROJECTs and PROJECT-SUPPLY are classified as non-mergeable /NAV86/, the referential integrity constraint PROJECT-SUPPLY[Part,Dealer] $\subseteq$ SUPPLY[Part,Dealer] must be stated explicitly in the integrated schema (Fig. 12a). If the canonical data model can support arbitrary many levels of aggregation PROJECT and PROJECT-SUPPLY may definitely be merged (Fig. 12b). This may be done for example by using relations with relation-valued attributes /SCH86/ - also known as NF^2-Relations - or by using property attributes with surrogate domains in the RM/T-Model. In the latter case the property attribute Supply$ of PROJECT-SUPPLY' has as domain the entity-surrogates of SUPPLY. The referential integrity constraint from above must no longer be stated explicitly, but it is enforced by a constraint inherent to the canonical data model - in this case by the property integrity rule of the RM/T-Model.

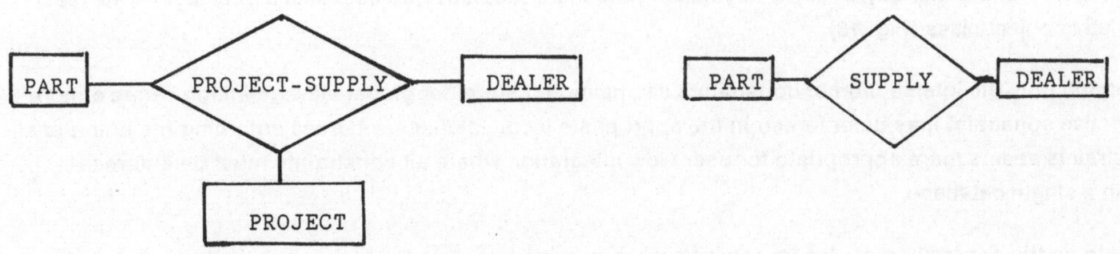

Referential integrity constraint:
    PROJECT-SUPPLY[Part,Dealer] $\subseteq$ SUPPLY[Part,Dealer]

<u>Figure 12a</u>: Non-mergeable relationships PROJECT-SUPPLY and SUPPLY in the ER-Model:

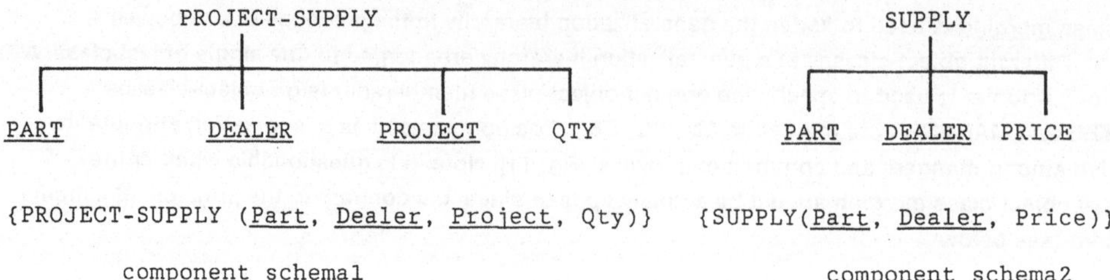

{PROJECT-SUPPLY (<u>Part</u>, <u>Dealer</u>, <u>Project</u>, Qty)}   {SUPPLY(<u>Part</u>, <u>Dealer</u>, Price)}

     component schema1   component schema2

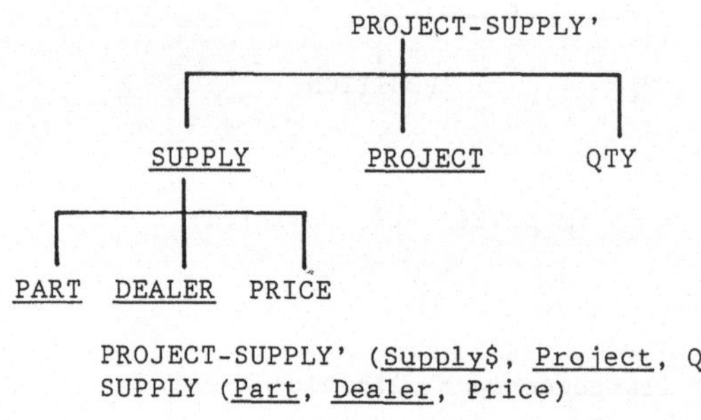

PROJECT-SUPPLY' (<u>Supply</u>$, <u>Project</u>, Qty)
SUPPLY (<u>Part</u>, <u>Dealer</u>, Price)

integrated schema

<u>Figure 12b</u>: Referential integrity constraints may be expressed directly
within the integrated schema, if a semantic data model which supports
arbitrary levels of aggregation is used as canonical data model

<u>Integrity constraints</u>: The integrity constraints considered by the analyzed view integration methodologies are essentially cardinality constraints and functional dependencies. Conflicts occur when different integrity constraints have been associated with concepts identified as being equal. We are mainly interested in the way how conflicting integrity constraints are handled:

(a) by choosing the more comprehensive (less stringent) representation, which basically means that in the integrated schema the intersection of the integrity constraints of the component schemas are enforced,

(b) by choosing a common representation which supports all constraints, i.e. in the integrated schema the union of the integrity constraints of the component schemas are enforced, and

(c) - in the case that the constraints associated with one object-class are subsumed by the constraints associated with another object class - by making the more restrictive object class a subclass of the less restrictive object class (Fig. 13).

Enforcing only the intersection of constraints seems more natural for global view definition where a more restrictive constraint may be enforced in the appropriate local database, whereas enforcing the union of all constraints seems more appropriate for user view integration where all constraints must be enforced within a single database.

To enforce the constraints of all component schemas in the integrated schema may imply component schema object-classes with empty extensions. One approach to that case is to drop "empty" object-classes automatically /CAS83/, another one is to treat the involved component schemas as "conflicting views" /BIS86/, which requires a conflict resolution decision by the user. Note: It has been proven recently that the conflictfreeness of a set of user views is undecidable /CON86/.

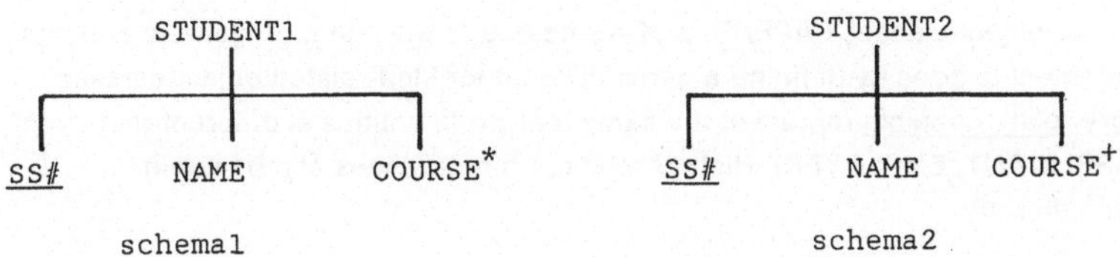

Integrated schema:

```
case  a)  chose more comprehensive representation: STUDENT1
      b)  chose more restrictive representation:   STUDENT2
      c)  make more restrictive representation subclass of
          less restrictive representation:
```

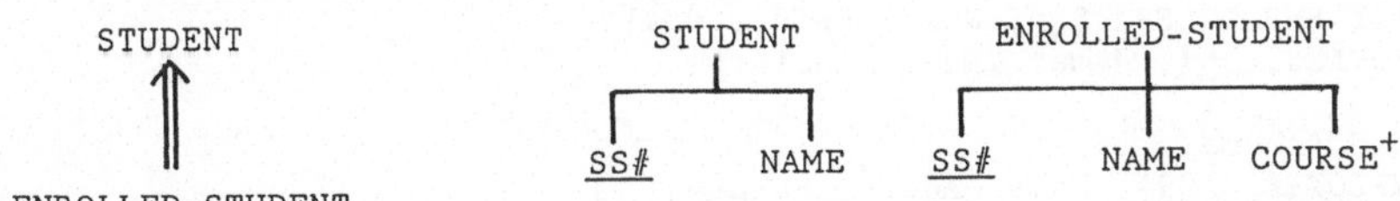


```
Note:  "+" multivalued attribute which may not be null
       inherited attributes, i.e. SS# and NAME, are shown with ENROLLED STUDENT
```

<u>Figure 13</u>: Conflicting integrity constraints

2.5 Interschema Relationships/Schema Enrichment

Schema enrichment is the process to capture implicit semantic relationships between different component schemas, i.e. interschema relationships, explicitly in the integrated schema. The interschema relationships we have analyzed can be classified as object-class relationships and attribute relationships.

<u>Object-class-relationships</u>: Object-classes of different component schemas may be role-related, kind-related or history-related. <u>Role-related objects</u> represent the same real world entity in a different situation or context (e.g.: Mr. Meier as a "carowner" and Mr. Meier as a "student"; or Mr. Smith as a "university employee" and Mr. Smith as a "IBM-employee"). The different context emerges from viewing the real world entity being in a certain relationship with one or more other entities (e.g.: STUDENTS are affiliated with a university, CAROWNERS own a car, Fig. 14a).

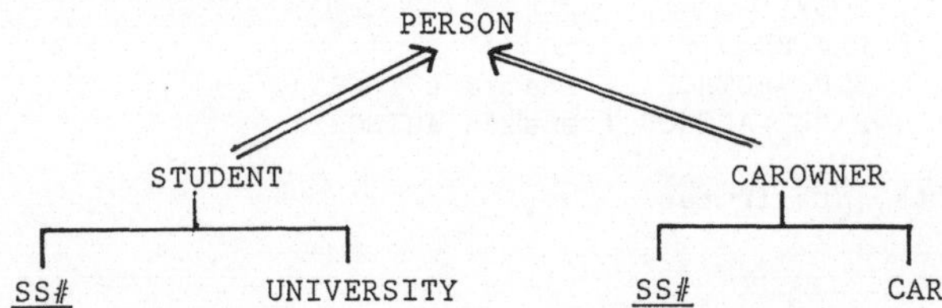


```
role-related objects: Mr. Meier as "student", Mr. Meier as "carowner"
```

<u>Figure</u> 14a: Role-related objects (objectclasses)

Schema enrichment is done by defining a superclass as a generalization of the role-related object-classes (e.g. PERSON, Fig. 14a). <u>Kind-related object-classes</u> have instances which can be perceived to belong to a common generic concept (e.g. object-classes PAPERS, BOOKS belong to the common generic concept "publications"). Schema enrichment is done by defining a generalization for kind-related object-classes (e.g. PUBLICATIONS). <u>History-related objects</u> represent the same real world entities at different real world times (e.g.: object-classes APPLICANT, EMPLOYEE). History-related object-classes can be again organized in a generalization hierarchy.

<u>Attribute relationships</u>: <u>Role-related attributes</u> represent the same type of property in a different situation or context (e.g. UAddr of UNIVERSITY-EMPLOYEES and IAddr of IBM-EMPLOYEES, see: Fig. 14; UAddr and Iaddr are not semantically equivalent (their values may be different for one real world entity, i.e. for one person) but role-related. Role-related attributes of the object-classes O1 and O2 are combined to a single attribute with the generic object-class of O1 and O2 (e.g. Addr of EMPLOYEES = union (UAddr, IAddr); or Salary of EMPLOYEES = USalary + ISalary, Fig. 14b).

```
UNIVERSITY-EMPLOYEES (SS#, Name, UAddr, USalary)
IBM-EMPLOYEES (SS#, Name, IAddr, ISalary)

Integrated Schema:
     EMPLOYEES (SS#, Name, Addr*, Salary)
          Addr = union (UAddr,IAddr)
          Salary = USalary + ISalary
      UGI (Sup                              Sub)
          EMPLOYEES    UNIVERSITY-EMPLOYEES
          EMPLOYEES    IBM-EMPLOYEES
```

<u>Figure 14b</u>: Role-related objects and role-related attributes

<u>Kind-related-attributes</u> represent real world properties which can be perceived to belong to a common generic property (e.g. Authored-Books of AUTHOR1 and Authored-Papers of AUTHOR2, Fig. 15). Kind-related attributes are integrated by first integrating the domains of the kind-related attributes (e.g. define PUBLICATIONS as generalization of BOOKS and PAPERS, Fig. 15), and then by combining the kind-related attributes to one attribute (e.g. Authored-Publications, Fig. 15).

```
Component Schemas:
    AUTHORS1 (Name,Authored-Books*)
    AUTHORS2 (Name,Authored-Papers*)

Integrated Schema:
    AUTHOR (Name, Authored-Publications*)
       UGI (Sup                   Sub)
            PUBLICATIONS    BOOKS
            PUBLICATIONS    PAPERS
            AUTHOR          BOOK-AUTHOR   (renamed AUTHOR1)
            AUTHOR          PAPER-AUTHOR  (renamed AUTHOR2)
```

<u>Figure 15</u>: Kind-related objects, attributes

3. THE ANALYZED METHODOLOGIES

The reader is referred to Tables 1 and 2 for an overview of the comparative analysis of the investigated view integration methodologies with respect to the criteria stated in the previous section. Due to space limitations we will in this section only address additional or specific features which can not be deduced from Tables 1 or 2.

3.1 Batini: Data Schema Integration, Entity Relationship Model

Batini's methodology for user view integration in the Entity-Relationship-Model consists of three phases: Conflict Analysis, Merging, Schema Enrichment & Restructuring. During Conflict Analysis representation conflicts are detected and resolved: Naming conflicts are handled by renaming in the component schemas. Structural differences are resolved by the application of schema transformation-operators (e.g.: entity to relationship, relationship to entity, attribute to relationship) to the component schemas. Conflicting integrity constraints are resolved by letting the user choose the more reliable ones. Merging is done simply by superimposing common concepts, which results in a three-colored drafted integrated schema, when two component schemas are to be integrated. During Schema Enrichment & Restructuring (a) new relationships are introduced in order to increase the clarity and expressiveness of the integrated schema, and (b) redundant relationships are removed by an analysis of "redundant cycles".

3.2 Navathe:Integrating User Views, Entity Category Relationship Model

Navathe's methodology for user view integration and global view definition is based on the Entity-Category-Relationship-Model, an Entity-Relationship-Model extended with the concept of generalization, and consists of the following phases: preintegration, object integration and relationship integration. During preintegration naming correspondences between objects (entities), attributes, relationships and roles are specified, as well as scale mappings and assertions on object-class extensions (identical, contained, overlapping, disjoint). Navathe's approach does not consider any structural differences between different component schemas: It is assumed that the same real world concept is represented with the same data model construct (entity, relationship, attribute) in every component schema.
Object integration: To integrate two object-classes A and B an object-class C is created, such that the set of attributes of C is the intersection of the sets of attributes of A and B, and the extension of C is the union of the extensions of A and B. A and B are made "subcategory object-types" of C, if they are not redundant. Redundant attributes of A and B are dropped.
Relationship integration (relationship merging): To integrate two relationships A-R-B and C-S-D, first A and C are integrated to E, B and D are integrated to F. Then R and S are integrated to E-T-F; R and S are made subrelationships of T, if they are not redundant. Relationships of different degrees are mergeable, if the lower degree relationship is derivable from the higer degree relationship. Note: It has been already outlined above, that because the ECR-Model does not support arbitrary many levels of aggregation in fact some "mergeable" relationships are classified as "non-mergeable".

3.3 Dayal: Multibase, Functional Data Model

Dayal uses the Functional Data Model to define a language for defining the integrated schema of a multidatabase system as a view of the component schemas. Dayal presents a query modification algorithm for modifying a query posed against the global view to a collection of subqueries to the component schemas. Representation conflicts are solved by views to component schemas[11]. In case of conflicting integrity constraints the more comprehensive ones are chosen, i.e. only the intersection of all constraints is enforced in the integrated schema. Object integration is done by defining supertypes as generalization of corresponding local entity types. Attribute integration is done by defining "superfunctions" as generalizations of corresponding functions of local entity types.

---

[11] In Dayal's methodology a view to a component schema consists of "virtual entities", which can be considered as object-classes whose extensions are derived from component schema object classes.

3.4 Yao: View Integration, Functional Data Model

Yao provides operations to transform the Functional Model during the view integration process. The transformations apply also to the operations specified by a Transaction Specification Language (TASL). Redundancy removal is done by (a) merging object-classes (nodes) with same extensions and (b) by flattening the generalization hierarchy (see above). Redundant attributes (functions) are detected by a heuristic redundancy test. No provisions are made for any kind of schema enrichments.

3.5 Casanova: Sound View Integration, Relational Data Model

Casanova assumes that the relations in the component schemas are in Boyce-Codd-Normal-Form (BCNF) and the only integrity constraints are those given by the keys or by inclusion/exclusion dependencies over keys. Such a "restricted schema" corresponds to a set of object-classes identified by their keys.

Integration constraints are defined during the "view combination step": The object-class-identity constraint and the subclass constraint are specified by inclusion dependencies on keys, e.g.: $R_i[K_i] \subseteq R_j[K_j]$. Attribute identity constraints are specified by so-called union functional dependencies, which are statements of the form $\{R_i:K_i -- > A1, R_j:K_j -- > A2\}$ or $R_i(A1) \sim R_j(A2)$, indicating that attributes A1 and A2 of the relations R_i and R_j with keys K_i and K_j are semantically equivalent. Mutual exclusion constraints are specified by exclusion dependencies on keys, e.g.: $R_i | R_j$.

Redundancy removal is done during the "optimization step": If $R_i \subseteq R_j$ and $R_i(A1) \sim R_j(A2)$ hold, then the redundant attribute A1 is dropped from R_j. If $R_i \subseteq R_j$ and $R_i \supseteq R_j$ hold, then the equivalent object-classes R_i and R_j can be merged. This is done by creating $R(\underline{K}XY)$, where X denotes the non key-attributes of R_i and Y those non key-attributes of R_j which are not synonymus to any attribute of R_i (R_i and R_j are dropped). If the semantically equivalent sets of attributes X and Y belong to object-classes (relations) R_i and R_j which are not related by any integration constraint, a generalization object-class (relation) with the common non-key-attributes of R_i and R_j is created, i.e. if $R_i(X) \sim R_j(Y)$ holds and the schemas of R_i and R_j are $R_i(\underline{K}XX')$ and $R_j(\underline{K}YY')$ then $R(\underline{K}X)$ is created and R_i and R_j are changed to $R_i'(\underline{K}X')$, $R_j'(\underline{K}Y')$.

If the specified constraints (key dependencies, inclusion dependencies and exclusion dependencies) can only be satisfied if a relation R has an empty extension then the R is dropped.

3.6 Biskup: Formal View Integration, Relational Data Model

Contrary to previous approaches Biskup draws a clear distinction between integrity constraints, which state time-invariable properties for meaningful databases over one integrated schema, and integration constraints, which state time-invariable connections between different component schemas. The component schemas are assumed to be "proper database schemas". This notion is an extension to the notion of a "restricted schema" as defined by Casanova: In addition to inclusion dependencies over keys key-based inclusion dependencies are allowed, i.e. if $R_i[Y] \subseteq R_j[Z]$, then either (a) $Z = K_j$ and $Y = K_j$ (subclass,generalization) or (b) $Z = K_j$, $Y \subseteq K_j$ or $Y \subseteq R_j \setminus K_j$ (referential integrity).

The following Integration Constraints are supported: The identity constraint, $R_i[\underline{K}X']$ ID $R_j[\underline{K}Y']$, is used to state object-class identity between R_i and R_j as well as attribute identity between the sets of attributes X' and Y'. The selection constraint, $R_i(Y)$ SEL (b R_j)[Z] - where b is a selection predicate over Rj -, is a special form of the subclass constraint. The containment constraint is either of the form (a) $R_i[X]$ CON $R_j[Y]$ and is used analog to the key-based inclusion dependency to assert a subclass constraint or referential integrity, or of the form (b) $R_i[\underline{K}X']$ CON $R_j[\underline{K}Y']$, when it is used to assert a subclass constraint between R_i and R_j as well as attribute identity between the sets of attributes X' and Y'. Biskup supports also the exclusion constraint.

View Integration is done by "equivalence preserving local schema transformations": integration constraints are replaced accordingly by integrity constraints and redundancies are removed: Object-class removal is done (a) in the presence of an identity constraint {if $R_i[\underline{K_i}X']$ ID $R_j[\underline{K_j}Y']$ holds for $R_i(\underline{K_i}XX')$ and $R_j(\underline{K_j}YY')$ then create $R(\underline{K_i}XX'Y)$ and drop R_i,R_j} or in the presence of a selection constraint {if $R_i(Y)$ SEL (b $R_j)[Z]$ holds then drop R_i}. Attribute removal is done in the presence of a containment constraint { if $R_i[\underline{K_i}X']$ CON $R_j[\underline{K_j}Y']$ holds then drop X' from R_i}. Note: in case of "disturbing" constraints, i.e. constraints which can not be changed accordingly when the schema is transformed, intended transformations may not be performable (see /BIS86/ for further detail). No provisions for schema enrichment are made. Conflicting integrity constraints: In the integrated schema the union of the integrity constraints of the component schemas is enforced. A set of views are in conflict if the unified integrity constraints would imply an empty relation in one of the views.

4. CONCLUSION

In this paper we have presented a comparative analysis of current view integration methodologies. The main tasks of the view integration process are
(a) to choose an appropriate canonical data model for the integrated schema, {We have argued that the canonical data model used in a view integration methodology should support arbitrary levels of aggregation and generalization.}
(b) to handle various representation problems,
(c) to define integration constraints which can be used to remove redundancies, and
(d) to capture implicit interschema relationships explicitly in the integrated schema.

Most of the investigated methodologies put heavy emphasis on principles for redundancy removal and schema enrichment once the integration constraints or interschema relationships have been defined. It is still an open research problem how integration constraints or interschema relationships can be recognized and detected efficiently. This problem becomes even harder in the presence of representation conflicts.

Furthermore, we think that the concept of integration constraints - as defined in section 2 - needs some reconsideration especially in a multidatabase system environment. For example, the objectclass-identity constraint is based on equality of the current extension of two objectclasses (for all point of times). In a multidatabase system, however, two intentionally equivalent objectclasses may yet have different current extensions (for example because of different organizational policies)

Another issue not yet considered in detail is what effects component schema changes - which may result from changes in the requirements and needs of a user group - have on the integrated schema and on the schema mappings. Has the view integration process to be started all over again or can partial solutions be backtracked?

It is evident that the view integration process can be never fully automated - one of the reasons therefore is the undecidability of the conflictfreeness of a set of views /CON86/, but knowledge-based view integration systems, dependent on good heuristics and on a constructive dialogue with the user, may still behave well on a number of practical view integration problems. We are currently investigating the fundamentals of such a system.

Table <u>1</u>: Comparative Analysis of View Integration Methodologies:

	BATINI	NAVATHE	DAYAL	YAO	CASANOVA	BISKUP
DATA MODEL	E-R-Model	E-C-R-Model	Funct.Model	Funct.Model	Relational	Relational
formal/informal	inf.	inf.	inf./form.	inf./form.	formal	formal
user view int.	+	+		+	+	+
global view def.		+	+			
mappings			+	+	+	+
query modific.			+	+		
REPR. PROBLEMS						
Naming	renaming in component schemas	renaming in component schemas	virtual entities	--	union funct. dep.	containment constraint
Scaling	--	conv. func. conv. tables	superfunct. (global scale)	--	--	--
Struct. Diff.: Aggregation	transformat. of component schemas	--	virtual entities	--	BCNF	BCNF
Specialization/ Decomposition	--	--	--	only decomposit.	--	--
Conflicting Integr. constr.	choose more reliable	make more constraint object-class subclass of less constraint one	choose more comprehensive	--	drop "empty" relation	conflictfree-ness of a set of views is undecidable

"+" ... the investigated methodology "addresses", "is applicable for" ...

Table 2: Comparative Analysis of View Integration Methodologies:

	BATINI	NAVATHE	DAYAL	YAO	CASANOVA	BISKUP
INTEGRATION CONSTRAINTS						
object-class-id	implicit[1]	+	implicit	implicit	incl. dep.	ID-constraint
attribute id.	implicit	+	implicit	implicit	union FD	CON-constraint
subclass const.		+	implicit	implicit	incl. dep.	CON-constraint SEL-constraint
referent. int.	indirect[2]	indirect	indirect	--	--	+
REDUNDANCY REMOVAL						
redundant objects	merge to 1 entity	merge to 1 entity	supertype	flatten gen.hier.	merge to 1 relation	merge to 1 relation
redundant attributes	+	+	+	heuristics for compositions	+	+
SCHEMA ENRICHMENT						
object-class relationships (role-,kind-rel.)	introduce new rel.sh.	category object-types	supertypes	--	--	--
attribute relationships (role-,kind-rel.)	schema restruct.	relationship merging	super- functions	--	--	--

1) not stated explicitly in the methodology, but implicitly used
2) not explicitly listed, but expressed (as far as possible) within the data model (see:text)

References

/BAT84/ Batini, C. and M. Lenzerini: "A Methodology for Data Schema Integration in the Entity-Relationship Model." In IEEE Transactions on Software Engineering, Vol.10, No. 6, 1984, pp. 650-664.

/BIS86/ Biskup J. and B. Convent: "A formal view integration method." ACM SIGMOD International Conference on Management of Data, 1986.

/BRO84/ Brodie, M. and D. Ridjanovic: "On the Design and Specification of Database Transactions." In: Brodie M., J. Mylopoulos, J. Schmidt (eds.): On Conceptual Modelling. Perspectives from Atrificial Intelligence, Databases, and Programming Languages Semantic Data Model Driven Design, Verification, Specification of Interactive Database Transactions. Springer-Verlag, Berlin, 1984., pp.277-307.

/CAS83/ Casanova, M. and V. Vidal: "Towards a sound view integration methodology", ACM-Sigact-Sigmod Symposium on Principles of Database Systems, 1983, pp. 36-47.

/CHE76/ Chen, P.P-S.: "The Entity-Relationship Model - Toward a unified view of data", ACM Transactions on Database Systems Vo. 1, No. 1, 1976, pp. 9-36.

/COD79/ Codd, E.F.: "Extending the Database Relational Model to Capture more Meaning." ACM Transactions on Database Systems, Vol.4, No. 4, 1979, pp. 377-387.

/CON86/ Convent, B.: "Unsolvable Problems Related to the View Integration Approach.", International Conference of Database Theory, Roma, Italy, 1986.

/DAY84/ Dayal U. and H. Wang: "View Definition and Generalization for Database Integration in a Multidatabase System." In IEEE Transactions on Software Engineering, Vol. SE- 10, No. 6, 1984, pp. 628-644.

/ELM85/ Elmasri, R. and J. Weeldreyer, A. Hevner: "The category concept: An extension to the entity-relationship model". In Data & Knowledge Engineering 1, North Holland, 1985, pp. 75-116.

/JAN85/ Jansen, C. G.: "A framework for representation." in: Bubenko J. and O. Olive (eds.): Information Systems. Theoretical and Formal Aspects. North-Holland, Amsterdam 1985, pp.127-144

/NAV86/ Navathe, S. and R. Elmasri, J. Larson: "Integrating User Views in Database Design. IEEE-Computer, Jan. 1986

/SHI81/ Shipman, D. W.: "The Functional Data Model and the Data Language DAPLEX. ACM Transactions on Database Systems, Vol. 6, No. 1, 1981, pp. 140-173.

/SMI77/ Smith, J.M. and D.C.P. Smith: "Database Abstraction: Aggregation and Generalization." ACM Transactions on Database Systems, Vol. 2, No. 2, 1977, pp. 105-133.

/SMI77b/ Smith, J.M. and D.C.P. Smith: Database Abstraction: Aggregation. Communications of the ACM, Vol. 20, No. 6 1977, pp. 405-433.

/SCH84/ Schrefl, M. and A.M.Tjoa, R.R. Wagner: "Comparison criteria for semantic data models." Proc. IEEE 1st International Conference on Data Engineering, Los Angeles, 1984, pp. 105-133.

/SCH86/ Schek, H. and M. H. Scholl: "The Relational Model with Relation-Valued Attributes." Information Systems Vol. 11, No.2,1986, pp.137-147.

/URB86/ Urban S. and L. Delcambre: "An analysis of the structural, dynamic and temporal aspects of semantic data models." Proc. IEEE 2nd International Confernece on Data Engineering, Los Angeles, 1986, pp.382-389.

/YAO82/ Yao S.B. and V.E. Waddle, B.C. Housel: "View Modeling and Integration Using the Functional Data Model." IEEE Transactions on Software Engineering, Vol.8 ,No.6, 1982, pp.544-553.

Der Einsatz der Modellierungssprache OBLOG zum Entwurf von Juristischen Expertensystemen im Wege des Prototyping am Beispiel eines Modells des Verfahrens der Eidesstattlichen Versicherung

Thomas F. Gordon

Forschungsstelle für Informationsrecht
Gesellschaft für Mathematik und Datenverarbeitung (GMD)
Postfach 1240, Schloß Birlinghoven
D-5205 Sankt Augustin 1

Gerald Quirchmayr

Institut für Informatik
Johannes Kepler Universität Linz
Altenbergerstraße 69
A-4040 Linz

Abstract Die hier zum Entwurf von Prototypen Juristischer Expertensysteme verwendete Modellierungssprache OBLOG ist ein mit KRYPTON oder KL-TWO vergleichbares hybrides Wissensrepräsentationssystem [BRACHMAN], [VILAIN]. Es vereint einen terminologischen Reasoner mit einem Horn-Klausel-Theorem-Beweiser. Ziel der terminologischen Komponente ist es, die Konstruktion von *type*- und *attribute*-Taxonomien zu unterstützen. Zur Darstellung fallspezifischer Informationen werden *entities* verwendet, die einem bestimmten *type* zugeordnet sind und verschiedene *attributes* haben. Prozeduren zur Bestimmung von *attribute*-Werten sind *type*-indizierte Horn-Klausel-*rules*. Die Menge der für eine *entity* anwendbaren *rules* wird von den bekannten *types* dieser *entity* bestimmt. Diese Menge verändert sich mit wachsender Verfeinerung des Wissens über eine Klasse von Objekten, womit eine Form des nicht-monotonen Reasoning unterstützt wird. Diese Struktur erlaubt die Aufteilung des Wissens über eine Klasse von Objekten in allgemeine Regeln und Ausnahmen, wobei allgemeine Regeln dazu dienen können, Heuristiken zum effizienten Auffinden wahrscheinlich richtiger Lösungen zu codieren. Nachstehender Beitrag soll mit Hilfe eines Beispiels zum Verfahren der eidesstattlichen Versicherung einen Überblick über den Einsatz von OBLOG im Bereich des Entwurfes Juristischer Expertensysteme im Wege des Prototyping geben.

1. Einleitung

Zum Entwurf des hier beschriebenen Prototyps eines Expertensystems zur Unterstützung im Bereich des Zivilprozeßrechtes wurde die Modellierungssprache OBLOG verwendet. Dieses an der Forschungsstelle für Informationsrecht der Gesellschaft für Mathematik und Datenverarbeitung entwickelte System ist eine Kombination aus Wissensrepräsentationssprache und nicht-monotonem Reasoning. Als Zielvorstellung bei der Entwicklung des Unterstützungssystems für den Bereich des Verfahrens der eidesstattlichen Versicherung diente ein analog den heutigen CAD-Systemen gestalteter Arbeitsplatz für Juristen, also eine Art Workstation für juristische Applikationen [FIEDLER].

Speziell die Problematik der Unterstützung des Juristen bei der Subsumtion beschäftigt seit längerer Zeit die Forschung auf dem Gebiet der Rechtsinformatik, da die Betrachtung dieses Vorganges als reine Deduktion einige bisher noch ungelöste Probleme mit sich gebracht hat. Eines dieser Probleme betrifft die Frage der Repräsentation juristischen Wissens in einer formalen Sprache, wobei derzeit weder geklärt ist, wie eine solche Repräsentationssprache aussehen müßte, noch ob es überhaupt möglich ist, eine solche zu konstruieren. Es müssen zum Beispiel erst Mittel und Wege gefunden werden, offene Konzepte rechtlicher Begriffe [HART], [McCARTY, SRIDHARAN], wie sie in Gesetzen sehr häufig vorkommen, zu modellieren. Ein zusätzliches Problem ergibt sich dabei daraus, daß die Bedeutung rechtlicher Begriffe oft erst im Zuge ihrer Anwendung eindeutig festgelegt werden kann. Kombinatorische Methoden wie das Durchprobieren aller möglichen Lösungen sind dabei wohl keine zufriedenstellende Hilfe, auf der anderen Seite können aber auch rein heuristische Verfahren das Problem nicht lösen, da sie nur zur Darstellung eines äußerst geringen Ausschnittes des möglichen Spektrums von Lösungen geeignet sind. Ziel der neueren Forschung auf diesem Gebiet ist es daher, einen in der Praxis anwendbaren Kompromiß zwischen beiden Extremen zu suchen, da einerseits eine möglichst hohe Effizienz des Problemlösungsalgorithmus und andererseits eine möglichst genaue Lösung erzielt werden sollen, um ein Höchstmaß an Gerechtigkeit der Entscheidung zu erreichen [PHILIPPS].

2. Das Verfahren der eidesstattlichen Versicherung und seine Struktur

Das Verfahren der eidesstattlichen Versicherung ist in den §§ 900 ff ZPO geregelt. Es beginnt mit dem Antrag des Gläubigers auf Bestimmung eines Termins und zur Ladung des Schuldners zur Abnahme der eidesstattlichen Versicherung. Dieser Antrag ist mündlich oder schriftlich einzubringen, die Einbringung kann auch durch einen Bevollmächtigten erfolgen. Sind dem Antrag alle nötigen Unterlagen beigelegt (vollstreckbarer Titel, ...), kann die Ladung des Schuldners mittels Zustellung an diesen erfolgen. Der Schuldner kann nun einige Einwendungen erheben (so etwa, daß er zur Abgabe der eidesstattlichen Versicherung nicht verpflichtet sei), oder glaubhaft machen, daß er binnen einer Frist von drei Monaten die Forderungen des Gläubigers tilgen werde, etc. Vom Rechtspfleger ist also eine Vielzahl von Prüfungen vorzunehmen. Grundsätzlich ist das Verfahren in folgende Abschnitte aufgliederbar: die Stellung des Antrages durch den Gläubiger, die Überprüfung der Zuständigkeit des Gerichtes und der Zulässigkeit des Verfahrens, die Überprüfung des eventuellen Vorliegens eines Voreintrages ins Schuldnerverzeichnis, der Terminsanberaumung und der Durchführung des Termins. Die Überprüfung der Zuständigkeit des Gerichtes und der Zulässigkeit des Verfahrens stellen dabei noch relativ einfache Probleme dar, wesentlich komplizierter sind die Anberaumung des Termins, da hier mögliche Vertagungsanträge zu behandeln sind und die Durchführung des Termins, in der die Einwendungen des Schuldners zu prüfen sind. Diese Einwendungen, die ein zentrales Problem darstellen, können verschiedenste Formen annehmen: sie können sich als Einwendungen im klassischen Sinn gegen die Zwangsvollstreckung selbst, gegen das Offenbarungsverfahren, gegen den Zeitpunkt des Verfahrens, oder gegen die Vollstreckungsklausel richten. Weitere Problembereiche betreffen die Unfähigkeit zur Abgabe der eidesstattlichen Versicherung und die Verpflichtung zur Wahrung von Berufsgeheimnissen. Eine etwas andere Art von Einwendungen sind Vertagungsanträge, die sich etwa auf die Zahlungsbereitschaft des Schuldners stützen können. Im Termin selbst kann der Schuldner schließlich noch begründete Widersprüche einbringen. Diese Struktur des Verfahrens, die die Gestalt

```
--->        Argument


            Gegenargument           <---


--->        Gegenargument gegen
            das Gegenargument


            .....................   <---
--->        .....................
            .....................   <---
```

hat, prädestiniert geradezu eine auf einem Regel-Ausnahmesystem [GORDON] basierende Modellierung. (Das klassische Beispiel aus dem Bereich der AI dazu lautet: Landtiere fliegen nicht - aber Vögel sind Landtiere, die fliegen - ja, aber ein Strauß ist ein Vogel, der nicht fliegen kann.) Diejenige Seite, die das speziellste Argument findet, wird also in einem solchen Modell den Prozeß gewinnen. Das entspricht auch der juristischen Praxis, da ein Jurist nur in seltenen Fällen versuchen wird, das Gegenteil der Behauptung seines Gegners zu beweisen, er wird vielmehr versuchen, in dieser Lücken zu finden. Außerdem ist es leichter, das Vorliegen von bestimmten Ausnahmen zu beweisen, als das Nichtvorliegen bestimmter Dinge zu zeigen. Dieser Weg der Verfahrensabwicklung unterstützt also neben dem Vorteil der relativ klaren Beweislastverteilung auch den Gedanken der Prozeßökonomie, da ein Argument umso schwerer zu untermauern ist, je spezieller es ist [RISSLAND]. Hat man dies jedoch einmal geschafft, liegt es am Gegner, den nötigen Aufwand zum Beweis einer Ausnahme zu investieren, was jedoch ab einem gewissen Punkt sicher nicht mehr lohnenswert ist. Gedacht ist an den Einsatz solcher Systeme im Bereich des Privatrechts, wo sich primär wirtschaftliche Interessen gegenüberstehen, in der Strafrechtspflege sollte jedoch die Suche nach der objektiven Wahrheit den Ausschlag geben, wobei dann eben die höheren Kosten für die Erbringung der schwierigeren Beweise unter dem Aspekt der maximalen Gerechtigkeit der zu treffenden Entscheidung akzeptiert werden müßten. Dies bedeutet, daß gerade Strafrechtsmodelle hohe Schachtelungstiefen erreichen, um alle Ausnahmen abdecken zu können. Speziell beim Verfahren der eidesstattlichen Versicherung ist es zusätzlich noch so, daß es eigentlich nur mit Hilfe des Regel-Ausnahme-Prinzips strukturiert dargestellt werden kann. Der Top-Down-Entwurf ist nämlich in diesem Beispiel nur bis zu einer bestimmten Ebene sinnvoll einsetzbar, da ab dieser keine klar definierten Teilmengen mehr gebildet werden können. Ab dieser Stufe kann aber, basierend auf den Ergebnissen der Top-Down-Analyse, mit Hilfe der Regel-Ausnahme-Struktur ein korrektes formales Modell der Verfahrensstruktur entwickelt werden. Zu beachten ist unbedingt, daß dieses Modell primär dazu dienen soll, den Juristen zu beraten van MELLE]. Das Hauptaugenmerk wird deshalb auf die die Modellierung des bereits vorhandene Wissens und dessen Struzktur (rectliche Vorschriften, fallspezifische Informationen) gelegt, von dem ausgehend dann weiteres Wissen mit Hilfe einer Inferenzmaschine hergeleitet werden kann.

3. Ein Modell des Prozeßablaufes

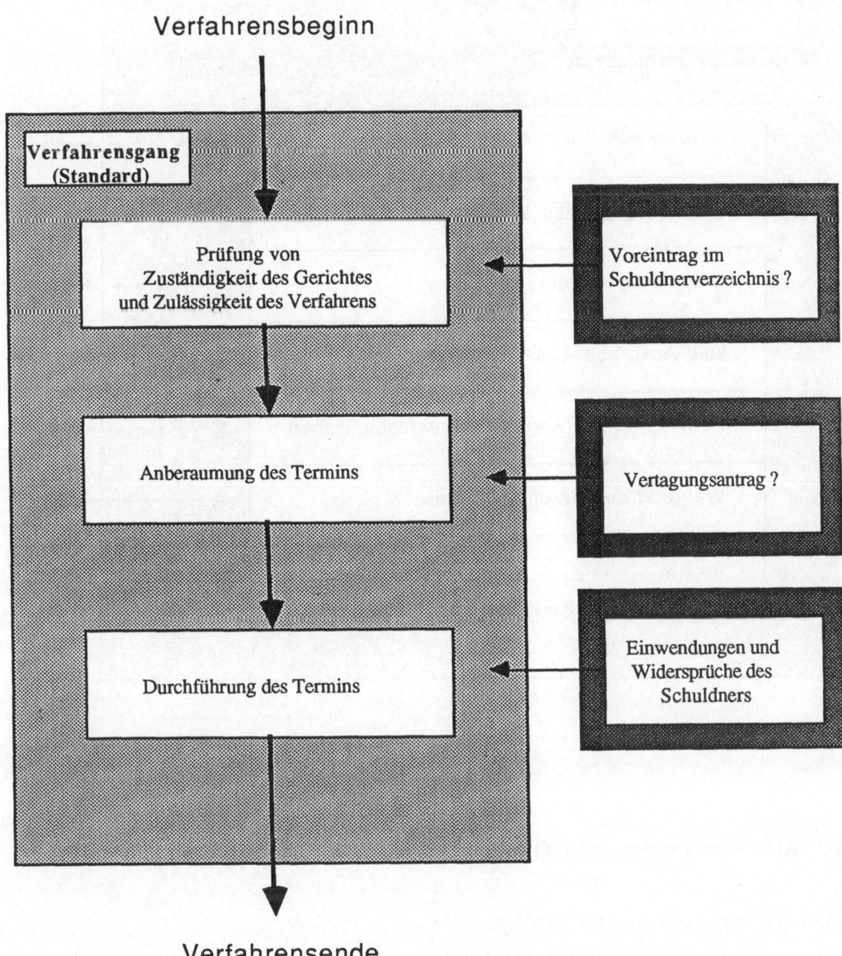

Obiges Modell zeigt in Form eines Blockdiagrammes den Standardfall des Verfahrensablaufes zusammen mit einigen Problemen, die, wenn sie auftreten, den normalen Verfahrensgang erheblich beeinflussen. Diese Einflußgrößen können aber ihrerseits wieder nur in Abhängigkeit von anderen Faktoren betrachtet werden, die ihre Wirksamkeit beeinflussen,was nachfolgende Skizze am Beispiel der möglichen Einwendungen und Widersprüche des Schuldners zeigt:

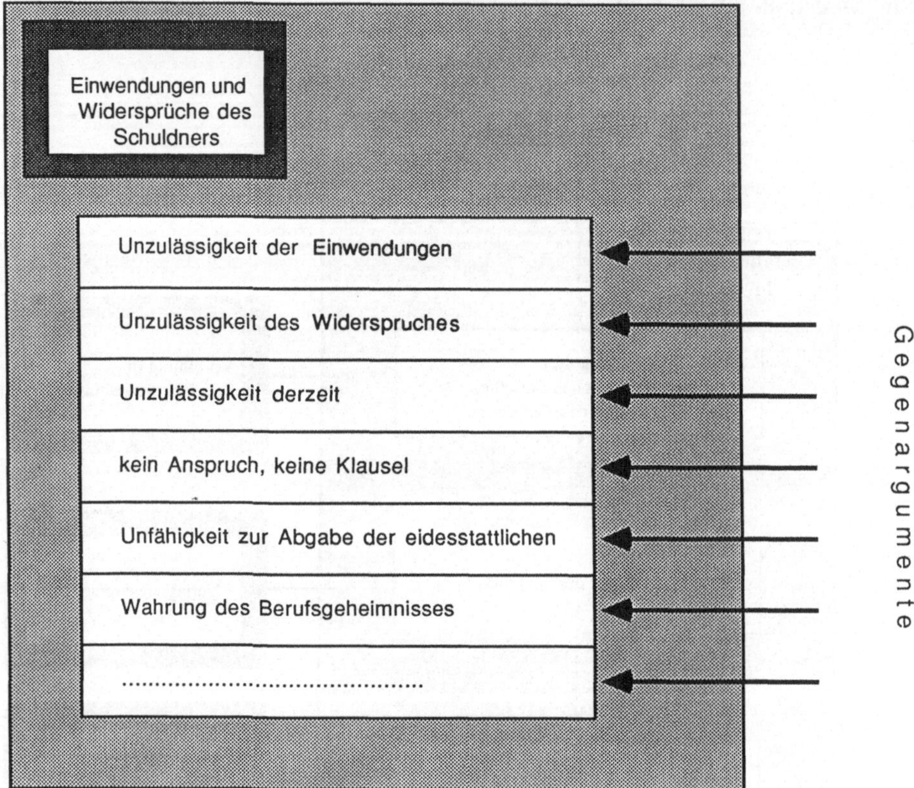

4. Das Modellierungssystem Oblog

4.1 Die Komponenten von Oblog

Das Modellierungssystem Oblog [GORDON, QUIRCHMAYR] besteht grundsätzlich aus zwei Teilen: den Ausdrucksmitteln, welche zur Darstellung von Gesetzestexten und deren Struktur dienen (Regeln), und jenen Sprachelementen, die zur Analyse und Modellierung fallspezifischer Informationen dienen (Enities). Aufbauend auf diesem Grundsystem kann eine Gesetzes- und eine Falldatenbank erstellt werden, die mit Hilfe von Editoren und einer Inferenzmaschine weiterbearbeitet werden können.

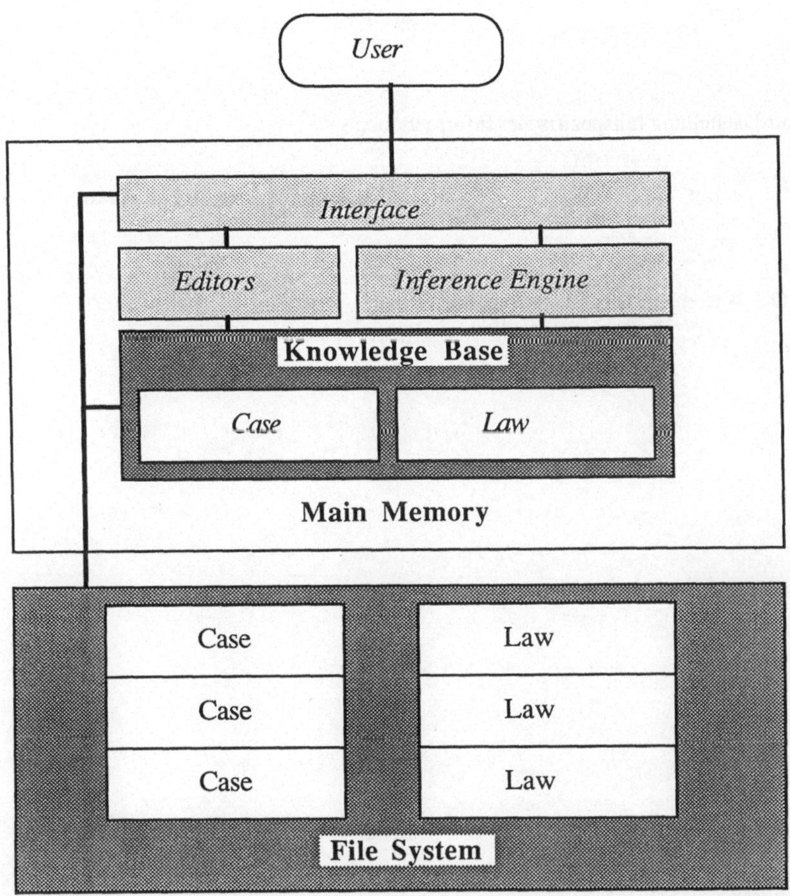

Ziel der Inferenzmaschine ist dabei primär die Zuordnung von *entities* eines Falles (---> fallspezifische Informationen) zu einzelnen *types*, mit deren Hilfe ein Gesetz modelliert wird. Über die einzelnen *types* ist abstraktes Wissen vorhanden, das dann auf die konkrete *entity* angewendet werden kann. Dazu noch ein kleiner Überblick über die Sprachkonstrukte von OBLOG:

a. zur Modellierung eines Gesetzes:

- type   [zur Darstellung eines Konzeptes, z.B. eines Vertrages]

- property / relation (attributes)   [zur Darstellung von Eigenschaften eines types]

- rule   [zur Modellierung von Regeln]

b. zur Darstellung fallspezifischer Informationen

- entity   [zur Modellierung der im Fall vorkommenden Fakten]

Eine OBLOG-Wissensbasis hat dann folgende Gestalt:

Case Specific Entities

Entity	Entity	Entity	Entity	Entity	Entity
Entity	Entity	Entity	Entity	Entity	Entity
Entity	Entity	Entity	Entity	Entity	Entity
Entity	Entity	Entity	Entity	Entity	Entity
Entity	Entity	Entity	Entity	Entity	Entity

Model of a Law

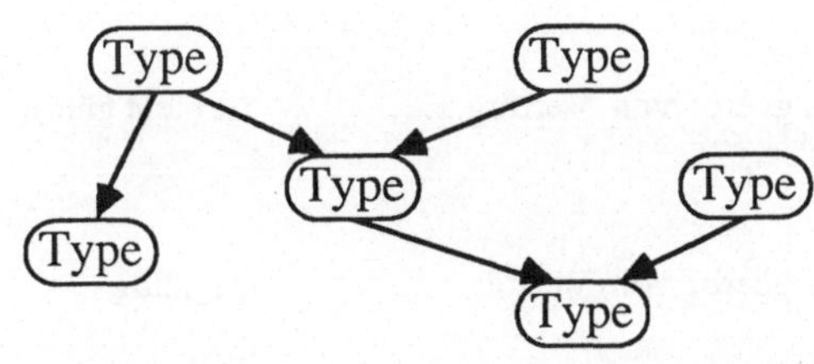

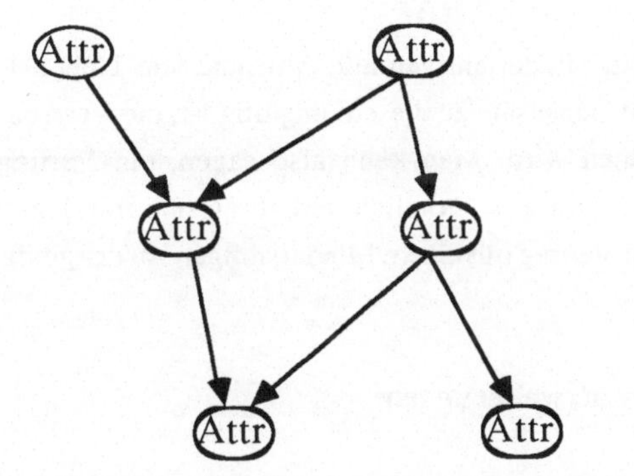

General Purpose Entities

Entity	Entity
Entity	Entity
Entity	Entity
Entity	Entity
Entity	Entity
Entity	Entity
Entity	Entity
Entity	Entity
Entity	Entity
Entity	Entity

4.2 Typenhierarchie und Regel-Ausnahmestruktur

Gesetzestexte sind im Normalfall als generelle Regeln mit Ausnahmen dargestellt. Zu diesen Ausnahmen kann es wieder Ausnahmen geben. Die einfachste Methode, eine solche Struktur darzustellen, ist der Aufbau einer Typenhierarchie, wie sie OBLOG zur Verfügung stellt. Dies wird hier am Beispiel der Hierarchie Vertrag - Vertrag mit einem Minderjährigen - genehmigter Vertrag mit einem Minderjährigen gezeigt (vgl. § 108 BGB):

Typedefinition	*Attribute, die für eine entity des types gültig sind*	
type Vertrag	Attribute 1 .... Attribute n-1,	ist gültig
type Vertrag mit Minderjährigem	...geerbt von Vertrag......,	ist nicht gültig
type genehmigter Vertrag mit Minderjährigem	...geerbt von Vertrag......,	ist gültig

Dies bedeutet, daß ein Vertrag mit einem Minderjährigen alle Attribute von 1 bis n-1 von seinem Obertyp Vertrag erbt, nur eben, daß er im Gegensatz zu diesem ungültig ist, die Vererbung bezüglich dieses einen Attributes also unterbrochen wird. Man kann also sagen, ein Vertrag mit einem Minderjährigen ist ein Vertrag, der nicht gültig ist. Ähnlich verhält es sich mit dem genehmigten Vertrag mit einem Minderjährigen, der ein Vertrag mit einem Minderjährigen ist, der gültig ist.

4.3 Die Offenheit des Modells für Erweiterungen

Die oben beschriebene Typenhierarchie erlaubt es, das Modell für Erweiterungen offenzuhalten. Es ist zum Beispiel leicht möglich, einen weiteren Typ einzufügen, wie etwa den eines unter Einfluß einer Drohung unterzeichneten Vertrages, der ebenfalls ungültig ist.

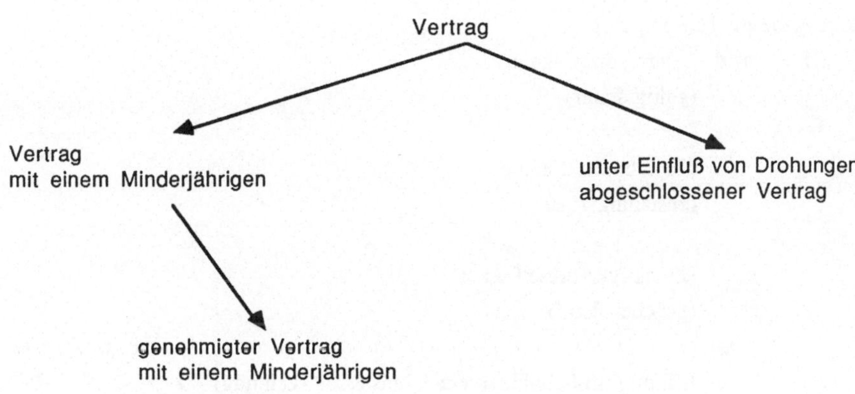

5. Die Funktionsweise des Prototyps

5.1 Die Modellierung des Gesetzes

Die Modellierung des Gesetzes erfolgt ausgehend von den in Kapitel 3 dargestellten Graphiken. So weit als möglich wird in Form einer Typenhierarchie das Verfahren der eidesstattlichen Versicherung dargestellt. Anschließend werden mit Hilfe des Regel-Ausnahmeprinzipes die Ausnahmen zu den allgemeinen Typen näher spezifiziert. Ist die Typenhierarchie erstellt, wird in Form von Regeln das Wissen modelliert, das zu den einzelnen Typen vorhanden ist. Diese Regeln können teilweise auch als Erkennungsregeln verwendet werden, um festzustellen, ob eine *entity* eines Falles ein Objekt eines bestimmten *types* ist.

Interessant ist vor allem die Frage, welche Voraussetzungen gegeben sein müssen, damit eine bestimmte Prozeßhandlung vorgenommen werden kann, in unserem speziellen Beispiel, ob ein Eintrag in das Schuldnerverzeichnis vorzunehmen ist, bzw. was an Stelle dieses Eintrages zu tun ist, wenn die nötigen Voraussetzungen nicht erfüllt sind. Für den Eintrag in das Schuldnerverzeichnis ist eine Abgabe der eidesstattlichen Versicherung erforderlich, die aber nur in bestimmten Fällen gültig ist. Die Bedingungen für die Gültigkeit werden in OBLOG wie folgt definiert, wobei man leicht zusätzliche Bedingungen in das Modell einfügen kann, wenn solche in einer der Vorversionen übersehen wurden, oder, was relativ häufiger vorkommt, sich der Gesetzestext ändert:

```
(rule Abgabe-im-Termin gültig
        (if     (and  (Antrag &self &antr)
                      (gültig &antr)

                      (Gericht &self &ger)
                      (zuständig &ger)

                      (Zulässigkeit &self &zul)
                      (gegeben &zul)

                      (Eintrag-im-Schuldnerverzeichnis &self &eintrag)
                      (or    (nicht-vorhanden &eintrag)
                             (and  (Wiederholung-nach-§903 &self &wdh)
                                   (zulässig &wdh)))

                      (Terminsbestimmung &self &tbest)
                      (korrekt &tbest)

                      (Vertagungsantrag &self &vantr)
                      (or    (fehlend &vantr)
                             (zurückgewiesen &vantr))

                      (Durchführung-des-Termins &self &df)
                      (zielführend &df)

                      (Termin &self &t)
                      (beendet &t))

        (gültig &self)))
```

Mittels eines Ausschnittes der obigen Regel soll nun die Semantik dieser gezeigt werden:

```
(rule Abgabe-im-Termin gültig
        (if     (and  (Antrag &self &antr)
                      (gültig &antr)

                      (Gericht &self &ger)
```

        (zuständig &ger)

        ....

        ....

        ....)

   (gültig &self)))

Eine Abgabe der eidesstattlichen Versicherung im Verfahrenstermin ist gültig, wenn ein Antrag vorliegt, der gültig ist und das Gericht, bei dem er einlangt, zuständig ist, und ... Zur Darstellung der Regeln wurde eine Prefix-Notation gewählt, da diese die logische Struktur relativ schön erkennen läßt. Dieser *type* der Abgabe einer eidesstattlichen Versicherung im Verfahrenstermin bildet die grundlegende Komponente für den Aufbau des Gesamtsystems, denn das eigentliche Ziel des Verfahrens - der Eintrag ins Schuldnerverzeichnis - kann nur dann errreicht werden, wenn zumindest ein erfolgreicher Verfahrenstermin vorliegt, der mit der gültigen Abgabe der eidesstattlichen Versicherung endet. In einer OBLOG-Typenhierarchie hat das Gesamtsystem die Form eines Baumes mit drei Ebenen, in dem die jeweils untere eine Ausnahme zur oberen bildet:

(type Abgabe-im-Verfahrensweg

    (type gehemmte-Abgabe (Abgabe-im-Verfahrensweg)

      (type durchgesetzte-Abgabe (gehemmte-Abgabe)

--->

   zunehmende Bestimmtheit des vorliegenden **types** durch wachsende Spezialisierung

Sollte man beim Test dieses Prototyps feststellen, daß noch Lücken vorhanden sind, so etwa, daß es noch Ausnahmen gibt, die nicht beachtet worden sind, können diese leicht in Form von neuen *types* in das vorhandene Modell eingebaut werden.

Das Wissen über die *types* ist in *rules* festgehalten, die mit dem *type* assoziiert sind;
die Erweiterung und Ergänzung dieser ist jederzeit möglich:

(rule Abgabe-im-Verfahrensweg erfolgreich (erfolgreich &self))   ist immer erfolgreich (**rule** gehemmte-Abgabe erfolgreich)   null rule, kann also niemals erfolgreich sein

(**rule** durchgesetzte-Abgabe erfolgreich (erfolgreich &self))   ist immer erfolgreich

Um festzustellen, welcher *type* der Abgabe der eidesstattlichen Versicherung im Verfahren nun vorliegt, werden Erkennungsregeln verwendet:

(**type** Abgabe-im-Verfahrensweg)   Standardannahme

(**type** gehemmte-Abgabe (Abgabe-im-Verfahrensweg)
      (**if**   (**and** (Abgabe-im-Verfahrensweg &abg)
                   (zweifelhaft &abg))
      (gehemmte-Abgabe &agb)

(**type** durchgesetzte-Abgabe (gehemmte-Abgabe)
      (**if**   (**and** (gehemmte-Abgabe &abg)
                   (Abgabe-im-Termin &self &abg-t)
                   (gültig &abg-t))
      (durchgesetzte-Abgabe &agb)

Man geht also davon aus, daß eine im Verfahrensweg erfolgte Abgabe der eidesstattlichen Versicherung gültig ist, es sei denn (Gegenargument), es bestehen Zweifel an der Gültigkeit der Abgabe. Diese Zweifel können dadurch ausgeräumt werden, daß das Vorliegen einer gültigen Abgabe der eidesstattlichen Versicherung in einem der Verfahrenstermine nachgewiesen wird (Gegenargument gegen obiges Gegenargument). Auf einer noch spezieller werdenden Stufe der Argumentation kann auch dieser Beweis durch Fakten widerlegt werden, die das Vorliegen einer Ausnahmesituation beweisen.

5.2 Die Darstellung fallspezifischer Informationen

Die Darstellung der Fakten eines Falles erfolgt in Form von *entities*, denen zusätzliches Wissen in Form von Attributen mitgegeben wird. Dies sieht etwa wie folgt aus, wobei die Attribute eine den

Typen vergleichbare Hierarchie bilden können (so ist etwa ein Stellvertreter eine Person mit besonderen Eigenschaften):

```
entity  p1(Person)
        (Alter a1)
        (Größe g1)
        (Körpergewicht k1))
```

Dazu ein Beispiel der Darstellung eines Falles zum Modell der eidesstattlichen Versicherung (zu dem in 4.2.2 gezeigten Ausschnitt des Modells):

```
(entity  abg (Abgabe-im-Verfahrensweg)
        (Abgabe-im-Termin abg-t)
        (zweifelhaft))
```

Es liegt also eine Abgabe im Verfahrensweg vor, über die bekannt ist, daß eine Abgabe der eidesstattlichen Versicherung in einem Verfahrenstermin erfolgte, und daß Zweifel an deren Korrektheit bestehen. Um beweisen zu können, daß die Abgabe der eidesstattlichen Versicherung erfolgreich ist, ist es nötig, dem System folgende weitere Informationen bezüglich der Abgabe im Termin bekanntzugeben:

```
(entity  abg-t  (Abgabe-im-Termin )
                (Antrag a)
                (Gericht g)
                (Zulässigkeit z
                (Eintrag-im-Schuldnerverzeichnis e)
                (Terminsbestimmung tb)
                (Vertagungsantrag v)
                (Durchführung-des-Termins d)
                (Termin t))
```

Über diese Elemente sind weitere Aussagen erforderlich:

```
    (entity  a (Antrag)
             (gültig))

    (entity  g (Gericht)
             (zuständig))

     (entity  z (Zulässigkeit)
             (gegeben))

    (entity  e (Eintrag-im-Schuldnerverzeichnis)
             (nicht-vorhanden))

    (entity  tb (Terminsbestimmun)
             (korrekt))

    (entity  v (Vertagungsantrag)
             (fehlend))

    (entity  d (Durchführung-des-Termins)
             (zielführend))

    (entity  t (Termin)
             (beendet))
```

Sollten im Laufe der Sachverhaltsprüfung weitere Informationen bekannt werden, können diese als neue *entities* der bisherigen Fallbeschreibung hinzugefügt werden. Es ist also durchaus möglich, die einzelnen Stadien des Wissensstandes während der Beweisaufnahme nachzubilden. Dies ist von größter Bedeutung, da je nach Umfang der Information das Urteil unterschiedlich ausfallen wird und es daher indiskutabel wäre, an einem einmal spezifizierten Ausgangszustand festhalten zu müssen.

5.3 Die Kommuniktion des Benutzers mit dem System

Die Eingabe der Fragen des Benutzers erfolgt derzeit noch über ein Command-line Interface, der Einbau einer graphischen Schnittstelle ist geplant. Typische Fragen, die der Benutzer an das Modell stellen kann sind

a) ob die Abgabe der eidesstattlichen Versicherung gültig zustande gekommen ist:

(and (Abgabe-im-Termin &x) (erfolgreich &x))

oder

b), ob bestimmte Elemente, wie etwa ein gültiger Antrag, vorliegen:

(and (Antrag &x) (gültig &x)).

Diese Schnittstelle ermöglicht es also dem Benutzer, sich in einer Art schrittweiser Verfeinerung zu den einzelnen Punkten durchzutasten, erlaubt es ihm aber auch, sich mit einer globalen Antwort zufrieden zu geben, oder gleich direkt die Details abzufragen. Abfragbar sind sowohl Fakten (b), als auch durch das System deduziertes Wissen (a).

6. Ausblick

Geplant ist die Implementation einer Reihe weiterer Prototypen in OBLOG, sowie die Verbesserung der Sprache selbst. Derzeit wird an einer Neuimplementierung der LISP-Version in PROLOG gearbeitet, da dadurch eine wesentliche Verbesserung der Laufzeiteffizienz zu erreichen ist. In einem nächsten Schritt wird dann eine graphische Schnittstelle entworfen, um dem Benutzer die Handhabung des Systems zu erleichtern.

7. Literatur

[BRACHMAN] Brachman, R.J.,   and Schmolze, J.G.,   *An   Overview · of the KL-ONE Knowledge Representation System*; Cognitive Science; 9(2); 1985; pp 171-216.

Brachman, R.J.;   Gilbert, V.P.; Levesque, H.J.; *An Essential Hybrid Reasoning System: Knowledge and Symbol Level Accounts of Krypton*; Proceedings of the Ninth International Joint Conference on Artificial Intelligence; 1985.

[FIEDLER] Fiedler, Herbert; *Expert Systems as a Tool for Drafting Legal Decisions*; Proceedings of the Second International Congress on Logic, Computer Science, and Law (*Logica, Informatica, Dirritto*); Florence; 1985.

[GORDON] Gordon, T.F.; *The Role of Exceptions in Models of the Law*; in *Formalisierung   im Recht und Ausätze juristischer Expertensysteme;* J. Schweitzer Verlag; München 1986.

[GORDON, QUIRCHMAYR] Gordon, T.F.; und Quirchmayr, G.; *OBLOG Eine Programmiersprache für juristische Expertensysteme;* Tübingen 1986. Gordon, T.F.; und Quirchmayr, G.; *OBLOG-2 Eine hybrides Wissensrepräsentationssystem zur   Modellierung rechtswissenschaftlicher Probleme;* 16. Jahrestagung der Gesellschaft für   Informatik; Berlin 1986.

[HART]   Hart, H.L.A.; *The Concept of Law;* Oxford University Press 1961.

[McCARTY, SRIDHARAN] McCarty, L.T. und Sridharan, N.S. *A Computational Theory of Legal Argument ; LRP-PR-13, Laboratory for Computer Science Research; Rutgers University 1982.

[PHILIPPS] Philipps, Lothar; *Der Computer als Hilfsmittel zu einer interessengerechten Normierung*; DVR Beiheft 17; J. Schweitzer Verlag; Munich; 1984.

[RISSLAND] Rissland, E.L.; *AI and Legal Reasoning ; Proceedings of the Ninth International Joint Conference on Artificial Intelligence* ; Los Angeles 1985.

[van MELLE] van Melle, William; *A Domain-Independent System that Aids in Constructing Knowledge-Based Consultation Programs*; Stanford Heuristic Programming Project; Report   No. STAN-CS-80-820; 1980.

[VILAIN]   Vilain, Marc; *The Restricted Language Architecture of a Hybrid Representation System*; Proceedings of the Ninth International Joint Conference on Artificial Intelligence; 1985.

PROTOTYPING ZUR UNTERSTÜTZUNG DES KONZEPTUELLEN ENTWURFS INTERAKTIVER INFORMATIONSSYSTEME

Frank Schönthaler[*], Andreas Oberweis[**],
Georg Lausen[**], Wolffried Stucky[*]

Schlüsselworte

Rapid Prototyping, Ausführbare Spezifikation, Software-Entwicklungsumgebung, Konzeptuelles Schema, Petri-Netze, Datenstrukturschema, Verhaltensschema, Zeitrestriktionen

Abstract

Als konzeptuelle Modellierung bezeichnet man üblicherweise das formale Beschreiben von Anforderungen für Informationssysteme, die unter Verwendung von Datenbanksystemen realisiert werden. Dieser Schritt ist im Life Cycle des Informationssystementwurfs zwischen der informalen bzw. semiformalen Spezifikation von Anforderungen und dem eigentlichen Systementwurf als Basis der Implementation angesiedelt. Das dabei erstellte konzeptuelle Schema sollte sowohl statische als auch dynamische Aspekte des zu entwickelnden Systems beschreiben. Es werden die Grundlagen des rechnergestützten Arbeitsplatzes *INCOME* skizziert, der eine konstruktive Methode zur konzeptuellen Modellierung mit Petri-Netzen unterstützt.

Um auch dem Endbenutzer eines zu entwickelnden Systems dieses formale Beschreibungsverfahren zugänglich zu machen, enthält *INCOME* eine Prototyping-Komponente, die die Ausführung der Spezifikation in jeder Phase des konzeptuellen Entwurfsprozesses ermöglicht. Es werden dabei alle Aspekte der konzeptuellen Modellierung berücksichtigt. Die Architektur und die Arbeitsweise dieser Komponente sowie die Auswirkungen des Prototyping auf die Qualität des konzeptuellen Entwurfs werden beschrieben. Eine Besonderheit der Komponente ist die Trennung in ein Interpretations- und ein Transformationssystem sowie die Möglichkeit zur Kombination des Tools mit Applikationsgeneratoren und Very High Level Languages verschiedener Zielumgebungen des zu entwickelnden Systems.

---

[*] Institut für Angewandte Informatik und Formale Beschreibungsverfahren, Universität Karlsruhe (TH), 7500 Karlsruhe
[**] Fachbereich Informatik, Technische Hochschule Darmstadt, 6100 Darmstadt

Diese Arbeit wurde teilweise von der Deutschen Forschungsgemeinschaft im Rahmen des Schwerpunktprogramms 'Interaktive betriebswirtschaftliche Informations- und Steuerungssysteme' unter der Nummer 'Stu 98/6' gefördert.

I. Einleitung

Das formale Beschreiben von Anforderungen für Informationssysteme, die unter Verwendung von Datenbanksystemen realisiert werden, bezeichnet man als *konzeptuelle
Modellierung*. Dieser Schritt ist im Life Cycle des Informationssystementwurfs
zwischen der informalen bzw. semiformalen Spezifikation von Anforderungen und dem
eigentlichen Systementwurf als Basis der Implementation angesiedelt (siehe Abbildung
1). Im Rahmen der konzeptuellen Modellierung wird das *konzeptuelle Schema* erstellt,
eine formale Beschreibung aller als relevant betrachteten Aspekte eines zu
entwerfenden Informationssystems, wobei auf die Betrachtung von Aspekten der
späteren Implementation bewußt verzichtet wird.

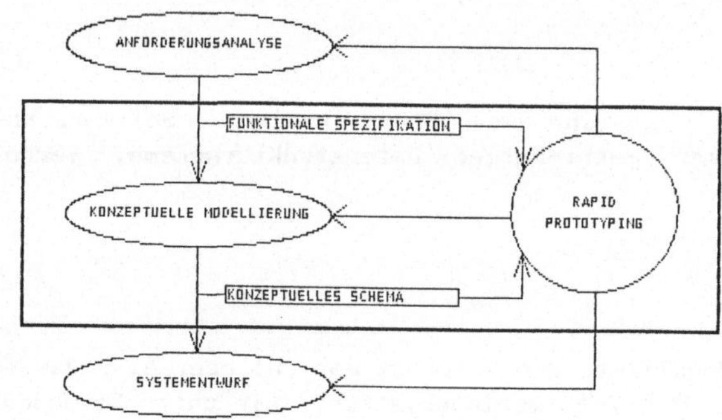

Abbildung 1: Lebenszyklus des Informationssystementwurfs

Nach [Gri82] sollte ein konzeptuelles Schema neben den *statischen* auch die
dynamischen Aspekte eines Systems berücksichtigen. Entsprechend wird das konzeptuelle Schema üblicherweise in eine statische und eine dynamische Komponente aufge-
teilt. *INCOME* (*In*teractive *CO*nceptual *M*odelling *En*vironment) ist ein rechnergestützter Arbeitsplatz, der eine methodische Vorgehensweise zur Konstruktion eines
konzeptuellen Schemas unterstützt.

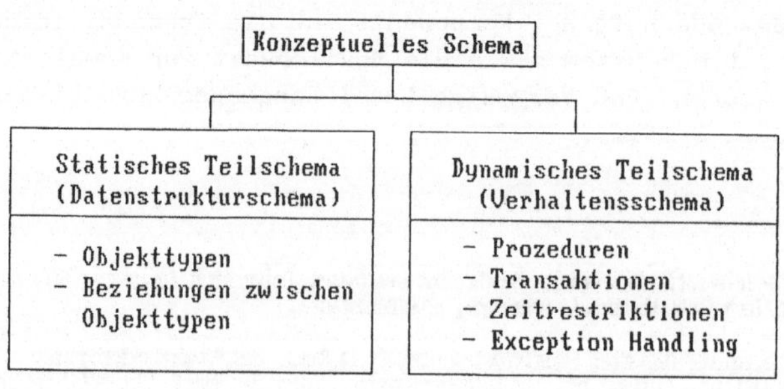

Abbildung 2: Gliederung des konzeptuellen Schemas

Das Schema wird dabei wie folgt gegliedert (siehe Abbildung 2): im statischen Teilschema, dem *Datenstrukturschema*, werden die relevanten Objekttypen angegeben sowie
ihre Struktur, die sich über die Beziehungen zu anderen Objekttypen ergibt. Im
dynamischen Teilschema, dem *Verhaltensschema*, werden die Systemabläufe (Prozeduren),
die elementaren Benutzeroperationen (Transaktionen) sowie Zeitaspekte und Mechanismen zur Regelung von Ausnahmesituationen (Exception Handling) spezifiziert. *Petri-
Netze* bilden einen einheitlichen Formalismus zur Beschreibung sowohl des statischen
als auch des dynamischen Teilschemas.

Ausgangspunkt der *INCOME*-Methode zur konzeptuellen Modellierung ist eine *funktionale
Anforderungsspezifikation*, die in Form einer Hierarchie von Objektflußdiagrammen
ähnlich SADT [Ros77], SA [DeM78], SSA [GaS79] oder ISAC [Lun82] gegeben ist.
Zusätzlich liegt ein *Glossar* vor, welches eine informale, textuelle Zusammenstellung
aller vorliegenden Informationen über Funktionen und Objektflüsse im zu entwerfenden
System darstellt. Aus der funktionalen Anforderungsspezifikation wird im nächsten
Schritt des konzeptuellen Entwurfsprozesses ein *konzeptuelles Datenstrukturschema*
abgeleitet. Es wird hierzu ein semantisch-hierarchisches Datenmodell, ähnlich SHM+
[BrR84] und THM [FuN86], verwendet. Die Objektflußdiagramme der untersten
Hierarchieebene werden als Petri-Netze interpretiert und gegebenenfalls so
modifiziert, daß die formale Netzschaltregel gilt, die die Beschreibung der System-
dynamik auf Benutzerebene erlaubt. Diese Netze werden zu einem globalen Netz – dem
Ablaufschema – verknüpft. Umgebungen des Ablaufschemas entsprechen elementaren
Benutzeroperationen, die durch Transaktionsnetze weiter verfeinert werden. Diese
Netze beschreiben das Systemverhalten auf Datenbankebene und bilden das
Transaktionsschema.

Ähnliche integrierte Ansätze zur konzeptuellen Modellierung, welche sowohl statische
als auch dynamische Aspekte der zu entwickelnden Systeme berücksichtigen, werden in
[AnL85, BrR84, OST83, OSV82, RiD82, SoK85, St.H85] beschrieben. Bei *INCOME* stehen die
Aspekte des Prototyping im Vordergrund. Um die formale Spezifikation eines Systems
auch dem Endbenutzer zugänglich zu machen, steht ein *Prototyping-Werkzeug* zur Verfügung. Dieses bietet die Möglichkeit, in jeder Phase des Entwurfsprozesses die
Abläufe des zu entwickelnden Systems zu simulieren. Damit wird eine verbesserte
Kommunikation zwischen Systemdesigner und Endbenutzer gewährleistet sowie eine
kontinuierliche Anpassung des Entwurfs an sich ändernde Anforderungen, die sich
einerseits aufgrund äußerer Einflüsse auf die Arbeitsabläufe ergeben, andererseits
aber auch durch ein im Laufe des Entwurfsprozesses zunehmendes Systemverständnis
aller Projektbeteiligten. Außerdem wird die frühzeitige Erkennung von Spezifikationsfehlern gefördert, die nicht anhand interner Analysen des Schemas aufgedeckt
werden können.

Das primäre Ziel des Prototyping ist nicht die Generierung eines weitgehend vollständigen Anwendungssystems, sondern die Unterstützung des konzeptuellen Entwurfs-
prozesses. Das Prototyping-Werkzeug kann dabei unabhängig von einer bestimmten
Zielumgebung der Applikation eingesetzt werden. Als Übergang von der konzeptuellen
Modellierung zur Implementationsphase bietet sich die Kombination des Tools mit
Applikationsgeneratoren oder Very High Level Languages der gewählten Zielumgebung
an.
Diese Arbeit ist wie folgt gegliedert: in Kapitel II wird das der *INCOME*-Methode
zugrundeliegende konzeptuelle Schema beschrieben. Ausführungen zur Architektur des
Arbeitsplatzes finden sich in Kapitel III. Die Prototyping-Komponente wird in den
Kapiteln IV und V beschrieben. Kapitel VI enthält eine kurze Zusammenfassung dieser
Arbeit sowie einen Ausblick auf unsere weiteren Forschungstätigkeiten.

II. Das konzeptuelle Schema

Der *INCOME*-Methode liegt ein konzeptuelles Schema zugrunde, das in ein statisches
(Datenstrukturschema) und ein dynamisches (Verhaltensschema) Teilschema gegliedert
ist. Als Beschreibungsmittel werden durchgängig formale Konzepte der Netztheorie
verwendet. Die Vorgehensweise zur Konstruktion des konzeptuellen Schemas wird in
dieser Arbeit nur skizziert. Detailliertere Informationen hierzu finden sich in
[LOS85, NSM87, OSL86].

II.1 Funktionale Anforderungsspezifikation

Der konzeptuellen Modellierung mit *INCOME* geht üblicherweise eine *Anforderungs-
analyse* voraus, als deren Ergebnis eine *funktionale Anforderungsspezifikation* in
Form einer Hierarchie von Objektflußdiagrammen sowie eine informale Beschreibung der
Funktionen und Objektflüsse des Systems in einem *Glossar* erstellt wird. Für diese
Anforderungsanalyse hat sich in einer praktischen Arbeit [Sch84] die folgende
Vorgehensweise als geeignet erwiesen: Der Systemdesigner, der sich bereits anhand
von Formular- und Dokumentenanalysen einen Einblick in das Anwendungsgebiet
verschafft hat, erstellt auf der Basis von Interviews mit den Endanwendern eine
informale textuelle Beschreibung des zu entwickelnden Systems. Auf der Basis dieser
Beschreibung entwirft er in einer Top-Down-Vorgehensweise eine erste Version der
Objektflußdiagramm-Hierarchie. Dieses Dokument wird in Zusammenarbeit mit dem Endan-
wender schrittweise korrigiert und zur funktionalen Anforderungsspezifikation des
Systems weiterentwickelt. Die Qualität dieser Spezifikation wird stark beeinflußt
von der Kommunikationsfähigkeit der am Entwicklungsprozeß beteiligten Personen.
Insbesondere hat es sich auch gezeigt, daß für die Spezifikation der elementaren
Teilaufgaben nicht der verantwortliche Manager sondern der direkt betroffene
Mitarbeiter der geeignete Gesprächspartner des Systemdesigners ist.

Objektflußdiagramme stellen ein einfaches, leicht verständliches Hilfsmittel für die
Beschreibung der Funktionen dar, die ein zu entwerfendes System erfüllen muß: sie
enthalten rechteckige Kästchen zur Darstellung der Funktionen und Pfeile zwischen
Kästchen zur Darstellung der Objektflüsse, die zwischen den betreffenden Funktionen
verlaufen. Hierarchien von Objektflußdiagrammen entstehen durch rekursives
Verfeinern einzelner Funktionen gemeinsam mit ihren jeweiligen Input- und Output-
flüssen durch neue Diagramme. Die Funktion der obersten Hierarchieebene stellt die
Gesamtsystemaktivität dar.

Eine solche semiformale Beschreibung eines System ist jedoch nur beschränkt
verwendungsfähig als Grundlage für die spätere Implementation, da Widersprüche,
Inkonsistenzen, Unvollständigkeiten, Ungenauigkeiten bzw. Mehrdeutigkeiten nicht
ausgeschlossen werden können. Vor der eigentlichen Implementation sollte daher
zunächst eine Prüfung des Entwurfs durchgeführt werden. Dies ist aber nur möglich,
wenn der Entwurf formal eindeutig und damit mathematischen Analysen zugänglich ist.

Wir verzichten bewußt darauf, durch die Verwendung zusätzlicher Symbole in den
Objektflußdiagrammen zusätzliche Semantik einzuführen (siehe hierzu z.B. [HHK77,
KPM85, War86]), damit die Diagramme auch für den Nicht-Fachmann verständlich
bleiben. Stattdessen bevorzugen wir eine Vorgehensweise, in der wir von den semiformalen Objektflußdiagrammen und den informalen textuellen Beschreibungen schrittweise
übergehen zum formalen Beschreibungsmittel der Petri-Netze (siehe dazu auch

[KrS81]). Diese bieten mit der Netztheorie einen mathematischen Formalismus an, welcher umfangreiche Analysen des zu entwerfenden Systems ermöglicht.

II.2 Datenstrukturschema

Zur Modellierung der Datenstrukturen werden Netze mit einer speziellen Interpretation eingesetzt: sogenannte *Datenstruktur-Netze*. Die S-Elemente stehen für Objekttypen, die die relevanten Realweltobjekte repräsentieren. Die Strukturen der Objekttypen werden durch Aggregationen, Gruppierungen und Generalisierungen definiert ([BrR84], [FuN86], [SmS77]), welche die T-Elemente im Netz bilden (vgl. Abbildung 3).

Die Aggregation konstruiert einen Objekttyp aus anderen Objekttypen, die ihm als Komponenten zugeordnet sind. Durch die Gruppierung werden Objekttypen definiert, deren Objekte Mengen von Objekten eines anderen Objekttyps sind. Mit der Generalisierung lassen sich Objekttypen unter einem gemeinsamen Gattungsbegriff zusammenfassen. Die Menge der Objekttypen und Beziehungen bildet das *konzeptuelle Datenstrukturschema*. Die grafische Darstellung der Objekttypbeziehungen zeigt Abbildung 3. Die Elemente des Wertebereichs eines Objekttyps OT ergeben sich im allgemeinen durch Anwendung von *Vererbungsregeln* als unnormalisierte Relationen [LaS87].

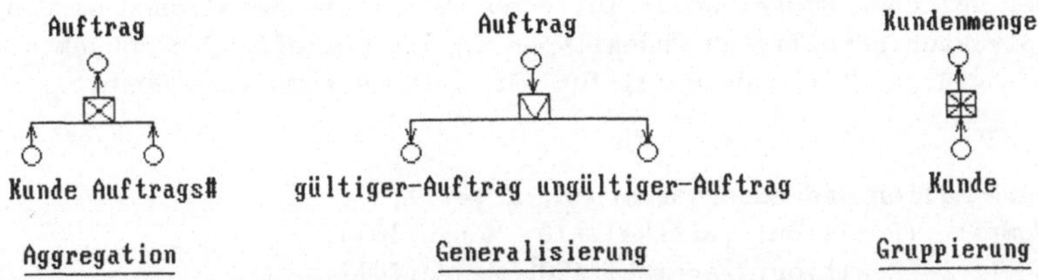

Abbildung 3: Grafische Darstellung der Objekttypbeziehungen

II.3 Verhaltensschema

Das *Verhaltensschema* stellt eine formale Beschreibung des Systemverhaltens dar. Wir betrachten das Systemverhalten auf zwei verschiedenen Ebenen: auf Benutzerebene und auf Datenbankebene. Dem Benutzer bleiben elementare Datenbankoperationen (wie 'delete', 'update', 'insert') verborgen; er arbeitet mit Benutzeroperationen, den sogenannten *Transaktionen*, die aus elementaren Datenbankoperationen zusammengesetzt sind. Verschiedene Transaktionen, die im Zusammenhang ausgeführt werden, bilden Systemabläufe, im folgenden auch als *Prozeduren* bezeichnet. Beim Entwurf des Verhaltensschemas wird entsprechend unterschieden zwischen dem Entwurf von Prozeduren im *Ablaufschema* und dem Entwurf von Transaktionen im *Transaktionsschema*.

II.3.1 Ablaufschema

Prozeduren setzen sich aus Transaktionen zusammen, die auf gleiche Resourcen oder
Objekte zugreifen, und werden entsprechend durch Angabe der Reihenfolgebeziehungen
sowie der Objektflüsse zwischen den Transaktionen spezifiziert. Zur formalen
Beschreibung dieser Zusammenhänge haben sich Petri-Netze als besonders geeignet
herausgestellt. Sie ermöglichen einmal die formale Beschreibung der Struktur von
Abläufen, d.h. es ist möglich, parallele, alternative bzw. sequentielle Teilabläufe
innerhalb eines Gesamtablaufs zu beschreiben. Durch Markierung der Stellen und
Einführung der formalen Schaltregel ist Systemdynamik eindeutig nachvollziehbar:
Objekte, die sich durch das System von Aktivität zu Aktivität bewegen, werden in
Petri-Netzen als Marken in Stellen symbolisiert.

Unsere Vorgehensweise der Ablaufmodellierung ist zunächst ähnlich den in [KrS81,
Rei85, RiD82] beschriebenen Methoden: ausgehend von einer semiformalen Beschreibung
der Abläufe in Form einer Hierarchie von *Kanal/Instanzen-Netzen* wird in einem
schrittweisen Formalisierungsprozeß ein *Prädikate/Transitionen-Netz* (*Pr/T-Netz*)
erzeugt, welches eine globale Beschreibung aller Systemabläufe darstellt.

Die wesentlichen Unterschiede sind die folgenden: Die Prädikate des Prädi-
kate/Transitionen-Netzes sind Variablen der im Datenstrukturschema definierten
Objekttypen. Die Objekte sind im wesentlichen unnormalisierte Relationen. Wir verwenden die in [BaK86] eingeführten Definitionen für 'komplexe Objekte'. Im Unterschied zu der üblichen Schreibweise für unnormalisierte Relationen werden die Namen
der an der Struktur beteiligten Objekttypen in die betreffenden Objekte hereinge-
zogen. Abbildung 4 zeigt ein Beispiel für ein solches komplexes Objekt.

[Auftrag: [Name:Müller, Adresse:Karlsruhe, Nr:4711,
          Rumpf: {[Position: [Artikel:A10, Menge:10]],
                  [Position: [Artikel:A20, Menge:70]],
                  [Position: [Artikel:A30, Menge:50]]}]]

Abbildung 4:   Ein komplexes Objekt vom Typ Auftrag

Das 'Hereinziehen' von Namen ermöglicht es, in der Beschriftungssprache den Namen
Variablen zuzuordnen, so daß in der Beschriftung die Struktur der Objekte in
natürlicher Weise ausgenutzt werden kann. Abbildung 5 zeigt ein nicht-triviales
Beispiel. Die Semantik des verwendeten Prädikats '$\leq$' ist die Teilobjektbeziehung
im Sinne von [BaK86]. Die ungerichtete Kante zwischen der Transition 'Erstellen-
Rückfrage' und dem Prädikat 'Artikeldaten' wird als abkürzende Notation wie in
[RiD82] verwendet und bedeutet, daß bei jedem Schaltvorgang die Menge der Artikeldaten entnommen und die gleiche Menge wieder zurückgelegt wird.

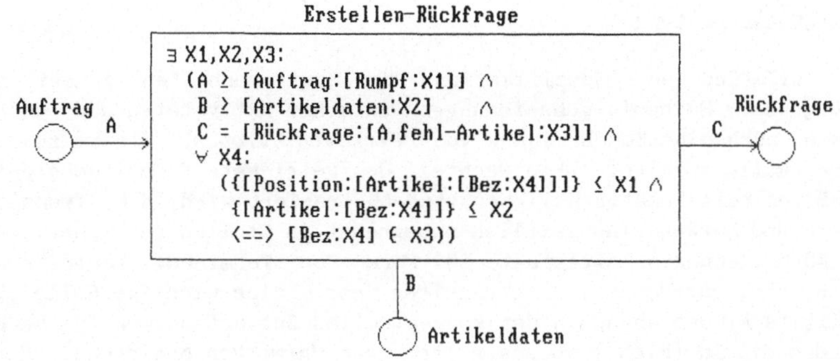

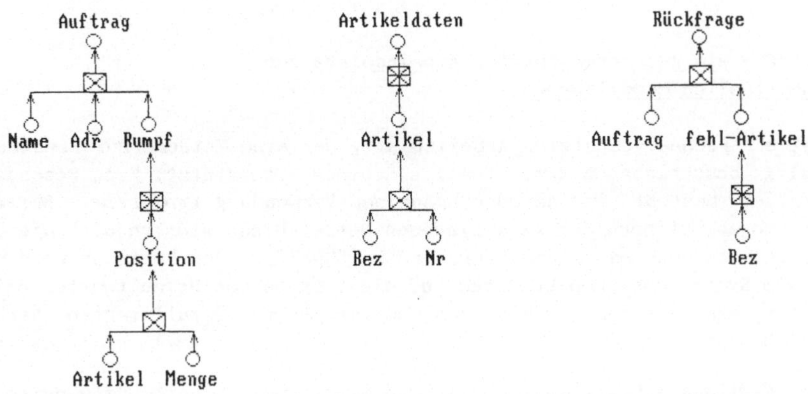

Abbildung 5: Beispiel für Pr/T-Netz Beschriftung und dazugehörige
Objekttypdefinition

II.3.2 Transaktionsschema

Im Ablaufschema wird das Systemverhalten nur bis zur Ebene der elementaren Benutzeroperationen (Transaktionen) hinab betrachtet. Zur Entwicklung des Tran-
saktionsschemas wird zu jeder Transaktion ein Verfeinerungsschritt durchgeführt: die
Transaktion wird durch *Abläufe von atomaren Datenbankoperationen* beschrieben. Da
hierbei die gleichen Beziehungen zwischen Teilabläufen bestehen können wie im Ablaufschema, bietet es sich an, den gleichen Beschreibungsmechanismus wie dort,
nämlich Prädikate/Transitionen-Netze, zu verwenden. Über die Beschriftung der Kanten
und Transitionen ist es möglich, Vor- und Nachbedingungen von Transaktionen zu
spezifizieren. Unsere Methode lehnt sich stark an die in [BrR84] beschriebene Vorgehensweise an. Die dort verwendete grafische Darstellungstechnik weist jedoch den
Nachteil auf, daß die genauen Reihenfolgebeziehungen zwischen den atomaren Datenbankoperationen nicht ersichtlich sind.

II.3.3 Zeitrestriktionen

Zu einer vollständigen Spezifikation von Systemverhalten gehört neben einer Beschreibung der Reihenfolgebeziehungen zwischen Aktivitäten und der relevanten Objektflüsse auch eine Beschreibung von *Zeitrestriktionen*, die im zu entwerfenden System einer Rolle spielen. Ein Nachteil des Petri-Netz-Formalismus besteht jedoch darin, daß von Zeitaspekten üblicherweise abstrahiert wird, d.h. Transitionen haben keine Dauern und Marken sind zeitlich unbegrenzt in Stellen verfügbar. Da insbeson-dere in Büroumgebungen Zeitaspekte in Form von Terminen, Verfügbarkeitszeiten, Fristen, Bearbeitungsdauern, Lieferzeiten etc. eine wichtige Rolle spielen, ist deren explizite Einbeziehung in den konzeptuellen Entwurf notwendig [BaP85, Gib85]. Wir verwenden die in [Ric85] vorgestellte, auf Uhrwerken basierende Vorgehensweise zur Modellierung von Zeitaspekten in Prädikate/Transitionen-Netzen. Dies wird ausführlich in [ObL86] dargestellt.

III. INCOME – ein rechnergestützter Arbeitsplatz zur konzeptuellen Modellierung

INCOME ist ein rechnergestützter Arbeitsplatz, der eine Methode zur Konstruktion des in Kapitel II beschriebenen konzeptuellen Schemas unterstützt. Eine Besonderheit des Arbeitsplatzes besteht in der durchgängigen Verwendung *grafischer Werkzeuge* zum Editieren und Abspeichern der verschiedenen Netze. Diese sichern auch die Konsistenz des konzeptuellen Schemas (siehe hierzu auch [LMN87]). Der Designer wird bei seinen Eingaben vom System über Pop-Up Menüs und die Vorgabe von Defaultwerten unterstützt, so daß für das Handling der Editoren zumeist keine detaillierten Vorkenntnisse erforderlich sind.

Die Architektur des Arbeitsplatzes, der prototypmäßig auf einem IBM-PC/AT unter MS-DOS installiert ist, zeigt die Abbildung 6. Die Steuerung des Systems ist über die *Operating Environment* realisiert. An der Benutzerschnittstelle steht neben Tastatur, Bildschirm und Drucker auch eine Maus zur Verfügung.

Die *INCOME Toolbox* enthält Werkzeuge, die die verschiedenen Konstruktionsphasen des konzeptuellen Schemas – Datenstrukturmodellierung, Systemablaufmodellierung, Trans-aktionsmodellierung – unterstützen. Außerdem steht ein Werkzeug zur funktionalen Anforderungsspezifikation mit Objektflußdiagrammen zur Verfügung. Um dem Endanwender bereits in den frühen Phasen des Entwicklungsprozesses Entwurfsentscheidungen anhand eines ablauffähigen Systems darzustellen, enthält *INCOME* eine Prototyping-Komponente, die sich in ein Interpretations- und Transformationssystem gliedert (siehe Kapitel IV). Zusätzlich bietet *INCOME* verschiedene Werkzeuge zur Dokumentation (Generierung von Systembeschreibungen, Pflichtenheften, Benutzerhand-büchern) und Analyse der Entwurfsdaten sowie zur konventionellen Programmentwicklung (Editor, Compiler, Linker, Library Manager, Debugger) an.

Die Kommunikation der Werkzeuge erfolgt über eine gemeinsame *Entwicklungsdatenbank*, die über das Datenbanksystem INOVIS-X86 (vormals DATENBANK-PASCAL) [Kar84] und das MS-DOS Filesystem verwaltet wird. Außerdem können sich die Werkzeuge gegenseitig aufrufen, wobei ein zusätzlicher Datenaustausch über einen Mechanismus erfolgt, der dem aus der UNIX-Welt bekannten Pipe-Mechanismus vergleichbar ist. *INCOME* bildet ein offenes System; neue Werkzeuge können jederzeit, nach Anpassung ihrer Schnitt-stellen, im System integriert werden.

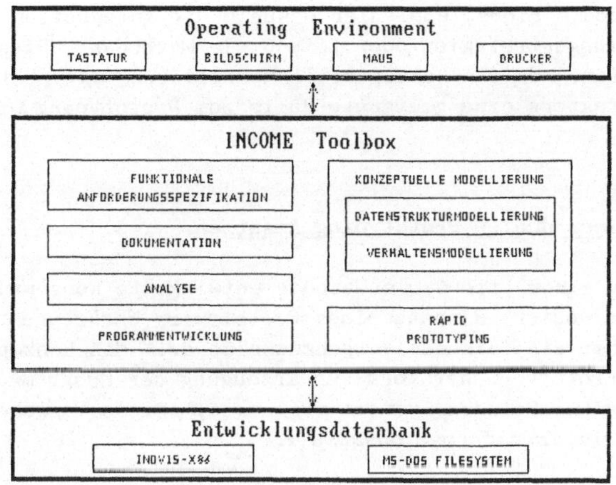

<u>Abbildung 6</u>:   **INCOME**-Architektur

IV. Das Prototyping-Werkzeug RAPPROT

Nachfolgend wird das Prototyping-Werkzeug *RAPPROT* beschrieben, das die Spezifikation der Benutzerschnittstelle (Formulare, Menüs) und der Prototypdatenbank, die Erweiterung unvollständiger konzeptueller Schemata sowie die Simulation der Abläufe des zu entwickelnden Systems ermöglicht. *RAPPROT* (*RAP*id *PRO*totyping *Tool*) ist dabei so konzipiert, daß es in jeder Phase des konzeptuellen Entwurfsprozesses eingesetzt werden kann. Die Zeitpunkte der Prototyp-Erstellung können somit vom Designer frei gewählt werden.

Die Vorteile des Einsatzes von Rapid Prototyping bei der Entwicklung interaktiver Informationssysteme werden heute weitgehend anerkannt (siehe [BKM84]). Prototyping unterstützt das frühzeitige Erkennen von Spezifikationsfehlern, die nicht anhand interner Analysen aufgedeckt werden können. Außerdem bildet die Arbeit mit den Prototypen eines Systems eine geeignete Kommunikationsbasis aller am Entwicklungsprozeß beteiligten Gruppen. Die Mitarbeit der Endbenutzer an der Entwicklung eines Informationssystems wirkt sich äußerst positiv auf die Akzeptanz dieses Systems bei der Übernahme in die betriebliche Praxis aus. Prototyping fördert zudem die kontinuierliche Anpassung des Entwurfs an sich ändernde Anforderungen während des Entwicklungsprozesses, die sich einerseits aufgrund äußerer Einflüsse auf das System oder aber durch ein umfassenderes Systemverständnis aller Projektbeteiligten ergeben können.

Nachteile ergeben sich dadurch, daß Prototyping auf der Basis unklarer Benutzerkonzepte auch eine Methode zum 'dirty programming' sein kann. Bei der Diskussion von Prototyping-Ansätzen müssen insbesondere auch die Probleme berücksichtigt werden, die bei Interessenkonflikten zwischen verschiedenen Benutzergruppen entstehen können [Ken84]. Tingley behandelt in seinem Beitrag [Tin84] zudem die Schwierigkeiten bei der Entwicklung von Systemen mittels Prototyping, die die Qualität des Arbeitsplatzes des Endbenutzers negativ beeinflussen.

Einige Autoren [Flo84, Rid84] empfehlen deshalb die Integration des Prototyping in geeignete Entwicklungsstrategien oder Life-Cycle-Methoden. Dieser Vorschlag wurde von uns aufgegriffen, da die konzeptuelle Modellierung mit Petri-Netzen aufgrund ihres formalen Charakters eine geeignete Basis zum Prototyping bildet.

IV.1 Motivation eines dualen Prototyping-Ansatzes

Um das im Rahmen einer Life-Cycle-Methode entwickelte konzeptuelle Schema eines Informationssystems unter Einsatz eines Prototyping-Werkzeuges testen zu können, bietet sich zunächst die folgende Vorgehensweise an: das konzeptuelle Schema wird als Eingabe eines Prototyp-Generators zur Erzeugung der Programmodule und der Meta-datenbank des zu entwickelnden Systems verwendet. Diese Vorgehensweise bezeichnet man üblicherweise als *Transformationsansatz*.

Bruno und Marchetto beschreiben in [BrM86] die Transformation von sogenannten PROT-Netzen, einer speziellen Modifikation der Petri-Netze, in ADA-Programmstrukturen, die die Basis des System-Prototyps bilden. In [BeU86] wird die Übersetzung einer Spezifikation abstrakter Datentypen in ein ausführbares Programm dargestellt. Hierzu werden eine Reihe von Transformationsregeln angegeben. Feather [Fea82] beschreibt die Umformung einer GIST-Spezifikation in eine Implementation, die durch Eingabe von Testdaten das Verhalten des spezifizierten Systems widerspiegelt. Es müssen hierzu für alle GIST-Konstrukte entsprechende Abbildungen (mappings) existieren.

Der Transformationsansatz hat für den Systementwickler einige wichtige Vorteile. Es ist für ihn nach der rechnergestützten Generierung jederzeit möglich, den Prototyp mit Hilfe konventioneller Werkzeuge zur Programmentwicklung (Editor, Compiler, Linker, Debugger, Library Manager) zu modifizieren bzw. zu bearbeiten. Es können beispielsweise bereits vorhandene Objektmodule aus Bibliotheken durch Aufruf und Binden problemlos im Prototyp integriert werden. In einer dem Systementwickler vertrauten Weise können so alle Möglichkeiten der Implementationssprache und des Datenbanksystems genutzt werden. Der erstellte Prototyp kann hierbei auch zum Ziel-system fortentwickelt werden.

Im Rahmen einer Diplomarbeit [Lan85] wurde ein solcher Ansatz für die Entwicklungsumgebung *INCOME* getestet. Hierbei tauchten jedoch einige grundlegende Probleme auf, die die Suche nach alternativen Vorgehensweisen erforderlich machten. Vor allem in den frühen Phasen der Softwareentwicklung muß die Spezifikation des Systems – und somit auch der entsprechende Prototyp – noch häufig geändert werden. Solche Änderungen gestalten sich sehr aufwendig, da zunächst der Quellcode des Systems modifiziert und meistens sogar völlig neu erstellt werden muß. Anschließend wird der Quellcode compiliert und das ganze System neu gebunden. Es ist außerdem recht schwierig, den Prototyp und die Spezifikation in einem konsistenten Zustand zu erhalten, falls konventionelle Werkzeuge zur Modifikation des Prototyps eingesetzt werden. Entweder muß der Prototyp nach jedem Einsatz eines solchen Werkzeuges auf Änderungen untersucht werden oder diese Werkzeuge müssen so konzipiert sein, daß alle Änderungen an das Prototyping-Werkzeug gemeldet werden. Beide Vorgehensweisen können jedoch während der konzeptuellen Modellierung eines Systems nicht als be-friedigend angesehen werden. Hierbei spricht gegen die erste Vorgehensweise vor allem der zeitliche Aufwand für Änderungen des Prototyps, während bei der zweiten Vorgehensweise der erhebliche Aufwand zur Entwicklung und Wartung solcher Werkzeuge beachtet werden muß.

Es ist deshalb ein Werkzeug wünschenswert, das die bereits vorliegende Spezifikation *interpretativ ausführt* und somit die Simulation des zu entwickelnden Systems ermöglicht. Dies hat den Vorteil, daß Änderungen des Prototyps direkt in der Spezifikation durchgeführt und somit bei der nächsten Ausführung sofort berücksichtigt werden können. Die Konsistenz der Spezifikation wird hierbei durch die Verwendung der entsprechenden Spezifikationswerkzeuge der *INCOME* Toolbox gewährleistet.

In der Literatur findet man einige Arbeiten, die sich mit der direkten Ausführung oder Interpretation von Spezifikationen beschäftigen. Zumeist werden dabei jedoch nur Teilaspekte des zu entwickelnden Systems berücksichtigt. Wasserman schlägt die Definition und Interpretation von Transitionsdiagrammen zur Simulation der Benutzerschnittstelle eines Systems vor, wobei die volle Funktionalität des Systems durch Aufruf und Ausführung von in verschiedenen Programmiersprachen implementierten Modulen erreicht wird [WPS86]. In [UUD85] werden mit der Spezifikationssprache DESCARTES zunächst die Beziehungen zwischen Ein und Ausgabedaten eines Programmes dargestellt. Die Spezifikation beschreibt also nicht, wie die Ausgabedaten aus den Eingabedaten ermittelt werden, sondern nur aus welchen Eingabedaten dies geschieht. Es ist somit lediglich eine abstrakte Ausführung der Spezifikationen möglich. McCoyd und Mitchell beschreiben in [McM82] die ereignisgesteuerte interpretative Ausführung einer Spezifikation, die in der Sprache PSLAIR1 vorliegt. Der Schwerpunkt liegt dabei auf einer Überprüfung des Systemverhaltens als Folge von Ereignissen und Prozessen.

Ansätze, die sowohl eine interpretative Ausführung als auch eine Transformation der Spezifikation ermöglichen, werden in [BlH82, Fea82] vorgeschlagen. Blum und Houghton [BlH82] regen den Einsatz eines Applikations- und Programm-Generators zum Prototyping an. Der Applikations-Generator ist ein interpretativ arbeitendes System, das in eine spezielle Entwicklungsumgebung eingebettet ist, während der Programm-Generator Programme erzeugt, die in andere Umgebungen portiert und von anderen Tools bearbeitet werden können. Für die Spezifikationssprache GIST wird in [CSB82] die Möglichkeit der direkten symbolischen Ausführung beschrieben. GIST wird zur Beschreibung des gewünschten (funktionalen) Verhaltens eines Systems als Menge von Objekten und möglichen Verknüpfungen zwischen diesen Objekten eingesetzt. Die Darstellung dieser Objekte an der Benutzerschnittstelle wird nicht spezifiziert. Die symbolische Ausführung hat zur Folge, daß das System nicht für konkrete Eingaben, sondern jeweils für bestimmte Klassen von Eingaben getestet wird. Zusätzlich wird für GIST in [Fea82] die Konvertierung der Spezifikation in eine entsprechende Implementation erläutert. Diese Implementation bietet, vor allem bezüglich ihres Laufzeitverhaltens, einige Vorteile beim Testen der Spezifikation.

Für die Entwicklungsumgebung *INCOME* wird ein solcher *dualer Ansatz* zum Prototyping verfolgt, der eine *transformatorische* und eine *interpretative* Vorgehensweise kombiniert. Während der Entwurfsphasen wird das konzeptuelle Schema wiederholt mit Hilfe der interpretativen Prototyping-Komponente getestet. Erst wenn der konzeptuelle Entwurfsprozeß beendet ist, wird über die Transformationskomponente die Spezifikation in Programmodule und eine Metadatenbank umgesetzt. Der in dieser Arbeit verfolgte Prototyping-Ansatz weist im Vergleich zu den bereits vorgestellten Ansätzen einige Besonderheiten auf: Prototyping wird nicht erst beim implementationsnahen Systementwurf sondern bereits im Rahmen des konzeptuellen Entwurfs eingesetzt. Hierbei können sämtliche Aspekte der konzeptuellen Modellierung - Datenstrukturen, Systemabläufe, Transaktionen - berücksichtigt werden. Die Konzeption sieht Prototyping vor allem auch bei unvollständigen Schemata vor, wobei Ergebnisse des Prototyping in nachfolgenden Entwurfsschritten verwendet werden können. Im Rahmen des Prototyping ist zudem bereits der Entwurf einer adäquaten Benutzer-schnittstelle möglich, für die eine Spezifikation generiert wird, die Basis der späteren Implementation sein kann. Über die Transformationskomponente ist die Kombination mit Applikationsgeneratoren und die Verwendung von Very High Level Languages möglich.

IV.2 Architektur des Prototyping-Werkzeuges RAPPROT

Die Architektur des Prototyping-Werkzeuges *RAPPROT*, das diesen Ansatz unterstützt, ist in Abbildung 7 dargestellt. *RAPPROT* ist integraler Bestandteil der Entwicklungsumgebung *INCOME* und verwendet als Datenbasis die zentrale Entwurfsdaten-bank.

IV.2.1 Allgemeiner Aufbau

Wie Abbildung 7 zeigt, besteht *RAPPROT* aus den Komponenten Interpretations- und Transformationssystem, den Schnittstellen zur Benutzer- und Datenbankebene sowie dem erstellten Applikationssystem.

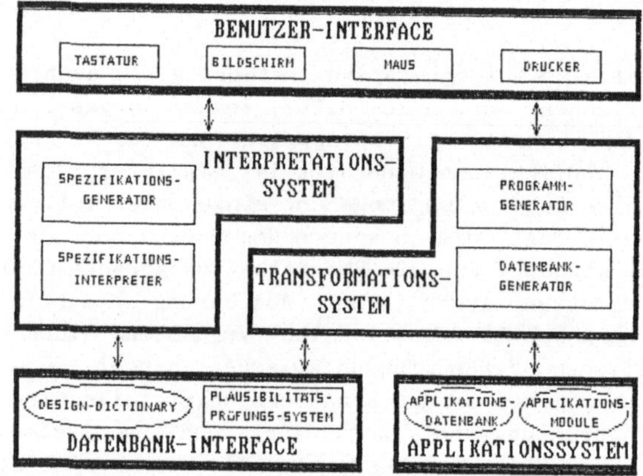

<u>Abbildung 7</u>: Architektur des Prototyping-Werkzeugs *RAPPROT*

Das *Interpretationssystem* wird für die Generierung der Benutzerschnittstelle, die Erweiterung unvollständiger konzeptueller Schemata sowie zur direkten Ausführung dieses Schemas unter Berücksichtigung aller Modellierungsaspekte verwendet. Es benötigt keine Übersetzungs- und Bindevorgänge, hat jedoch den Nachteil, daß kein Quellcode der Applikation erstellt wird.

Für diese Aufgabe steht das *Transformationssystem* zur Verfügung. Es besteht aus einem Programm-Generator, der die Programmodule eines spezifizierten Systemaus-schnitts generiert sowie aus dem Datenbank-Generator, der das Data-Dictionary der Applikation mit Informationen zur externen, logischen und internen Datenbank-Struktur erstellt. Das Transformationssystem wird üblicherweise erst nach Abschluß der konzeptuellen Modellierung eingesetzt, nachdem unter Verwendung des Interpretationssystems bereits mit einigen Prototypen gearbeitet wurde.

Über das Transformationssystem erfolgt die Konfigurierung des Prototyping-Tools für verschiedene Zielumgebungen. Das bedeutet, daß beim Wechsel der Zielumgebung des zu entwickelnden Systems oder bei der Entwicklung von Subsystemen für verschiedene Zielumgebungen nicht das gesamte Tool, sondern nur diese Komponente ausgetauscht bzw. modifiziert werden muß.

Da bei der Anwendung des Werkzeuges Entscheidungsprozesse erforderlich sind, die für den Designer transparent dargestellt werden müssen, werden hohe Anforderungen an die *Benutzerschnittstelle* gestellt. Außerdem muß die Benutzerführung sowohl den Anforderungen eines erfahrenen Systementwicklers als auch – vor allem im Rahmen des Spezifikationsinterpreters – denen des Endbenutzers der Applikation genügen. Bei der Implementation der Schnittstelle wird deshalb auf den Einsatz von grafischen Hilfsmitteln und Fenstertechniken großen Wert gelegt.

Eine wichtige Eigenschaft des Tools ist die Kontrolle von Erstellung und Ausführung des Prototyps über die Entwurfsdatenbank, das sogenannte Design-Dictionary. Diese Datenbank enthält neben den Informationen zum konzeptuellen Schema auch die Spezifikation der Benutzerschnittstelle der Applikation, die mit dem Spezifikationsgenerator erstellt wird. Alle Komponenten weisen eine einheitlich ausgelegte *Datenbankschnittstelle* auf. Das Plausibilitätsprüfungs-System gewährleistet dabei, unter Anwendung des Prinzips der Datenkapselung für die Manipulationsoperationen, die Konsistenz der Entwicklungsdaten (siehe hierzu auch [LMN87]).

Im folgenden werden nun die beiden Komponenten Interpretations- und Transformationssystem näher beschrieben.

IV.3.2 Das Interpretationssystem

IV.3.2.1 Aufbau des Interpretationssystems

Abbildung 8 illustriert den Aufbau und die Arbeitsweise des Interpretationssystems.

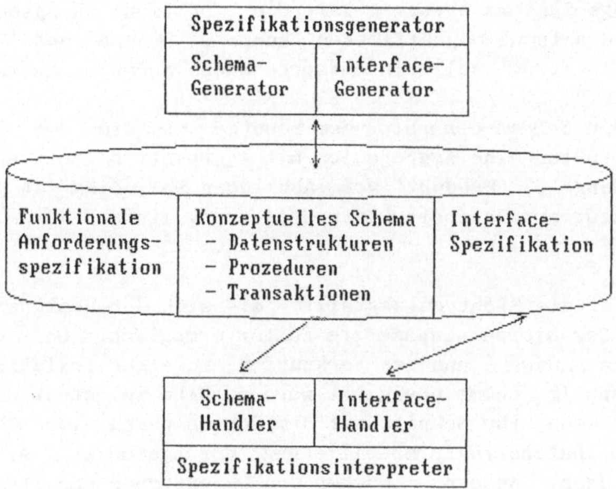

Abbildung 8: Aufbau des Interpretationssystems

Es besteht aus einem Spezifikationsgenerator und einem Spezifikationsinterpreter. Der *Spezifikationsgenerator* erzeugt aus bereits vorhandenen Informationen der Entwurfsdatenbank zusätzliche, zur Ausführung notwendige Teile der Spezifikation des Systems. Es ist somit gewährleistet, daß *RAPPROT* auch dann eingesetzt werden kann, wenn einzelne Phasen der konzeptuellen Modellierung noch nicht abgeschlossen sind.

Der Generator wird zur interaktiven Definition der Benutzerschnittstelle (Menüs, Formulare, Felder) eingesetzt. Diese Definition enthält neben *statischen* (Layout der Formulare und Menüs, Beziehungen der Schnittstellenobjekte zum konzeptuellen Schema) auch *dynamische* Elemente. So können für Felder in Formularen Aktionen spezifiziert werden, die zur Interpretationszeit ausgeführt werden. Der Spezifikationsgenerator gewährleistet die Konsistenz zwischen Schnittstellendefinition und konzeptuellem Schema. Detaillierte Informationen bezüglich dieser Schnittstellendefinition finden sich in Kapitel V.

Der *Spezifikationsinterpreter* ermöglicht die direkte Ausführung der Spezifikation, wobei alle Aspekte der konzeptuellen Modellierung berücksichtigt werden. Die Mensch/Maschine-Interaktion wird über die mit dem Spezifikationsgenerator erstellte Benutzerschnittstelle abgewickelt, deren Layout zum Interpretationszeitpunkt manipuliert werden kann. Für alle strukturellen Änderungen der Benutzerschnittstelle, die das konzeptuelle Schema nicht verändern, wird der Interpreter verlassen und der Spezifikationsgenerator aufgerufen. Alle Manipulationen, die den Ablauf des Prototyps, die zugrundeliegende globale Datenstruktur oder aber die Transaktionsebene betreffen, können nur mit den entsprechenden *INCOME*-Konstruktionswerkzeugen durchgeführt werden, die die Konsistenz des konzeptuellen Schemas sichern.

Die Arbeitsweise der beschriebenen Komponenten soll nun anhand kleiner Beispiele erläutert werden.

(a) Spezifikationsgenerator

In der Entwurfsdatenbank liege nur die funktionale Anforderungsspezifikation eines Auftragsbearbeitungs-Systems vor. Für die Funktion 'Eingeben-Auftrag' ·(siehe Abbildung 9a) mit den Input-Objektflüssen 'Kunde', 'Menge' und 'Produkt' sowie dem Output-Objektfluß 'Auftrag' soll ein entsprechendes Formular definiert werden.

Hierzu schlägt der *Schema-Generator* dem Benutzer als die dem Formular zugrundeliegende Sichtenstruktur eine Aggregation mit Aggregattyp 'Auftrag' und Komponententypen 'Kunde', 'Menge', 'Produkt' vor (Abbildung 9b). Dies ist derselbe Vorschlag, den auch das Werkzeug zur Datenstrukturmodellierung liefern würde.

In Abbildung 9c ist die Sicht dargestellt, die sich der Designer daraus interaktiv erstellen wird. Der hierzu eingesetzte Editor ermöglicht bei vorhandenem Datenstrukturschema die Auswahl und das Verknüpfen einzelner Teilstrukturen aus diesem Schema. Hierzu kann im Schema navigiert werden. Neue Teilstrukturen dürfen nur dann eingefügt werden, wenn ihr Schnitt mit dem Schema genau einen Objekttyp aufweist. Wurde noch keine Datenstrukturmodellierung durchgeführt, sind alle denkbaren Operationen – Einfügen, Ändern, Löschen von Objekttypen und Strukturen – zulässig. Die Sicht wird vom Schema-Generator im Design-Dictionary abgelegt. Detaillierte Informationen zum Sichtenentwurf finden sich in [NSM87].

Für die dargestellte Sicht bildet der *Interface-Generator* ein Formular, indem er alle elementaren Objekttypen (Quellen des Datenstrukturschemas), die über Aggregationen mit einer Senke der Sicht verknüpft sind, mit ihrem Bezeichner und einem Wertefeld in das Formular einträgt. Für Gruppierungen werden Tabellen vorgesehen, in deren Kopfzeilen die Bezeichner der entsprechenden Elementtypen stehen. Gegebenenfalls werden auch geschachtelte Tabellen erstellt. Der Designer wird nun das Layout des vorgeschlagenen Formulars überarbeiten. Außerdem hat er noch die Möglichkeit, zusätzliche lokale Felder, Aktionen für alle Felder sowie Darstellungattribute zu definieren (im Detail siehe Kapitel V). Das Ergebnis dieses Schrittes zeigt die Abbildung 9d. Zu dem dargestellten Formular erstellt der Interface-Generator automatisch eine entsprechende Spezifikation (siehe Kapitel V) und legt diese in der Entwurfsdatenbank ab. Die Spezifikation enthält jedoch nur solche Informationen, die zum Interpretations- oder Transformationszeitpunkt nicht aus dem konzeptuellen Schema abgeleitet werden können.

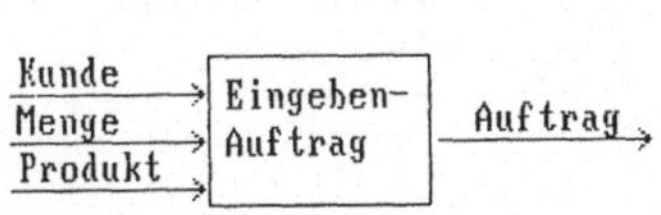

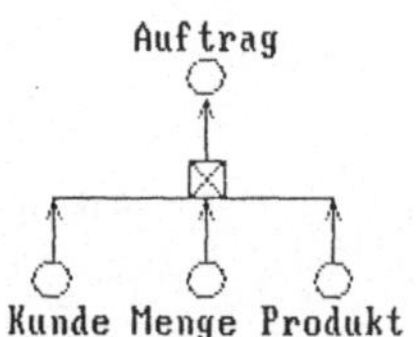

(a) Funktion 'Eingeben-Auftrag' der Anforderungsspezifikation

(b) Vorschlag des Schema-Generators

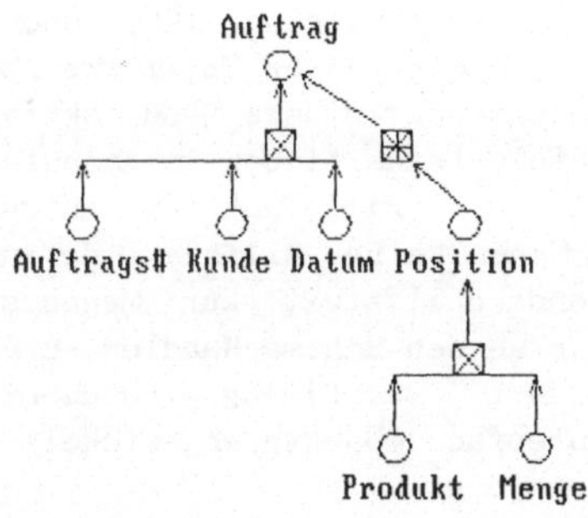

(c) Definition der Sicht durch den Designer

(d) Definition eines Formulars mit dem Interface-Generator

<u>Abbildung 9</u>: Arbeitsweise des Spezifikationsgenerators

(b) <u>Spezifikationsinterpreter</u>

Die Arbeitsweise des Spezifikationsinterpreters soll am Beispiel einer Menüauswahl gezeigt werden. In der Entwurfsdatenbank ist der in Abbildung 10a dargestellte Ausschnitt eines Ablaufschemas abgelegt. Vom Kunden gehen Aufträge und Anfragen ein, die unter dem Gattungsbegriff 'Kunden-Nachricht' zusammengefaßt werden können. Zur Interpretation eines Ablaufschemas werden die Transitionen durch die entsprechenden Verfeinerungen aus dem Transaktionsschema ersetzt. Das Prädikat 'Kunden-Nachricht' sei eine Quelle des Ablaufschemas. Der Benutzer hat nun zum Interpretationszeitpunkt die Möglichkeit, dieses Prädikat mit Marken zu belegen. Hat der Benutzer eine Marke im Prädikat 'Kunden-Nachricht' abgelegt, versucht der *Schema-Handler* eine schaltfähige Transition zu bestimmen. In unserem Beispiel findet er die beiden Transitionen 'Eingeben-Auftrag' und 'Bearbeiten-Anfrage', so daß der Benutzer entscheiden muß, welche dieser Transitionen geschaltet werden soll.

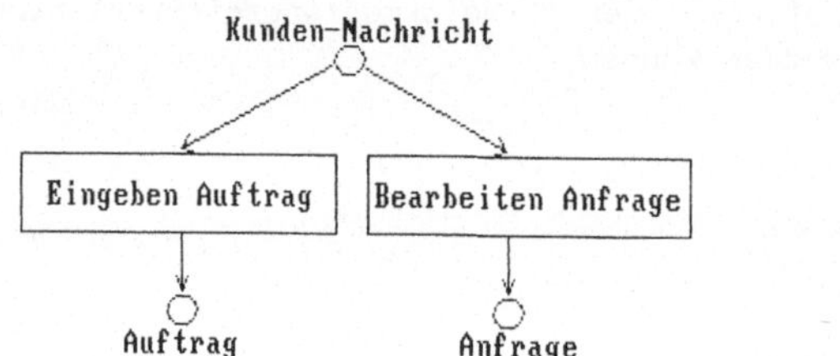

(a) Ausschnitt des Ablaufschemas

(b) Menü zur Auswahl der weiteren Schaltfolge

<u>Abbildung 10</u>: Arbeitsweise des Spezifikationsinterpreters

Mit dem Interface-Generator wurde zum Generierungszeitpunkt bereits ein Menü für die vorliegende Markierung des Ablaufschemas erzeugt (siehe Abbildung 10b) und eine entsprechende Spezifikation in der Entwurfsdatenbank abgelegt. Der *Interface-Handler* wird nun vom Schema-Handler zur Abwicklung des Dialogs über dieses Menü aktiviert. Der Benutzer hat neben der Auswahl der beiden Nachfolgetransitionen im Ablaufschema (Funktionstasten F1 bzw. F2) noch die Möglichkeit, die Hilfefunktion aufzurufen (F9). Hat der Benutzer bei der Spezifikation des Menüs keinen Hilfstext definiert, so erscheint bei Aufruf der Hilfefunktion ein Standardhilfstext zur Menüauswahl. Die Auswahl des Benutzers wird vom Interface-Handler an den Schema-Handler zurückgemeldet, der nun die entsprechende Schaltfolge ausführt. Der Dialog wird dabei über die mit den schaltenden Transitionen verbundenen Interface-Objekte abgewickelt (z.B. Ein- und Ausgabe von Werten in Feldern von Formularen).

IV.3.3 Das Transformationssystem

Den Aufbau und die Arbeitsweise des Transformationssystems veranschaulicht Abbildung 11. Dies kann jedoch nur in sehr allgemeiner Form geschehen, da dieser Aufbau im Detail, abhängig von der Zielumgebung, stark variieren kann. Als Zielumgebung beschränken wir uns im Rahmen unserer Entwicklungsarbeit auf eine Personal-Computer-Umgebung, in der als Betriebssystem MS-DOS und als Datenbanksystem INOVIS-X86 (vormals DATENBANK-PASCAL) [Kar84] zur Verfügung steht.

Beim Aufruf des Transformationssystems muß spezifiziert werden, welcher Ausschnitt der Entwurfsdatenbank bearbeitet werden soll. Dies ist deshalb notwendig, da für Subsysteme eventuell mehrere verschiedene Zielumgebungen gefordert sein können.

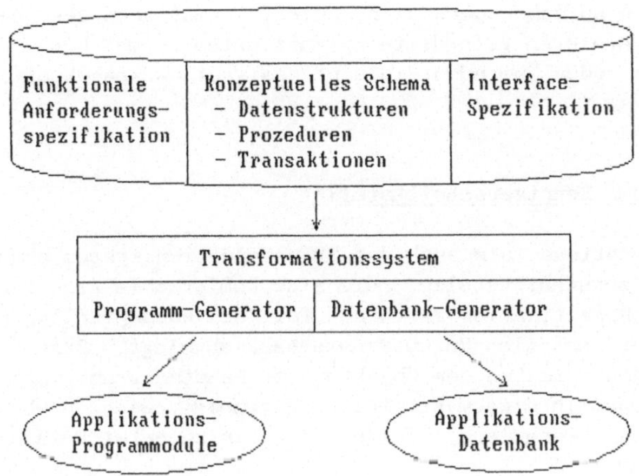

<u>Abbildung 11</u>: Aufbau des Transformationssystems

Der *Programm-Generator* erstellt aus der vorliegenden Spezifikation eine Reihe von Programmodulen im Quellcode. Die Modularisierung wird dabei interaktiv auf der Basis eines Rechnervorschlags vorgenommen. Der Generator enthält Tools zum Übersetzen und Binden des Systems. Er ermöglicht außerdem die Auswahl bereits vorhandener Module aus Bibliotheken und die Integration dieser Module in der Applikation. Die Auswahl der Module wird derzeit vom Benutzer anhand von Bibliotheksverzeichnissen weitgehend manuell durchgeführt. In einer zukünftigen Implementation ist eine geeignete Spezifikation der Module vorgesehen, die es ermöglicht, ihre Auswahl rechnergestützt durchzuführen.

Mit dem *Datenbank-Generator* wird aus den Informationen der Entwurfsdatenbank ein Data-Dictionary der Applikation abgeleitet, welches Informationen zur externen, logischen und internen Datenbankstruktur enthält. Falls die Möglichkeit zum Führen eines solchen Data-Dictionaries in der Zielumgebung nicht gegeben ist, müssen die entsprechenden Informationen über den Programm-Generator im Quellcode berücksichtigt werden.

Die beiden Komponenten des Transformationssystems stellen eine Umgebung zum Einsatz von Werkzeugen bereit, die für die Zielumgebung zur Verfügung stehen. Werden mit diesen Werkzeugen (z.B. Editor, Compiler, Linker, Debugger) Änderungen am Applikationssystem durchgeführt, kann die Konsistenz mit dem Design-Dictionary nicht mehr automatisch gewährleistet werden. Möglichkeiten zur Beseitigung dieses Problems wurden bereits in Kapitel IV.1 diskutiert.

Falls neben *RAPPROT* für die Zielumgebung bereits Applikationsgeneratoren zur Verfügung stehen (z.B. DMS [IBM80a], ADF [IBM80b]) oder Very High Level Languages (z.B. NATURAL [MöS84], INOVIS-X86 [Kar84]) verwendet werden, kann das Transformationssystem die Aufgabe übernehmen, die Informationen des Design-Dictionaries in das von den Generatoren geforderte Entwurfsdaten-Format bzw. in Konstrukte der Programmiersprachen oder zumindest in eine geeignete aussagekräftige Dokumentation umzusetzen.

V. Spezifikation der Benutzerschnittstelle

Sowohl das Interpretations- als auch das Transformationssystem benötigen eine Spezifikation der Benutzerschnittstelle, die eine komfortable Arbeit mit dem Prototyp ermöglicht. Diese Spezifikation ist nicht Teil des konzeptuellen Schemas, wird aber wie dieses in der zentralen Entwurfsdatenbank abgelegt. Zusätzlich enthält die Datenbank Beziehungen zwischen den Objekten der Benutzerschnittstelle und Teilen des konzeptuellen Schemas. In diesem Kapitel wird gezeigt, wie die Objekte der Benutzerschnittstelle (Menüs, Formulare, Felder) für ein zu entwickelndes System spezifiziert werden können.

Ähnliche Vorgehensweisen finden sich praktisch bei sämtlichen Applikationsgeneratoren und Very High Level Languages. Hierbei werden jedoch die Interface-Objekte nicht auf der Basis eines konzeptuellen Schemas, sondern frei durch den Benutzer definiert. Die Spezifikation wird dabei zumeist direkt im Data-Dictionary des zugrundeliegenden Datenbanksystems abgelegt und kann nur von den dazugehörigen Treibern verwendet werden. Die Definition von Interface-Objekten wird auch bei den Ansätzen zum Prototyping praktiziert, in denen Prototypen über Szenarien als Folge von Bildschirmseiten erstellt werden (siehe z.B. ACT/1 [MaC83], ELECTRONIC FORM SYSTEM [Geh82]).

Um *RAPPROT* als Prototyping-Werkzeug für unterschiedliche Zielumgebungen einsetzen zu können, ist es notwendig, die Spezifikation in einer implementationsunabhängigen Form in der Entwurfsdatenbank abzulegen. Es wurde hierzu die Sprache *RAPPROT-ISL* definiert, die nachfolgend beschrieben wird. Die Syntax der Sprache muß vom Designer nicht erlernt werden, da er die Spezifikation interaktiv mit dem Interface-Generator erstellen kann, der für den überwiegenden Teil der notwendigen Eingaben Pop-Up-Menüs und Defaultwerte anbietet. Selbstverständlich besteht aber für den erfahrenen Systementwickler auch die Möglichkeit, diese Spezifikation direkt über einen Texteditor zu erfassen. Zu beachten ist hierbei, daß RAPPROT-ISL nicht zur vollständigen Spezifikation der Benutzerschnittstelle, sondern nur zur Definition einzelner Objekte dieser Schnittstelle verwendet werden kann. Die vollständige Spezifikation ist erst gegeben durch die Verknüpfung der Objekte untereinander und mit Teilen des konzeptuellen Schemas. Diese Verknüpfungen werden bei der interaktiven Generierung von RAPPROT-ISL Spezifikationen im Design-Dictionary aufgebaut. Die erstellte Schnittstellenspezifikation dient der Interpretation durch den Interface-Handler sowie als Eingabe des Programm-Generators bei der Ableitung einer Applikation.

Der Endbenutzer arbeitet an der Schnittstelle mit Ausprägungen eines *Interface-Objekttyps*, die in drei Gruppen gegliedert werden können: Formulare, Menüs und Felder. Unter einem *Formular* verstehen wir nicht nur die Repräsentation eines bestimmten Ausschnitts der Datenbasis (Maske), sondern auch die Darstellung mehrerer gleichartiger Tupel (Report). Über ein *Menü* wird der Benutzer vom System zu einer Entscheidung aufgefordert, indem ihm verschiedene Auswahlmöglichkeiten angeboten werden. Ein Formular ist aus mehreren *Feldern* aufgebaut, die zur Ein- und Ausgabe variabler Daten verwendet werden. Außerdem kann ein Formular auch konstante Datenfelder und Textinformationen enthalten.

Nachfolgend wird die Struktur des Interface-Objekttyps anhand der Abbildung 12 erläutert. Zur Darstellung der Struktur wird das zur Datenstrukturmodellierung eingesetzte semantisch-hierarchische Datenmodell verwendet.

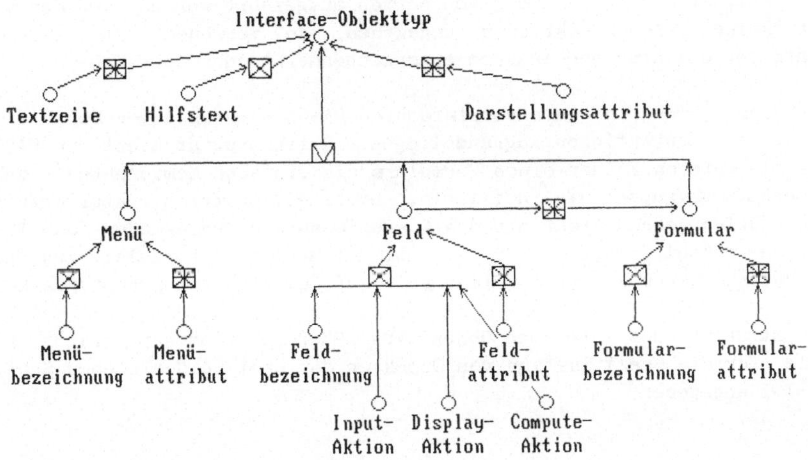

Abbildung 12: Struktur des Interface-Objekttyps

Für alle Ausprägungen des Interface-Objekttyps wird eine Menge von *Darstellungsattributen* angegeben. Es handelt sich dabei zum Beispiel um die Größe des belegten Bereichs am Bildschirm oder um Informationen darüber, ob ein Rahmen gezeichnet oder der Bildschirm gelöscht werden soll. Außerdem ist es möglich, *Textzeilen* mit entsprechender Positionierung und Darstellungsform zu definieren. Ebenso ist für jedes Objekt die Angabe eines *Hilfstextes* vorgesehen, der in einem spezifizierten Fenster angezeigt werden kann.

Zu jedem der Interface-Objekte wird eine *Bezeichnung* definiert. Über diese Bezeichnung können die Menüs und Formulare identifiziert werden, während die Felder über ihre Bezeichnung und über die Beziehung zu einem Formular identifiziert werden. Eine genauere Spezifikation der Objekte erfolgt jeweils über eine Menge von Attributen. Für Menüs und Formulare werden zur Steuerung der Verarbeitung durch die Interpretations- und Transformationskomponente ein Typ sowie das Ein- und Ausgabemedium angegeben.

Bei den Feldern werden lokale und globale Felder unterschieden. Nur *globale Felder* stehen unmittelbar zu einem Attribut einer, aus dem konzeptuellen Datenstrukturschema abgeleiteten (siehe [NSM87]), Relation der Prototypdatenbank in Beziehung. *Lokale Felder* werden nicht in der Datenbank abgelegt; ihr Geltungsbereich wird über die Beziehung zu einem Formular spezifiziert, während dessen Bearbeitung die Felder definiert sind. Sie werden häufig zur Anzeige von aus anderen Feldern errechneten Zusatzinformationen oder zur Eingabe von Werten verwendet, die zur Ermittlung von Defaultwerten globaler Felder benötigt werden. Man unterscheidet außerdem *konstante Felder*, die nicht verändert werden können, und *variable Felder*, deren Werte zur Ausführungzeit variieren können. Außerdem können für Felder z. B. Wertebereiche (bei globalen Feldern müssen dies Teilmengen der entsprechenden globalen Wertebereiche sein), Bearbeitungsrestriktionen (Ein-, Ausgabe-, berechnetes Feld) oder feste Defaultwerte angegeben werden.

Für die Felder von Formularen ist die Definition von *Aktionen* vorgesehen, die bei Eingabe, Ausgabe oder Berechnung von Werten ausgeführt werden. Wurden vom Designer explizit keine solchen Aktionen angegeben, so verwendet die Interpretations-komponente für die Ein- und Ausgabe entsprechende Standardroutinen.

Die Aktionen werden in einer vereinfachten PASCAL-Syntax angegeben (siehe hierzu Anhang B). Als den Aktionen zugrundeliegende Datenstruktur dient ein PASCAL-Record, der die elementaren Felder eines Formulars als einfache Komponenten enthält sowie die Wiederholungsgruppen als indizierte, eventuell weiter strukturierte Felder. Die Aktionen dürfen jedoch nicht mit den Operationen und Bedingungen des Transaktions-schemas verwechselt werden, da sie nur auf der dem Formular zugrundeliegenden lokalen Datenstruktur arbeiten, nicht aber auf der globalen Prototypdatenbank.

Um die Struktur des Interface-Objekttyps näher zu erläutern, sind in Anhang A Beispiele für die Spezifikation von Objekten der drei verschiedenen Subtypen in der RAPPROT-ISL angegeben.

VI. Zusammenfassung und Ausblick

In der vorliegenden Arbeit wurden die Grundlagen des rechnergestützten Arbeits-platzes *INCOME* skizziert, der eine Methode zur konzeptuellen Modellierung mit Petri-Netzen unterstützt. Im konzeptuellen Schema werden dabei sowohl statische (Daten-strukturen) als auch dynamische Aspekte (Prozeduren, Transaktionen) des zu entwickelnden Systems beschrieben.

Um das formale Beschreibungsverfahren auch dem Endbenutzer zugänglich zu machen, enthält *INCOME* als integralen Bestandteil die Prototyping-Komponente *RAPPROT*, die zur interpretativen Ausführung des konzeptuellen Schemas und damit zur Simulation des zu entwickelnden Systems verwendet wird. Die Konzeption dieser Komponente wurde beschrieben. *RAPPROT* kann während aller Entwurfsphasen eingesetzt werden und berücksichtigt sämtliche Aspekte der konzeptuellen Modellierung. Für den Prototyp kann außerdem eine komfortable Benutzerschnittstelle spezifiziert werden, über die zur Ausführungszeit die Mensch/Maschine-Interaktion abgewickelt wird. Als Übergang zur Implementationsphase der Applikation enthält *RAPPROT* zusätzlich eine Komponente, die die Spezifikation in Programmodule und eine Metadatenbank transformiert. Der Einsatz des Prototyping-Werkzeuges trägt damit entscheidend bei zur Verbesserung der Qualität des konzeptuellen Schemas sowie zu dessen Verwertung beim eigentlichen Systementwurf bzw. bei der Implementation.

Die im Rahmen des *INCOME*-Projektes bereits implementierten Werkzeuge zur funktionalen Anforderungsspezifikation sowie zum konzeptuellen Datenstrukturentwurf werden derzeit anhand praktischer Fallstudien getestet. Darüberhinaus wurden als Teile des Prototyping-Werkzeues die Komponenten Interface-Generator und Interface-Handler sowie ein Datenbank-Generator realisert.

Schwerpunkte zukünftiger Arbeiten werden die Berücksichtigung der im Verhaltensschema spezifizierten Zeitrestriktionen beim Prototyping sowie eine eingehende Behandlung der Konsistenzproblematik zwischen konzeptuellem Schema und erstelltem Prototyp während des gesamten Entwurfsprozesses sein. Ziel ist es, die bisher nur eingeschränkt vorhandene Möglichkeit zum manipulativen Eingriff im konzeptuellen Schema zum Interpretationszeitpunkt zu erweitern.

VII. Literaturverzeichnis

[AnL85]   Antonellis, De V., und Leva, Di A. DATAID-1: A database design methodology. *Inform. Systems 10*, 2 (1985), 181 - 195.

[BaK86]   Bancilhon, F., und Khoshafian, S. A calculus for complex objects. In *Proc. Fifth ACM SIGACT-SIGMOD Symp. on Principles of Database Systems* (Cambridge, Mass., March 24-26). ACM, 1986, 53 - 59.

[BaP85]   Barbic, F., und Pernici, B. Time modeling in office information systems, *ACM SIGMOD RECORD 14*, 4 (1985), 51-62.

[BeU86]   Belkhouche, B., und Urban J.E. Direct implementation of abstract data types from abstract specifications. *IEEE Trans. Softw. Eng. SE-12*, 5 (May 1986), 649-661.

[BKM84]   Budde, R., Kuhlenkamp, K., Mathiassen, L., und Züllighoven, H., Eds. *Approaches to Prototyping.* Springer-Verlag, Berlin, Heidelberg, 1984.

[BlH82]   Blum, B.I., und Houghton R.C. Rapid prototyping of information management systems. *ACM Softw. Eng. Notes 7*, 5 (Dec. 1982), 35-38.

[BrM86]   Bruno, G., and Marchetto, G. Process-translatable Petri nets for the rapid prototyping of process control systems. *IEEE Trans. Softw. Eng. SE-12*, 2 (Febr. 1986), 346-357.

[BrR84]   Brodie, M.L., und Ridjanovic, D. On the design und specification of database transactions. In *On Conceptual Modelling. Perspectives from Artificial Intelligence, Databases, and Programming Languages*, M.L. Brodie, J. Mylopoulos, und J.W. Schmidt, Eds. Springer-Verlag, New York, 1984.

[CSB82]   Cohen, D., Swartout, W., und Balzer R. Using symbolic execution to characterize behavior. *ACM Softw. Eng. Notes 7*, 5 (Dec. 1982), 25-32.

[DeM78]   De Marco, T. *Structured Analysis and System Specification.* Yourdon Press, New York, 1978.

[Fea82]   Feather, M.S. Mappings for rapid prototyping. *ACM Softw. Eng. Notes 7*, 5 (Dec. 1982), 17-24.

[Flo84]   Floyd, C. A systematic look at prototyping. In *Approaches to Prototyping*, R. Budde, K. Kuhlenkamp, L. Mathiassen, und H. Züllighoven, Eds. Springer-Verlag, Berlin, Heidelberg, 1984.

[FuN86]   Furtado, A.L., und Neuhold, E.J. *Formal Techniques for Data Base Design.* Springer-Verlag, Berlin, Heidelberg, 1986.

[GaS79]   Gane, C., und Sarson, T. *Structured Systems Analysis: Tools and Techniques.* Prentice-Hall, Englewood Cliffs, NJ, 1979.

[Geh82]   Gehani, N.H. A study in prototyping. *ACM Softw. Eng. Notes 7*, 5 (Dec. 1982), 71-74.

[GeL81]   Genrich, H.J., und Lautenbach, K. System modelling with high-level petri nets. *Theoretical Computer Science*, 13 (1981), 109 - 136.

[Gib85]   Gibbs, S.J. Conceptual modelling and office information systems. In *Office Automation - Concepts and Tools*, D.C. Tsichritzis, Ed. Springer-Verlag, New York, 1985.

[Gri82]   Griethuysen, J.J. Ed. Concepts and Terminology for the Conceptual Schema and the Information Base, Report of the ISO/TC97/SC5/WG3, Publication No. ISO/TC97/SC5 - N 695, March 1982.

[HHK77]   Hammer, M., Howe, W.G., Kruskal, V.J., und Wladowsky, I. A very high level programming language for data processing applications. *Communications of the ACM 20*, 11 (Nov. 1977), 832–840.

[IBM80a]   IBM. Dvelopment Management System/Customer Information Control System/ Virtual Storage: General Information Manual. IBM Manual No. GH20-2195-2, IBM, White Plains, NY, 1980.

[IBM80b]   IBM. IMS Application Development Facility, General Information Manual, IBM Manual No. GB21-9869-1, IBM, White Plains, NY, 1980.

[Jör84]   Jörgensen, A.H. On the psychology of prototyping. In *Approaches to Prototyping*, R. Budde, K. Kuhlenkamp, L. Mathiassen, und H. Züllighoven, Eds. Springer-Verlag, Berlin, Heidelberg, 1984.

[Kar84]   Karszt, J. DATENBANK-PASCAL: Ein ausbaubares Datenbanksystem nach einem ER-Modell für Personal-Computer-Anwendungen. Dissertation, Univ. Karlsruhe, 1984.

[Ken84]   Kensing, F. Property determination by prototyping. In *Approaches to Prototyping*, R. Budde, K. Kuhlenkamp, L. Mathiassen, und H. Züllighoven, Eds. Springer-Verlag, Berlin, Heidelberg, 1984.

[KPM85]   Kerner, H., Pitrik, R., Motschnig, H., und Trattnig W. EDDA-S, eine graphische, strukturierte Datenflußsprache für den Software-Entwurf. In *GI/OCG/ÖGI-Jahrestagung Wien 1985, Informatik Fachbericht 108*, H.R. Hansen, Ed. Springer-Verlag, Berlin, Heidelberg, 1985.

[KrS81]   Krämer, B., und Schmidt H.W. Interaktive Softwareentwicklung durch schrittweise Formalisierung. In *Software-Engineering – Entwurf und Spezifikation*, C. Floyd, und H. Kopetz, Eds. B.G. Teubner, Stuttgart, 1981.

[Lan85]   Lange, J. INCOME – Rapid Prototyping zur Überprüfung und Weiterentwicklung von funktionalen Anforderungsspezifikationen. Diplomarbeit Univ. Karlsruhe, 1985.

[LaS87]   Lausen, G., und Schek, J.: Semantic Specification of Complex Objects. In *Proceedings of IEEE-CS Symposium on Office Automation*, Gaithersburg, USA 1987.

[LMN87]   Lausen, G., Müller, H., Németh, T., Oberweis, A., Schönthaler, F., und Stucky, W. Integritätssicherung für die datenbankgestützte Software- Produktionsumgebung INCOME, In *Proceedings BTW87 Darmstadt*, Springer- Verlag Berlin, Heidelberg 1987.

[LOS85]   Lausen, G., Oberweis, A., und Schönthaler, F. Formale Beschreibung von Anforderungen: Eine netzorientierte Vorgehensweise zur konzeptuellen Modellierung von Informationssystemen. In *GI/OCG/ÖGI-Jahrestagung Wien 1985, Informatik Fachbericht 108*, H.R. Hansen, Ed. Springer-Verlag, Berlin, Heidelberg, 1985.

[Lun82]   Lundeberg, M. The ISAC approach to specification of information systems. In *Information Systems Design Methodologies: A Comparative Review*, T.W. Olle, H.G. Sol, und A.A. Verrijn-Stuart, Eds. North-Holland Publ. Comp., 1982.

[MaC83]   Mason, R.E.A., und Carey, T.T. Prototyping interactive information systems. *Communications of the ACM 26*, 5, (May 1983), 347–354.

[McM82]   McCoyd, G.C., und Mitchell, J.R.. System sketching: the generation of rapid prototypes for transaction based systems. *ACM Softw. Eng. Notes 7*, 5 (Dec. 1982), 127–132.

[MöS84]   Mönckemeyer, M., und Spitta, T. Concept and experiences of prototyping in a software-engineering-environment with NATURAL. In *Approaches to Prototyping*, R. Budde, K. Kuhlenkamp, L. Mathiassen, und H. Züllighoven, Eds. Springer-Verlag, Berlin, Heidelberg, 1984.

[NSM87]   Németh, T., Schönthaler, F., Müller, H., und Stucky, W. INCOME: Von der funktionalen Anforderungsspezifikation zur Prototypdatenbank – Ein methodischer Ansatz. In *Proceedings der GI-Fachtagung Requirements Engineering RE '87* (St. Augustin, Germany, May 20–22). 1987, to appear.

[ObL86]   Oberweis, A., und Lausen, G. Temporal aspects in office information systems. In *Proc. IFIP TC-8 Working Conference – Office Systems: Methods and Tools* (Pisa, Italy, Oct. 22–24). IFIP, 1986.

[OSL86]   Oberweis, A., Schönthaler, F., Lausen, G., und Stucky, W. Net based conceptual modelling and rapid prototyping with INCOME. In *Proc. of the 3rd Conference on Software Engineering* (Versailles, France, May 27–30). A.F.C.E.T., Paris, France, 1986, pp. 165–176.

[OST83]   Olle, T.W., und Tully, C.J., Eds. *Information Systems Design Methodologies: a Feature Analysis.* North-Holland Publ. Comp., 1983.

[OSV82]   Olle, T.W., Sol, H.G., und Verrijn-Stuart, A.A., Eds. *Information Systems Design Methodologies: a Comparative Review.* North-Holland Publ., 1982.

[Rei85]   Reisig, W. Systementwurf mit Netzen, Springer-Verlag, Berlin, Heidelberg, 1985.

[Ric85]   Richter, G. Clocks and their use for time modeling. In *Information Systems: Theoretical and Formal Aspects*, A. Sernadas, J. Bubenko jr., und A. Olive, Eds. IFIP, 1985.

[RiD82]   Richter, G., und Durchholz, R. IML-inscribed high-level petri nets. In *Information Systems Design Methodologies: A Comparative Review*, T.W. Olle, H.G. Sol, und A.A. Verrijn-Stuart, Eds. North-Holland Publ. Comp., 1982.

[Rid84]   Riddle, W.E. Advancing the state of the art in software system prototyping. In *Approaches to Prototyping*, R. Budde, K. Kuhlenkamp, L. Mathiassen, und H. Züllighoven, Eds. Springer-Verlag, Berlin, Heidelberg, 1984.

[Ros77]   Ross, D.T. Structured analysis (SA): a language for communicating ideas. *IEEE Trans. Softw. Eng. SE-3*, 1 (Jan. 1977), 16–34.

[Sch84]   Schönthaler, F. Problemanalyse und konzeptueller Datenbankentwurf der Schroff S.A.R.L., Betschdorf. Studien- und Diplomarbeit, Univ. Karlsruhe, 1984.

[SmS77]   Smith, J.M., und Smith, D.C.P. Database abstractions: aggregation and generalization. *ACM Trans. Database Syst. 2*, 2 (1977), 105–133.

[SoK85]   Solvberg, A., und Kung, C.H. On structural and behavioural modelling of reality. In *Database Semantics (DS-1)*, T.B. Steel, und R. Meersman, Eds. North-Holland Publ. Comp., 1985.

[StH85]   Studer, R., und Horndasch, A. Modeling static and dynamic aspects of information systems. In *Database Semantics (DS-1)*, T.B. Steel, und R. Meersman, Eds. North-Holland Publ. Comp., 1985.

[Tin84]   Tingley, G.A. Comments on [Jör84]. In *Approaches to Prototyping*, R. Budde, K. Kuhlenkamp, L. Mathiassen, und H. Züllighoven, Eds. Springer-Verlag, Berlin, Heidelberg, 1984.

[UUD85]   Urban, S.D., Urban, J.E., und Dominick, W.D. Utilizing an executable specification language for an information system. *IEEE Trans. Softw. Eng. SE-11*, 7 (July 1985), 598–605.

[War86]   Ward, P.T. The transformation schema: an extension of the data flow diagram to represent control and timing. *IEEE Trans. Softw. Eng. SE-12*, 2 (Febr. 1986), 198–210.

[WPS86]   Wassermann, A.I., Pircher, P.A., und Shewmake, D.T. Building reliable interactive information systems. *IEEE Trans. Softw. Eng. SE-12*, 1 (Jan. 1986), 147–156.

Anhang A: Beispiele für die Spezifikation von Interface-Objekten

(a) Spezifikation eines Menüs

Die Abbildung 13 zeigt die Spezifikation des Menüs 'Auftragsbearbeitung' der Abbildung 10b.

Für dieses Interface-Objekt wird der Typ 'Funkey' (function key) angegeben und als Eingabemedium die Tastatur. Die Auswahl muß somit durch Drücken von Funktionstasten erfolgen. Das Menü belegt am Bildschirm den durch die linke obere Ecke (1, 1) und die rechte untere Ecke (27, 7) angegebenen Bereich. Das Attributbyte 32 bezeichnet die Hintergrundfarbe. Es wird ein Rahmen gezeichnet (FRAME = 15); der nicht vom Menü belegte Bereich des Bildschirms wird nicht gelöscht, und der überschriebene Bereich wird nach Verlassen des Menüs wieder am Bildschirm angezeigt (ERASE = No). Der Text wird zeilenweise unter Angabe der Anfangsposition und des Attributbytes für die Bildschirmdarstellung angegeben. Der Hilfstext wird zusammen mit dem durch ihn belegten Bildschirmbereich definiert.

```
INTERFACE_OBJECT Auftragsbearbeitung;

    SPECBEGIN

        MENUE =
           TYPE = Funkey;
           MEDIUM = Keyboard;

        ATTRIBUTES =
           AREA = ( 1, 1, 27, 7, 32 );
           ERASE = No;
           FRAME = 15;

        TEXT =
           LINE = ( 5, 1, 112, 'Auftragsbearbeitung');
           LINE = ( 3, 3,   7, 'F1   Eingeben Auftrag');
           LINE = ( 3, 4,   7, 'F2   Bearbeiten Anfrage');
           LINE = ( 3, 5,   7, 'F9   Hilfe');

        HELP =
           AREA = ( 14, 6, 32, 10, 32 );
           FRAME = 15;
           @ Drücken Sie bitte
             die gewünschte
             Funktionstaste ! @;

    SPECEND;
```

Abbildung 13: Spezifikation eines Menüs

(b) **<u>Spezifikation eines Formulars</u>**

Die Abbildung 14 zeigt die Spezifikation des Formulars aus Abbildung 9d, das als Maske am Bildschirm dargestellt wird. Zu bemerken ist dabei, daß die Formularfelder mit den zugehörigen Textzeilen und Hilfstexten gesondert spezifiziert werden (siehe Abbildung 15). Die Beziehungen zwischen dem Formular und den darin enthaltenen Feldern werden bei der interaktiven Spezifikation der Interface-Objekte vom Interface-Generator automatisch aufgebaut und in der Entwurfsdatenbank abgelegt.

```
INTERFACE_OBJECT Eingeben-Auftrag;

   SPECBEGIN

      FORM =
         TYPE = Mask;
         MEDIUM = Screen;

      ATTRIBUTES =
         AREA = ( 1, 1, 36, 12, 32 );
         ERASE = Yes;
         FRAME = 15;

      TEXT =
         LINE = ( 11, 1, 112, 'Eingeben-Auftrag');
         LINE = ( 3, 8, 7, '----------------------------------');

   SPECEND;
```

<u>Abbildung 14</u>: Spezifikation eines Formulars

(c) **Spezifikation eines Feldes**

Die Spezifikation eines Feldes wird am Beispiel des Feldes 'Kunde' im Formular 'Eingeben-Auftrag' dargestellt (siehe Abbildung 14). Das Feld wird als globales variables Feld vereinbart. Außerdem ist ein Bereich zulässiger Werte (DOMAIN = 1000..2000) angegeben, der eine Teilmenge des im Datenstruktur-Schema spezifizierten Wertebereichs sein muß. Das Feld darf nur zur Eingabe verwendet werden (USAGE = Input); der Defaultwert bei der Eingabe ist 1000 (DEFAULT = 1000); die Werte werden rechtsbündig angezeigt (JUSTIFIED = Right).

Neben der Spezifikation der Darstellungsattribute, der Textzeile und des Hilfstextes ist noch eine Aktion angegeben, die zur Eingabe von Werten im Feld 'Kunde' ausge-führt wird. Hierfür wird eine vereinfachte PASCAL-Syntax verwendet.

```
INTERFACE_OBJECT Kunde;

   SPECBEGIN

      FIELD =
         TYPE = Global, Variable;
         DOMAIN = 1000 .. 2000;
         USAGE = Input;
         JUSTIFIED = Right;
         DEFAULT = 1000;
         ACTION (INPUT) =
            ACTBEGIN
               read (Kunde);
               IF Kunde = 1000 THEN
                  BEGIN
                     Produkt [1] := 'Interne Verrechnung';
                     Menge   [1] := 1;
                     write (Produkt [1], Menge [1])
                  END
            ACTEND;

      ATTRIBUTES =
         AREA = ( 13, 5, 34, 5, 32 );

      TEXT =
         LINE = ( 3, 5, 7, 'Kunde');

      HELP =
         AREA = ( 15, 4, 31, 7, 32 );
         FRAME = 15;
         @ Identifikation
           des Kunden @;

   SPECEND;
```

Abbildung 15: Spezifikation eines Feldes

Eine Prototyp-Entwicklung auf der Basis eines relationalen DBMS

Wolfgang Hesse, Softlab GmbH, München

Inhalt:

Zusammenfassung

1   Einleitung

2   Prototyping: Ziele, Vorgehensweisen, Werkzeugauswahl

3   Prototyp-Entwicklung auf relationaler Basis

4   Die Anwendung: Depotverwaltung im Wertpapiergeschäft

5   Konzeption und Realisierung des Prototyps

6   Bewertung und Schlußfolgerungen

Literatur

Zusammenfassung

"Prototyping auf der Basis eines relationalen Datenbanksystems" war der Gegenstand eines Projekts, das Softlab in Zusammenarbeit mit der Firma ORACLE kürz-
lich durchgeführt hat. Es hatte zum Ziel, an einem Anwendungsbeispiel die Vor
gehensweise des "prototyping" praktisch zu erproben, dabei ein Prototyp-
Entwicklungswerkzeug einzusetzen und auf seine Verwendbarkeit hin zu untersuchen sowie Folgerungen daraus für eine künftige methodische Vorgehensweise
und die dafür benötigte Werkzeugunterstützung zu ziehen. Als Anwendungsbeispiel diente die Depotverwaltung von Wertpapieren bei Banken.

Der Artikel beleuchtet die durchgeführte Prototyp-Entwicklung unter vier
Aspekten:

- Grundsätzliches zum Thema "Prototyping" (Ziele, Vorgehensweisen, Hilfsmittel, ..)

- Bedeutung des relationalen Ansatzes für das Prototyping

- Definition, Entwurf und Realisierung des Prototyps "Depotverwaltung"

- Erfahrungen aus der Prototyp-Entwicklung und Schlußfolgerungen

1   Einleitung

"**Rapid prototyping**" ist eines der neueren Schlagworte in der Softwaretechnik,
dem es wie vielen neuen Ideen und einigen seiner Vorgänger ergangen ist: Zunächst lieferte es einen Denkanstoß dafür, bis dahin als unverrückbar aner-
kannte methodische Grundsätze in Frage zu stellen und dabei besonders die
Struktur des "software life cycle" neu zu überdenken. Sodann folgte eine Phase
der Euphorie, in der man mit dieser neuen Idee nun endlich das Zaubermittel
zur Lösung vieler Probleme gefunden zu haben glaubte. Diese mußte dann nahezu
zwangsläufig einer gewissen Ernüchterung weichen, als sich nämlich zeigte, daß
der erhoffte Zauber ausblieb und daß auch dieser neue Ansatz seine Grenzen
hat.

In diesem Beitrag möchte ich von Erfahrungen berichten, die wir mit einem
Prototyp-Entwicklungswerkzeug zu einem Zeitpunkt gemacht haben, als die
"Prototyping-Fieberkurve" ihre weitesten Ausschläge (Euphorie bzw. Ent-
täuschung) bereits hinter sich hatte und man sich dem Thema "prototyping"
wieder ganz unbefangen nähern konnte.

Bei dem Projekt, von dem ich berichten möchte, ging es uns darum,

- an einem Anwendungsbeispiel die **Vorgehensweise** des "prototyping" praktisch
  zu erproben und mit den bekannten Verfahren der "konventionellen" Softwaretechnik zu vergleichen,

- ein **Prototyp-Entwicklungswerkzeug** einzusetzen und auf seine Verwendbarkeit,
  seine Stärken und Schwächen hin zu untersuchen,

- herauszufinden, ob und wenn ja für welche **Anwendungen** "prototyping" eine
  geeignete Vorgehensweise ist und welche Art von Werkzeugen für welche
  Aufgaben einsetzbar sind bzw. noch benötigt werden.

Das zu wählende **Anwendungsbeispiel** sollte aus der Welt der kommerziellen
Informationssysteme stammen und sowohl von der Thematik als auch vom Umfang
her für eine Kundendemonstration geeignet sein. Wir entschieden uns daher für
die Depotverwaltung von Wertpapieren (genauer: Aktien) bei Banken. Dazu ist
anzumerken, daß diese Anwendung für uns reinen Demonstrationscharakter hat und
daß es uns nicht um spezielle inhaltliche Aspekte der Anwendung ging.

Die praktische Verwendbarkeit des "prototyping"-Ansatzes steht und fällt mit
der **Werkzeugunterstützung**. Es hat sich eingebürgert, hier von "Werkzeugen der
vierten bzw. fünften Generation" zu sprechen (wobei die ersten drei Generationen der "konventionellen" Programmentwicklung zugerechnet werden). Gemeinsam ist den Sprachmitteln der beiden "fortgeschrittenen" Generationen das
"sehr hohe" Niveau ("very high level"). Durch den Vorzug deskriptiver Be-
schreibungsformen vor prozeduralen versucht man sich besser an die natürliche
Denk- und Ausdrucksweise der Anwendungs-Programmierer oder gar der Endbenutzer
anzupassen. Werkzeuge der sogenannten vierten Generation sind datenbasiert,
arbeiten also in der Regel auf der Basis eines Datenbanksystems, während
Werkzeuge der fünften Generation wissensbasiert (d.h. auf der Grundlage von
"Fakten" und "Regeln") arbeiten.

Unser Ziel war es (und hat letztlich auch die Auswahl des Anwendungsbeispiels
mitbestimmt), Prototyping auf der Basis eines Datenbanksystems durchzuführen.
Hierfür bietet sich aus verschiedenen, unten näher erläuterten Gründen der
relationale Ansatz (vgl. /COD 70/) vorrangig an. Bei den verfügbaren Werkzeugen fiel unsere Wahl auf das System ORACLE des gleichnamigen Herstellers.

Dabei ging es uns aber mehr darum, die Vorzüge und Grenzen von relationalen Systemen für das Prototyping allgemein zu ergründen als spezifische Erkenntnisse über das ORACLE-System zu gewinnen (wenngleich diese natürlich als Nebenprodukt mit abfielen).

Bei der näheren Beschäftigung mit dem Thema "Prototyping" und bei der Entwicklung unseres Prototyps stellte sich unter anderem heraus, daß

- Prototypen unter sehr unterschiedlichen Zielsetzungen entwickelt werden können, die entsprechend unterschiedliche Vorgehensweisen und Hilfsmittel erfordern, daß es also **kein universelles Prototyp-Entwicklungswerkzeug** geben kann,

- Prototyping keineswegs bedeutet, alle erlernten Grundsätze der Softwaretechnik über Bord zu werfen, sondern daß sich vielmehr eine Synthese zwischen beiden Ansätzen finden läßt, ja sogar, daß **"methodisches prototyping"** nach sehr ähnlichen Mustern verläuft wie herkömmmliche Software Entwicklung,

- der relationale Ansatz in recht eleganter Weise die Umsetzung eines logischen Datenmodells in einen lauffähigen Prototyp unterstützt,

- es problematisch ist, erfahrenen Anwendungsprogrammierern und (DV-technisch "unbedarften") Endbenutzern das gleiche Werkzeug anzubieten.

In den folgenden Abschnitten soll die vorliegende Prototyp-Entwicklung unter vier Aspekten beleuchtet werden:

1) Was **bedeutet** "Prototyping", welche Zielsetzungen erfordern welche Vorgehensweisen und welche Hilfsmittel (Abschnitt 2)

2) Der **relationale** Datenbank-Ansatz und seine Bedeutung für das Prototyping (Abschnitt 3)

3) **Bericht** über Definition, Entwurf und Realisierung des Prototyps "Depotverwaltung" (Abschnitte 4 und 5)

4) **Erfahrungen** aus der Prototyp-Entwicklung und Schlußfolgerungen (Abschnitt 6).

2   Prototyping: Ziele, Vorgehensweisen, Werkzeugauswahl

Was versteht man unter "prototyping" ?

Der Begriff des "Prototyps" ist uns aus der Fertigungsindustrie wohl bekannt als vorwegegenommene Einzelanfertigung eines (möglichen) Endprodukts, an dem man bestimmte Eigenschaften studieren will, ehe man in die Massenproduktion geht. Bei der Software-Entwicklung, wo Massenproduktion nicht diese Rolle spielt, versteht man darunter einen Teil eines SW-Systems oder -Bausteins, an dem man bestimmte Eigenschaften des zu entwickelnden Systems bzw. Bausteins untersuchen will.

Mit der Idee, Software prototypisch zu entwickeln, versucht man, gewisse Schwierigkeiten im Umgang mit dem klassischen "software life cycle" zu überwinden. Mögliche Ursachen für solche Schwierigkeiten können z. B. sein:

- der lange **Zeitraum** zwischen der Aufgaben-Definition für ein Softwaresystem im sog. "Pflichtenheft" und der ersten laufenden Systemversion,

- zu geringe **Einflußmöglichkeiten** der oder des Auftraggeber(s) auf den Ent- wicklungsprozeß nach der Abnahme des Pflichtenhefts,

- fehlende oder unzureichende **Einbindung der Benutzer** in den Entwicklungs- zyklus,

- fehlende oder unzureichende Möglichkeiten zur **Anpassung** an sich ändernde **Anforderungen** in einem dynamischen, sich kontinuierlich weiterentwickelnden Systemumfeld.

Dazu kommt die gestiegene Bedeutung der **frühen Projektphasen** (Analyse und Definition) und das Bedürfnis, ihnen einen entsprechend größeres Gewicht zu verleihen. Dies ist Gegenstand des sogenannten "Requirements Engineering", d.h. der systematischen Ermittlung, Festlegung und Bewertung von **System-An- forderungen**. Bei kommerziellen Informationssystemen spielt hier die **Informa- tionsbedarfs-Ermittlung** und **-analyse** eine besondere Rolle. Durch Prototyping können Auftraggeber und Benutzer in diese Aufgaben einbezogen werden, Anwendungsbeispiele und Lösungsmodelle können vorgeführt werden und am konkreten, greifbaren Objekt analysiert und weiterentwickelt werden.

Mögliche Zielsetzungen beim Prototyping

Aus den genannten Kritikpunkten an der herkömmlichen Vorgehensweise läßt sich eine Reihe von Zielsetzungen herleiten, die man durch ein "Prototyping"- Vorgehen möglicherweise besser erreichen könnte:

- Erforschung (neuer Funktionen, Lösungen, Techniken, ..)

- Sammlung von Erfahrungen (mit neuen Anforderungen, Lösungen, Techniken; Erkennen von Grenzen; Vermeiden von Fehlentwicklungen, ..)

- Anforderungs-Analyse und -Festlegung, Ermittlung des Informationsbedarfs

- Studie und Bewertung bestimmter System-Eigenschaften (z.B. Benutzerfreund- lichkeit)

- Vorgabe für weitere Systementwicklung (etwa als "Spezifikation")

- Schnelle Verfügbarkeit (zumindest für Teilfunktionen)

- Demonstration (z.B. der Benutzer-Schnittstelle)

- Lehre (z.B. Benutzer-Schulung)

In jedem Falle ist es das oberste Ziel beim "prototyping", mit geringem Zeit- und Personalaufwand etwas "Vorzeigbares" erstellen.

Klassifizierung von Prototyping-Methoden

Schon ein Blick auf die Liste möglicher Zielsetzungen (die sich natürlich noch ausdehnen ließe) zeigt ein keineswegs einheitliches Bild. So resultieren z.B. aus den Zielsetzungen "Erforschung" und "Vorgabe für weitere Systementwicklung" ganz unterschiedliche Anforderungen, die in der Regel auch zu ganz unterschiedlichen Prototypen führen werden.

Ch. Floyd unterscheidet 3 Klassen von "prototyping"-Ansätzen (/FLO 84/):

- **explorativ**: der Prototyp dient der Erforschung von noch unbekanntem Terrain, z.B. von System-Anforderungen, Informationswünschen, erwarteten System-Eigenschaften o.ä.

- **experimentell**: der Prototyp wird benutzt, um (für eine bereits bekannte Zielsetzung) Lösungsmöglichkeiten zu untersuchen, zu bewerten und zu vergleichen.

- **evolutionär**: der Prototyp dient als Zwischenschritt auf dem Wege zu einem sich "evolutionär" (d.h. schrittweise, in Interaktion mit seiner Umwelt) entwickelnden System.

Strategien für die Funktions-Auswahl

Da sich ein Prototyp in der Software-Entwicklung normalerweise auf ein (womöglich nur sehr kleines) Teilsystem beschränkt, ist es besonders wichtig, nach welchen Kriterien ein solches Teilsystem ausgewählt wird.

Geht man von einer Gesamtsystem-Architektur in Schichten aus, (wobei eine Schicht als umso "höher" angesehen wird, je mehr sie mit der Anwendung und je weniger sie mit dem gewählten Basissystem zu tun hat), so erstreckt sich ein Prototyp entweder auf eine oder wenige Schichten des geplanten Gesamtsystems ("horizontales prototyping") oder auf eine bestimmte Funktion oder Menge von Funktionen quer durch alle Schichten ("vertikales Prototyping", vgl. Abb. 1.) Zwischen diesen beiden grundsätzlichen Möglichkeiten gibt es natürlich Mischformen.

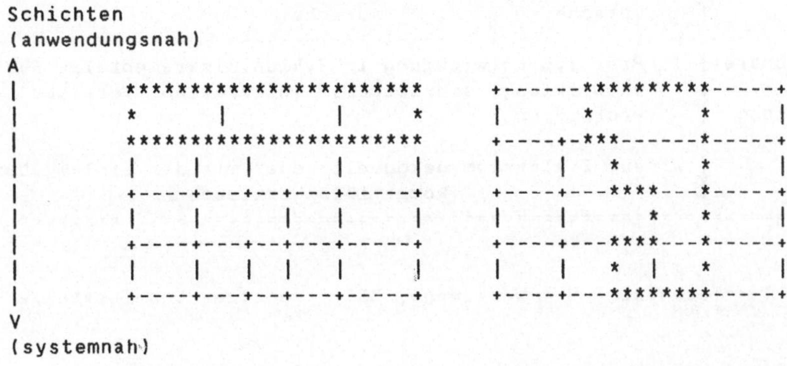

Abb. 1: Horizontales und vertikales Prototyping

Auswahl geeigneter Techniken und Werkzeuge

Die folgende Tabelle gibt einen Anhalt für die Auswahl geeigneter Prototyping-Techniken und -Werkzeuge abhängig von der Zielsetzung und dem Gegenstand für das Prototyping:

```
 +        Gegen- | Benutzer-          | Benutzer-          | (ausgewählte)       |
    +     stand | Schnittstelle      | Schnittstelle      | Funktionen          |
 Ziel    +      |                    | + Funktionen       |                     |
 ---------------+--------------------+--------------------+---------------------+
 Exploration    | T: horizontales    |T: gemischtes       |T: vertikales        |
                | Prototyping,       |   Prototyping      |   Prototyping,      |
                | Schichten-         |                    |   funktionale       |
                | Simulation         |                    |   Simulation,       |
                |                    |                    |   Skelett-Pro-      |
                |                    |                    |   grammierung       |
                |                    |                    |                     |
                | W: BSS-Entw./      |W: Integrierte      |W: DB + Zugriffs-    |
                | Simulations-       |   Werkzeuge        |   werkzeuge,        |
                | Werkzeuge          |   (DB + Zugriffe   |   PROLOG o.ä.       |
                | (Menüs, Mas-       | + BSS-Entw.)       |                     |
                | ken, windows,      |                    |                     |
                | Dialog             |                    |                     |
                |                    |                    |                     |
                | flexible, vielseitig verwendbare, anpaßbare Werkzeuge        |
                |              (zielsystem-unabhängig)                         |
 ---------------+--------------------+--------------------+---------------------+
 Experiment     | T+W: wie oben      |T+W: wie oben       |T+W: wie oben        |
                |                    |                    |                     |
                | an Zielumgebung angepaßte / angenäherte oder "real"          |
                |              simulierende Werkzeuge                          |
 ---------------+--------------------+--------------------+---------------------+
 Vorgabe für    | T: Prototyp =      | T: Prototyp =      | T: Prototyp =       |
 (Weiter-)      | BSS-Spezifi-       | BSS + funkt.       |    funktionale      |
 entwicklung    | kation             | Spezifikation      |    Spezifikation    |
                |                    |                    |                     |
                | W: BSS-Entwurfs-   | W: "ausführbare" Spezifikations-         |
                | sprache            |    sprache                               |
 ---------------+--------------------+--------------------+---------------------+
 evolutionäre   | T: Prototyp-Entwicklung in Zyklen, inkrementelle System-    |
 System-        |    entwicklung, schrittweise Integration "fertiger"         |
 entwicklung    |    Prototypen                                               |
                |                                                             |
                | W: ans Zielsystem gekoppelte oder mit der Zielumgebung       |
                |              kompatible Werkzeuge                           |
 ===============+====================+====================+=====================+
```

Legende: T = Techniken, W = Werkzeuge, BSS = Benutzer-Schnittstelle

Tab 1.: Techniken und Werkzeuge für die Prototyp-Entwicklung

3   Prototyp-Entwicklung auf relationaler Basis

Bei der Anwendung, von der hier berichtet werden soll, handelt es sich um
einen funktionalen Ausschnitt aus einer (gedachten) größeren Bankanwendung,
die etwa die Abwicklung des gesamten Wertpapiergeschäfts betreffen könnte. Die
Entwicklung einer Benutzer-Schnittstelle stand nicht im Mittelpunkt, diesbe-
zügliche Gestaltungsfragen sollten aber auch nicht gänzlich unbeachtet bleiben. Unsere Zielsetzung war primär "experimentell": Es ging uns darum, bestimmte Vorgehensweisen selbst auszuprobieren und dabei den Nutzen angebotener
Werkzeuge zu untersuchen.

Wie die obenstehende Tabelle zeigt, ist für diese Art des "gemischten" Prototypings das Arbeiten mit "echten" Daten, d.h. solchen, die wirklich funktional
verarbeitet (und nicht nur an einer Benutzer-Schnittstelle "vorgezeigt")
werden, unerläßlich. Es lag daher nahe, ein Werkzeug zur Prototypentwicklung
auf der Basis eines **Datenbanksystems** zu benutzen, um dort echte Daten halten
zu können.

Verschiedene Gründe sprachen dafür, ein **relationales** DB-System zu benutzen,
u.a. die folgenden:

- Relationale Datenbanken entsprechen in ihrem Aufbau weitgehend dem **logischen
  Datenmodell**, auf dem nach unserer Vorgehensweise die Aufgaben-Definition
  (bzw. der "funktionale Entwurf" oder das "Fachkonzept") für ein Softwaresystem aufbaut.

- Die **Datenzugriffe** sind einfach, Navigationsprobleme in der DB bleiben dem
  Prototyp-Entwickler erspart.

- **Anwendungen** lassen sich sehr schnell realisieren und ändern.

- Ein Übergang vom Prototyp zu einem **Produktionssystem** (d.h. eine Weiterentwicklung im "evolutionären" Sinne) ist zumindest dann möglich, wenn ein relationales DB-System auch für den Produktionsbetrieb zur Verfügung steht.

- Relationale DB-Systeme bieten die Möglichkeit des "aktiven", d.h. in die DB-
  Verwendung integrierten **Datenlexikons**.

Unsere Wahl fiel auf das System **ORACLE** des gleichnamigen Herstellers. ORACLE
bietet (in der von uns benutzten VAX/VMS-Version 4.3) neben dem eigentlichen
Datenbankverwaltungssystem (DBMS) und dem integrierten Datenlexikon (DD) verschiedene Werkzeuge an. Die wichtigsten sind:

IAF (Interactive application facility), bestehend aus dem

- **IAG** (Interactive application generator), einem Anwendungs-Entwicklungswerk-
  zeug,

- **FASTFORM**, einer verkürzten Fassung des IAG für die schnelle Einrichtung von
  Anwendungen in standardisierter Form sowie dem

- **IAP** (Interactive application processor), einem Werkzeug, mit dem man Anwendungsfunktionen ablaufen läßt.

UFI (User friendly interface): Dieses Werkzeug gestattet den schnellen Aufbau
von Tabellen und direkte Tabellen-Abfragen mittels SQL-Anweisungen.

Dazu kommen Report-Generatoren, Text-Formatierer, Graphik- und Dokumenten-Aufbereitungsprogramme und Programmiersprachen-Schnittstellen (z.B. zum Anschluß von C-Programmen).

Wir haben uns vorrangig mit den Werkzeugen IAF sowie UFI befaßt.

Abb. 2 gibt einen Überblick über die Arbeitsweise und Zusammenhänge der wichtigsten ORACLE-Werkzeuge.

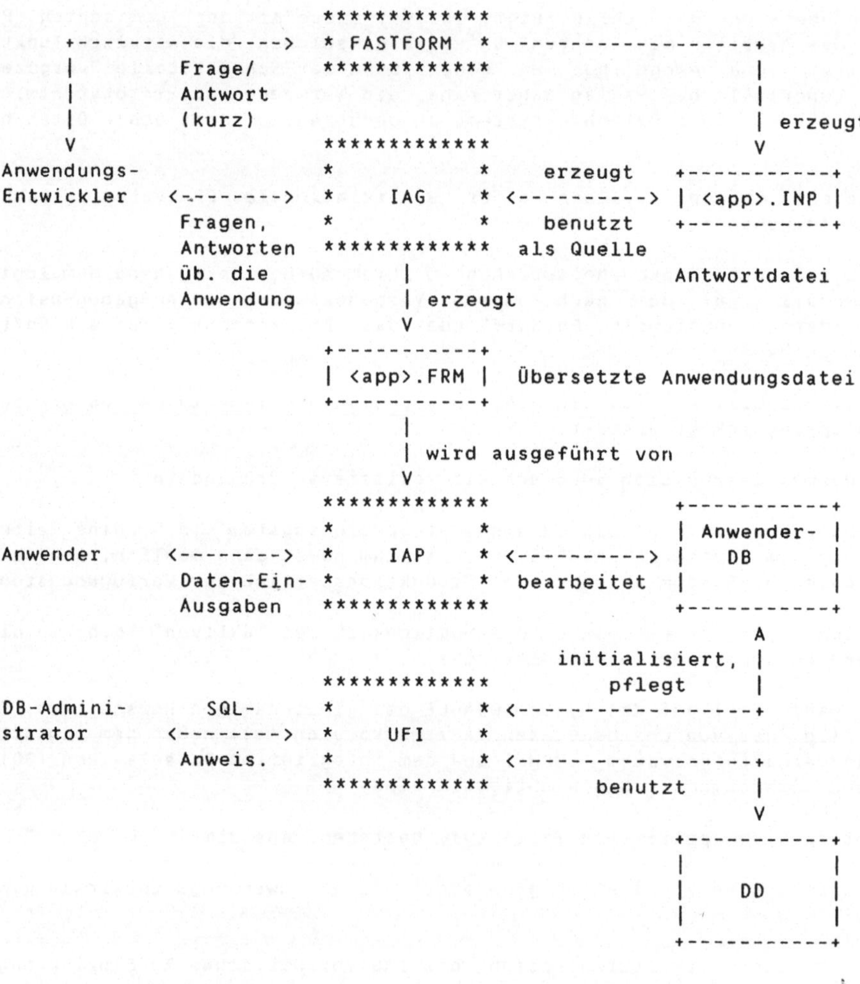

Abb. 2: Arbeitsweise der wichtigsten ORACLE-Werkzeuge

Vorgehensweise beim Prototyping

Unsere Vorgehensweise läßt sich durch den folgenden "Prototyp-Entwicklungs-zyklus" beschreiben:

- Analyse des Anwendungsgebiets

In dieser ersten Phase unterscheidet sich "Prototyping" kaum von einer "konventionellen" Systementwicklung. Da die Prototyp-Auswahl selbst von dem Ergebnis dieser Analyse abhängt, kann hier in der Regel noch kaum eine funktionale Selektion stattfinden, d.h. die Analyse bezieht sich auf das Gesamtsystem oder zumindest auf größere Teile davon. Die Analyse enthält eine Abgrenzung des Anwendungsgebiets, eine Beschreibung des **Ist-Zustands**, der **Schwachstellen** und **Wünsche** sowie ein **Soll-Konzept** für das zukünftige System. Um dessen Funktionen leichter benennen und erklären zu können, ist es zweckmäßig, schon hier ein (meist noch rudimentäres) Datenmodell einzuführen und zu benutzen.

Ein entscheidender Vorteil des "prototyping"-Anatzes liegt darin, daß man den Prototyp selbst zur (weiteren) Analyse einsetzen kann. Das heißt, in einem zweiten (und weiteren) Iterationsschritt(en) kann man dem Benutzer anhand des Prototyps mögliche Systemleistungen vorführen und gemeinsam mit ihm mögliche Erweiterungen und Alternativen ausprobieren. Diese Vorgehensweise bietet sich besonders an, wenn es darum geht, den Informationsbedarf des Anwenders zu ermitteln und die Funktionen eines Informationssystems festzulegen. Softlab setzt zur Zeit einen an anderer Stelle entwickelten Prototyp auf ORACLE-Basis für diese Aufgaben ein.

Da es sich bei unserem Projekt um ein reines Demonstrationsprojekt handelte, war diese Phase am wenigsten "lebensnah". Wir beschränkten uns auf die Festlegung des Anwendungsgebiets und eine grobe Abgrenzung des zu behandelnden Funktionsumfangs. Bei einer "echten" Entwicklung, z.B. für einen Kunden, hätten hier umfangreiche Abstimmprozesse mit Vertretern des Kunden, namentlich den potentiellen Systembenutzern gestanden.

- Prototyp-Definition:

Diese umfaßt die Funktionsauswahl für den Prototyp, d.h. damit wird die funktionale Einschränkung des Prototyps gegenüber dem Gesamtsystem festgelegt. Von hier ab beziehen sich die Entwicklungsschritte nur noch auf den Prototyp, nicht mehr auf das gesamte System. Wie bei der "klassischen" Systementwicklung folgen die Schritte der **Funktions- und Datenmodellierung.** Für die Funktions-Beschreibungen des Prototyps wird ein Datenmodell aufgestellt, das sich zunächst auf die Beschreibung der vom Prototyp verwendeten Daten beschränken kann. Allerdings sollte das Datenmodell schon so konzipiert sein, daß es ohne Schwierigkeiten für das Gesamtsystem weiterverwendet bzw. weiterentwickelt werden kann.

- Prototyp-Spezifikation:

Oft wird an dieser Stelle ein fundamentaler Gegensatz zwischen dem "prototyping"-Ansatz und der "klassischen" Systementwicklung gesehen. Wir können diese Meinung nicht teilen. Nach unserer Einschätzung ist ein Prototyp ein Stück Software wie jedes andere und sollte daher auch spezifiziert werden. Die bekannten Gründe, die für eine Spezifikation sprechen (wie z.B. als Grundlage für funktionale und Leistungs-Analyse, Weiterentwicklung, Test, "Wartung", Benutzerdokumentation und -Schulung etc.) sind für einen Prototypp nicht weniger bedeutungsvoll als anderswo.

Selbstverständlich bezieht sich die Spezifikation zunächst nur auf den Prototyp selbst, bezüglich der Erweiterungsmöglichkeiten gilt aber das oben Gesagte sinngemäß.

- Prototyp-Konstruktion

Diese besteht in der Umsetzung der Spezifikation in maschinenverarbeitbare Form, entspricht also der herkömmlichen Programierung. Bei der Besonderheit der angebotenen Sprachen und Werkzeuge wird man hier allerdings kaum noch von "Programmierung" sprechen. Je formaler und weitgespannter die eingesetzten Sprachen und je mächtiger die Werkzeuge sind, desto mehr läßt sich dieser Schritt automatisieren.

Es folgt der Test, ggf. mit Simulation nicht realisierter Komponenten und die Einbindung des Prototyps in eine Umgebung, die entweder mit der Zielumgebung identisch ist oder diese simuliert.

- Prototyp-Bewertung

Dieses ist der entscheidende Schritt, von dem die Weiterentwicklung bzw. zukünftige Verwendung des Prototyps abhängt. Hier ist die Zusammenarbeit mit den (künftigen) Benutzern besonders wichtig: Beim praktischen Umgang mit dem vorliegenden Prototyp sind sie sehr viel leichter in der Lage, Entwurfsentscheidungen zu bewerten und ihre eigenen Vorstellungen zu entwickeln und zu artikulieren als anhand eines Stück Papiers, das das künftige System lediglich in Worten beschreibt.

In unserem speziellen Fall wurde diese Phase durch eine Bewertung der angewendeten Prototyping-Techniken und -Werkzeuge ersetzt, deren Ergebnis u.a. dieser Beitrag darstellt.

Schon an dieser Stelle können wir das Fazit ziehen, daß sich Prototyp-Entwicklung und klassische Systementwicklung (wie etwa in /HES 80/ beschrieben) keineswegs so krass voneinander unterscheiden, wie das öfters behauptet wird. Das wird durch die oben beschriebene Vorgehensweise bestätigt, an die wir uns bei unserer Entwicklung - abgesehen von den erwähnten Abweichungen - gehalten haben.

In unserem Ansatz, den wir "methodisches Prototyping" nennen möchten, sehen wir vielmehr neben den offenkundigen Unterschieden auch deutliche Analogien zum "klassischen" Systementwicklungsprozess. Der wesentliche Unterschied besteht darin, daß sich die genannten "Phasen" bzw. Tätigkeiten nicht mehr auf das Gesamtsystem, sondern nur auf einen für die Prototypentwicklung ausgewählten Teil bezieht. Mehrmaliger Durchlauf dieses Zyklus gestattet die Prototypentwicklung weiterer Teile bzw. das "evolutionäre" Ausbauen des Prototyps zu dem beabsichtigten Gesamtsystem.

4   Die Anwendung: Depotverwaltung im Wertpapiergeschäft

Die Aufgabenstellung für den hier beschriebenen Prototyp betraf die Verwaltung
und Verarbeitung von Daten über

- Kunden,

- Wertpapiere (Aktien) und deren

- Depots (Kundendepots und Sachdepots, d.h. kunden- bzw. wertpapierbezogene
  Aufstellungen des Wertpapierbestands),

- Kurse   sowie die

- Bestellungen von Aktien.

Von dem Prototypen sollten u.a. die folgenden Anwendungsfunktionen zur Verfügung gestellt werden:

- Neue Kunden aufnehmen

- Neue Depots einrichten

- Aktiendaten (Emittent, Nennwert, Dividende, ..) aufnehmen

- Bestellungen zum Kauf/Verkauf von Aktien aufnehmen

- Aktienkurse archivieren

- Gekaufte Aktien in Depot übernehmen

- Verkaufte Aktien aus Depot löschen

- Auskünfte über
  . alle Depots eines Kunden
  . alle Wertpapiere eines Sachdepots
  . alle Wertpapiere eines Kundendepots
  . Gesamtwert aller Wertpapiere eines Kunden/Kundendepots
  . Kursverlauf einer Aktie

5   Konzeption und Realisierung des Prototyps

Mit der genannten Aufgabenstellung als Ausgangspunkt waren die folgenden
hauptsächlichen Aufgaben zu erledigen:

- Entwicklung eines Datenmodells für die geplante Anwendung
- Spezifikation der Anwendungsfunktionan
- Festlegung der Prototyp-Struktur
- Realisierung des Prototyps

Nach der oben vorgeschlagenen Vorgehensweise entspricht der erste Schritt der
Prototyp-Definition, der zweite der Prototyp-Spezifikation, der dritte und
vierte der Prototyp-Konstruktion.

Selbstverständlich liefen die genannten Tätigkeiten nicht in strenger zeitlicher Folge, sondern eher miteinander verzahnt ab. Trotzdem ist es sinnvoll, sie logisch und begrifflich (und auch in der Darstellung) voneinander zu trennen. Diese zeitliche Verzahnung der Tätigkeiten ist bereits aus der "klassischen" Systementwicklung wohlbekannt, spielt aber beim Prototyping eine besondere Rolle und wird durch den begrenzten Systemumfang und die flexiblen Werkzeuge erleichtert.

Entwicklung eines Datenmodells für die geplante Anwendung

Dieser Schritt unterscheidet sich zwar im Umfang, nicht aber im Inhalt von der klassischen Datenmodellierung. Wir konnten hier auf vertrauten Begriffen und Vorgehensweisen aufbauen (vgl. dazu z.B. /VRT 82/, /F-H 84/, /HES 87/)

Zunächst waren geeignete Kandidaten für **Objekttypen** zu finden wie z. B.

- Kunde
- Wertpapier
- Depot
- Bestellung
- Kursarchiv

Objekte sind miteinander durch **Beziehungen** verknüpft. Beispiele dafür sind:

- Ein Kunde besitzt mehrere Depots (1 : n).

- Ein Wertpapier ist in mehreren Depots enthalten, ein Depot kann mehrere Wertpapiere enthalten (m : n).

- Auf ein Depot können sich mehrere Bestellungen beziehen (1 : n).

- Zu einem Wertpapier gibt es mehrere Bestellungen (1 : n).

- Ein Kunde kann mehrere Bestellungen erteilen (1 : n).

- Zu einem Wertpapier gibt es mehrere archivierte Kurse (1 : n).

Normalisierungs-Überlegungen führten uns dazu, den ursprünglichen Objekttyp "Depot" in zwei Objekttypen

- Depotverzeichnis (Zuordnung Kunde / Depot) und
- Depotinhalt (Zuordnung Depot / Wertpapier)

aufzuspalten.

Damit waren wir in der Lage, die für die Anwendung benötigten **Relationen** zu definieren (vgl. Tab. 2).

Eine graphische Darstellung der Beziehungen liefert Abb. 3:

```
+----------------------------------------------------------------------
|
| Kunde:        (Kd_Nr, Name, Vorname, Tel, Plz, Ort, Strasse)
|
| Depot_Verz: (Depot_Nr, Kd_Nr)
|
| Depot_Inh:  (Depot_Nr, Kenn_Nr, Stück)
|
| Wertpapier: (Kenn_Nr, Emittent, Nennwert, Dividende, Kurs, Datum)
|
| Kursarchiv: (Kenn_Nr, Kurs, Datum)
|
| Bestellung: (Best_Nr, Datum, Kd_Nr, Depot_Nr, Kenn_Nr, Stück, Limit)
|
+----------------------------------------------------------------------
```

Tab. 2: Relationen der Anwendung (unterstrichen: Schlüssel-Attribute)

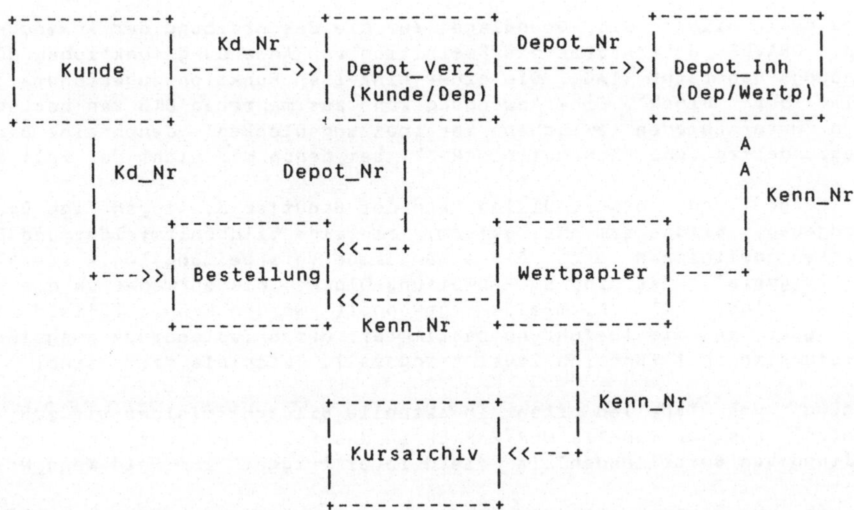

Legende: --->> 1:n-Beziehung (mit verbindendem Fremdschlüssel)

Abb. 3: Graphische Darstellung der Beziehungen

Mit Hilfe von UFI lassen sich die den Relationen entsprechenden Tabellen pe
SQl-Anweisungen direkt erzeugen. Ein Beispiel:

```
+-------------------------------------------------------------------+
| CREATE TABLE WERTPAPIER (KENN_NR    NUMBER (6),                    |
|                          EMITTENT   CHAR (30),                     |
|                          NENNWERT   NUMBER (3)                     |
|                          DIVIDENDE  NUMBER (3,2)                   |
|                          KURS       NUMBER (6,2)                   |
|                          DATUM      DATE);                         |
+-------------------------------------------------------------------+
```

INSERT-Anweisungen erlauben eine Vorbesetzung der Tabellen, wie z.B.

WERTPAPIER

```
+---------+----------------------+-------+-------+--------+------------+
| Kenn_   | Emittent             | Nenn- | Divi- | Kurs   | Datum      |
| Nr      |                      | wert  | dende |        |            |
+---------+----------------------+-------+-------+--------+------------+
| 202000  | Allianz              | 50    | 9     | 2900   | 05-JUN-86  |
| 202001  | Münchner_Rück        | 50    | 9     | 3300   | 16-MAY-86  |
| 606000  | BASF                 | 50    | 9     | 310    | 28-MAY-86  |
| 606001  | BASF ju.             | 50    | 0     | 295    | 03-Jun-86  |
| 303000  | Daimler              | 50    | 10.5  | 1215   | 16-MAY-86  |
| 404000  | Siemens              | 50    | 10    | 616    | 16-MAY-86  |
+---------+----------------------+-------+-------+--------+------------+
```

Spezifikation der Anwendungsfunktionen

Das Datenmodell bildet die Grundlage für die Beschreibung der Anwendungsfunktionen. ORACLE unterstützt die Definition von Anwendungsfunktionen durch
den Anwendungs-Generator IAG. Die einer einzelnen Funktion zugeordnete IAG-
Einheit ist der "Block". Eine Anwendung kann aus mehreren Blöcken bestehen.
Dabei wird unterschieden zwischen "Verarbeitungsblöcken", denen eine Basistabelle zugrundeliegt und "Kontrollblöcken", bei denen das nicht der Fall ist.

In einem Frage- und Antwort-Dialog kann der Benutzer die zugehörige Basistabelle angeben, Bildschirm-Anzeigeform, einzelne Bildschirmfelder und Ein-
/Ausgabemasken definieren etc. Die eigentliche Verarbeitungslogik steckt in
den sog. "triggers". Das sind SQL-Anweisungsblöcke, die entweder an die Verarbeitung einzelner Bildschirmfelder gekoppelt werden können ("field level
triggers") oder an die Ausführung bestimmter, durch Tastendruck ausgelöster
DB-Zugriffsfunktionen ("function level triggers"). Beispiele dafür sind:

- Übertragung von Tabellenwerten in aktuelle Bildschirmfelder wie z.B. den
  "Emittenten" aus der Tabelle WERTPAPIER in das Feld "Emittent" der Funktion
  "Bearbeitung von Bestellungen" (= "field level trigger" zum Feld Kenn_Nr).

- Abfrage, ob zu einem gegebenen Kunden, dessen Kundenstammdaten gelöscht
  werden sollen, noch Depots existieren. Ausgabe einer Fehlermeldung, falls
  dies der Fall ist (= "function level trigger" des Typs "PRE-DELETE" für die
  Funktion "Bearbeitung der Kundenstammdaten)

Bei der Arbeit mit dem IAG zeigte sich, daß das IAG-Dialogprotokoll als Spezifikation der Anwendungsfunktionen nicht geeignet ist. Das liegt u.a. daran,
daß

- das Dokument durch das umständliche Frage-/Antwortspiel unübersichtlich
  wird,

- der Maskenaufbau nicht im Zusammenhang, sondern nur durch Angabe einzelner
  Bildschirmpositionen dargestellt wird,

- die Zusammenhänge der Funktionen untereinander schwer erkennbar sind,

- SQL als "Spezifikationssssprache" nur bedingt geeignet ist (vgl. unten).

Blockbeschreibung:

```
+------------------------------------------------------------------+
| NAME (kurz): KUNDE1                                               |
+------------------------------------------------------------------+
| NAME (lang): Bearbeitung der Kundenstammdaten                    |
+------------------------------------------------------------------+
| Basistabelle: Kunde                                              |
+------------------------------------------------------------------+
| ERSTELLUNGSDATUM: 21.4.86                                        |
+------------------------------------------------------------------+
| ART DES BLOCKS: Verarbeitungs-Block                             |
+------------------------------------------------------------------+
| AUSLÖSER: Menu: "Bearbeitung der Kundenstammdaten"              |
+------------------------------------------------------------------+
| DURCHFÜHRUNGSBEDINGUNGEN, FREQUENZ: Benutzerfunktion zur        |
|    Kundendatenerfassung und -information                         |
+------------------------------------------------------------------+
| MASKE: KD_1                                                      |
|                                                                  |
| Anzeigeform: Multiple record                                     |
|                                                                  |
|    Feld      |key| Typ      | Länge   | Verwend. | Beschreibung   |
|    ----------+---+----------+---------+----------+--------------- |
|    Kd_Nr     | * | NUMBER   | 6       | BE       | eindeutige Nr. |
|              |   |          |         |          | eines Kunden   |
|    Name      |   | CHAR     | 30      | BE       | Nachname d.K.  |
|    Vorname   |   | CHAR     | 30      | BE       | Vorname d.K.   |
|    Tel       |   | CHAR     | 15      | BE       | Tel.-Nr. d.K.  |
|    Plz       |   | NUMBER   | 4       | BE       | Postleitzahl   |
|    Ort       |   | CHAR     | 30      | BE       | Wohnort d.K.   |
|    Straße    |   | CHAR     | 30      | BE       | Straße d.K.    |
|    (BE = Benutzer-Eingabe)                                        |
+------------------------------------------------------------------+
| VERARBEITUNG:                                                    |
|                                                                  |
| Insert:                                                          |
|    Kundennr. muß eindeutig sein                                  |
|    Kundennr. muß feste Länge (6 Ziffern) haben                   |
|    Kundennr. und Nachname müssen eingegeben werden               |
|                                                                  |
| Update:                                                          |
|    Ändern Kundennr. nicht möglich                               |
|                                                                  |
| Delete:                                                          |
|    Löschen ist nur möglich, wenn der Kunde keine Depots          |
|    und keine laufenden Bestellungen besitzt.                     |
|                                                                  |
+------------------------------------------------------------------+
| BEMERKUNGEN:                                                     |
|                                                                  |
+------------------------------------------------------------------+
```

Abb. 4: Spezifikation einer Anwendungsfunktion

(Anmerkung: Die hier benutzte Version war ORACLE VAX/VMS 4.3. Einige der angeführten Punkte sind bereits oder werden durch jüngere ORACLE-Versionen hinfällig.)

Wir verwendeten deshalb zur Spezifikation ein Muster, das in ähnlicher Form in "klassischen" Projekten schon vielfach eingesetzt wurde (vgl. Abb. 4)

Festlegung der Prototyp-Struktur

Bei dieser dritten Aufgabe spielten die Randbedingungen des von uns benutzten Werkzeugs eine noch größere Rolle als bei der vorhergehenden. Die uns zur Verfügung stehende ORACLE-Version bot lediglich die folgenden Möglichkeiten zur Strukturierung des Prototyps:

- Einstufige Menüs
- Zuordnung von Blöcken zu den Menüpositionen

Das Fehlen von Möglichkeiten zur "Modularisieruung", d.h. zur Zusammenfassung von mehreren Funktionen zu "Anwendungspaketen", um diese z.B. für mehrfachen Gebrauch zur Verfügung zu stellen, machte uns besonders zu schaffen.

So blieben als einzige Strukturierungs-Hilsmittel die Menüpositionen und die ihnen zugeordneten Blöcke, deren Zahl aus technischen Gründen auf maximal zwei pro Menüposition beschränkt bleiben mußte. Die folgende Liste der Menüpositionen spiegelt grob das Funktionsangebot des Prototyps wider:

- Bearbeitung der Kundenstammdaten
- Bearbeitung der Aktienstammdaten
- Anzeige eines Sachdepotinhaltes
- Auswertung des Kursverlaufs
- Bearbeitung der Kundendepots
- Bearbeitung eines Kundendepotinhalts
- Erfassung von Bestellungen
- Bearbeitung von Bestellungen

Auch in diesem Punkt bringen neuere ORACLE-Versionen teilweise Verbesserungen. So entfällt z.B. beim Einsatz der "Dynamic Menu Facility" die Einschränkung auf einstufige Menüs.

Realisierung des Prototyps

Die Realisierung des Prototyps lief in den folgenden Schritten ab:

- Bearbeitung der einzelnen Verarbeitungsblöcke (zunächst separat)

  pro Verarbeitungsblock:
  . Zuordnung der Basistabelle
  . Erzeugung eines Standardblocks (mit FASTFORM)
  . (iteriert:) Modifikation des Standardblocks. dabei
    .. Individuelle Bildschirmgestaltung
    .. Einbau von "triggers" ("field Level" und "function Level")

- Integration der Verarbeitungsblöcke

  . Aufbau des Menüs für die Gesamtanwendung

  . Einbau von Kontrollblöcken (die u.a. das Weiterreichen von default-Werten
    von einem Block zum nächsten ermöglichen)

  . Berücksichtigung "anwendungsübergreifender" Zusammenhänge (wie z.B. Lö-
    schung von Kunden-Stammdaten erst, nachdem der betreffende Kunden keine
    Depots mehr besitzt)

Zum Abschluß seien einige Projekt-Kenngrößen genannt: Die Anwendung umfaßte
acht Bildschirmmasken, vierzehn IAG-Blöcke (darunter 5 Kontrollblöcke) und ca.
5000 Zeilen IAG-Dialog. Der dafür geleistete Aufwand betrug ca. 10 Mannwochen
(2 Bearbeiter), wovon ca. 1/3 als Einarbeitungszeit gelten kann.

6 Bewertung und Schlußfolgerungen

Da es sich bei unserer Prototyp-Entwicklung um ein reines Demonstrationsprojekt handelte, soll an die Stelle der hier normalerweise zu erfolgenden
Auswertung und Entscheidung über die Weiterverwendung des Prototyps ein kurzes
Resummee über den von uns eingeschlagenen Weg beim Prototyping und die dabei
eingesetzten Techniken und Werkzeuge treten.

Zum Prototyping auf relationaler Basis:

Der Ansatz, eine Anwendung auf der Basis eines relationalen Datenbanksystems
zu entwickeln, erwies sich für den gewählten Anwendungsbereich als tragfähig.
Die in Abschnitt 3 genannten Argumente (für ein relationales DB-System) wurden
im großen und ganzen bestätigt. Die Einfachheit und Durchsichtigkeit der
Datenhaltung in den Tabellen ist bestechend.

Für unser Vorhaben, "gemischtes Prototyping" (vgl. Abschnitt 2) zu betreiben,
erwies sich das ORACLE-System als geeignet. Lediglich auf der Seite des Prototypings der Benutzer-Schnittstelle hätten wir uns eine größere Unterstützung
und Flexibilität gewünscht.

Zur Sprache SQL:

SQL ist eine "ideal" auf das relationale Konzept abgestimmte DB-Sprache. Ta-
bellenaufbau, relationale Operationen und direkte (unkonditionierte) DB-Opera-
tionen lassen sich mit Hilfe von SQL in einfacher und eleganter Weise formulieren.

Die Absicht, jegliche "prozeduralen" Elemente aus SQL zu verbannen und damit
einen non-prozeduralen "Programmier"stil zu erzwingen, ist als solche lobens-
wert. Jedoch sind dieser Absicht auch Sprachkonzepte zum Opfer gefallen, deren
Fehlen den Umgang mit SQL sehr erschweren und die zu sehr unnatürlichen Um-
schreibungen führen. Dazu zählen wir das Fehlen von Parameter-Mechanismen und
von Konstruktionen zur Fallunterscheidung, was sich besonders deutlich bei der
Fehlerbehandlung auswirkt. So halten wir z.B. ein if-then-else Konstrukt für
keineswegs so "prozedural", daß es die hinter SQL stehende Grundidee gestört
hätte. Bei der sog. "funktionalen" (nicht-prozeduralen !) Programmierung
spielt dieses Konstrukt sogar eine zentrale Rolle.

In diesem Zusammenhang wäre es eine Überlegung wert, ob man nicht SQL zu einer funktionalen Sprache ausbauen könnte, etwa durch die Möglichkeit, "Funktionen" als Zusammenfassung mehrerer SQL-Anweisungen, mit und ohne Parameter zu definieren und "aufzurufen". (Wohlgemerkt: als Funktionsaufruf, nicht etwa im Sinne von normalen Prozeduraufrufen mit Seiteneffekten !). Damit ließen sich auch rekursive SQL-Anfragen formulieren.

Selbstverständlich können die angesprochenen Probleme auch durch die Anbindung an eine prozedurale Programmiersprache wie PASCAL oder C gelöst werden - nur stehen dann alle prozeduralen Sprachelemente zur Verfügung (und werden natürlich auch benutzt), womit gegenüber dem konventionellen Programmierstil nichts gewonnen ist.

Eine alternative (und der klareren Struktur wegen eventuell vorzuziehende) Möglichkeit besteht darin, eine solche funktionale Sprachumgebung für SQL als eigenständige Komponente zu schaffen oder SQL mit einer vorhandenen funktionalen oder logischen Sprache zu koppeln. Möglichkeiten dazu werden z.B. in /DAD 86/ diskutiert.

Als Spezifikationssprache ist SQL aus den oben genannten Gründen nur bedingt geeignet. Modularisierungs-, Funktionsdefinitions- und Parametermechanismen (oder gleichwertige Konzepte) halten wir für eine solche Verwendung für unerläßlich.

SQL in UFI/IAF

ORACLE liefert eine vollständige SQL-Implementierung. Es erlaubt zusätzlich die Bearbeitung baumartiger Strukturen (CONNECT BY / START WITH -Konstrukt).

UFI erlaubt direkte DB-Zugriffe per SQL-Anweisungen und ist damit ein sehr bequemes und mächtiges, aber auch gefährliches Werkzeug. Es wird normalerweise dem DB-Administrator vorbehalten bleiben.

In IAF kommen SQL-Anweisungen als "field level-" und "function level-triggers" vor. Abgesehen von den oben angesprochenen Problemen, namentlich mit der Fehlerbehandlung und der Daten-Weitergabe von Block zu Block, erweist sich dieses Konzept als tragfähig.

IAF-Eigenschaften

IAF wurde mit dem Anspruch entwickelt, auch dem DV-unerfahrenen "End"benutzer die Entwicklung von Anwendungen zu ermöglichen. Auf dieser Idee beruht z.B. der IAG-Dialog. Der Umgang mit IAG zeigt,

- daß einerseits die stereotye Beantwortung eines länglichen Fragenkatalogs ermüdend ist und wohl auch dem Endbenutzer bald auf die Nerven geht,

- daß man dagegen mit FASTFORM sehr schnell und bequem Standard-Anwendungen erzeugen kann, die aber umfängliche Modifikationen erfordern und

- daß andererseits die weitere Arbeit mit dem (z.B. mit FASTFORM erstellten) Dialogprotokoll keineswegs trivial ist, sondern ein tieferes Verständnis für den Aufbau des Dialogs erfordert.

Der Entwurf der Bildschirmmasken per Positionsangaben für die einzelnen Felder war umständlich und unübersichtlich, wird aber mit dem Einsatz des "Screen-painters" jetzt besser gelöst.

Insgesamt erscheint uns das Konzept des Frage/Antwort-Dialogs für die Anwendungsentwicklung weniger gut geeignet. Es ist zu fragen, ob diese überhaupt dem Endbenutzer allein überlassen werden soll oder ob nicht gerade auf diesem Gebiet die Zusammenarbeit mit einem DV-Fachmann sinnvoller ist. Für die SQL-Einschübe ist ein solcher Fachmann sowieso schon notwendig. Dann ließe sich die Anwendung insgesamt auf einem mehr "technischen" Niveau, aber mit flexibleren und mächtigeren Mitteln beschreiben.

ORACLE geht mit seinen neuesten Versionen einen andren Weg: Hier versucht man, mit Menü- und Fenstertechnik dem Endbenutzer eine "schmackhafte" Schnittstelle zu bieten und die Sprache SQL vor ihm zu verstecken. Die Zukunft wird zeigen müssen, ob dieser Weg der erfolgreichere ist.

Die Transaktionsbehandlung ist bei IAF denkbar einfach gelöst: sie beruht auf der COMMIT-Taste. Das heißt, der Datenbank-Anwender kann per Betätigung von Funktionstasten Anfragen machen, Daten "lokal" verändern und löschen, ohne die eigentliche Datenbank zu berühren. Das geschieht erst, wenn er eine spezielle Taste ("COMMIT") betätigt. Die Folge ist eine sehr schwerfälliges Systemverhalten im Fehlerfall. Tritt ein (Bediener-) Fehler auf, der eine Zwischen-Transaktion erfordert, so ist die begonnene Transaktion erst durch ein "Roll back" abzubrechen, was dann später dazu führt, daß die bereits eingegebenen Daten nochmals eingegeben werden müssen. In der neuesten ORACLE-Version wurde die Transaktionsbehandlung grundlegend verändert.

Auf die fehlenden Strukturierungsmöglichkeiten (Modularisierung, Abstraktion, Information Hiding etc.) wurde oben bereits hingewiesen.

Zusammenfassend läßt sich sagen, daß für die hier ausgewählte Anwendung das anvisierte Ziel mit vertretbarem Aufwand (vgl. die oben genannten Kenndaten) erreicht wurde und daß sich der dabei eingeschlagene Weg (trotz der genannten Kritikpunkte) insgesamt als erfolgreich erwies. Inwieweit die eingesetzten Werkzeuge für eine wesentlich größere Anwendung und/oder für eine breitere Zielsetzung (etwa im Sinne des "evolutionären prototypings") geeignet sind, läßt sich aus den hier gemachten Erfahrungen allein noch nicht abschließend beurteilen.

Wir sind aber davon überzeugt, daß der "Prototyping"-Ansatz einen wachsenden Anhängerkreis finden wird, was sicher noch zu einem vermehrten Angebot an Werkzeugen führen wird. So sehen wir eine gewisse Tendenz zur Entwicklung großer "Prototyping-Werkzeugkisten" mit Spezialwerkzeugen für die verschiedenen Zielsetzungen und mit guten Modularisierungs- und Integrationsmöglichkeiten, die den Zusammenbau von mehreren kleineren Prototypen zu größeren optimal unterstützen.

In einer solchen Werkzeugkiste könnten sich Werkzeuge der sogenannten fünften Generation neben solchen der vierten in "friedlicher Koexistenz" finden. Ein Ziel weiterer bei Softlab begonnener Untersuchungen ist es, Prototyping auch mit wissensbasierten Techniken zu betreiben, dabei die Stärken und Schwächen der beiden Ansätze miteinander zu vergleichen und die jeweiligen am besten geeigneten Einsatz- und Anwendungsgebiete herauszufinden.

Dank

Für die Mitarbeit in dem beschriebenen Projekt, die Durchsicht des Manuskripts
und für viele fruchtbare Diskussionen danke ich meinem Kollegen Florian Bünte.

7   Literaturhinweise

/BUD 84/   BUDDE, R. et al. (Eds.) Approaches to prototyping, Springer 1984

/COD 70/   CODD, E.F.:   A relational model of data for large shared data
                banks, CACM 13.6 (1970)

/DAD 86/   DADAM, P: Forschung und Entwicklung im Datenbank-Management-
                System-Bereich, GI - 16. Jahrestagung, Vol. 1, Informatik-Fach-
                berichte 126, pp. 63-89, Springer 1986

/DAT 81/   DATE, C.J.: An introduction to database systems, Third edition,
                Addison-Wesley 1981

/FLO 84/   FLOYD, Ch.: A systematic look at prototyping, in: /BUD 84/

/F-H 84/   FRÖLICH, R., HUPPERTZ, B.:   Daten- und Funktionsmodellierung,
                zwei Jahre Technologieentwicklung und Piloteinsatz beim Anwen-
                dungsentwurf von Informationssystemen, in /INF 84/

/HES 80/   HESSE, W.: Das Projektmodell - eine Grundlage für die ingenieur-
                mäßige Software-Entwicklung, GI - 10. Jahrestagung, Informatik-
                Fachberichte 33, pp. 107-122, Springer 1980

/HES 84/   HESSE, W.:   S/E/TEC - Software-Produktionsumgebung von Softlab,
                in: Moderne Software-Entwicklungssysteme und -werkzeuge, Biblio-
                graphisches Institut 1984

/HES 87/   HESSE, W.: Ein verallgemeinertes Anwendungsmodell für die Ent-
                wicklung von DV-Systemen (zur Veröffentlichung eingereicht)

/INF 84/   GI/ACM-Fachtagung "Modellierung und Konstruktion bei der Ent-
                wicklung von Informationssystemen", Informatik-Fachberichte,
                Springer 1984

/ORA 84/   ORACLE Overview and introduction to SQL, Oracle Corp. 1984

/VRT 82/   VINEK, G., RENNERT, P.F., TJOA, A M.: Datenmodellierung, Theorie
                und Praxis des Datenbankentwurfs, Physica 1982

Werkzeuge zum Entwurf von verteilten Informationssystemen im Büro
- State-of-the-Art und Ansätze zur Methodenintegration -

von

Dr. Joachim Niemeier, Dipl.-Ing. A.J. Ness, Dipl.-Inform. F. Reim

Fraunhofer-Institut für Arbeitswirtschaft und Organisation (IAO)
Holzgartenstr. 17, D-7000 Stuttgart 1

Informationsbedarfsermittlung und -analyse - Allein ein Problem der Softwareentwicklung?

Die Notwendigkeit einer effizienten und effektiven methodischen und instrumentellen Unterstützung von Prozeßen der Planung und Einführung von Informationssystemen hat auf dem Gebiet der Softwareentwicklung zu einer eigenständigen Softwaretechnologie geführt (vgl. HÖRING (1987), S. 28.4.03). Der Bedarf an umfassenden organisatorisch-technischen Analyse- und Planungsmethoden für den technischen und administrativen Bürobereich erfordert immer mehr, organisatorische Fragen einzubeziehen (vgl. SCHÖNECKER UND NIPPA (Hrsg., 1987). Die Ursachen für diese neuen Anforderungen können anhand der folgenden drei Thesen dargestellt werden (vgl. KIESER (1986), S. 124 f):

These 1

Die neuen Informations- und Kommunikationstechnologien führen zu einer beträchtlichen Ausweitung des *organisatorischen Gestaltungsspielraums.*

These 2

In der Praxis läßt sich eine Tendenz beobachten, diesen Gestaltungsspielraum *nicht* zu nutzen. Die neuen Informations- und Kommunikationstechnologien werden meist im Rahmen *raditioneller Organisationskonzepte* implementiert. Insoweit kann man von einem *organisatorischen Konservatismus* sprechen.

These 3

Der organisatorische Konservatismus kann durch *neue Analyse- und Gestaltungsmethoden* überwunden werden.

Für die folgenden Betrachtungen soll unter dem Begriff *Büro* ein sozio-technisches System als Teil einer größeren Organisation verstanden werden, z. B. eine Abteilung in einer Unternehmung. Es sollen hier nicht nur administrative Büros, wie z. B. die Finanzbuchhaltung, die Materialwirtschaft, oder Sekretariate betrachtet werden, sondern auch technische Büros, wie z.B. Produktentwicklung, Konstruktion, Arbeitsvorbereitung oder Produktionssteuerung.

Unter einem *verteilten Bürosystem* als Ressource wird ein Netzwerk verbundener Rechner verstanden, das zur Unterstützung der Büroarbeit eingesetzt wird. Diese Definition geht ausdrücklich über die oft vorgefundene hinaus, die "Bürosystem" für ein komfortables Textsystem verwendet, mit dem auch Dokumentablage und Elektronische Post möglich sind und dessen Hauptzweck die Effizienzsteigerung im Sekretariatsbereich ist.

Im Rahmen des ESPRIT-Forschungsprogramms befassen sich speziell vier Projekte mit dem Einsatz und der Gestaltung von Informationssystemen im Büro. Außer COMANDOS ("Construction and Management of Distributed Office Systems"), aus dessen Rahmen diese Arbeit stammt, sind das FAOR (vgl. SCHÄFER u.a. (1986)), OSSAD (vgl. de ANTONELLIS, BODEM UND COCCIA (1985), DUMAS, DE PETRA UND CHARBONNEL (1986)) und TODOS (vgl. CEC-ITTTF (1986), PERNICI UND VOGEL (1986)). COMANDOS zielt darauf ab, eine effiziente und leicht zu bedienende Umgebung für die Entwicklung und den Betrieb von verteilten Anwendungen im Büro zu schaffen (CEC-ITTTF (1986)). Dazu gehören ein verteiltes Betriebssystem, das auf heterogenen Rechnern läuft, ein verteiltes Datenmanagementsystem, das sowohl ein Dateisystem als auch ein verteiltes Datenbanksystem umfaßt, und verschiedene Managementwerkzeuge. Die Hauptaufgaben dieser Managementwerkzeuge sind die Unterstützung der Gestaltung des verteilten Bürosystems zugeschnitten auf die Bedürfnisse der Anwenderorganisation, die Konfiguration, die Verwaltung und der Betrieb des Systems, sowie Zugangssicherung und Datenschutz.

Klassische Organisationsmethoden und -werkzeuge reichen nicht aus, wenn mehr gefragt ist als die Rationalisierung einer Arbeitsinsel

Verschiedene Angebote im Methodenbereich sollen eine höhere Professionalität der Organisationsarbeit im technischen und adminisatrativen Büro ermöglichen. Die Angebotsvielfalt an Methoden bedingt zwangsläufig ein Auswahl- und Beurteilungsproblem. Dabei spielt für die Organisationspraxis weniger ein theoretischer Perfektionismus als vielmehr eine pragmatische Orientierung an der Aufgabenstellung des Organisators und Planers eine entscheidende Rolle. Angesichts weit entwickelter Methoden zur Arbeitsstrukturierung in der Produktion, zur Entwicklung von DV-Verfahren in abgegrenzten Verwaltungsbereichen (Lohn- und Gehaltsbuchhaltung, Fertigungsplanung und –steuerung etc.) und zur organisatorischen Strukturierung auf Arbeitsplatzebene macht sich das Fehlen von umfassenden organisatorisch-technischen Gestaltungsmethoden für den technischen und administrativen Bürobereich immer deutlicher bemerkbar. Methoden, welche in klassischen Organisationsprojekten zu einer isolierten Betrachtung von Arbeitsplätzen, Aufgaben und Tätigkeiten und in DV-Projekten zur isolierten Betrachtung einzelner Anwendungsgebiete eingesetzt wurden, sind nicht für Gestaltungsaufgaben im Büro "portierbar". In der Organisationspraxis zeigt sich dieses Defizit in:

    o der unzureichenden Berücksichtigung eines funktions- und arbeitsplatzübergreifenden Denkens in Arbeitsprozessen und Netzwerken. Typische Stichworte für die sich daraus entwickelnden Konsequenzen sind "Insellösungen" und "Medienbrüche".

    o der Dominanz der Ist-Analyse im Gestaltungsprozeß. Dadurch werden bestehende Ablaufstrukturen in ähnlicher Form rechnerunterstützt abgebildet. Wurden bislang Bürotätigkeiten beispielsweise auf der Grundlage von Formularen, die im Arbeitsablauf auszufüllen waren, durchgeführt, so werden bis heute auf technische Systemen dieselben Arbeitsabläufe auf Formularbasis abgebildet. Durch eine "Elektrifizierung der Ist-Situation", wie Zangl (vgl. ZANGL (1986), S. 236) es treffend formuliert, werden jedoch keine oder nur geringe Wertschöpfungsvorteile erzielt. Für diese übereinfachte Vorgehensweise wurde jedoch häufig mit dem Argument der Benutzerakzeptanz argumentiert. Man ging davon aus, daß sich die Sekretärin oder der Sachbearbeiter mit der Arbeit am Bildschirm leichter vertaut machen würde, wenn auch hier im übertragenen Sinne mit Formularen, Dokumenten, Aktenschränken, Postkörben, Schreibtischen und Papierkörben gearbeitet wird. Wäre mit Hilfe dieser "Desk-Top-Methaper" vor 20 Jahren ein rechnerunterstützter Ingenieurarbeitsplatz entwickelt worden, dann hätte dieser sicherlich große Ähnlichkeit mit einem Rechenschieber gehabt.

o der Orientierung an reinen Produktivitätssteigerungen als Wirtschaftlichkeitsmaßstab anstelle einer Promotion von qualitativen Verbesserungen der Büroleistungen. Dies fördert die Argumentation, daß der Einsatz von knappen finanziellen Mitteln in der Produktion ertragreicher sei, da erfahrungsgemäß hier mit einem Faktor 2 bis 3 in der Wirtschaftlichkeit gerechnet werden kann, während im Bürobereich nach Einführung der Textverarbeitung schon 20-30 % Produktivitätssteigerung einen guten Rationalisierungserfolg darstellen. Die in den letzten Jahren auf diesem Gebiet durchgeführten Untersuchungen zeigen diesen Trend eindeutig (vgl. z.B. IDC (1985)). Ansätze für eine Einbeziehung von weiteren Größen der Wettbewerbsfähigkeit in dem Planungs- und Bewertungsprozeß von Bürosystemen werden zunehmend gesucht (vgl. auch zur konzeptionellen Problematik BULLINGER (1986)).

o einer mehr "intuitiven" und sehr aufwendigen Erfassung der Problemstellung, die sich in einer langen Projektdauer und einer hohen Belastung der Nutzerbereiche niederschlägt. Bei Bürorationalisierungsprojekten sind häufige Vorstudien und Ist-Analysen von über einem Jahr Länge zu beobachten. Die Ergebnisse derartiger Studien haben häufig dann aufgrund der schnellen Veränderungen im Büro nur noch historischen Wert.

Man kann nicht auf Entwicklungstrends im Methodenbereich eingehen, ohne auf die von Universitäten, Forschungsinstituten, Berufsverbänden und Computerherstellern in Gang gesetzten Entwicklungen im Hinblick auf den Abbau dieses Methodendefizits einzugehen. Die bereits am Markt angebotenen Methoden, so die Argumentation, seien bei einer sinnvollen, unternehmungsspezifisch maßgeschneiderten Kombination für eine professionelle Organisationsarbeit im Büro ausreichend. Diese Professionalität wird dabei ausgehend von verschiedenen Wurzeln begründet:

o Professionalität durch Berücksichtigung allgemeiner Prinzipien der Systemanalyse

Die Systemanalyse für die klassische Datenverarbeitung untersucht die Ablauforganisation von Prozeßketten (vgl. HÖRING (1987), S. 28.4.03). Die Erfahrung aus der Entwicklung von Software fördert die Argumentation nach einem strikten, planmäßigen und zielorientierten Vorgehen, das auf allgemeinen Prinzipien wie Abstraktion, Strukturierung, Hierarchisierung und Modularisierung aufbaut. Die Nutzung systemtheoretischen Gedankenguts zur Lösung betriebswirtschaftlicher Gestaltungsprobleme ist im Rahmen des Entwurfs betrieblicher Informationssysteme erprobt. Hier sind in vielen Unternehmungen weitreichende Standardisierungsbemühungen erfolgt, die in Richtung (vgl. HANSEN (1980), Sp. 2181):

- eines Übergangs von einer individuell geprägten Entwicklung von Informationssystemen zur Anwendung strukturierter ingenieurmäßigen Methoden,

- einer Vereinheitlichung und Koordination von Vorgehensweisen in der Systemanalyse,

- einer Verwendung von vielfach verwertbaren Bausteinen und Hilfsmitteln und

- einer Automatisierung formalisierbarer Tätigkeiten des Systementwicklungsprozesses

erfolgt sind. Die Erfahrungen haben gezeigt, daß diese Vorgehensweise immer dann erfolgreich sein kann, wenn im Untersuchungsfeld repetitive, formalisierbare Aufgaben durchgeführt werden. Bei großen Systemen können jedoch schnell einige tausend Bausteine und Hilfsmittel identifiziert werden, deren große Zahl schon für sich genommen die Entwicklung von Informationssystemen vor große Probleme stellt. Insbesondere wenn die Planung Arbeitsprozeße von Führungs- und Fachkräften einbezieht, müßen unstrukturierte und wenig formalisierbare Prozeße berücksichtigt werden, deren Ausprägung von der jeweiligen Problemsituation sowie den menschlichen Problemlösungsfähigkeiten beeinflußt werden und deren zukünftige Nutzung schwer vorhersehbar ist (vgl. HÖRING (1987), S. 28.4.03). Allgemein gilt: "Aus der Nutzung der Technik ergeben sich neue Strukturen der Arbeit; die Nutzung der Technik im Arbeitszusammenhang bestimmt deren Leistung" (WELTZ (1986), S. 1121).

o Professionalität durch eine Vorgehensweise nach Phasenmodellen

Die Vorgehensweise nach Phasenmodellen ist häufig die Grundlage der Dienstleistungsangebote von Beratern. Hier werden Stufenkonzepte (z.B. Vorstudie, Ist-Analyse, Soll-Konzept, Implementierung) als Problemlösungen vorgetragen. In diesem Zusammenhang wird jedoch häufig betont, daß für eine konstruktive Beratung die Einbeziehung der "angestoßenen Prozesse" weit wichtiger ist, als die bei der Beratung verwendeten Instrumente oder ihr Bezugsrahmen. Diese "angestoßenen Prozesse", die nach der Gestaltung und Durchführung der Beratung beim Management und bei den Mitarbeitern ablaufen, sind insbesondere für die spätere Akzeptanz und Anwendung wichtig. Sie werden jedoch nicht in ein Phasenkonzept miteinbezogen. Dies bedarf häufig geradezu einer Reduzierung der technokratischen Elemente im Beratungsprozeß, da sonst Aushandlungs-, Konsensbildungs-, aber auch Machtausübungsprozesse die Problemlösung dominieren.

o Professionalität durch Projektmanagement

Beim Projektmanagement stehen methodisch-instrumentelle Kenntnisse im Hinblick auf die Planung, Steuerung und Kontrolle von Büroprojekten im Vordergrund. Damit kann die Effizienz von Büroprojekten gesteigert werden, nicht jedoch deren Effektivität. Die Zugrundelegung eines Projektmanagementkonzeptes allein kann nicht sicherstellen, daß das Richtige getan wird, allenfalls, daß das was getan wird, wirtschaftlich durchgeführt wird und sei es auch noch so falsch.

o Professionalität durch den Einsatz von Methodenpaketen

Methoden und Methodenpakete werden oft unreflektiert übernommen und als die Problemlösung postuliert. So ist die "Kommunikationsanalyse" als Methodenpaket ein heute weit verbreitetes Angebot. Beim näheren Betrachten zeigt sich jedoch schnell, daß die Methodenpakete häufig inhaltlich nicht vergleichbar sind und nur das gleiche Etikett tragen. Methoden für sich genommen führen zu keinen erfolgreichen Lösungen ohne ein umfassendes Organisationskonzept, auch wenn sie als ausgereift bezeichnet oder in Form von Organisationssoftware rechnerunterstützt zur Verfügung gestellt werden. Letztendlich sind die Zielsetzung eines Projektes und eine adäquate Berücksichtigung der spezifischen Unternehmungsgegebenheiten der entscheidende Prüfstein für eine Methodenbeurteilung. Dazu HÖRING (1987, S. 28.4.05): "In der Analyse ist es daher wichtig, die Natur der Problemstellung nicht bereits vorzu-disponieren und somit an den falschen Problemen anzusetzen, d.h. den "Fehler der dritten Art" zu begehen. Dies geschieht oft bereits durch fest vorgegebene Schrittfolgen und Inhalte einer Analysemethode, die nur unzureichend an die vorgegebene Situation angepasst sind."

o Professionalität durch Nutzung von integrierten Hard-, Soft- und Orgwareangeboten.

In den letzten Jahren sind mehrere (rechnerunterstützte) Organisationsmethodenpakete von Computersystemherstellern entwickelt worden, die zur Unterstützung des Vertriebsmarketings eingesetzt werden. PLAKOM, MOSAIK (beide SIEMENS AG, zu MOSAIK vgl. SIEMENS AG (1986), SCHAIBLE (1986), BERGMANN (1987)), SOPHOPLAN (Philips Kommunikations Industrie AG, vgl. PHILIPS AG (1986a) und PHILIPS AG (1986b)), und KSS (IBM) sind hierfür herausragende Vertreter. Die Erfahrungen bei erfolgreichen Einführungsprozessen von technischen Systemen im Büro zeigen, daß die Herausbildung einer dominanten Koalition zwischen Organisator/Planer einerseits und Vertriebsbeauftragten andererseits einen wesentlichen Erfolgsfaktor darstellen (zu empirischen Untersuchungen der Bedeutung von "Third-Party Interventionen" siehe BRABANDER UND THIERS (1984)). Im Vergleich zu den oben dargestellten Phasenmodellen ist dabei eine Erweiterung über die Erstimplementation in Richtung "ständige Betreuung" eine grundsätzlich Voraussetzung.

Es soll allerdings auch schon Vertriebsbeauftragte gegeben haben, die sich nach Abwicklung des Moduls "Bestelldatenerfassung" aus dem aktiven Prozeß zurückgezogen haben. In diesem Zusammenhang ist wichtig, daß die beteiligten Organisatoren aus der Anwenderunternehmung die Möglichkeit haben, sich in einem solchen Planungs- und Organisationsprozeß zu qualifizieren um die Werkzeuge später in eigener Regie nutzen zu können.

Zusammenfassend kann man folgende Problemfelder im Methodenbereich feststellen:

o   Die Ist-Analyse nimmt bis heute eine zu dominierende Stellung ein.

o   Herkömmliche Wirtschaftlichkeitsbetrachtungen reichen nicht aus.

o   Die Kooperation der am Planungsprozeß Beteiligten (z.B. Fachabteilungen, Organisa-tions- und Planungsbereiche, DV-Abteilungen, Berater) ist unzureichend.

o   Für Organisationsvorhaben im Bürobereich stehen zu wenige und/oder nicht in aus-reichendem Maß qualifizierte Mitarbeiter zur Verfügung.

o   Es magelt an einem Bewußtsein für neuartige Lösungsperspektiven und Verfahren.

Rechnergestützte Werkzeuge zur Gestaltung von Informationssystemen im Büro - Ein Überblick zum Entwicklungsstand

Als Ausgangspunkt für die Definition und Spezifikation der Werkzeuge zur Unterstützung der Gestaltung eines verteilten Bürosystems wurde im Rahmen von COMANDOS eine Übersicht über repräsentative Werkzeuge und Methoden erarbeitet (zum Überblick an rechnergestützten Werkzeugen siehe insbesondere SCHÖNECKER UND NIPPA (Hrsg., 1987). Auf "baugleiche Werkzeuge" wird nicht näher eingegangen. Da in COMANDOS die Zielsetzung ist, die Gestaltungsunterstützung in Form von in das System integrierten Werkzeugen zu realisieren, und diese Werkzeuge eine direkte Anbindung an die Konfiguration und den Betrieb des Systems haben sollen, wurden speziell computerunterstützte Methoden und Werkzeuge untersucht (vgl. NESS, REIM, MEITNER UND NIEMEIER (1986)). Daneben wurden auch kommerzielle und experimentelle, verteilte Bürosysteme im Hinblick auf ihre Systemarchitektur und ihre Einbindungssätze von Gestaltungs- und Konfigurationswerkzeugen betrachtet.

Für die Untersuchung von Gestaltungsmethoden und -werkzeugen kann die Aufgabe der Planung und Gestaltung eines Bürosystems in vier miteinander verknüpfte Grundaufgaben zerlegt werden (Bild 1). Die *organisatorische Gestaltung* des Büros ist beeinflußt durch dessen Aufgabe, durch die Umgebungsbedingungen, wie zum Beispiel Außenkontakte, Gesetze, etc., und durch interne Bedingungen. Diese internen Bedingungen können die Größe, die Qualifikation der Mitarbeiter und die verfügbaren Ressourcen des Büros sein.

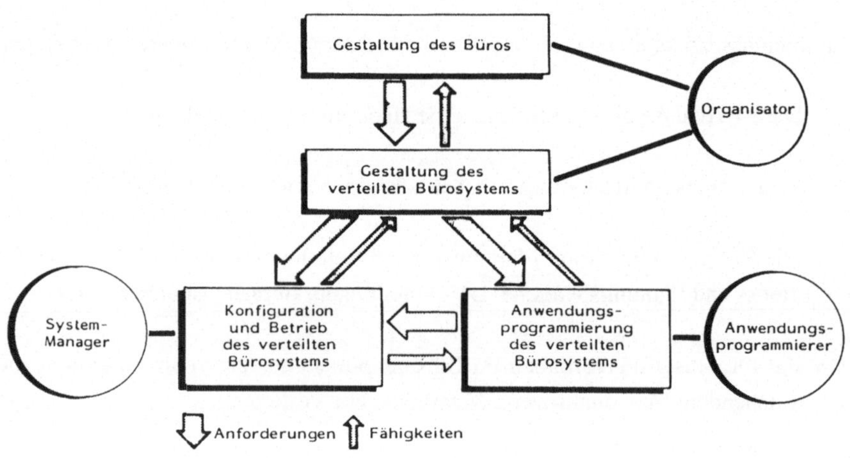

Bild 1: Die Grundaufgaben bei der Gestaltung eines Bürosystems

Die *Gestaltung eines verteilten Bürosystems* umfaßt die Auswahl der geeigneten Systemkomponenten und die konzeptuelle Spezifikation des Hardware- und Softwaresystems. Diese Aufgabe kann als technische Gestaltung des Büros verstanden werden und ist somit ein Bestandteil der Gestaltung des Büros.

Die *Konfiguration* und der Betrieb realisieren die konzeptuelle Spezifikation in einem operationalen System. Die *Anwendungsprogrammierung* implementiert die für eine bestimmte Büroumgebung erforderliche Software im verteilten Bürosystem.

In Bild 1 sind zwischen den Grundaufgaben zwei Arten von Beziehungen identifiziert: Anforderungen und Fähigkeiten. Die organisatorische Gestaltung definiert Anforderungen an die Gestaltung des technischen Systems und muß dabei dessen potentielle Fähigkeiten kennen und berücksichtigen. Die Gestaltung des verteilten Systems definiert Anforderungen an die Konfiguration und den Betrieb des Systems und kennt dabei die verfügbaren Komponenten und deren Leistungsmerkmale. Ebenso werden die Anforderungen an die Anwendungsprogrammierung definiert. Die Anwendungsprogrammierung stellt umgekehrt Leistungen und Fähigkeiten zur Verfügung, die bei der Gestaltung eines verteilten Bürosystems berücksichtigt werden müssen.

Die Grundaufgaben und davon insbesondere die Gestaltungsaufgaben können als komplexe Entscheidungen betrachtet werden. Simon teilte Entscheidungen in die drei Phasen Aufklärung, Gestaltung und Auswahl ein (vgl. SIMON (1960)). Später wurde diese Phaseneinteilung je nach Anwendungszusammenhang um weitere Phasen ergänzt (vgl. zum Beispiel GROCHLA (1982)). Der Begriff der Phase beinhaltet jedoch eine zeitliche oder kausale Reihenfolge, die insbesondere bei komplexen Gestaltungsentscheidungen nicht eingehalten werden kann. Daher wurde für die Untersuchung der Gestaltungswerkzeuge eine Einteilung in fünf funktionale Komponenten vorgenommen (Bild 2), ohne dabei einen zeitlichen oder kausalen Zusammenhang vorzuschreiben.

Die funktionale Komponente "Lösungsauswahl" wurde ausdrücklich von der "Bewertung der Lösung" und von der "Implementierung" unterschieden. Die "Bewertung der Lösung" kann teilweise erfolgen, d. h. daß nicht alle möglichen oder relevanten Gesichtspunkte herangezogen werden. Die "Lösungsauswahl" dagegen kann weitere Merkmale und Verfahren heranziehen, die nicht bei der "Bewertung der Lösung" berücksichtigt waren, z. B. persönliche Gründe. Darüberhinaus beinhaltet die "Lösungsauswahl" die tatsächliche Entscheidung und die Verantwortung dafür.

Zusammen mit den Grundaufgaben spannen diese funktionalen Komponenten einen zweidimensionalen Rahmen zur Klassifikation der untersuchten Werkzeuge auf. Innerhalb dieses Rahmens werden insbesondere die Paradigmen und zugrundeliegenden Annahmen, sowie die verwendeten Modelle der Methoden und Werkzeuge betrachtet.

Aufklärung	Informationsakquisition (Beschaffung und Aufbereitung von Daten), Identifikation von Problemen und Möglichkeiten, genaue Aufgabendefinition
Lösungen erstellen	Verstehen des Problems, Modellierung, Erfinden und Entwickeln möglicher Lösungen
Lösungen bewerten	Prüfung der erstellten Lösungen auf Machbarkeit, Bewertung der erstellten Lösungen im Hinblick auf die Gestaltungsziele
Lösungsauswahl	Auswahl einer bestimmten Lösung, Verantwortung dieser Entscheidung
Implementierung	Operationale Realisierung der ausgewählten Lösung

Bild 2: Die funktionalen Komponenten der Gestaltungsentscheidungen

Es wurde untersucht, wie die Werkzeuge in eine Methode eingebunden sind, welche generellen Ansätze in den Methoden gemacht werden und welche Annahmen über das Büro oder das verteilte Bürosystem den Ansätzen zugrunde liegen. Mit generellen Ansätzen ist z.B. ein Phasenkonzept, ein inkrementelles Vorgehen im Gegensatz zu einem einmaligen, abgeschlossenen Gestaltungsprozeß, ein Lebenszyklusansatz, oder eine hierarchische Aufgabenzerlegung gemeint. Diese Betrachtung der Paradigmen und zugrundeliegenden Annahmen ist notwendig, um die Einsetzbarkeit und Leistungsfähigkeit eines Werkzeugs für eine bestimmte Aufgabe besser beurteilen zu können. Weiterhin wurde untersucht, welche Modelle des Büros und des Bürosystems bei den Werkzeugen verwendet werden. Insbesondere war von Bedeutung, welche Aspekte des Büros und welche Konzepte und Bestandteile modelliert wurden. Daneben war weiterhin von Bedeutung, welcher Formalismus oder welche Sprache zur Präsentation der Modelle verwendet wurde und wie dieser implementiert war.

Die in die Untersuchung einbezogenen rechnerunterstützten Werkzeuge waren:

MOSAIK (Modulares, organisationsbezogenes System zur Analyse und Implementierung von Kommunikationstechnik), Siemens AG, München

MOSAIK ist eine Methode zur Ermittlung und Analyse von Kommunikationsdaten im Büro (vgl. SIEMENS AG (1986), SCHAIBLE (1986), BERGMANN (1987)). Es unterstützt die Auswahl zwischen unterschiedlichen technischen Lösungsmöglichkeiten und die Implementierung der Lösung. MOSAIK verfolgt einen prozeßorientierten Ansatz zur Kommunikations-Netzwerk-Analyse in mehreren hierarchischen Ebenen der untersuchten Organisation. Das Hauptziel von MOSAIK ist die Gestaltung einer effizienten technischen Unterstützung der Büroarbeit, worunter auch die *Gestaltung des verteilten Bürosystems* fällt.

Von den funktionalen Komponenten der Gestaltung wird die Aufklärung und das Erstellen von Lösungen durch computerbasierte Werkzeuge unterstützt, letzteres allerdings nur was das Verständnis des Problems betrifft. Die übrigen Gestaltungsfunktionen werden dem Organisator überlassen.

PLAKOM (Planungsverfahren zur Erarbeitung von Kommunikationskonzepten), Siemens AG, München

PLAKOM ist eine computerbasierte Methode zur Analyse und Repräsentation von Kommunikationsstrukturen im Büro (vgl. SIEMENS AG (1984), (1985a), (1985b). Im Gegen-satz zu MOSAIK, das einen prozeßorientierten Ansatz verfolgt, wurde ein aufgabenorientierter Ansatz gewählt. PLAKOM zielt besonders auf eine breite, flächendeckende Betrachtung ab, ohne einzelne Bereiche sehr detailliert zu untersuchen. Es besteht aus den drei Modulen zur Informationssammlung, graphischen und tabellarischen Auswertung und zur Gegenüberstellung mit Gerätedaten.

PLAKOM unterstützt die technische Bürogestaltung. Dies beinhaltet die *Gestaltung des verteilten Bürosystems,* worunter hier im wesentlichen Kommunikationsdienste wie Telefon oder Telex zu verstehen sind. Es werden Empfehlungen für Hardware und Dienstleistungen zur Unterstützung der analysierten Büroarbeit gegeben. Die *Aufklärungskomponente* der Gestaltung wird unterstützt. Für die *Erstellung und Bewertung von Lösungen* wird nur eine sehr rudimentäre Unterstützung geboten.

SOPHO-PLAN, Philips Kommunikationsindustrie AG, Siegen

SOPHO-PLAN unterstützt die Einführung von Bürokommunikationsgeräten in bestehende Büroumgebungen (vgl. PHILIPS AG (1986a), (1986b)). Dazu existieren verschiedene Werkzeuge, von denen nur eines, Proplan zur Aggregation und Präsentation der Analysedaten, computerunterstützt ist.

Die *Gestaltung des verteilten Bürosystems* wird auf einer sehr generellen Ebene, nämlich der reinen Hardware-Auswahl, unterstützt. Zur Gestaltung des Büros selbst bietet SOPHO-PLAN nur rein beschreibende Informationen. Eine Änderung der bestehenden Organisationsstruktur ist nicht Gegenstand SOPHO-PLAN's. Auch SOPHO-PLAN unterstützt fast ausschließlich die *Aufklärung.* Lediglich einige Hinweise auf mögliche Schwächen in Informationsketten, die vom Modul Proplan gegeben werden, deuten in Richtung der anderen funktionalen Entscheidungskomponenten.

VERIKS (Verbesserung der innerbetrieblichen Kommunikationssysteme), INFORA, Köln

VERIKS bietet Unterstützung bei der Verbesserung interner Informations- und Kommunikationssysteme (vgl. REINDL (1986)). Eine computerunterstützte Analysemethode hilft bei der Identifizierung von Kommunikationsbedürfnissen für jede Rolle oder Funktion, die innerhalb einer Organisation wahrgenommen wird.

Die organisatorische Gestaltung des Kommunikationssystems wird unterstützt. Dies entspricht der *Gestaltung des Büros*. Technische Gestaltungsentscheidungen werden nicht betrachtet. VERIKS unterstützt die Entscheidungskomponente *Aufklärung*. Durch unterschiedliche Arten von Analysen, die mit Hilfe der Werkzeuge durchgeführt werden können, soll beim Organisator ein besseres Problemverständnis erreicht werden.

KSA (Kommunikations-Struktur-Analyse), TU Berlin

KSA ist eine computerunterstützte Methode zur Verbesserung von Informations- und Kommunikationsbeziehungen in einer Organisation (vgl. KRALLMANN, FEITEN, HOYER und KÖLZER (1986)). Verschiedene Module, die im wesentlichen auf einer hierarchischen Zerlegung der Bürotätigkeiten aufbauen, arbeiten auf einer Datenbank, die eine Repräsentation der organisatorischen Struktur beinhaltet.

KSA hilft bei der *Gestaltung des Büros*. Die Leistungsfähigkeit des Büros wird durch eine Optimierung bei den Elementaraufgaben und eine Umstrukturierung der Bürotätigkeiten erreicht. Die *Gestaltung des verteilten Bürosystems* ist Teil der Optimierung der Elementaraufgaben. Dateneingabe-, sowie Analyse- und Aggregationswerkzeuge unterstützen die *Aufklärung*. Durch die Auswertewerkzeuge und einen Simulator wird auch Unterstützung beim *Erstellen von Lösungen* geboten.

ISMOD (Information System Model and Architecture Generator), IBM

ISMOD dient zur Analyse von Informationsbedürfnissen einer Unternehmung (vgl. HEIN (1985)). Es identifiziert Prozesse, die eine logisch zusammenhängende Menge von Aktivitäten umfassen. Basierend auf Datenflüssen in der Unternehmung hilft ISMOD bei der Bildung von Subsystemen, die aus mehreren Prozessen bestehen. Durch Simulation auf den erhobenen Daten kann die Auswirkung einer neuen Subsystem-Struktur auf die Organisation untersucht werden. Als Maß dient dabei die "Benutzerzufriedenheit".

ISMOD unterstützt die *Gestaltung des Büros*. Dabei wird eine Zerlegung der Unternehmung in mehr oder weniger isolierte Subsysteme vorgenommen. Im wesentlichen wird die *Aufklärung* und das *Erstellen von Lösungen* unterstützt. Die Bewertung unterschiedlicher Lösungsansätze wird teilweise durch die Simulation unterstützt. Allerdings werden dabei nur Teilaspekte betrachtet. Die Realisierbarkeit einer Lösung wird beispielsweise nicht in Erwägung gezogen.

OFFIS (Office Information Specification), University of Arizona, USA

OFFIS verfolgt einen etwas weitergehenden Ansatz in Richtung der Erstellung von Lösungen, als die oben beschriebenen Systeme, verzichtet jedoch auf die Unterstützung der Datenakquisition. Es ist ein interaktives System, das eine Sprache zur Beschreibung eines Büromodells und einen Analysator (Auswerteprogramm) umfaßt (vgl. BRACKER und KONSYNSKI (1981). KONSYNSKI, BRACKER und BRACKER (1982)). Der Analysator verwaltet eine Datenbank mit dem aktuellen Büromodell und den Anforderungen an das Büro. Damit können Reports über vorgeschlagene Bürospezifikationen erstellt werden.

OFFIS unterstützt sowohl die *Gestaltung des Büros* als auch die *Gestaltung des verteilten Bürosystems*. Aus der verfügbaren Literatur kann vermutet werden, daß der Schwerpunkt mehr bei der Bürogestaltung liegt. Auch hier stehen Kommunikationsaspekte der Büroarbeit im Vordergrund. Durch die OFFIS-Beschreibungssprache wird das *Erstellen von Lösungsalternativen* unterstützt. Es können existierende und auch vorgeschlagene, zukünftige Systementwürfe formal dargestellt werden. Mit Hilfe des Analysators können diese auf Vollständigkeit und Konsistenz überprüft werden. Allerdings beschränkt sich diese Prüfung im wesentlichen auf die Syntax. Was darüber hinausgeht wird dem menschlichen Gestalter überlassen.

PLEXSYS, University of Arizona, USA

PLEXSYS wurde entwickelt, um Computer-Unterstützung für den gesamten Systementwicklungsprozeß, beginnend mit der Problemdefinition bis hin zur Code-Erzeugung zu bieten (vgl. KONSYNSKI und NUNAMAKER (1984)). Bekannte Methoden und Werkzeuge werden dabei benutzt, z. B. Business Systems Planning (vgl. ZACHMANN (1982)), PSL/PSA (vgl. BALZERT (1982)) und CSF (vgl. ROCKART (1979)).

In der verfügbaren Literatur über PLEXSYS wird die Unterstützung bei der *Gestaltung des Büros* beschrieben. Die *Aufklärung* wird im Rahmen der Problemdefinition und des Business System Planning auf konzeptueller Ebene unterstützt. Dabei soll PLEXSYS die Möglichkeit bieten, alternative Perspektiven und Gesichtspunkte bei der Präsentation von Informationen aufzuzeigen. Mit der formalen PLEXSYS-Sprache zur Anforderungsbeschreibung und -analyse wird das *Erstellen von Lösungen* und bis zu einem gewissen Grad auch deren Bewertung unterstützt. Diese Sprache basiert auf PSL. Leider sind keine detaillierten Angaben über die Unterstützung bei der *Implementierung* verfügbar.

Quinault, Xerox PARC, USA

Quinault ist ein interaktives Programmpaket, das sich aus Werkzeugen zum Erzeugen und Editieren von Information Control Nets (vgl. ELLIS (1979)), zu deren Analyse, Transformation und Simulation zusammensetzt (vgl. NUTT (1981), NUTT und RICCI (1983)). Eine Erweiterung umfaßt inzwischen auch eine Simulation, die auf einem Netzwerk von homogenen Rechnern abläuft.

Quinault unterstützt sowohl die *Gestaltung des Büros* als auch die *Gestaltung des verteilten Bürosystems*. Mit Hilfe des verteilten Simulators kann ein verteiltes Bürosystem sehr wirklichkeitsnah modelliert und analysiert werden. Im wesentlichen wird das *Erstellen von Lösungsalternativen* mit Hilfe der prozeßorientierten ICN's unterstützt. Die *Bewertung der Lösungen* wird durch Auswertefunktionen, z. B. die Pfadanalyse, und durch den ICN-Simulator unterstützt.

Taxis, University of Toronto, Canada

Taxis verfolgt einen objektorientierten Ansatz zum Entwurf von interaktiven Informationssystemen. Es wurden Sprachen, Werkzeuge und Methoden entwickelt (vgl. BARRON (1982), MYLOPOULOS, BORGIDA, GREENSPAN und WONG (1984)).

Taxis geht von einem bestehenden Büro einschließlich seiner Aufgabenbeschreibungen aus. Die Hardware-Auswahl und deren Konfiguration werden nicht behandelt. Durch SADT (vgl. BALZERT (1982)) und die Anforderungsspezifikationssprache RML wird die *Gestaltung des Informationssystems* unterstützt. Für den daran anschließenden Schritt, die *Anwendungsprogrammierung*, wird die prozedurale (Datenbank-) Programmiersprache Taxis in einer umfangreichen Programmier- und Prototyping-Umgebung zur Verfügung gestellt. Das *Erstellen von Lösungen* wird durch die rein deskriptiven Hilfsmittel RML und Taxis unterstützt. Dadurch wird jedoch keine bestimmte Vorgehensweise vorgegeben. Die *Bewertung von Lösungen* wird durch semantische Überprüfungen auf Taxis-Programmen und einen Taxis-Interpreter erleichtert. Die Implementierung wird durch die Automation der Transformation von der konzeptuellen Ebene (RML) auf Taxis und ein ausführbares Programm angestrebt. Bisher kann von einer formalen Beschreibung in Taxis ein lauffähiges Programm kompiliert werden.

XSEL / XCON (Expert Seller / Expert Configurer), Digital Equipment Corp., USA

XCON ist ein wissensbasiertes System zur Konfiguration von DEC Computern. Eingabe ist die (detaillierte) Kundenbestellung, ausgegeben wird eine Reihe von Diagrammen, die z. B. die räumliche Anordnung der Komponenten und die nötige Verkabelung angeben (vgl. MCDERMOTT (1980), (1981); KRAFT (1984); BUNGERS und GROTH (1984)). XSEL ist der Versuch, XCON so zu erweitern, daß der Verkäufer direkt unterstützt wird (vgl. MCDERMOTT (1982)).

XCON führt die *Konfiguration* durch. XSEL soll bei der *Gestaltung des Bürosystems* unterstützen. Diese Unterstützung ist allerdings nur sehr rudimentär realisiert. Die *Erstellung und Bewertung von Lösungen* und impliziert auch die Auswahl werden von XSEL/XCON durchgeführt. Dies ist deshalb möglich, weil von der Existenz einer einzigen Lösung ausgegangen wird. Sollten mehrere Lösungen existieren, so sind diese als gleichwertig angenommen.

SICONFEX (Siemens Configuration Expert), Siemens AG, München

SICONFEX ist ein wissensbasiertes System zur interaktiven Konfiguration des Siemens Betriebssystems SICOMP, das im Bereich der Prozeßdatenverarbeitung eingesetzt wird (vgl. LEHMANN U.A. (1985), HAUGENEDER, LEHMANN und STRAUSS (1985)). Es werden Parameterkarten zur Konfiguration erzeugt. Dazu werden Angaben über Hardware und Software-Spezifikation erfragt. Basierend auf diesen Angaben bestimmt SICONFEX die Konfiguration, partitioniert den Hauptspeicher und weist Software-Paketen bestimmte Speicherbereiche zu.

Die *Konfiguration* wird unterstützt. Alle Eigenschaften des Computers sind bekannt. SICONFEX *erstellt Lösungen*. Es geht von der Annahme einer geschlossenen Welt aus. Die Bewertung und Auswahl einer Lösung wird ebenfalls implizit durchgeführt, da auch hier von der Existenz einer einzigen Lösung ausgegangen wird.

Eine Klassifikation der rechnerunterstützten Werkzeuge

Bild 3 stellt den Versuch dar, die untersuchten Werkzeuge entsprechend der oben eingeführten orthogonalen Konzepte, funktionale Komponenten der Gestaltung und Grundaufgaben der Gestaltung, einzuordnen. Dabei ist zu berücksichtigen, daß die Einordnung vom aktuellen, d.h. realisierten Entwicklungsstand zu Untersuchungszeitraum abhängig ist und eine Vielzahl der Werkzeuge weiterentwickelt werden. Das Schaubild sollte daher unter einem qualitativen Aspekt betrachtet werden. Selbstverständlich stellen die Linien keine exakten Markierungen auf einer Skala dar. Auch die relative Größe der Rechtecke ist nur ein qualitativer Indikator für Wichtigkeit der Unterstützung der entsprechenden funktionalen Komponente oder Aufgabe. Trotz dieser quantitativen Einschränkungen lassen sich einige interessante Beobachtungen machen. So sind fünf unterschiedliche Gruppen von Werkzeugen zu erkennen.

Die *erste Gruppe* umfaßt MOSAIK, SOPHO-PLAN und VERIKS. Diese Werkzeuge sind charakterisiert durch die Absicht, die Aufklärung der Gestaltung des Büros und des verteilten Bürosystems zu unterstützen. Ihnen liegt das Paradigma zugrunde, neue Geräte zur Verbesserung der Kommunikation in eine existierende Organisation einzuführen. Die verwendeten Methoden sind nicht in die Organisation integriert, sondern laufen gewissermaßen als Batch-Job nebenher. Die Methoden gliedern sich alle in mehrere aufeinanderfolgende Phasen, wobei besondere Bedeutung auf die Datenerhebung im Büro gelegt wird. Die zugrundeliegenden Modelle des Büros, auf denen die Datenerhebung und die Auswertungen basieren, weisen große Ähnlichkeit auf. Sie unterscheiden Aufgaben, Information, die zwischen den Aufgaben ausgetauscht wird, Prozesse, bestehend aus einer Reihe von Aufgaben und Organisationseinheiten, denen verschiedene Aufgaben zugeordnet sind. Die Computer-Unterstützung besteht im wesentlichen aus einer Datenbank, die die erhobenen Daten verwaltet und den entsprechenden Eingabe- und Auswerteprogrammen. Die Interpretation dieser Auswertungen wird dem Organisator überlassen. Einige dieser Werkzeuge unterhalten zusätzlich eine Datenbank mit technischen Daten von Informationssystemen, die aber keine integrierte Schnittstelle zu den anderen computerbasierten Modulen hat.

Die *zweite Gruppe* der Werkzeuge besteht aus KSA und ISMOD. Diese Werkzeuge unterscheiden sich von denen der ersten Gruppe dadurch, daß sie zusätzlich Unterstützung bei der Erstellung von Lösungen bieten. Beide haben eine prozeßorientierte Betrachtung des Büros. Nach der Datenerfassung setzen sie auf einer detaillierten Beschreibung der aktuellen Situation auf und versuchen eine bessere Gestaltung zu erreichen. Eine Datenbank verwaltet den aktuellen Entwurfszustand. Um unterschiedliche Lösungsalternativen bewerten zu können, werden Mechanismen wie z.B. Auswerte- und Simulationsprogramme zur Verfügung gestellt. Das Kriterium zur Bewertung ist bei ISMOD die "Benutzerzufriedenheit", bei KSA im wesentlichen die "Durchlaufzeit". KSA geht stärker als ISMOD von einer iterativen Vorgehensweise beim Erstellen und Bewerten von Lösungen aus.

OFFIS, PLEXSYS und Quinault bilden die *dritte Gruppe*. Diese Werkzeuge konzentrieren sich auf die Erstellung von Lösungen und deren Bewertung. Eine detaillierte Analyse der aktuellen Situation, beschrieben in einer formalen Sprache, wird vorausgesetzt. Basierend darauf kann der Benutzer Lösungen erzeugen und testen. Quinault bietet auch die Möglichkeit der verteilten Simulation auf mehreren Prozessoren. Die Bewertung der Lösungen erfolgt aufgrund von Prozeßzeiten, "Workloads" und Intensität von Informationsflüssen.

Die *vierte Gruppe* besteht nur aus einem Werkzeug, Taxis. Sie umfaßt die Erstellung von Lösungen, deren Bewertung und die Implementierung im Rahmen der Anwendungsprogrammierung und der Gestaltung des verteilten Bürosystems. Es wird ein globaler Modellierungsrahmen für alle während des Designs benutzten Modelle verwendet. Ihm liegen eine Objektorientierung und die schrittweise Verfeinerung als Hauptparadigmen zugrunde. Die Verfeinerung von der Problembeschreibung zum konzeptuellen Entwurf wird hauptsächlich vom Menschen gemacht - mit Unterstützung von Werkzeugen, beispielsweise zur Konsistenzprüfung. Die Transformation vom konzeptuellen Design, ausgedrückt in einer formalen Sprache, zum lauffähigen Anwendungsprogramm ist automatisiert.

Die *fünfte Gruppe* setzt sich aus XSEL/XCON und SICONFEX zusammen. Die Werkzeuge decken die Erstellung, Bewertung und die Auswahl von Lösungen ab. Sie befassen sich im wesentlichen mit der Konfiguration und behandeln nur partiell die Gestaltung des verteilten Bürosystems. Das zugrundeliegende Paradigma dieser Gruppe ist die Suche nach einer stets eindeutig auffindbaren, besten Lösung. Durch eine angemessene Zerlegung der Gestaltungsregeln kann die Lösung daher ohne Interaktion mit dem Benutzer gefunden werden. Darin unterscheidet sie sich wesentlich von den übrigen Gruppen, wo immer potentiell mehrere Lösungen auf unterschiedlichen Suchpfaden erreicht werden können.

Diese beschreibende Klassifikation kann und soll keine Auskunft über Vor- und Nachteile der untersuchten Werkzeuge geben. Die Werkzeuge sind nicht an sich gut oder schlecht, ihre Qualität kann nur hinsichtlich eines Verwendungszusammenhangs beurteilt werden. Dieselbe Eigenschaft eines Werkzeugs kann in unterschiedlichen Verwendungszusammenhängen einmal ein Vorteil sein, das andere Mal ein Nachteil. Der Klassifikationsrahmen und die Beschreibung der Werkzeuge kann jedoch in einer Verwendungssituation die Werkzeuge einer Bewertung leicht zugänglich machen und darüberhinaus ihren Zusammenhang aufzeigen. Aus der Beschreibung der verfügbaren Werkzeuge zusammen mit den oben genannten Anforderungen und Problemen, die beim Einsatz verteilter Systeme im Büro eingehalten bzw. gelöst werden müssen, können Ansatzpunkte für die Entwicklung mächtiger Werkzeuge und für deren Integration abgeleitet werden.

Die Kopplung zwischen den Werkzeugen und dem verteilten Bürosystem in Bild 3 wird von oben nach unten und von links nach rechts enger. Die Werkzeuge der ersten Gruppe, die sich mit der Aufklärung für die Gestaltung des Büros und auch des verteilten Bürosystems befassen, sind weitgehend unabhängig vom technischen System. VERIKS, SOPHO-PLAN und MOSAIK beanspruchen für sich system- und herstellerunabhängig zu sein. Die Modellierung und das Wissen über das Bürosystem müssen detaillierter und umfangreicher werden, je näher die Aufgabe des Werkzeugs an die Konfiguration und die Programmierung des Systems heranrückt und je stärker die Unterstützung für die Bewertung und Implementierung einer Lösung wird. Das zeigt sich insbesondere bei den Konfigurationswerkzeugen XSEL/XCON für Hardware und SICONFEX für Software, sowie bei Taxis zur Unterstützung der Anwendungsprogrammierung. Die Bewertung einer Lösung beinhaltet das Wissen über die Auswirkungen eines verteilten Bürosystems auf seine Umgebung. Dafür werden sehr genaue Informationen über die Eigenschaften eines Bürosystems benötigt. Neben XSEL/XCON und SINCONFEX, die von einer stets auffindbaren besten Lösung ausgehen, sind OFFIS und Quinault Beispiele für die Einbeziehung dieses Wissens..

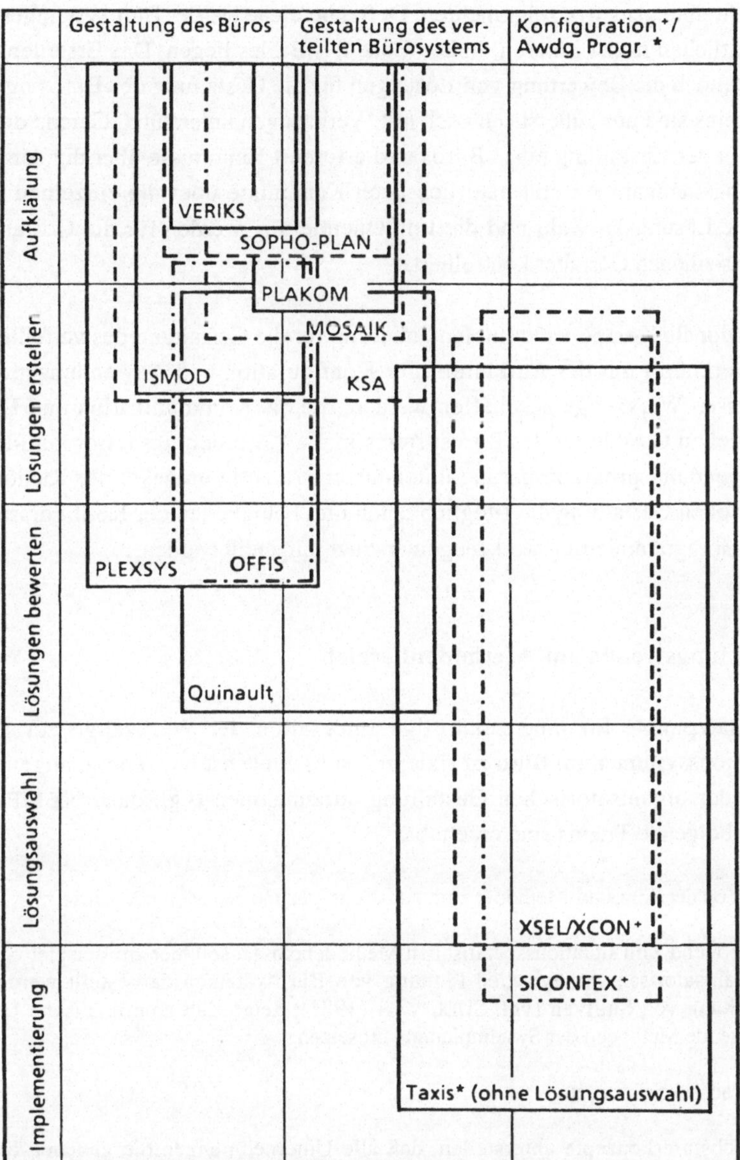

Bild 3: Die Einsatzbereiche der untersuchten Werkzeuge

Die Beschreibungsmatrix zeigt mehrere Defizitbereiche bei der Bürosystemgestaltung auf, die im wesentlichen in der unteren, linken Ecke des Bildes liegen. Das Erstellen von Lösungen und mehr noch die Bewertung von Lösungen für die Gestaltung des Büros und des verteilten Bürosystems sind nur äußerst schwach mit Werkzeugen unterstützt. Gerade dieser Bereich ist zentral bei der Gestaltung eines Büros und erfordert Kenntnisse über die Auswirkungen von Gestaltungsmaßnahmen und natürlich auch Kenntnisse über die einzelnen Ressourcen im Büro. Die Lösungsauswahl und die Implementierung werden für die Gestaltung des Büros vom menschlichen Gestalter kontrolliert.

Die funktionale Komponente Implementierung für die Gestaltung des verteilten Bürosystems ist eng verknüpft mit der Aufklärung für Konfiguration und Anwendungsprogrammierung. Hier müssen Werkzeuge geschaffen werden, die die Kommunikation und Übersetzung der konzeptuellen Gestaltung des Bürosystems in die Anforderungsdefinition für Konfiguration und Anwendungsprogrammierung unterstützen. Auch in umgekehrter Richtung müssen der konzeptuellen Gestaltung die Möglichkeiten und Fähigkeiten der Konfiguration und der Anwendungsprogrammierung werkzeugunterstützt mitgeteilt werden.

Entwicklungstrends im Methodenbereich

Um Ansatzpunkte für eine zukünftige Integration der Werkzeuge zur Gestaltung von Informationssystemen im Büro zu fixieren, ist es zunächst notwendig, allgemeine Trends im Bereich der organisatorischen Gestaltung aufzunehmen (vgl. dazu NEMEIER und NESS (1986)). Folgende Trends sind erkennbar:

    o Von der Allround-Methodik zum situationsspezifischen Methodeneinsatz

Der Trend zum situationsspezifischen Methodeneinsatz soll hier am Beispiel von Methoden zur organisatorisch-strategischen Planung von Bürosystemen dargestellt werden. Eine Untersuchung von Sullivan (vgl. SULLIVAN (1985)) zeigt, daß amerikanische Unternehmungen folgende Methoden der Systemplanung einsetzen:

- Wachstumskonzepte

Wachstumskonzepte unterstellen, daß alle Unternehmungen die gleichen Stadien (z.B. das Konzept der fünf Phasen der Bürorationalisierung (vgl. BULLINGER (1984)) durchlaufen und daher eine Unternehmung von den Erfahrungen der anderen profitieren kann.

- Ansätze des Informations-Ressource-Managements

Ansätze des Informations-Ressource-Managements konzentrieren sich weniger auf die Entwicklung organisatorischer Strukturen als auf die Entwicklung und Gestaltung der unternehmungsweiten Informationsressourcen. Ein typischer Ansatz für Methoden des Informations-Ressource-Managements ist KSS (Kommunikations-System-Studie) von IBM. Wesentliche Anwendungsvoraussetzungen für diese Methode sind "rationale" Datenstrukturen und eine zentralisierte Rechnerumgebung.

- Methode der Kritischen Erfolgsfaktoren

In einer dezentralen Systemwelt mit einer Vielzahl von Informationsbeständen tritt die Frage nach dem individuellen und organisatorischen Informationsbedarf in den Vordergrund. Hierzu wird von der methodischen Vorgehensweise beispielsweise die Methode der Kritischen Erfolgsfaktoren eingesetzt. Die Methode geht von der Annahme aus, daß für ein maßgeschneidertes, d.h. situativ angepasstes Informationsmanagement die Wettbewerbsumwelt einer Unternehmung und damit Trends, Chancen und Gefahren verfolgt werden müssen. Die Kenntnis der aktuellen Wettbewerbsumwelt und ihrer dominaten Merkmale dient dazu, erste robuste Ansatzpunkte für den Einsatz von Informations- und Kommunikationstechnologien zu identifizieren. Ein Erfolgsfaktor ist beispielsweise die Zeitspanne zwischen Auftragserstellung und Auslieferung ab Werk, welche kürzer sein muß als bei den Konkurrenten oder aber die Fähigkeit, ein bestimmtes Standardprodukt innerhalb kürzester Zeit zu variieren (vgl. MERKEL (1986), S. 100).

Die Frage, welche dieser Methoden die effektivste ist, beantwortet Sullivan vor dem Hintergrund der Dimensionen "Infusion" und "Diffusion". Infusion bezeichnet dabei den Umfang, indem die Informationstechnologie die Unternehmung in Hinblick auf die Bedeutung, Auswirkung oder Reichweite durchdrungen haben. Diffusion bezeichnet dabei den Umfang der Dezentralisation des Technikeinsatzes bzw., den Umfang, in welchem Technik über die gesamte Unternehmung verbreitet ist.

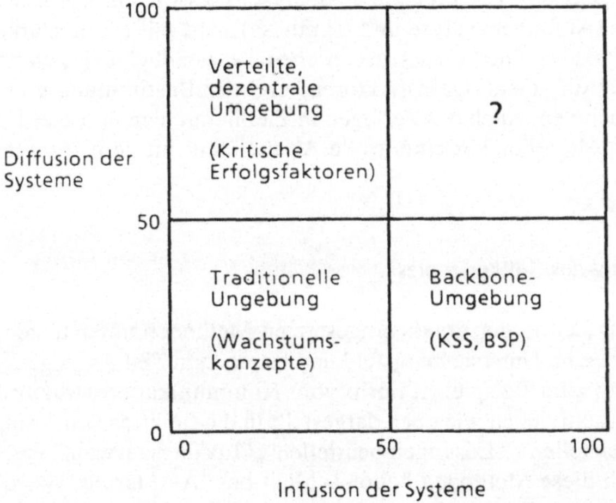

Abb. 4: Systemplanungsansätze in der Infusions-/Diffusionsebene (aus SULLIVAN (1985))

Die beiden Dimensionen "Infusion" und "Diffusion" zeigen eine hohe Korrelation mit erfolgreich eingesetzten Planungsmethoden. Die Ergebnisse dieser Untersuchung sind zusammenfassend in Schaubild 4 dargestellt.

Diese Ergebnisse deuten auf die Notwendigkeit einer situationsspezifischen Methodenauswahl hin und lenken den Blick auf ein methodisch noch leeres Feld, eine komplexe Umgebung, in der sowohl eine hohe Diffusion als auch eine hohe Infusion verliegt. Diese Situation ist typisch für die Zukunft vieler Unternehmungen und muß daher dringend methodisch angegangen werden. In diesem Feld werden rechnerunterstützte Werkzeuge ein wichtige Rolle spielen, wenngleich diese allein konzeptionelles Denken nicht sicherstellen.

o Hin zu prozeßorientierten Modellen

Bei der Einführung der Textbe- und Textverarbeitung stellen Schriftgutanalysen die dominante Aufgabe im Methodenbereich dar. Im nächsten technologischen Schritt wurden die Geräte kommunikationsfähig, damit trat an die Stelle der Schriftgutanalyse die Kommunikationsanalyse. In Unternehmungen, die Erfahrungen mit der Schriftgutanalyse hatten, wurden diese zur Untersuchung kommunikativer Aspekte (woher, wohin, unter welchen Bedingungen) erweitert, so daß sich eine "gewachsene" Aufgabenstruktur im Methodenbereich herausbildete. Unternehmungen, die keine methodischen Vorerfahrungen hatten, gingen rasch auf den Trend der Kommunikationsanalyse ein, oftmals mit den Erwartungen, mit den Ergebnissen der Kommunikationsanalyse eine umfassende Infrastrukturplanung durchführen zu können. Allein Informationen wie "Die Unternehmung hat 70% interne Kommunikation, davon sind 30% speicherungswürdig", sagt zwar etwas über den Charakter der Unternehmung aus, nicht jedoch etwas über die zukünftige Stoßrichtung der Organisationsarbeit. Der Büroprozeß geht in dieser Betrachtungsweise verloren. Ähnlich wie bei dem Versuch, die Schriftgutanalyse zur Untersuchung kommunikativer Aspekte einzusetzen wird heute versucht, auf die Kommunikationsanalyse Netzmodule aufzusetzen, die das Erkennen von Büroprozessen ermöglichen sollen.

In Analogie zur oftmals unreflektierten Ersetzung der Schriftgutanalyse durch eine Kommunikationsanalyse, treten heute autonome Büroprozessanalysen an die Stelle von Kommunikationsanalysen. Im Modellbereich läßt sich ein Trend ausgehend von datenorientierten Modellen (Schriftgutanalyse, Kommunikationsanalyse) hin zu prozeßorientierten Modellen (Büroprozeßanalyse, Durchlaufzeitanalysen) feststellen. Der Einsatz der Aufgabengliederungstechnik (Aufgabenanalyse und -synthese) wird mit einem stärkeren Eingehen auf aktorenorientierte Modelle eine Renaissance erleben. Letztendlich läßt sich ohne die Zuordnung von Aufgaben und Aufgabenträgern (Aktoren) und der Bestimmung von Kapazitätsgrößen keine Planung vornehmen. Auch das Zerlegen in Zielhierarchien und Ziel-Mittel-Relationen in aktorenorientierten Modellen hat eine große Ähnlichkeit mit dem Vorgehen der Aufgabengliederungstechnik.

o Stärkere Betonung des Sollkonzeptes

Die meisten der zur Zeit in der Praxis eingesetzten Methoden unterstützen hauptsächlich die Informationserhebung im Untersuchungsfeld und bieten zum Teil Aggregations- und Repräsentationsunterstützung zum Beispiel in Form vom Kommunikationsstrukturdiagrammen. Teilt man die Gestaltungsaktivitäten wie oben dargestellt in die funktionalen Komponenten "Aufklärung", "Lösungen erstellen", "Lösungen beurteilen", "Lösungsauswahl" und "Implementation" ein, so finden sich diese Methoden hauptsächlich bei "Aufklärung" wieder. Die Kernkomponenten "Lösungen erstellen und beurteilen" und insbesondere das systematische Erkennen von Chancen und Schwächen einer Situation oder eines Lösungsvorschlages, die zu einem Sollkonzept führen, sind nur wenig unterstützt.

Mit dem stärkeren Einsatz von Techniken der Künstlichen Intelligenz (artificial intelligence, wobei "intelligence" bezeichnenderweise mit Aufklärung übersetzt werden kann, z. B. in CIA) für Designaufgaben, wie beispielsweise von der Rechnerhardware und Betriebssystemkonfiguration bekannt, und der stärkeren Verwendung von Simulationstechniken, kann insbesondere in diese Bereiche vorgestoßen werden. Es ist zu erwarten, daß neben der Schaffung von rechnerunterstützten Gestaltungshilfsmitteln eine Strukturierung und eine Aufarbeitung der Gestaltungsarbeit einhergehen werden, die zu einem besseren Verständnis beitragen können.

o Stärkere Berücksichtigung bestehender Strukturen

Mit der zunehmenden Verbreitung von Informationssystemen in Büros und ihrer Einbindung in organisatorische Abläufe, z.B. rechnerbasierte Lohn- und Finanz-buchhaltung, Fakturierung, Auftragsabwicklung etc., werden Strukturen und Werte geschaffen, die bei der organisatorischen Umgestaltung, insbesondere beim Entwurf von technischer Infrastruktur, berücksichtigt werden muß.

In der Praxis trifft man heute oft die Aussage "Sie dürfen vollkommen auf der grünen Wiese planen, Hauptsache die technische Lösung ist mit unseren bestehenden IBM-Rechnern kompatibel und wir können unsere gekauften und in 300 Mannjahren Entwicklungsaufwand erstellten Programmpakete weiter verwenden. Aber im Bürobereich müssen wir dringend etwas tun".

Die Organisationsmethoden werden daher in Zukunft weniger die Neueinfuhrung von Computertechnik in Büros zum Ziel haben können, sondern vielmehr die Umgestaltung und Anpassung von bestehender Informationstechnik-/infrastruktur an neue Rahmen- und Randbedingungen. Dies wird sich insbesondere in der Änderung der Aufklärungsvorgehensweise weg von der einmaligen Totalerhebung hin zu inkrementeller Informationsbeschaffung unter Einbeziehung des bestehenden verteilten Bürosystems als Informationsquelle auswirken.

o Der Trend zur Methodenmodularität

Als Weiterentwicklung einer Aufgabengliederung in Systementwicklungsphasen kann die Modularisierung von Analysemethoden gesehen werden (vgl. zum Beispiel MOSAIK). Sie ermöglicht einen differenzierten, teilweisen Einsatz einer Analysemethode, angepaßt an die jeweilige Situation und Aufgabenstellung im Untersuchungsfeld. Die Modularisierung selbst kann jedoch noch kein inkrementelles Analysevorgehen ermöglichen, bei dem mit geringem Aufwand in kürzeren Zeitabständen die Analyseergebnisse akutalisiert werden können, aufbauend auf vorherigen Untersuchungen.

Ansatzpunkte für eine Werkzeugintegration

Im folgenden werden Ansätze für die Schaffung von mächtigeren Gestaltungswerkzeugen diskutiert, wie sie für den Einsatz verteilter Systeme im Büro erforderlich sind. Diese Ansätze lassen sich aus der obigen Klassifikation bestehender Werkzeuge ableiten und berücksichtigen ausdrücklich die oben genannten Probleme beim Einsatz verteilter Bürosysteme. Sie definieren auch die Gestaltungsparadigmen des COMANDOS Projekts. COMANDOS zielt in erster Linie auf die wirksame Unterstützung der Erstellung und Bewertung von Lösungen für die Gestaltung eines verteilten Bürosystems und auf die Anbindung dieser konzeptuellen Gestaltung an die Konfiguration und die Anwendungsprogrammierung ab.

o Genaue Kenntnis des Systems

Für die angestrebte Werkzeugintegration, die eine durchgängige Verknüpfung aller Methoden und Werkzeuge von der Gestaltungsunterstützung bis zum Management des laufenden Systems umfaßt, ist die genaue Kenntnis des Systems erforderlich. Die Systemarchitektur, die einzelnen Komponenten, deren Eigenschaften und ihre Verknüpfung müssen bekannt sein.

Eine Betrachtung verschiedener experimenteller und kommerzieller verteilter Systeme für den Bürobereich (vgl. NESS, REIM, MEITNER und NIEMEIER (1986)) hat ergeben, daß eine dreischichtige Architektur vorherrscht: "Host", "Workstation" und "Desktop". Die "Hosts" sind die eingesetzten Rechner - die Hardware und eventuell ein "Host"-Betriebssystem. Die "Workstations" sind Software-Umgebungen, die auf dem "Host" laufen und die der Unterstützung des "Desktops" dienen. Die "Desktops" sind Prozeßumgebungen, die explizit auf die Arbeitsumgebung eines Büroarbeiters abgebildet sind. Bei einigen der betrachteten Systeme können diese "Desktops" zwischen den "Workstations" migrieren, was höhere Flexibilität auf Anwenderseite bedeutet.

o Verwendung von Information aus dem laufenden System

Kommerziell eingesetzte, verteilte Systeme verfügen über einfache Konfigurationswerkzeuge, die im laufenden Betrieb eine Änderung der Konfiguration, sowohl der Hardware, als auch der Software zulassen. Leistungsmodellierung und Leistungsoptimierungswerkzeuge, wie sie von zentralisierten Großrechnern bekannt sind, wurden bisher bei verteilten Systemen noch nicht eingesetzt. Gerade hier sind weitere Werkzeuge zur Gestaltung und zur Verwaltung eines komplexen, verteilten Systems mit einigen hundert Knoten notwendig. Sie sollten auf den existierenden Administrationswerkzeugen und den "manuellen" Konfigurationswerkzeugen aufsetzen. Die Integration der Werkzeuge zur Gestaltung, zur Konfiguration und zum Betrieb des Systems bietet nicht nur die Möglichkeit einer direkteren Umsetzung der organisatorischen Anforderungen und eine Unterstützung bei der Handhabung der Komplexität. Sie erlaubt auch die Übernahme und die Verarbeitung von Informationen, die im Betrieb und bei der tatsächlichen Konfiguration anfallen. Dies sind z.B. quantitative Daten über Kommunikationsströme, Statistiken über Fehlerorte und –häufigkeiten, Aussagen zur Lastverteilung oder über Zustände von Vorgängen. Außerdem können Angaben über Leistungsschätzungen verschiedener Systemstrukturen eingebracht werden.

o Komplexitätsreduktion durch Aufgabenzerlegung

Es hat sich besonders bei den Werkzeugen der vierten und fünften Gruppe, Taxis, XSEL/XCON und SICONFEX gezeigt, daß eine geeignete Aufgabenzerlegung notwendig ist (z.B. mit hierarchischer Struktur), um mit der Komplexität fertig zu werden. Darüberhinaus ist ein genereller Modellierungsrahmen sinnvoll, in dem die einzelnen Modelle konzeptuell eingebunden sind. Dadurch sollte auch die Definition von Schnittstellen erleichtert werden. Es kann nicht erwartet werden, daß ein einziges Modell den gesamten Aufgabenbereich sinnvoll umfassen kann.

o Gestaltung als symbiotischer Prozeß zwischen Mensch und Maschine

Die Werkzeuge in der oberen linken Ecke des Bildes 3, die sich vor allem mit der Gestaltung der Büros und des verteilten Bürosystems befassen, unterstützen gut strukturierte "low-level" Tätigkeiten wie z.B. die Datenpräsentation. Sie überlassen jedoch die normativen und interpretativen Anteile am Gestaltungsprozeß dem Organisator. Diese Klasse der Werkzeuge weist daher ein hohes Maß an Interaktion zwischen dem Organisator und dem Programm auf. Dies hängt zum einen mit der Vielzahl subtiler und schlecht formalisierbarer Details in diesem Bereich zusammen, zum anderen wohl auch mit der leichteren sensorischen Zugänglichkeit der Büroumgebung für einen menschlichen Beobachter, der hier einem Computerprogramm weit überlegen ist.

Die Werkzeuge, die sich dagegen mit der Konfiguration und der Anwendungsprogrammierung befassen, benötigen wesentlich weniger Interaktion. Diese Aufgaben sind stärker strukturiert und enger eingrenzbar. Die angewandten Techniken reichen von prozeduralen zu regelbasierten

Programmen. Da die Aufklärung als Teilkomponente der Gestaltung nicht unterstützt wird, ist eine sehr genaue Problemdefinition durch den Benutzer erforderlich. Es kann erwartet werden, daß die durchgängige Gestaltungsaktivität in einer Symbiose zwischen dem menschlichen Gestalter und einem Unterstützungssystem ablaufen wird.

o Inkrementelle Vorgehensweise

Da eine komplette Neugestaltung des Büros in der Realität selten vorkommt, sollte ein Gestaltungsprozeß unterstützt werden, der von einem bestehenden Büro oder einem vorhandenen verteilten Bürosystem ausgeht. Darauf aufbauend wird iterativ ein neuer Entwurf entwickelt. Diese Vorgehensweise erscheint auch deshalb sinnvoll, weil in einer Büroumgebung häufig Änderungen auftreten. Dadurch wird eine inkrementelle Anpassung auch des laufenden, verteilten Bürosystems erforderlich.

Voraussetzungen zur Kommunikation von Problemen und Lösungen

Abschließen sollen einige wesentliche Voraussetzungen skizziert werden, welche eine Kommunikation von Problemen und Lösungen sowohl innerhalb des Unternehmens als auch die Entwicklung integrierter Werkzeuge zur Gestaltung von Informationssystemen im Büro erst ermöglichen werden:

o Entwicklung neuer Kooperationsstrukturen zwischen Fachwelt, Fachbereichsorganisator und technischer Bürowelt (Applikationsprogrammierer, Systemmanager)

Über die Grenzen der herkömmlichen Arbeitsteilung bei der Systemgestaltung ist schon häufig geschrieben worden (vgl. dazu beispielsweise WELTZ (1986), S. 1122). Es ist danach nur noch eingeschränkt möglich, daß der Systemexperte plant und strukturiert, während die Anwender die Informationen liefern. Hier soll der Focus jedoch noch erweitert werden, um auf weitere Kooperationsnotwendigkeiten aufmerksam zu machen. Der Fachbereich ist dafür zuständig, daß die operativen Geschäfte abgewickelt und Problemlösungen als Form der Anpassung an eine neue Aufgabenumwelt initiiert werden. Dabei unterstützt ihn der Organisator. Der Applikationsprogrammierer kam immer dann ins Spiel, wenn Abläufe rechnerunterstützt realisiert wurden. Der Systemmanager sorgte für die Aufrechterhaltung der Systemleistungen meist größerer Systeme und nahm die Anpassung im technischen System vor (Einrichten von Benutzeraccounts, Verwaltung der Speicher etc.) Jede dieser Aufgaben führte zu einer hohen Professionalisierung. Da die Aufgaben bislang weitgehend unabhängig voneinander wahrgenommen werden konnten, hatte ein Fachbereich unterschiedliche Ansprechpartner.

Mit dem technischen Trend hin zu verteilten technischen Bürosystemen kann diese Aufgabenteilung nicht mehr in der ursprünglichen Form beibehalten werden. Der Organisationsgestalter definiert mit dem organisatorischen Soll-Konzept Anforderungen an das technische System in Form einer funktionalen Spezifikation. Dabei muß er gleichzeitig die Kapazität und Leistungsfähigkeit des technischen Systems berücksichtigen. Im nächsten Schritt werden diese Informationen in die technische Konfiguration umgesetzt. Diese Aufgabe nimmt der Systemmanager wahr, der für die Konfiguration und operationale Steuerung der Hardware, des Betriebssystems und der Systemdienste, z. B. Lastverteilungen, und Leistungsparameter des technischen Systems liefern wiederum Informationen, die bei der Planung der Organisation zu berücksichtigen sind. Mit dem Entwurf eines Bürosystems werden für die Anwendungsprogrammierung funktionale Anforderungen festgelegt, die durch eine detaillierte Software-spezifikation auszufüllen sind. Die Anwendungsprogrammierung stellt umgekehrt Leistungen und Fähigkeiten zur Verfügung, die beim Entwurf eines verteilten Bürosystems berücksichtigt werden müssen.

o Stärkere und schnellere Nutzbarmachung von wissenschaftlichen Konzepten für die Organisationspraxis und Interdisziplinarität

Es kann häufig beobachtet werden, daß neue Konzepte und Ideen sehr lange brauchen, bis sie die Forschungsszene verlassen und in praktischen Einsatz kommen. So wurde zum Beispiel Ende der siebziger Jahre von Michael Hammer am Massachussetts Institute of Technology das "Focal Objekt" als abstraktes Beschreibungselement für einen Büroprozeß (procedure) vorgeschlagen, das kurz darauf als zentrales Konzept in ein funktionales, prozeßorientiertes Modell von Büroarbeit einging (vgl. MIT-LCS (1980)).

Dieses Konzept entstand allerdings nicht in einer betriebswirtschaftlichen Fakultät, sondern in einem Computer Science Laboratory aus der Arbeit an höheren Programmiersprachen heraus (vgl. HAMMER, HOWE, KRUSKAL und WLADAWSKI (1977)). Wesentlich später wurde dieses Prinzip als "Büroprodukt" in einer prozeßorientierten Betrachtung der Büroarbeit beispielsweise in MOSAIK neu entdeckt. Interessant ist in diesem Zusammenhang, daß die ursprünglich in der Computer Science entwickelte Bürobeschreibungssprache rein deskriptiv war (vgl. SUTHERLAND und SIRBU (1983), MIT-LCS (1980)) und dort erst später die Notwendigkeit von normativen Elementen erkannt wurde. 1983 wurde dann die Beschreibungssprache um normative Konzepte erweitert (SUTHERLAND (1983)).

Diese Erweiterung wurde von dem an der Sloan School of Management, also an einer betriebswirtschaftlichen Fakultät, entwickelten Ansatz der Kritischen Erfolgsfaktoren (ROCKART (1979)) abgeleitet. Diese Beispiele deuten darauf hin, daß für die notwendige schnelle Umsetzung von Forschungsergebnissen in praktische Methoden, ein interdisziplinärer Austausch und besser noch ein interdisziplinäres Zusammenarbeiten erforderlich ist.

o Neue Kompetenzfelder für Organisatoren und Planer

Die zunehmende Anwendung von Methoden für die organisatorische Gestaltung führen dazu, daß der Organisator neue, zusätzliche methodische und methodologische Ansätze, neue Instrumente und Modellansätze und vor allem auch neue rechnerunterstützte Hilfsmittel zur Verfügung haben wird und beherrschen muß. Bislang werden in einem arbeitsplatzweisen Vorgehen vom Organisator mit Papier und Bleistift Arbeitsumgebungen mit hoher Kostenverantwortlichkeit gestaltet. Durch eine prozeßorientierte Betrachtung bei der arbeitsplatz- und funktionsübergreifenden Gestaltung von Arbeitssystemen werden Komplexitätsprobleme aufgeworfen, die vor allem aus der großen Anzahl der zu betrachtenden Elemente und Zusammenhänge herrühren. Diese erfordern Rechnerunterstützung im Hilfsmittelbereich, wodurch jedoch keinesfalls konzeptionelles Denken ersetzt werden kann.

Für die Anwenderorganisation entsteht zum einen durch die Änderung des Aufgaben-, Betrachtungs- und Methodenumfeldes und der Hilfsmittel und zum anderen durch die zunehmende Anzahl der vorgeschlagenen Methoden und angebotenen Hilfsmittel ein Ordnungsbedarf. Es müssen, individuell angepaßt auf die Unternehmungssituation, Ordnungsrahmen geschaffen werden. Diese legen ähnlich einer Methodologie fest, welche methodischen Vorgehen, welche Instrumente und welche Hilfsmittel legitim sind und wie sie eingesetzt werden sollen. Für den Organisator ergeben sich hieraus neue Kompetenzfelder zusätzlich zu den bisherigen, wie zum Beispiel Moderations- oder Strukturierungskompetenzen. Die neuen Kompetenzfelder betreffen in erster Linie drei Bereiche, die Ordnungskompetenz, die Methodenkompetenz und die Werkzeugkompetenz.

Eine ähnliche Entwicklung konnte im letzten Jahrzehnt im Ingenieurbereich mit der zunehmenden Rechnerunterstützung beobachtet werden. Gemeinsam mit dem Potential neuer Hilfsmittel änderten sich die Möglichkeiten im Methodenbereich und schufen neue Kompetenzen für die Ingenieure in einem positiven Rückkopplungskreis. Dieser Kompetenzzuwachs führte zu einer Berufsbilderweiterung, was sich auch auf die Ausbildung ausgewirkt hat, indem zuerst Numerik und Programmiersprachen und später CAD, CAM und CIM Eingang in die Studienpläne gefunden haben und finden werden.

Literatur

Balzert, H. (1982), Die Entwicklung von Software-Systemen, Bibliographisches Institut, Mannheim, Wien, und Zürich 1982

Barron J. (1982), Dialogue and Process Design for Interactive Information Systems using Taxis, in: Proceedings of ACM SIGOA Conference on Office Systems, New York 1982, S. 108-116

Bergmann, M. (1987), Moasik: ein modulares und rechnergestütztes Methodenpaket zur effizienten Gestaltung der Büroarbeit, in: Fähnrich, K.-P. (Hrsg., 1987)

Brabander, B. D. E. und Thiers, G. (1984), Successful Information System Development in Relation to Situational Factors which Affect Effective Communication between MIS-Users an EDP Specialities, in: Management Science, 30, 1984, 2, S. 137-155

Bracker, L. C., Konsynski, B. R. (1981), The OFFIS System - A Tool in Automated Office Design, in: Proc. 1981 Office Autom. Conf. Dig., AFIPS Press, S. 417-419

Bullinger, H.-J. (1984), Die Durchdringung der Unternehmung mit integrierten Bürosystemen - Die Phasen der Bürorationalisierung, in: Bullinger, H.-J. (Hrsg., 1984), S. 549-582

Bullinger, H.-J. (Hrsg., 1984), Integrierte Bürosysteme - zukunftssichere Strategien und Anwendungen, Berlin, Heidelberg, New York, Tokyo 1984

Bullinger, H.-J., (1986), Wettbewerbsvorteile durch Informationsmanagement, in: Bullinger (Hrsg., 1986), S. 55 - 119

Bullinger, H.-J. (Hrsg., 1986), Informationsmanagement für die Praxis, Berlin, Heidelberg, New York, Tokyo 1986

Bungers, D., Groth, K. (1984), Das Expertensystem R1, In: Bungers D., Müller B. S., Raulefs P. (Hrsg., 1984): Beiträge aus einem Workshop zur Aufarbeitung der State-of-the-Art: Architektur und Funktionsanalyse, Arbeitsberichte der GMD Nr. 120, S. 114-120

CEC-ITTTF (1986), Commission of the European Communities Information Technology and Telecommunications Task Force, ESPRIT Project Synopsis, Office Systems, Januar 1986

Cook, C. (1980), Streamling Office Procedures - An Analysis using the Information Control Net Modul, in: Proceedings AFIPS National Computer Conference, 1980, S. 555-565

De Antonellis, V., Bodem, H. und Coccia, A. (1985), Relevance of Models for Office Support Systems Analysis, in: Commission of the European Communities (Hrsg., 1985) Preprints of the ESPRIT Technical Week'85

Dumas, P., de Petra, G., Charbonnel, G. (1986), Toward a Methodology for Office Analysis, Reprints of the ESPRIT Technical Week'86

Ellis, C. A. (1979), Information Control Nets: A Mathematical Model of Office in: Proc. Conf. Simulation, Measurement and Modeling Computer Systems, Boulder, CO, August 1979, S. 225-239

Fähnrich, K.-P. (Hrsg., 1987), Fortschritte der neuen Informations- und Kommunikationstechniken, ONLINE 87, Velbert 1987

Grochla, E. (1982), Grundlagen der organisatorischen Gestaltung, Poeschel, Stuttgart, 1982

Hammer, M., Howe, W. G., Kruskal, V. J. und Wladawski, I. (1977), A Very High-Level Programming Language for Data Processing Application, in: Comm. ACM, Vol 20, No 11, S. 832-840, 1977

Hansen, H. R. (1980), Systemanalyse, in: Grochla (Hrsg., 1980), Handwörterbuch der Organisation, Stuttgart 1980, Sp. 2171-2183

Haugeneder, H., Lehmann, E., Strauss, P. (1985), Knowledge-Based Configuration of Operating Systems - Problems in Modeling the Domain Knowledge, in: Brauer, W. und Radig, B. (1985), Wissensbasierte Systeme, GI-Kongreß 1985, Informatik-Fachberichte 112, Springer-Verlag, S. 121-134

Höring, H. (1987), Neue Methoden und Instrumente zur Planung und Einführung fortschrittlicher IuK-Systeme, in: Fähnrich, K.-P. (Hrsg., 1987), S. 28.4.01 - 28.4.13

Hein, K. P. (1985), Information System Model and Architecture Generator, in: IBM Systems Journal, Vol. 24, Nos 3/4, 1985, S. 213-235

IDC (1985), Office '86, Der Deutsche Markt für Büroinformationssysteme 1984-1990, IDC Deutschland GmbH, Eschborn 1986

Kieser, A. (1986), Organisationskonzepte. Wege zu einer methodengestützten Analyse und Planung von Bürosystemen, in: Bullinger (Hrsg., 1986), S. 123 - 125

Konsynski, B. R.; Bracker, L. C.; Bracker, J. R. (1982), A Model for Specification of Office Communications, in: IEEE Trans. Communications, Vol. 30, No. 1, Januar 1982, S. 27-36

Konsynski, B. R. und Nunamaker, J. F. (1984), Decision Suppurt in Enterprise Analysis, in: Chang, S.-K. (Hrsg. 1984), Management and Office Information Systems, New York, London 1984, S. 119-132

Kraft, A. (1984), XCON: An Expert Configuration System at Digital Equipment Corporation, in: Winston P. H., Prendergast, K. A. (Hrsg., 1984), The Commercial Uses of Artificial Intelligence, Cambridge, MA, The MIT Press, S. 41-49

Krallmann, H., Feiten, L., Hoyer, R., Kölzer, G. (1986), Konzeption der Kommunikationsstrukturanalyse, Interner Bericht, TU Berlin, 1986

Krallmann, H. (Hrsg., 1986), Planung, Einsatz und Wirtschaftlichkeitsnachweis von Büroinformationssystemen, Berlin 1986

Lehmann E. u.a (1985), SICONFEX ein Expertensystem für die Konfigurierung eines Betriebssystems, in: Hansen, H. R. (Hrsg., 1985), GI/OCG/OGI - Jahrestagung 1985, Springer-Verlag, S. 792-805

McDermott, J. (1980), R1: A Rule-Based Configurer, Carnegie-Mellon, 1980

McDermott, J. (1981), R1: The Formative Years AI Magazine, 1981, S. 21-29

McDermott J. (1982), XSEL: A Computer Sales Person's Assistant, in: Hayes, J. E., Michie, D., Pao, Y.-H. (Hrsg., 1982)), Machine Intelligence 10, Ellis Horwood Limited, S. 325-337

Merkel, H. (1986), Die Beantwortung der Frage nach der Wirtschaftlichkeit von Informationssystemen. Eine Herausforderung an das Informationsmanagement, in: Krallmann, H. (Hrsg., 1986), S. 93 - 101

MIT-LCS (Hrsg., 1980), Annual Progress Report Office Automation Group, Massachusetts Institute of Technology, Laboratory for Computer Science, 1980

Mylopoulos, J., Borgida, A., Greenspan, S., Wong, H. K. T. (1984): Information System Design at the Conceptual Level - The Taxis Project, in: IEEE Database Engineering, Vol. 7, No. 4, December 1984, S. 4-9

Ness, A. J., Reim, F., Meitner, H. und Niemeier, J. (1986), Decision Support System for Planning and Design of Distributed Office Systems, Deliverable FHG-D 1-T1.1-860829 des ESPRIT-Projekts 834 (Comandos) Universität Stuttgart, Fraunhofer-Institut für Arbeitswirtschaft und Organisation, Stuttgart 1986

Niemeier, J. und Ness, A. (1986), Modelle zur Analyse und Planung von Bürosystemen - Entwicklungstrends im Methodenbereich, in: Bullinger, H.-J. (Hrsg., 1986), S. 241-271

Nutt, G. J. (1983), An Experimental Distributed Modeling System, 1983, in: ACM Trans. Off. Inf. Syst., Vol. 1, No. 2, S. 117-142

Nutt, G. J., Ricci, P. A. (1981), Quinault: An Office Modeling System, in: Computer, Vol. 14, No. 5, S. 41-57

Palm, S. U. (1985), An Office Investigation and Analysis Method, in: Roukens, J. und Renuart, J. F. (Hrsg., 1985), ESPRIT '84: Status Report of Ongoing Work, Amsterdam, New York, Oxford, S. 283-294

Pernici, B., Vogel, W. (1986), An Integrated Approach to OIS Development, Beitrag zur ESPRIT Technical Week'86, (wird veröffentlicht)

Philips AG (1986a), SOPHO-PLAN Methodik zur gezielten Planung und Einführung von Bürokommunikation, Kurzbeschreibung, Philips Kommunikations Industrie AG, Siegen-Weidenau, 807/86024,0/PRO, 1986

Philips AG (1986b), SOPHO-PLAN als Planungsmethode für integrierte Informationssysteme, Philips Kommunikations Industrie AG, 1986

Reindl, E. (1986), INFORA-VERIKS - ein DV-gestütztes Verfahren für die Analyse und Gestaltung der Bürokommunikation, Fachseminar Instrumente der Bürosystemplanung, 30./31. Jan. 1986, BIFOA, Köln

Rockart, J. F. (1979), Chief Executive define their own Data Needs, in: Harvard Business Review, March-April 1979, S. 81-93

Schäfer, G. u.a. (1986), FAOR: A Multiperspective Requirements Approach, Beitrag zur ESPRIT Technical Week '86, (wird veröffentlicht)

Schaible, A. F. (1986), PLAKOM und MOSAIK - Über die Analyse von Kommunikation und Funktion zum Anforderungsprofil von Bürosystemen, in: Bullinger, H.-J. (Hrsg. 1986)

Schönecker, H.G. und M. Nippa (Hrsg., 1987), Neue Methoden zur Gestaltung der Büroarbeit - Computergestützte Organisationshilfen für die Praxis, München 1987

Siemens AG (1984), PLAKOM, Planungsverfahren zur Erarbeitung von Kommunikationskonzepten, Kurzbeschreibung, Siemens AG, Berlin, München, Version 3.0, July 1984

Siemens AG (1985a), PLAKOM, Das Werkzeug für die organisierte Bürokommunikation, Version 3, Siemens AG, München, Juli 1985

Siemens AG (1985b), PLAKOM Erhebungsbogen, Version 3.0, Siemens AG, München, Oktober 1985

Siemens AG (1986), MOSAIK, "Wirtschaftliche Lösungen für die Bürokommunikation ganzheitlich gestalten mit MOSAIK", Siemens AG München, Juni 1986

Simon, H. (1960), The New Science of Management Decision, Harper and Row, New York

Sirbu, M., Schoichet, S., Kunin, J. and Hammer, M. (1981), OAM: An office Analysis methodology, in: MIT, Office Automations Group Memo OAM-016, 1981

Sirbu, M. A., Schoichet, S. R., Kunin, J. S., Hammer, M. M. Sutherland, J. B. und Zarmer, C. L. (1983), Office Analysis Methodology and Case Studies, Massachusetts Institute of Technology 1983

Sullivan, C. H. (1985), System Planning in the Information Age, in: Sloan Management Review, Winter 1985, S. 3-12

Sutherland, J. (1983), An Office Analysis and Diagnostic Methodology, MS Thesis, Technical Report MIT/LCS/TR-290, Massachusetts Institute of Technology, 1983

Sutherland, J. und Sirbu, M. (1983), Evaluation of an Office Analysis Methodology, OAM-043, MIT, LCS of Computer Science, 1983

Weltz, F. (1986), Was ist neu an der neuen Bürotechnik? Überlegungen zum Einsatz und Nutzen technischer Unterstützung der Bürokommunikation, in: Office Management, 1986, 11, S. 1120 - 1123

Zachmann, J. A. (1982), Business Systems Planning and Business Information Control Study: A Comparison, in: IBM Systems Journal, Vol. 21, No. 1, S. 31-53

Zangl, H. (1986), Transparenz der Zusammenhänge im Büro, Durchlaufzeiten (DZA) zur Untersuchung und Gestaltung von Arbeitsabläufen, in: Bullinger, H.-J. (Hrsg. 1986), S. 223 - 240

<u>Informationsbedarfsermittlung
für die Gestaltung eines Bürgeramtes</u>

Herbert Stuhlmann
Gesellschaft für Mathematik und Datenverarbeitung mbH
Bonn 5205 Sankt Augustin, Schloß Birlinghoven

Ausgangsüberlegungen

Ausgangspunkt des Forschungsvorhabens war ein 1978 von der Stadt Unna begonnenes Pilotprojekt "Offenes Rathaus", das erste Überlegungen anstellte, wie mehr Bürgernähe in der Kommunalverwaltung realisiert werden konnte. Seit Herbst 1980 wurde ein Projekt als gemeinsames Forschungsvorhaben der Gesellschaft für Mathematik und Datenverarbeitung (GMD), Sankt Augustin, und der Stadt Unna mit Unterstützung des Bundesministeriums für Forschung und Technologie (BMFT) durchgeführt. Die Problemstellung des gemeinsamen Forschungsvorhabens der GMD und der Stadt Unna knüpfte an die Vorarbeiten des Pilotprojektes an.

Im Verhältnis von Bürgern und Verwaltung haben eine Reihe von bedeutsamen Veränderungen stattgefunden.

Die Gebietsreformen haben zwar dafür gesorgt, daß das Leistungsangebot der Kommunen umfassender und einheitlicher werden konnte, die dabei erfolgte Zentralisierung der Verwaltung bewirkte jedoch zwangsläufig "Bürgerferne". Bürgerferne blieb jedoch nicht auf die räumliche Dimension beschränkt, obwohl auch die vielerorts länger gewordenen Wege den Kosten– und Zeitaufwand für den Bürger beträchtlich erhöhten.

Einige der wichtigsten Faktoren, die darüber hinaus das Verhältnis Bürger/Verwaltung verändert haben, sollen hier aufgezählt werden:

– Der gesellschaftliche Wandel (wachsende Mobilität der Bevölkerung, abnehmendes Interesse an öffentlichen Angelegenheiten, steigende Anforderungen an die öffentliche Daseinsfürsorge) beeinflußte das Verhältnis zwischen Bürger und Verwaltung.

– Die Verwaltung machte durch die gesetzgeberischen Vorgaben einen Wandel von der Ordnungsverwaltung zur Leistungsverwaltung durch, der viele Umstellungs– und Anpassungsprozesse erforderte.

– Die Organisationsstrukturen der Kommunalverwaltungen sind aufgabenorientiert, nicht bürgerbezogen.

– bei denen mehr Bürgernähe unter Wahrnehmung der Mitarbeiterinteressen erreicht
  werden sollte

– die zugleich als Grundlage für die Fortentwicklung und Vereinheitlichung der Aufgaben– und Verwaltungsgliederung der Gemeinden gleicher Größenklasse in den
  Ländern der Bundesrepublik dienen konnten

– wobei der Einsatz   von Informationstechnik eine notwendige Voraussetzung für die
  Realisierung sein sollte.

Für die Entwicklung, Durchsetzbarkeit und Realisierung eines so angedachten Bürgeramtes waren eine Reihe von

– Informationsquellen so zu bilden, daß die zu Beginn des Vorhabens noch sehr heterogenen, in der Regel nur implizite und aus den unterschiedlichsten Blickwinkeln und
  Interessengruppierungen heraus bewerteten Informationen einer objektiven Bearbeitung
  zugänglich gemacht werden konnten.

– Entscheidungsgremien zu bilden, durch die die unterschiedlichsten Interessen ausgewogen   berücksichtigt und die Ergebnisse auf breiter Basis mitgetragen werden
  konnten.

Ausgangsmaterial

Als Ausgangsmaterial für die Entwicklung eines Bürgeramtes unter Einbeziehung der
Informationstechnik wurden alle Informationen angesehen,

– die geeignet waren als Kriterium zu dienen, ob und in welchem Umfang Aufgaben für
  ein Bürgeramt geeignet waren und inwieweit ein DV–Einsatz hierfür als sinnvoll erschien.
– die für die hardware– und Softwaremäßige Gestaltung eines optimalen DV–Systems
  zur Erledigung der für das Bürgeramt ermittelten Aufgaben erforderlich waren und die
  dafür notwendig vorzuhaltenden Daten.

In diesem Sinne standen die folgenden Materialien und Fundgruben zur Verfügung:

Informationen, die in expliziter Form zugänglich waren:

– Der Aufgabengliederungsplan der Kommunalen Gemeinschaftsstelle für Verwaltungsvereinfachung (KGSt), ansonsten der Aufgabengliederungsplan der Stadt Unna von 1974.

- Die Zuständigkeitsbereiche der einzelnen Ämter und Behörden sind für den Bürger wegen der zunehmenden Aufgabenzersplitterung (verwaltungsintern und zwischen den verschiedenen Verwaltungsebenen) nicht mehr erkennbar.

- Die Rechtsvorschriften werden für den Bürger wie auch für die Sachbearbeiter immer unüberschaubarer.

- Die Informationsaufnahme der Verwaltung wird durch organisatorische Kriterien und die technischen Hilfsmittel bestimmt. Formulare sind daher in der Regel nach verwaltungsinternen Erfordernissen gestaltet und schwer verständlich. Das gleiche gilt für "Bescheide" und die häufig unnatürliche Sprache, die für Mitteilungen und Bitten ("Bescheide" und "Ladungen", typische obrigkeitsstaatliche Ausdrücke) verwendet wird.

- Die Art des DV–Einsatzes in der öffentlichen Verwaltung zwingt den Bürger häufig, sich den Bedingungen der Technik unterzuordnen; Formulare müssen DV–gerecht ausgefüllt werden, Bescheide sind kaum lesbar und unübersichtlich, weil verschlüsselte Angaben übersetzt werden müssen.

Da die Verwaltung –   wie die Bürger – ein Interesse an einer möglichst problemlosen Fallabwicklung hat, die vorgefundenen Umstände dies aber nicht gewährleisteten, ging man davon aus, daß "Bürgernähe" nicht allein eine Forderung der Bürger an die Verwaltung ist.

Als Beispiel für einen neueren theoretischen Ansatz zum Verhältnis zwischen Bürger und Verwaltung wurde das Konzept einer Bielefelder Soziologengruppe (Kaufmann, Grunow, Hegner) herangezogen. Ihr "relationales Konzept" geht von der wechselseitigen Abhängigkeit von Bürger und Verwaltung aus. Der persönlichen Kontaktsituation beider Seiten wird dabei besondere Beachtung geschenkt mit dem Ziel, ein Interaktionssystem zu finden, das die Handlungschancen des einzelnen Bürgers gegenüber der Verwaltung soweit verbessert, daß er deren Leistungen seinen Ansprüchen gemäß voll ausschöpfen kann.

Die Folgen der bei den Bürgern und Verwaltungen entstandenen Veränderungen müssen durch die Verwaltung bewältigt werden. Als einen möglichen Lösungsweg dieses Problems schlug das Pilotprojekt der Stadt Unna eine teilweise Neuorganisation der Verwaltung mit dem Ziel vor, die Bürgernähe des Verwaltungshandels zu erhöhen.

Ziel des Vorhabens

Ziel des Vorhabens war es, alternative Organisationsmodelle für Kommunalverwaltungen zu entwickeln,

- Die gesetzlichen Grundlagen für die Aufgabenerledigung, Verordnungen und teilweise Arbeitsanweisungen.

- Berichte über Organisationsuntersuchungen anderer Gemeinden und Städte für bestimmte Ämter.

- Unterlagen, die bei der Erledigung von Aufgaben entstehen: Formulare, Akten, Karteien, Übersichten und Pläne.

- Datenstrukturen und Daten, die für spezielle Aufgaben systematisch erstellt worden waren; z.B. die Einwohnermeldedaten, das Fundbuch und das Fischereibuch.

- Die Situation der Datenverarbeitung in Unna:
  - Geräteeinsatz
  - Datenstrukturen und Mengengerüste
  - Wo und in welcher Form bereits eingesetzt.

Informationen, die in impliziter Form zugänglich waren:

- Das Fachwissen der Dezernenten, Amtsleiter und Sachbearbeiter der Stadt Unna.

- Das Partialwissen über Wünsche oder Aussagen zu Schwachstellen, erreichbar über

  - politische Mandatsträger
  - Bürger (insbesondere der artikulationsschwachen Bürger und Minderheitengruppen)
  - Verwaltungsmitarbeiter der Stadt Unna
  - Gremien und Institutionen mit bestimmten Zielrichtungen zur

    - Verwaltungsvereinfachung
    - Standardisierung
    - Einhaltung des Datenschutzes
    - Vertretung der Arbeitnehmerinteressen
    - Gewährleistung der Portabilität und Wartung des Systems

  - Wissen der Mitarbeiter innerhalb der beiden Projektgruppen in

    - DV – technischen
    - juristischen
    - soziologischen
    - sozialen
    - verwaltungstechnischen Fragen.

Konkretisierung der Struktur des Vorhabens

Zu Beginn des Vorhabens wurde eine dreitägige Klausurtagung durchgeführt, die den folgenden Zwecken diente:

– Den beteiligten Partnern sollte die Möglichkeit geboten werden, sich untereinander kennenzulernen.

– Es sollten die Ergebnisse der Vorstudie vorgestellt und die Zielvorstellungen aus unterschiedlichen Blickwinkeln erläutert und diskutiert werden (Stadt Unna, GMD im Zusammenhang mit den Förderungszielen).

– Für die Teilnehmer sollte ein gemeinsamer Informationsstand für die weitere Mitarbeit geschaffen werden.

– Der Absteckung der Gesamtziele des Vorhabens, der Bildung von Mitwirkungsgremien und des Ablaufs der Arbeiten in der ersten Phase (Festlegungen, Notwendigkeiten) sollten konkretisiert werden.

Die Sitzungen der Klausurtagung wurden mit Hilfe der Metaplan–Gesprächstechnik geführt. Es handelt sich hierbei um eine Methode des "Schriftlichen Diskutierens" mit Hilfe von Schlagwortkärtchen. Diese Methode verbindet die schriftliche Fixierung – sie liefert damit eine visuelle Unterstützung während der Diskussion – mit der Möglichkeit, seine Meinung zu äußern, ohne darauf warten zu müssen, daß einem das Wort erteilt wird. Durch diese Methode wird auch die Zahl der möglichen Diskussionsbeiträge vervielfacht, weil die schriftliche Form einen echten Parallelablauf ermöglicht, und im Gegensatz zu einer herkömmlichen Diskussion keine Beiträge mehr untergehen, weil sie unter Umständen im Moment als nicht sehr relevant empfunden wurden oder weil sie in der Rednerfolge durch einen Vorredner aus dem Aktualitätskreis gedrängt wurden. Ein Moderator überwacht die Einhaltung des thematischen Fadens und sorgt für die Umsetzung der Diskussionsbeiträge in Entscheidungssituationen und schafft so Entscheidungszwänge.

Diese Methode wurde im Verlaufe des Vorhabens in gewissen Varianten noch häufiger angewendet, um aus nur implizite vorhandenen, aus schriftlich nicht fixierten, aus den verschiedensten Anlässen aufgenommenen und aus den innerhalb einer Gruppe gestreuten Informationen relativ rasch zu konkreten Informationen und Aussagen zu kommen.

Auf der Klausurtagung wurden zu den folgenden Auslösefragen Informationen gesammelt bzw. Ergebnisse erarbeitet:

– Verfahren zur Ermittlung der Bürger– und Mitarbeiterbedürfnisse

– Verfahren der Istaufnahme

– Inhalte der Istaufnahme

– Aufgaben und Zusammensetzung des Beratungsgremiums

– Beteiligung von Bürgern und Mitarbeitern

– Grenzbeispiele aus verschiedenen Ämtern

– Was sind Kriterien für Aufgaben des Bürgeramtes?

– Was soll Bürgernähe bedeuten?

Die Zusammensetzung der Teilnehmer entscheidet nicht unerheblich über die Qualität der Ergebnisse. An dieser Klausurtagung nahmen teil,
von der Stadt Unna:

– der Stadtdirektor
– 2 stellvertretende Bürgermeister
– 1 Beigeordneter der Stadt
– 2 Vertreter des Personalrats
– 1 Gewerkschaftsvertreter ÖTV
– 7 Mitarbeiter der Stadtverwaltung (aus unterschiedlichen Ämtern)

von der GMD:

– 10 wissenschaftliche Mitarbeiter
  davon – 5 DV – Spezialisten
         – 2 Sozialwissenschaftler
         – 1 Verwaltungsjurist
         – 1 Betriebswirt
         – 1 Psychologe

– 2 Moderatoren der Firma Metaplan.

Ergebnisse der Klausurtagung (Beispielhaft)

Ergebnisse waren die als Maßstab für die Eignung einer Aufgabe als Bürgeramtsaufgabe entwickelten folgenden Kriterien, die Richtschnur für die Fragenkomplexe der Amtsleiterinterviews und der Istaufnahme wurden:

- Die Aufgabe ist einfach und ohne großen Aufwand an Zeit und Hilfsmitteln zu erledigen.

- Die Aufgabe ist sofort und abschließend zu erledigen.

- Es sind keine oder nur einfache Entscheidungen bei der Abwicklung der Aufgabe zu fällen.

- Für die Aufgabe sind keine Einzelakten zu führen.

- Die Anzahl der Vorgänge pro Jahr ist hinreichend groß.

- Es sind keine oder nur wenige andere Stellen einzuschalten.

- Der Informationsbedarf zur Aufgabenbearbeitung ist gering und einfach.

- Es ist überwiegend persönlicher Kontakt mit dem Bürger erforderlich.

- Die Dauer des Bürgerkontaktes ist gering.

- Es handelt sich um eine Aufgabe mit Auskunfts- und Beratungscharakter.

- Die Diskussionsergebnisse bildeten die Grundlage für die Konstruktion und für das geplante Zusammenwirken der Beteiligungsgremien.

Das Vorhaben wurde von je einer Projektgruppe bei der GMD und der Stadt Unna durchgeführt.

Für beide Projektgruppen wurde ein gemeinsamer Lenkungsausschuß eingerichtet, der das Vorhaben über die gesamte Laufzeit begleitete und als Beratungsgremium für den BMFT einen Beitrag zur Steuerung innerhalb des festgelegten Rahmens leistete.

Entscheidungen von besonderer Tragweite für die beiden Projektgruppen der Stadt Unna und der GMD wurden durch das Projektgremium getroffen, das sich aus dem Stadtdirektor der Stadt Unna und dem Vorstand der GMD zusammensetzte.

Um die Übertragbarkeit der Verfahren und der Ergebnisse des Vorhabens sicherzustellen, wurde ein Gutachterausschuß bei der Kommunalen Gemeinschaftsstelle für Verwaltungsvereinfachung (KGSt) eingerichtet.

Der Beirat der Stadt Unna bestand aus fünf Mitgliedern der im Rat vertretenen Fraktionen. Der Beirat wurde zur Beratung der Projektgruppen in kommunalpolitischen Fragen eingeschaltet. Der Rat wurde durch ihn über den Fortgang des Vorhabens unterrichtet und beraten, darüber hinaus bereitete er die Entscheidungen des Rates vor.

Durch die Mitarbeiter – Arbeitsgruppe konnte die direkte kontinuierliche Mitarbeiterbeteiligung während der Laufzeit des Vorhabens sichergestellt werden.

Der Bürger – Arbeitskreis wurde erst nach Abschluß der Ist – Analyse gebildet. Die Mitarbeit der Bürger wurde über eine Publikumsbefragung und über eine Bürgerumfrage erreicht. Der Bürger – Arbeitskreis begleitete das Vorhaben beratend während der restlichen Laufzeit.

Das Beratungsgremium war das Gremium, das am engsten mit den Projektgruppen zusammenarbeitete und folgende Aufgaben wahrzunehmen hatte:

– Einbringung von Bürger – und Mitarbeiterinteressen,
– Einbringung von Sachkunde,
– Beratung zur Lösung von Konflikten und
– Erörterung der Aufgaben, Ergebnisse und nächsten Schritte des Vorhabens.

Das Beratungsgremium setzte sich zusammen aus zwei Ratsmitgliedern, zwei Personalratsmitgliedern, drei Mitarbeitern aus der Stadtverwaltung, einer Bürgeranwältin und einem Gewerkschaftsvertreter.

Organisation von Partizipation

Das Projekt Bürgeramt hatte wegen der realtiv großen Zahl von Gruppen mit unterschiedlichen Funktionen und/oder Interessen eine vergleichsweise komplizierte Beteiligungsorganisation. Damit alle zunächst einmal ihre Interessen unverfälscht bestimmen konnten, hatten Mitarbeiter und Bürger ihre eigenen Gremien. Auf jeder Seite wurden Untergruppen gebildet, die z.B. auf der Bürgerseite unabhängig voneinander arbeiteten. Diese Gruppen wurden im Beratungsgremium wieder zusammengeführt.

Ist – Aufnahme und Ist – Analyse

Konzept der Ist – Aufnahme

Entsprechend einer klassischen Isterhebung erkennt man aus der Übersicht neben einer gewissen Vorbereitung (A) eine allgemeine Erhebung (B) und daran anschließend eine vertiefte Ist – Aufnahme (C).

Die Zielsetzung des Vorhabens Bürgeramt bedingte, die Erwartungen und Bedürfnislagen der Bürgerschaft (als das potentielle oder aktuelle Verwaltungspublikum) und des Verwaltungspersonals mit den Anforderungen an einen ordnungsgemäßen und wirtschaftlich vertretbaren Verwaltungsvollzug in Einklang zu bringen. Damit sind die drei für das Vorhaben Bürgeramt wesentlichen "Sichtweisen" und damit die Informationsbedarfe benannt. Die Vielfalt der Informationsbedarfe führte zur Vielfalt der Informationsquellen, die auch in sich heterogen sein konnten.

Es gehört zu den Selbstverständlichkeiten der Methodenlehre der empirischen Sozialforschung, daß sich Auswahl und Ausgestaltung eines Erhebungsinstruments nach der Untersuchungsfrage und den Merkmalen der Untersuchungspopulation zu richten haben. Immer dann, wenn die Population nicht auf die Untersuchungsfrage hin "zugeschnitten" werden kann, oder wenn es nicht die "eine" Untersuchungsfrage gibt, so wie es im

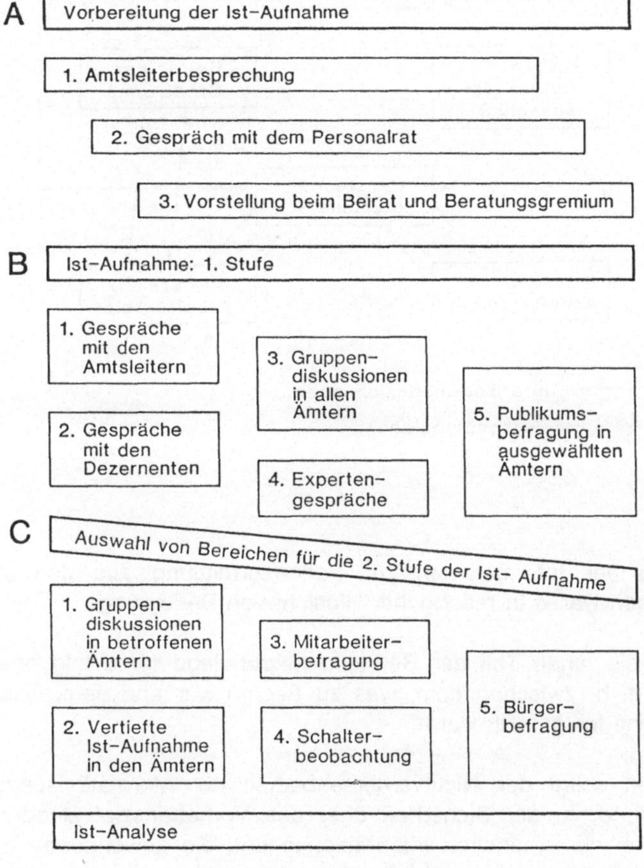

Übersicht über die Ist-Aufnahme

Vorhaben Bürgeramt der Fall ist, bewahrt allein ein Methodenmix vor voreiligen und verkürzten Antworten. Jeder Untersuchungsschritt liefert dabei einen Teil der vorhabensrelevanten Informationen. Die Ergebnisse ergänzen einander und relativieren sich gegenseitig.

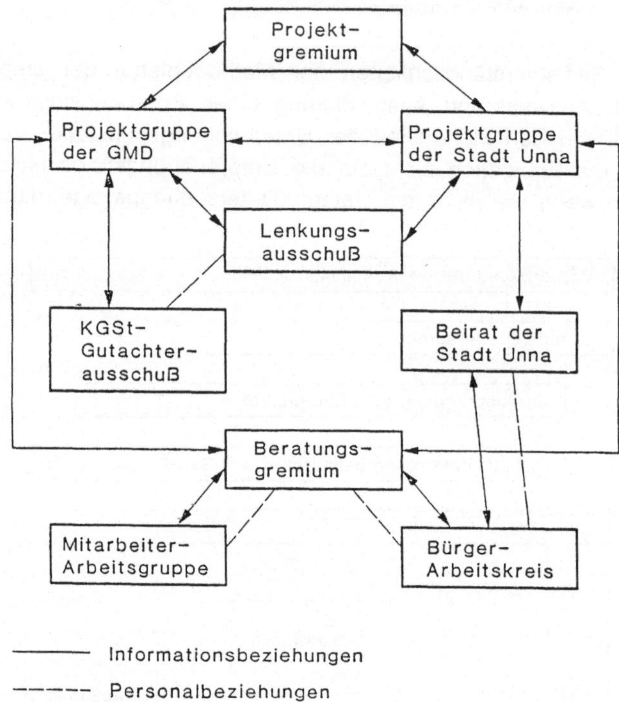

Die Aufbereitung der Informationen zur Bedarfsermittlung aus den unterschiedlichen Beteiligungsgruppen waren in mehrfacher Hinsicht von Bedeutung:

- So bildeten sie einen Teil der Beurteilungsgrundlage für Erfolg oder Mißerfolg des Vorhabens; d. h. zwischen dem, was zu Beginn war und dem, was nach Abschluß des Vorhabens festgestellt wurde.

- Zum anderen sollte der Nichtvorhersehbarkeit an Informationsbedarf entgegengewirkt werden; d. h. der Sicherheit über das Vorhabensziel stand die Unsicherheit gegenüber, ob die ermittelten Informationen und die gewonnenen Erkenntnisse, die aus bestimmten Blickwinkeln und Erfahrungen ermittelt wurden, mit denen der Betroffenen auch tatsächlich übereinstimmten.

- Wegen der relativ aufwendigen Informationsermittlungen und weil es unmöglich war, zum Zeitpunkt der Vorbereitung einer Datensammelaktion – unabhängig von Methode und Technik – alle im weiteren Verlauf des Entwicklungsvorhabens noch entstehenden Informationsbedarfe zu antizipieren, war es notwendig, die zu einem Zeitpunkt gesammelten Informationen so aufzubereiten, daß im Verlauf der weiteren Arbeiten entschieden werden konnte, ob diese Informationen zur Beantwortung einer offenen Frage beitragen konnten.
- Im politischen Raum – und der wurde bei diesem Vorhaben stark tangiert – wird mit Informationen relativ häufig parteiisch umgegangen. Fragen und Antworten, die den eigenen Interessen und Absichten abträglich zu sein scheinen, werden unter Umständen verworfen. Hier sollte eine gewisse Objektivierung der Informationen dem entgegenwirken.

Verfahren der Gruppendiskussion

Wird – wie in diesem Fall – praktisch die gesamte Verwaltung als mehr oder minder betroffen angesehen, dann sind intensive, zeitaufwendige Diskussionen mit allen Betroffenengruppen praktisch ausgeschlossen. In einer frühen Phase der Systementwicklung, wo noch Alternativen überlegt werden und die Zahl der einbeziehbaren Arbeitsabläufe und Mitarbeiter vergleichsweise groß ist, wird eine solche Situation häufig gegeben sein. Intensive Gruppendiskussionen werden ebenfalls ausgeschlossen sein, wenn der Akzent auf die Erfassung eines breit angelegten "Stimmungsbildes" in der Belegschaft gesetzt wird. Auch die Schwerpunktsetzung auf eine erste "authentische" Information eines größeren Kreises von potentiell betroffenen Mitarbeitern erfordert eine breit angelegte Durchführung. Läßt sich umgekehrt der Kreis der Betroffenen relativ eng begrenzen oder lassen sich sogar einzelne Probleme als besonders interessant aus dem Gesamtkontext herausbrechen, dann liegt eine zeitlich eher unbegrenzte Diskussion mit einer überschaubaren Zahl von wirklich aussagefähigen Mitarbeiter näher.

Diese Überlegungen zeigen, daß es keinen eindeutigen Zweck von Gruppendiskussion gibt.

Als erste Gruppendiskussion in einer Reihe zukünftiger Folgeveranstaltungen fanden in den Monaten April bis September 1981 mit 31 Gruppen (insgesamt 229 Mitarbeiter) Diskussionen über das Bürgeramt und über Bedenken gegen dessen Realisierung aus der Sicht der Mitarbeiter statt. Diese Diskussionen wurden von den Projektgruppen vorbereitet und geleitet. Grob gesehen, bestand die Gruppendiskussion aus zwei Teilen. Im ersten Teil wurden anhand von Schaubildern mögliche Umrisse des Bürgeramtes vorgestellt. Im zweiten Teil konnten die Mitarbeiter auf aus Ihrer Sicht bedeutende Schwierigkeiten und Auswirkungen des vorgestellten Planungsmodells hinweisen. Dieser Teil der Gruppendiskussion wurde durch 5 sogenannte "Auslösefragen" strukturiert. Die Auslösefragen waren:

Welche Aufgaben aus Ihrem Amt könnten für das Bürgeramt in Frage kommen?

Welche Aufgaben aus Ihrem Amt sollten nicht in das Bürgeramt übernommen werden?

Welche fachlichen, organisatorischen und technischen Probleme gibt es aus Ihrer Sicht für die Einrichtung des Bürgeramtes?

Welche Vorteile und Chancen vermuten Sie in einem Bürgeramt für sich selbst? Welche Nachteile und Probleme vermuten Sie in einem Bürgeramt für sich selbst?

Bei der Vielzahl der Nennungen (ca 1000) war eine Auswertung innerhalb der bereits blockbildenden Auslösefragen nur über eine sich aus den Nennungen selbst ergebenden Einteilung in Kategorien möglich.

Die Zusammenstellung vermittelt zunächst eine Art Stimmungsbild, in dem skeptische Beurteilungen und entsprechende Forderungen der Mitarbeiter überwiegen.

Gruppendiskussionen zu einem frühen Zeitpunkt des Vorhabens sollten nicht als exakte Erhebungsinstrumente angesehen werden. Häufigkeitsunterschiede in der Nennung sollten in einer Anfangsphase mehr im Sinne des Abbildes eines mehr oder weniger vorhandenen Problembewußtseins gedeutet werden.

Grundsätzlich sollte nicht davon ausgegangen werden, daß die häufig genannten Probleme auch die wichtigsten sind. Die häufige Nennung ergibt sich unter Umständen aus einer zufällig intensiveren Diskussion einzelner Probleme.

Bürgerumfrage

Mit der Bürgerumfrage, die als Teil der vertieften Ist–Aufnahme durchgeführt wurde, waren zwei Ziele verbunden:

– Die Ergebnisse der Publikumsbefragung sollten inhaltlich abgesichert und ergänzt werden. Die Ergebnisse der Bürgerumfrage sollten

  – in die Diskussion um das Soll–Konzept für ein Bürgeramt einfließen und

  – eine Grundlage für die nach Abschluß des Vorhabens vorgesehene Erfolgskontrolle bilden.

– Auf der Vorgehensebene sollten durch die Bürgerumfrage

  – die Bemühungen unterstützt werden, das Vorhaben Bürgeramt in der Öffentlichkeit bekanntzumachen

  – Bürger zur Beteiligung angeregt werden und

  – die Wirksamkeit der bisherigen Öffentlichkeitsarbeit überprüft werden.

Die genannten Ziele wurden unter Berücksichtigung von Aufwand und Kosten durch eine breit angelegte schriftliche Umfrage verwirklicht.

In der Publikumsbefragung konnten die Fragen unmittelbar an den Erwartungen des gerade bevorstehenden Amtsbesuches und an die Erlebnisse bei diesem Amtsbesuch anknüpfen. In der Bürgerumfrage wurde berücksichtigt, daß Personen mit flüchtigen, seltenen oder lang zurückliegenden Verwaltungskontakten genauso zu Wort kamen wie Personen mit intensiven, häufigen oder aktuellen Verwaltungskontakten. Ebenso wurden Personen angesprochen, die sich in der Kommunalpolitik unterschiedlich interessiert zeigten und mit deren Ergebnissen unterschiedlich zufrieden waren. Deswegen wurden in der Bürgerumfrage Erfahrungen mit Ämtern und Behörden genauso angesprochen wie Meinungen und Vorstellungen über die öffentliche Verwaltung im allgemeinen, die Stadtverwaltung Unna im besonderen und – dem Vorhabensschwerpunkt entsprechend – den Einsatz von Informationstechnik. Die Fragegegenstände sind als thematische Blöcke in der Abbildung auf der nächsten Seite zusammengefaßt.

Im Stichprobenplan wurde der Stichprobenumfang auf etwa 4000 Personen festgelegt, um bei einer erwarteten Rücklaufquote von 20% bis 25% den angestrebten Rücklauf von etwa 1000 ausgefüllten Fragebögen zu erreichen. Um bei diesem Rücklauf differenzierte Auswertungen gerade für die als problematisch erkannten Gruppen älterer Personen und Vorortbewohnern zu ermöglichen, wurden beide Gruppen in der Stichprobe stärker berücksichtigt, als es ihrem tatsächlichen Anteil an der Wohnbevölkerung in Unna entsprach (geschichtete Zufallsstichprobe). Die Stichprobe wurde auf Personen im Alter zwischen 16 Jahren und 75 Jahren begrenzt.

Insgesamt wurden 1190 Fragebögen zurückgeschickt. Unter diesen befanden sich 28 nicht ausgefüllte Bögen, in denen teilweise Gründe für die Verweigerung genannt wurden. Bezogen auf die 4336 Fragebögen, von denen angenommen werden konnte, daß sie den Adressaten erreicht haben, betrug die Rücklaufquote gut 27% (zurückgesandte Fragebögen insgesamt). Gleiches Antwortverhalten unterstellt, entsprach die Rücklaufquote von 27% einer Rücklaufquote von etwa 30% im Fall einer ungeschichteten Zufallsstichprobe.
Die Bürgerumfrage war nicht als Meinungs – oder Image – Studie angelegt. Trotzdem wurden überwiegend subjektive Einschätzungen verschiedener Aspekte der Verwaltungsorganisation, der Informationstechnik und Merkmale des Verwaltungspersonals in Form von Meinungsaussagen, Zufriedenheitsurteilen, Erwartungen und Vorstellungen erfragt.

Umfrageergebnisse gelten dann als zutreffend, wenn sie in die eigene Argumentation passen, sie gelten als nicht zutreffend, wenn sie die Argumente des Dikussionsgegners zu stützen scheinen. Bei dieser Umfrage wurde die Aussagekraft der Ergebnisse an prägnanten Beispielen unter den Gesichtspunkten geprüft: Was läßt sich mit subjektiven Urteilen

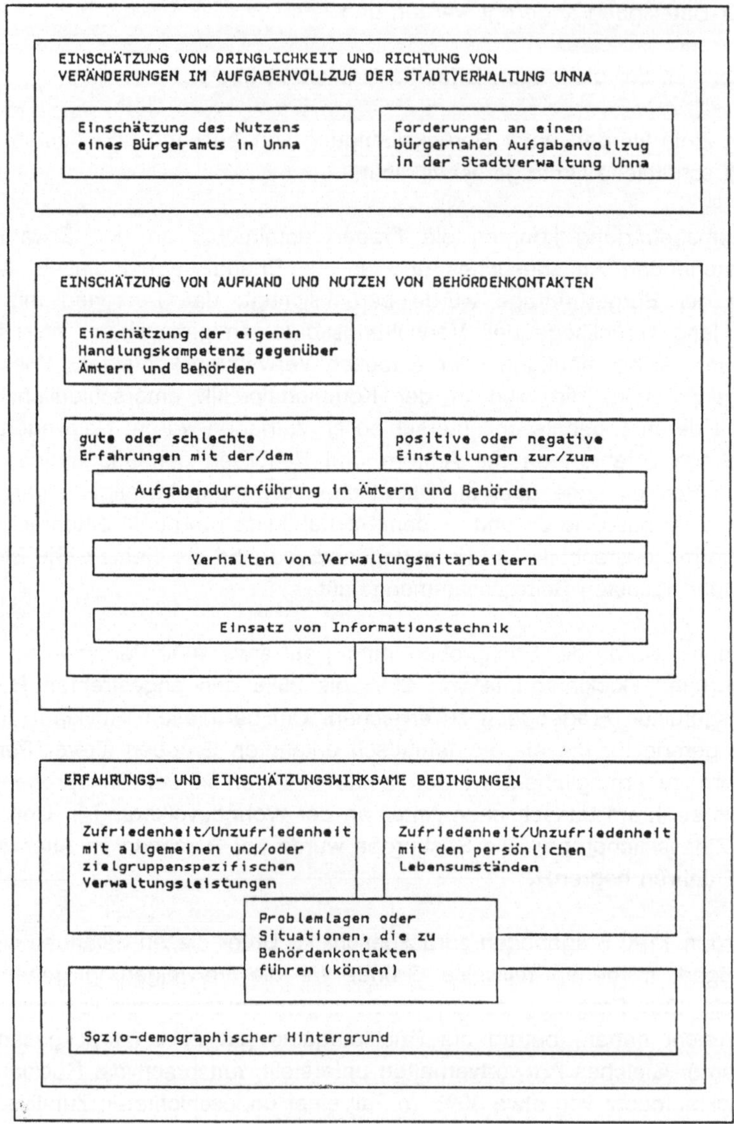

Themenbereich der Bürgerumfrage

an objektiven Gegebenheiten tatsächlich belegen und was läßt sich damit nicht belegen. Die Daten der Fragebögen wurden DV–gestützt aggregiert; zum Teil wurden sie in eine tabellarisch auswertbare Form gebracht, zum Teil wurden sie als freie Antworten und Kommentare thematisch gebündelt und als Leitsätze formuliert.

Die Ergebnisse der Bürgerumfrage wiesen auf einige Bedingungen hin, von denen der Vorhabenserfolg abhing und die zum Teil über den engeren Bereich des Bürgeramtes hinausgingen.

Beispiele:

– "Reparatur" bisher stark mängelbehafteter informationstechnik–gestützter Verfahren

– "Dienender", nicht "steuernder" Einsatz von Informationstechnik

– Personelle Einheit von Verwaltungszuständigkeit und Verwaltungsverantwortung

– Transparenz des Umgangs mit persönlichen Daten

Bürgeranwältin (Anwaltsplanerin)

Die Bürgeranwältin sollte diejenigen Bevölkerungsgruppen unterstützen, die aufgrund unzureichender Voraussetzungen weniger gut in der Lage waren, ihre Anliegen, Probleme und Interessen zu äußern bzw. durchzusetzen. Das Konzept der Anwaltsplanung setzte an sozioökonomisch ungleich verteilten Partizipationsvoraussetzungen bzw. –chancen der Bürger an. Die Tätigkeit der Bürgeranwältin erstreckte sich auf die Ermittlung von Gewohnheiten, Problemen, Barrieren usw. im Umgang der Bürger mit der Verwaltung, auf die Unterstützung der Bürger bei der Artikulation und u.U. der Organisation ihrer Interessen sowie auf eine Mitarbeit im Beratungsgremium. Dabei legte sie besonderes Augenmerk auf die Bedürfnisse solcher Gruppen von Bürgern, die von ihrer sozialen, materiellen, gesundheitlichen oder von ihrer in sonstiger Weise beeinträchtigten Lage her Probleme in der Wahrnehmung von Rechten und Pflichten gegenüber der öffentlichen Verwaltung hatten.

Auskunfts– und Informationssystem

Das Auskunfts– und Informationssystem setzt jeden der im Bürgeramt tätigen Mitarbeiter in den Stand, Auskünfte über Zuständigkeiten, Öffnungszeiten und notwendige Unterlagen bezüglich aller Aufgaben der gesamten eigenen Verwaltung und richtungsweisende Informationen bezüglich anderer Behörden, Organisationen und Vereinigungen des Einzugsgebietes zu geben.

Der Einstieg in das System erfolgt über eine alphabetisch geordnete Schlagwortdatei, die nach Angabe eines Buchstabens oder bis hin zum vollständigen Schlagwort entweder den Umgebungsbereich des Schlagwortes zur weiteren Auswahl anzeigt oder, wenn es sich um ein in der Datei geführtes Schlagwort handelt, direkt in die Informationsdatei verzweigt.

Die Inhalte der Informationsdatei gliedern sich in die Abschnitte

- Kurzbeschreibung
- Unterlagen und Besonderheiten
- Zuständigkeiten
- ausführliche Beschreibung
- Aufgaben – Erledigung
- Individuelle Beratung.

Dem Auskunftssuchenden Bürger wird ein Formular ausgedruckt, auf dem er die für ihn nötigen Daten findet, insbesondere den Namen des zuständigen Sachbearbeiters, welche Unterlagen er mitbringen muß und die Angabe einer Gebäude – Nummer, die auf der Rückseite die örtliche Lage auf einem Stadtplan anzeigt.

Fazit partizipativer Projektgestaltung

Organisatorische Änderungen und/oder die Einführung neuer Technologien können unterschiedlichen Zielen mit entsprechend unterschiedlichen Auswirkungen dienen. Ziel der Beteiligung ist es, eine einseitige Festlegung der Systementwicklung innerhalb eines potentiell immer vorhandenen Gestaltungsspielraumes zu verhindern. Dies ist eine klassische Aufgabe von Partizipation: Interessen verschiedener, durch eine organisatorische und/oder technische Veränderung betroffener Gruppen sollen in den Entwicklungsprozeß eingebracht und berücksichtigt werden. Im Ergebnis sollen breiter abgestimmte und damit bessere Systeme entstehen. Außerdem wird mit der Partizipation ein "Frühwarnsystem" installiert, das Lösungen verhindern soll, die später nicht akzeptiert würden.

Partizipation kann dabei nicht als ein immer und überall erstrebenswertes Ideal betrachtet werden. Angesichts der immens großen Zahl von Handlungsalternativen ist zumindest für das Individuum Nicht – Partizipation der Normalfall. Arbeitsteilung sowie die Entwicklung einer gewissen Routine sind als Grundlage für die intensive Beschäftigung mit problematischen Veränderungen der Umwelt notwendig. Funktional wird Partizipation bei der Systementwicklung – ähnlich wie bei anderen Prozessoren – vor allem dann relevant, wenn das gesamte Vorhaben mit großen Unsicherheitsfaktoren verknüpft ist. In "turbulenten" Politikfeldern drohen routinehafte Vorgehensweisen, wie sie auch die Systementwicklungen zum Teil kennzeichnen, an ihre Grenzen zu stoßen.

Einen besonderen Aspekt der "Partizipation bei der Systementwicklung" bildet die unterschiedliche Verteilung des projektrelevanten Wissens. "Technisches" und "fachliches" Wissen fallen personell auseinander. Während sich die Systementwickler in der Regel auf allgemein zugängliche Quellen des fachlichen Wissens beziehen können und/oder sich durch die Weiterbildung von "Fachleuten" zu Programmierern helfen können, fehlen solche Ausgleichsmöglichkeiten insbesondere für die betroffenen Bürger und auch weitgehend für die Mitarbeiter. Eine spezielle "Partizipation bei der Systementwicklung", die über traditionelle Formen der Beteiligung an organisatorischen Veränderungen hinausgeht, kann sich nur entwickeln, wenn es zu einer Zusammenarbeit von Systementwicklern und Betroffenen kommt. Die Unterstützung dieser Kooperation, zunächst in der Form von Beobachtung und Analyse und später in Form der Entwicklung von Hilfsmitteln, ist insofern ein wichtiger Bestandteil der Entwicklung von Partizipation als "Methode".

Literatur

Ehrenberg, Ute; Kaeten – Ammon, Hans; Tepper, August

Beteiligung von Bürgern und Mitarbeitern an der Entwicklung eines kommunalen Bürgeramtes. Zwischenbericht.
Sankt Augustin: Selbstverlag Gesellschaft für Mathematik und Datenverarbeitung mbH Bonn 1983. (= Arbeitspapier der GMD, Nr.69).

Dunker, Klaus; Noltemeier, Albert (Hrsg.)
Organisationsmodelle für ein Bürgeramt und deren Realisierung in der Stadt Unna.
Schlußbericht.
GMD – Studie Nr. 95, 18985, 412 Seiten, ISBN 3 – 88457 – 091 – 9

Liedtke, Bernd;
Einrichtung eines Bürgeramts aus Bürgersicht.
Bürgerumfrage Unna 1982. Konzept und Durchführung.
GMD – Studie Nr. 83, 1984, 136 Seiten, ISBN 3 – 88457 – 059 – 5

Liedtke, Bernd;
Einrichtung eines Bürgeramts aus Bürgersicht
Ergebnisse der Publikumsbefragung 1981 und der Bürgerumfrage 1982 in Unna
GMD – Studie Nr. 92, 1984, 125 Seiten, ISBN 3 – 88457 – o88 – 9

Tepper, August;
Gruppendiskussionen als Verfahren der partizipativen Systementwicklung. Probleme einer bürgerfreundlichen Verwaltung aus der Sicht von Verwaltungsmitarbeitern.
Sankt Augsutin: Gesellschaft für Mathematik und Datenverarbeitung mbH Bonn (GMD), Mai 1982. (= Interner Bericht GMD – IPES.82.02.83).

ENTWICKLUNG EINES DOKUMENTATIONSSYSTEMS FÜR DIABETESPATIENTEN

R. Engelbrecht, I. Kunze, J. Schneider
Institut für Medizinische Informatik und Systemforschung (MEDIS)
Gesellschaft für Strahlen- und Umweltforschung mbH (GSF) München

Einleitung

Die Dokumentation von Anamnese, Befund, Diagnose und Therapie stellt in der Medizin die Basis für das ärztliche Handeln dar. Deshalb war die medizinische Dokumentation auch das erste Anwendungsgebiet in der medizinischen Informatik. In den 60er Jahren wurde von der GMDS der allgemeine Krankenblattkopf (7) für die Basisdokumentation entwickelt. Die darauf aufbauenden Arbeiten, vor allen Dingen an den Universitätskliniken z. B. in Hannover und München, ergaben Systeme, die im Batchbetrieb liefen und auf besonders ausgebildete medizinische Dokumentare angewiesen waren. Außerdem fand selten eine vollständige Integration der Daten in den Klinikablauf statt. Hauptziel war die Verwendung der Daten bei Wiederaufnahme des Patienten und für epidemiologische Studien, d. h. für die medizinische Forschung nach Krankheitsursachen. Im Rahmen von Bundesprojekten wurden die Systeme BAIK (5, 9) und KRAZTUR (2, 8) entwickelt, die als autonome Lösungen auf Mini- und Personal Computern vielfältig im Einsatz sind.
Die Einbeziehung der Dokumentation in die klinische Routine blieb ein Ziel, das deswegen häufig nicht erreicht wurde, weil die entwickelten Lösungen nicht arztgerecht waren, d. h. von Ärzten nicht benutzt wurden. Es gibt spezifische Designprobleme (3) und Lösungsmöglichkeiten. Dazu gehört vor allen Dingen die aktive Einbeziehung der späteren Benutzer der Systeme in den Design- und Realisierungsprozeß. Dies ist in den letzten Jahren durch den Einsatz von integrierten Entwicklungswerkzeugen und leicht verfügbarer Hardware in Form von Personal Computern (PC) möglich geworden. Am Beispiel der Entwicklung des Dokumentationssystems des Projekts DIACONS für Diabetespatienten soll der Einsatz eines solchen Werkzeuges gezeigt und bewertet werden.

Projekt DIACONS

DIACONS (DIAbetes CONSultant) ist ein Projekt zur Unterstützung der Diabetesbehandlung im Krankenhaus.
Die Aufgaben umfassen :

- Medizinische Dokumentation

- Diagnostik- und Therapieberatung

- Ausbildung und Schulung

Im medizinischen Bereich spielt die Erfassung und Auswertung von Daten eine entscheidende Rolle. Insbesondere bei Krankheiten wie Diabetes mellitus entstehen im jahrelangen Krankheitsverlauf große Datenmengen. Diese Datenmengen müssen zur Verfügung stehen und ausgewertet werden, um eine aktuelle Differentialdiagnose zu erstellen und die entsprechende Therapie einzuleiten. Die Probleme der Diabetesbehandlung liegen im Monitoring und in der Einstellung des Blutzuckers der Patienten sowie in der Beratung und Schulung von Patienten und medizinischem Personal. Bedingt durch die Langzeitkontrolle des Diabetes spielt die Dokumentation eine wichtige Rolle. Für das Projekt DIACONS bedeutet dies, ein geeignetes Datenbanksystem zu finden. Dazu ist es für eine gute Planung sinnvoll, einen Prototypen zu entwickeln. Er dient der Informationsbedarfsermittlung und -analyse und liefert demzufolge wertvolle Information u. a. über Art und Anzahl der zu erfassenden Daten und Layout der Bildschirmmasken und Ausdrucke. Als Werkzeug zur Erstellung eines solchen Prototyps wurde das PC-Datenbanksystem DATAEASE (1) gewählt.

Das Entwicklungssystem DATAEASE

DATAEASE ist ein integriertes System zur Erstellung von Anwendungen und basiert auf einem relationalen Datenbankmodell. In menügesteuerter Form werden dem Benutzer Funktionen zur Erstellung und Wartung einer Problemlösung angeboten.

Diese Funktionen umfassen folgende Bereiche:

- Definition und Änderung der relationalen Datenbankbeschreibung und Bildschirmmasken
- Verknüpfungen der Relationen
- Datenbankwartung
- Listenerstellung
- Dateneingabe
- Datenausgabe
- Menü-Erstellung
- Systemverwaltung
- Hilfsprogramme

Datenbankkenntnisse sind nicht erforderlich, denn anhand dieser durch weitere Menüs genauer spezifizierten Funktionen (s. Abb. 1) kann der Benutzer in einfacher und schneller Weise seine Datenbank erstellen und verwalten.

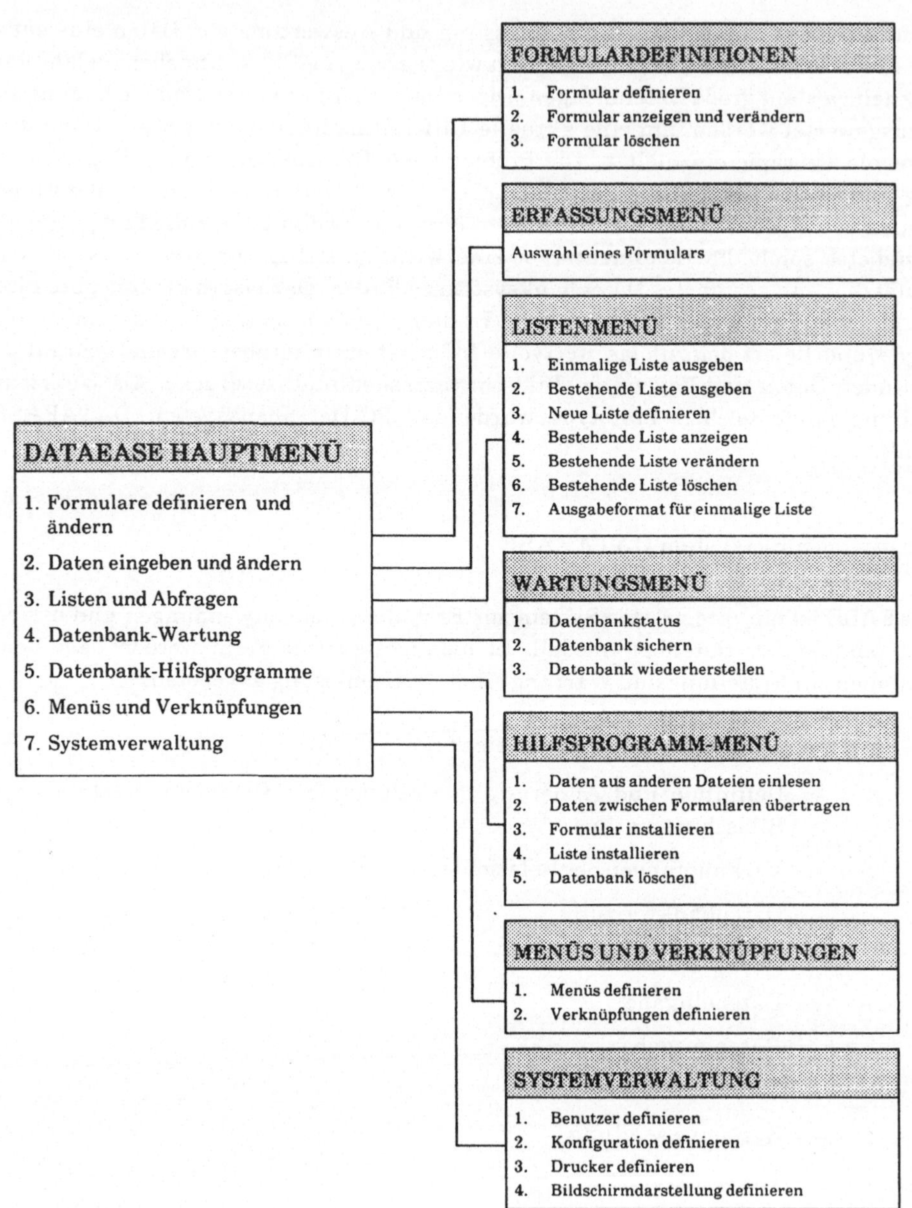

Abb. 1 DATAEASE Menüstruktur

Formulardefinition

Zur Definition der Daten-Relationen werden auf dem Bildschirm Formulare entworfen, die aus festen Texten und Ein-/Ausgabefeldern bestehen. Die festen Texte enthalten Informationen, die dem späteren Anwender die notwendigen Hinweise für die Eingabe der Daten liefern. Sie können an beliebiger Stelle des Bildschirms positioniert werden. Die Eingabedatenfelder werden im Dialog mit dem DATAEASE-System festgelegt, d.h. DATAEASE fragt nach Feldeigenschaften wie Datentyp, Feldlänge, Eindeutigkeit, Eingabezwang und Zugriff (s. Abb. 2). Für die Datentypen stehen folgende Möglichkeiten zur Verfügung: Text, Nummer, Zahl, Datum, Uhrzeit, Auswahl, Ja- oder -Nein-Feld.

```
FORMULAR BZ-Werte Stat
Bitte Taste EINGABE, LOESCHEN oder AENDERN betaetigen
     Feldname :                                 Patnrid
     Feldart :                                  Nummer
     Ist es eine formatierte Nummer ?           kein Format
     Maximale Laenge des Feldes                 5
     Restliche Fragen mit EINGABE, AENDERN oder LOESCHEN uebergehbar
     Besteht in diesem Feld EINGABEZWANG ? :               Ja
     Erfordert dieses Feld schnellen (INDIZIERTEN) Zugriff?:  Nein
     Ist dies ein EINDEUTIGES Feld ? :                     Nein
     Erfordert dieses Feld eine BEREICHSUEBERPRUEFUNG ? :  Nein
     Ist dieses Feld ABGELEITET (berech./such./zaehl./Vorgabe)?:Ja
     Ableitungsformel :                      suche Karteikarte patnrid


     Eingabe in dieses Feld VERHINDERN ? :                 Nein
```

Abb. 2 Felddefinition

Es ist ebenfalls möglich, eine Bereichsüberprüfung sowie die Ableitung des Inhalts eines Feldes anzugeben. Der Inhalt kann auf mehrere Arten abgeleitet werden:

- durch Vorgabe eines bestimmten Wertes

- für Text- und Nummernfelder durch automatisches Zählen ab einem bestimmten Anfangswert

- durch Berechnung aus dem Inhalt eines oder mehrerer anderer Felder

- durch Übernahme eines Feldes aus einem anderen Formular

- durch Tabellenauswahl

Die im Dialog festgelegte Felddefinition kann jederzeit sowohl geändert als auch gelöscht werden. Es besteht jedoch keine Möglichkeit, die Position des Datenfeldes über einen einfachen Befehl oder Tastendruck innerhalb der Bildschirmmaske zu verändern, sondern nur durch Löschen des Feldes und anschließende neue Definition mit denselben Angaben an der gewünschten Stelle. Bei bereits bestehenden Datensätzen hat eine veränderte Position keine Auswirkung, da die Zuordnung des Datenfeldes zu den Daten über den Feldnamen erfolgt und an der Definition nichts geändert wird. Die Änderung der Spezifikation für ein Datenfeld, wie beispielsweise eine Änderung des Feldnamens oder des Feldtyps, bewirkt die Löschung des bestehenden Feldes bzw. der mit diesem Feld verbundenen Daten.

Die Vorgehensweise, daß Bildschirmformulare vom Benutzer entworfen werden und vom System daraus die Datenbankstruktur abgeleitet wird, ist typisch für DATAEASE. Im Gegensatz dazu stehen Systeme (wie z. B. EASY SQL von Oracle und dBASE III), bei denen die Datenbankstruktur vom Benutzer festgelegt wird und das System daraus (recht starre) Bildschirmmasken als Benutzerschnittstelle generiert.

Listenerstellung

Eine zweite Darstellungsmöglichkeit für die Relation ist die Liste. Durch die Selektionsmöglichkeit von Datensätzen können Verarbeitungen auf eine bestimmte Gruppe von Daten bezogen werden. Zur Analyse können Berechnungen und statistische Operationen herangezogen werden. Es wird interaktiv ein SQL-ähnliches Abfrage-Statement erstellt.

Datenerfassung

Datensätze werden mit Hilfe der vorher definierten Formulare eingegeben. Jedes Formular ist die Darstellung einer Relation im Datenmodell. Für die Ein-/Ausgabefelder werden bestimmte Wertebereiche festgelegt. Die Relation ist eine Teilmenge des Kreuzprodukts dieser Wertebereiche. Ein über den Bildschirm eingegebener Datensatz bildet ein Tupel der Relation. Die Beziehung zwischen Relationen wird erst durch Verknüpfungen festgelegt.

Verknüpfungen

Verknüpfungen werden benutzt, um Beziehungen zwischen Relationen herzustellen. Sie werden durch gleiche Attribute in verschiedenen Relationen ausgedrückt. Auf diese Art können in den Formularen Daten aus anderen Formularen automatisch übernommen werden. Ebenso wird die Verbindung hergestellt zwischen den Listen und den Relationen.

Menüs

Mit DATAEASE kann der Benutzer eigene Menüs erstellen, die in gleicher Weise wie die von DATAEASE bereitgestellten Standard-System-Menüs arbeiten. Die erstellten Formulare und Listen können dann direkt aufgerufen werden unter Umgehung der von DATAEASE zur Verfügung gestellten Menüs. Es können andere Programme und Betriebssystembefehle sowie Dienstprogramme oder Datenbank-Pflegeprogramme durch Menü-Auswahl aufgerufen werden. Die Menü-Organisation kann sich über mehrere Ebenen erstrecken. Es ist möglich, spezielle Menüs auf die Benutzer und ihre Anwendung zuzuschneiden. Durch verschiedene Zugriffsberechtigungen kann man zwischen Gruppen von Anwendern unterscheiden.

Datenbankwartung

Die Datenbank besteht aus den Relationen und ihren Verknüpfungen. Der Benutzer kann DATAEASE nach dem gesamten Status der Datenbank abfragen und Informationen über alle Relationen in der Datenbank ausdrucken. Weiterhin steht ihm eine Funktion zur Sicherung der Datenbestände sowie zur Wiederherstellung gesicherter Daten zur Verfügung.

Systemverwaltung

Für jede Datenbank, die von DATAEASE bearbeitet wird, existiert eine Liste von Benutzern. Die Benutzerdaten umfassen Name, Passwort, Zugriffsberechtigung und den Namen des Startmenüs, das dem jeweiligen Benutzer bei Aufruf der Datenbank gezeigt wird. Weiterhin gibt es Funktionen, um Konfiguration, Drucker und Bildschirmdarstellung zu definieren.

Hilfsprogramme

Diese Programme unterstützen den Benutzer bei der Übernahme von fremden Datenbeständen in die Datenbank, der Installation von Formularen und Listen in andere DATAEASE-Datenbanken und der Übertragung von Daten zwischen verschiedenen Relationen einer Datenbank.

Informations- und Kommunikationsbedarf

Im Rahmen des Projekts DIACONS wurde ein Prototyp entwickelt, der der medizinischen Dokumentation von Daten der Diabetespatienten im Krankenhaus dient. Dieser Prototyp ist als Teil eines Gesamtsystems zu sehen, etwa als Teil eines Krankenhausinformationssystems mit Patientenverwaltung, bei dem durch entsprechende Kommunikation und Steuerung für optimale Diagnostik und Therapie des Patienten gesorgt werden soll.
Bereits bei Einlieferung eines Diabetespatienten ist in den meisten Fällen eine Fortsetzung der Therapie notwendig, bevor Untersuchungen eingeleitet werden können und die Therapie eventuell geändert werden muß. War der Patient bereits in diesem Krankenhaus, stehen Daten über Therapie, Ausmaß der Folgeschäden und Zusatzerkrankungen in der Krankenakte zur Verfügung. Im Fall der Neuaufnahme muß bei Patienten, deren Diabetes bereits behandelt wird, die Art ihrer Therapie erfaßt werden, d.h. ob und mit welchen Medikamenten sie behandelt werden, ob sie Diät einhalten müssen oder Insulin spritzen.
Zu den Untersuchungen, die durchgeführt werden, gehören in erster Linie die Blutzuckermessung sowie die Blut- und Urinuntersuchung. Die Blutzuckermessungen werden direkt auf der Station zu bestimmten Uhrzeiten durchgeführt (in der Regel siebenmal pro Tag), die anderen Analysen erfolgen im Labor. Ein Anschluß eines Laborsubsystems ist denkbar, aber in diesem Projekt nicht vorgesehen. Neben den vielen Blutzuckerwerten fallen noch andere Daten an, wie beispielsweise Befunde, Laborergebnisse, Diagnosen.
Im Rahmen der Systemanalyse eines Informationssystems geht es in erster Linie darum, den Bedarf an Information und Kommunikation zu ermitteln. Der Informationsbedarf kann als Quintupel von folgenden Elementen beschrieben werden:

- Art der Information

- Umfang

- Verknüpfung der Informationselemente

- Ort der Entstehung und Verwendung

- Zeit.

Für jedes Element gibt es unterschiedliche Methoden der Ermittlung und Beschreibung (6).

Ein Beispiel für den zu beschreibenden Informationsbedarf ist die Insulindosis-Empfehlung für Patienten zu Hause, die mit subcutaner Insulininfusion therapiert werden. Auf Grund der täglichen Blutzuckerselbstkontrollen und der Therapieerfahrungen der jeweils letzten Tage wird eine der Kohlenhydratzufuhr angepaßte Insulindosierung errechnet und dem Patienten empfohlen. Ein Prototyp ist bereits auf Taschenrechnerbasis realisiert. Nachstehend sind die einzelnen Elemente des oben angegebenen Quintupels genannt:

- Meßwerte Blutzucker

- Umfang der Daten entsprechend den täglichen Messungen

- verknüpft mit Insulindosierung

- zu Haus, benötigt für Ermittlung der Insulindosierung

- täglich zu festgelegten Zeitpunkten.

Das System ist durch Evaluation auf größerem Rechner verifiziert.

Wichtig ist neben der statischen Beschreibung der Information auch deren Weiterverwendung, angefangen bei der Eingabeprüfung und Abspeicherung in der Datenbank, über das Retrieval bis hin zur Präsentation. Desgleichen ist der Kommunikationsbedarf zu ermitteln, wobei Kommunikation als Transport von Information zwischen

- Orten, z.B. Station, Krankenhäuser

- Personen, z.B. Pflegedienst, Ärzte

- Funktionen, z.B. Verwaltung, Pflege

definiert ist. Die Kommunikation läßt sich als Matrix der Kommunikationspartner darstellen (4). Beispielsweise wird bei der Matrix Funktionen-Funktionen der Informationsbedarf der einzelnen Funktionen beschrieben und die Kommunikation durch Beschreibung der Aktion und des Informationskanals dargestellt.
Typische Informationsquellen im Krankenhaus sind die Labors und andere zentrale Service-Einrichtungen. Im Falle eines Diabetespatienten entstehen Laborwerte im klinisch-chemischen Labor und in den Stationslabors. Diese Werte gelangen über Datenleitung auf Stationsdrucker, wo sie ausgedruckt und in die Krankengeschichte einsortiert werden. Die Konsultationsbefunde anderer Fachdisziplinen (Retinopathie, Angiologie, ...) werden als Original in die Krankenakte eingeheftet. Zur Beurteilung des Zustandes des Patienten und seiner weiteren Behandlung werden beide Informationen gemeinsam herangezogen.
Der entwickelte Prototyp enthält diese Information und liefert somit ein klinisches Gesamtbild des Patienten. Er mißt also einerseits das Informationsaufkommen und durch das Retrieval des Arztes andererseits den Bedarf an Information. Die Information wird interaktiv und in Form von Listen wieder zur Verfügung gestellt. Dabei kann davon ausgegangen werden, daß jede (in Service) entstehende Information vom Arzt benötigt wird, da er die Untersuchungen und Konsultationen angefordert hat. Im Rahmen eines Krankenhauskommunikationskonzepts läßt sich so über die Anforderung von Leistungen *ein* Teil des Bedarfs an Information messen. Der *andere* leitet sich aus Beobachtungen und Ermittlungen, aus angeordneten Therapien und Therapiekontrollen ab, die jene Personen durchführen, die direkt an der Behandlung des Patienten beteiligt sind, nämlich Arzt und

Schwester. Ferner wird der gesamte Bedarf an Information bzw. deren Speicherung durch die Dokumentationspflicht des Arztes festgelegt, wobei es vor allem auch die Kriterien für die Dauer der Aufbewahrung der Information (in einzelnen Fällen bis zu 30 Jahren) zu beachten gilt. Durch die angewandten Verfahren der Untersuchung und der Therapie sind die Datenstrukturen im wesentlichen festgelegt. Es geht also darum, sie im Detail zu beschreiben, ihre Häufigkeiten zu ermitteln, wieviel große Blutbilder etwa pro Patient und Aufenthalt auftreten können, und sie in ein Datenbankdesign und Design von Beratungskomponenten eines Diabetes-Konsultationssystems (DIACONS) einzubringen.

Mit dem entwickelten Prototyp soll ebenfalls die Akzeptanz und die Durchführbarkeit eines solchen Systems getestet werden. Unter anderem geht es dabei um eine sinnvolle Bildschirmaufteilung und eine Menüsteuerung, die es dem Krankenhauspersonal erlaubt, in einfacher und bequemer Weise das System zu bedienen.

Entwicklung des Prototyps mit DATAEASE

Der Prototyp wurde interaktiv über mehrere Schritte entwickelt. Die Systemerstellung erfolgte hauptsächlich im MEDIS-Institut, während die Besprechungen im Krankenhaus Bogenhausen, dem späteren Einsatzort, stattfinden mußten.

Ausgangspunkt waren die von einem Stationsarzt vorgeschlagenen Erfassungsformulare mit Personendaten, anamnestischen Daten, Daten über Arztbesuche, Therapiekontrolle, Blutzuckerwerte sowie Daten zu den Spätkomplikationen.
Entsprechend der Vorlage wurden zuerst drei Formulare erstellt:

- das Formular ''Karteikarte''
  mit Personendaten, anamnestischen Daten über Diabetestyp und Therapie
  sowie Daten über letzte Arzt- bzw. Krankenhausbesuche

- das Formular ''Therapiekontrolle''
  mit Tagesprofil des gemessenen Blutzuckers

- das Formular ''Blutzuckerwerte''
  mit Angaben über Kohlenhydrate, gespritzte Insulindosis, Spritz-Eßabstand, usw.

Am Beispiel des Formulars ''Blutzuckerwerte'' soll die Vorgehensweise zur Systemerstellung demonstriert werden. Abb. 3 zeigt die erste nach der Vorlage des Arztes entwickelte Version.
Das Formular besteht aus drei Bereichen:

- Kopf mit allgemeiner Systeminformation

- Patiententeil

- Datenteil

Der Patiententeil enthält eine laufende Nummer, die automatisch vom System vergeben wird, sowie den Namen des Patienten. Im Datenteil werden die für die jeweilige Erfassung notwendigen Eingabefelder festgelegt. Im Fall des Blutzuckerformulars sind es Tag und Uhrzeit der Messung, der Blutzuckerwert, die Zeit postprandial, die Menge der Kohlenhydrate, die Dosis des gespritzten Insulins und der Spritz-Eßabstand.

```
Städt. Krankenhaus Bogenhausen      D I A C O N S     MEDIS-Institut der GSF
                                    Blutzucker Werte

Pat. Nr. : 00001 Patient


Tag       : 30/05/86
Zeit      : 17:00:00

mg/dl     : 215
Zeit pp   : 120

BE        : 6
Dosis     : 6
Spritz-Ess-
Abstand   : 20
```

Abb.3 Formular "Blutzuckerwerte" (1. Version)

Für die erste Rücksprache mit dem Arzt wurde ein Ausdruck der Bildschirmmasken vorbereitet, um zu klären, ob die von ihm vorgeschlagenen Erfassungsformulare richtig dargestellt wurden. Dabei stellte sich heraus, daß die beiden Formulare "Therapiekontrolle" und "Blutzuckerwerte" nicht den Vorstellungen des Arztes entsprachen. Der Grund lag darin, daß einige Angaben, wie etwa das Tagesprofil, nicht als Eingabe gedacht waren, sondern als Ausgabe, d. h. als Liste. Aus den Vorlagen war dies jedoch nicht ersichtlich. Die Eingabedatenfelder wurden neu festgelegt, ebenso ihre Anordnung auf dem Bildschirm sowie die für die Felddefinition notwendigen Angaben über Art und Größe des Feldes bis hin zur Bereichsangabe.

Die Formulare wurden entsprechend der neuen Vorlage geändert. Das Formular "Karteikarte", das vorher aus drei Bildschirmseiten bestand und anamnestische Daten enthielt, wurde auf eine Seite reduziert, die nur noch die Personendaten enthielt. Für die anamnestischen Daten über Diabetestyp und Therapie, die sich häufiger ändern, wurde ein eigenes Formular eingerichtet.
Da der Blutzucker mehrmals täglich gemessen wird (meistens zu bestimmten Uhrzeiten), wurde für alle Messungen eines Tages eine Relation angelegt und abgespeichert, während in der vorigen Form des Formulars für jede Messung eine Relation angelegt wurde. Die neue Relation ist auf dem Bildschirm als Tabelle dargestellt (s. Abb. 4).

```
┌─────────────────────────────────────────────────────────────────────────────┐
│ Städt. Krankenhaus         D I A C O N S          MEDIS-Institut der GSF      │
│ Bogenhausen      * B Z - W E R T E   S T A T I O N Ä R *   20/03/87 16:29:45  │
├─────────────────────────────────────────────────────────────────────────────┤
│ Pat. Nr. :  00001  1 Is I                    Name :  E. Patient              │
├─────────────────────────────────────────────────────────────────────────────┤
│ Datum    :  31/05/86          RR1 : ___/___   RR2 : ___/___    Puls : ___    │
│                                                                               │
│   Uhrzeit       BZ-Wert      Zeit pp       Kohlen-       Dosis     Spritz-Ess- │
│   (hh:mm)       (mg/dl)      (min)      hydrate (BE)      (E)     Abstand (min) │
│   ─────────────────────────────────────────────────────────────────────────  │
│     2:___        199          ___           ─            ___          ──       │
│     6:___ (nü)   220          ──            ─            ──           ──       │
│     7:30         ──           ──            4            20           10       │
│     9:30         181          120           3            ──           ──       │
│    11:30         176          ──            4            ──           ──       │
│    13:30         220          ──            ──           ──           ──       │
│    17:___        210          ──            6            6            10       │
│    22:___        230          ──            2            7            ──       │
│     :            ──           ──            ─            ──           ──       │
│     :            ──           ──            ─            ──           ──       │
└─────────────────────────────────────────────────────────────────────────────┘
```

Abb.4 Formular "Blutzuckerwerte" (2. Version)

Im Patiententeil der Formulare wurde die Patientennummer neu festgelegt. Sie setzt sich aus vier Teilen zusammen:

- einer Identifikationsnummer, die automatisch bei Eingabe eines neuen Datensatzes hochgezählt wird

- einer zweistelligen Zahl für die Anzahl der Aufenthalte im Krankenhaus

- einem Auswahlfeld für die Angabe der Diabetestherapie und

- einem Auswahlfeld für die Angabe des Diabetestyps.

Diese Angaben werden bei Aufnahme eines neuen Patienten in dem Formular "Kartei-karte" abgespeichert. Die Identifikationsnummer ist als eindeutiges Feld festgelegt worden, und über diese Nummer sind alle Relationen verknüpft. Auf diese Weise ist es möglich, Daten aus einem durch die Identifikationsnummer eindeutig bestimmten Datensatz der "Karteikarte" in andere Formulare zu übernehmen. In diesem Fall werden nach Angabe der Nummer die restlichen Felder (Anzahl der Aufenthalte, Diabetestherapie und -typ) vom System automatisch ergänzt. Es besteht aber auch die Möglichkeit, sie wieder zu über-schreiben.

Das nächste Treffen fand einige Tage später wieder im Krankenhaus statt. Diesmal wurden die geänderten und neu erstellten Formulare am Bildschirm gezeigt, denn DATAEASE war auf einem tragbaren PC installiert und die Datenbank dort eingerichtet. Auf diese Weise bekamen die Ärzte einen besseren Überblick über den menügesteuerten Ablauf bei der Eingabe und über die Aufteilung des Bildschirms bei den einzelnen Formularen. Kleine Veränderungen konnten auf diese Weise sofort durchgeführt werden. Die größeren, d. h. aufwendigeren Änderungen wurden im Institut erledigt.
Etwa zwei- bis dreimal pro Woche fand ein Treffen mit dem Stationsarzt im Krankenhaus statt, um das Layout der Bildschirmmasken und die Erstellung neuer Formulare zu besprechen. Nach einem Zeitraum von vier Wochen war eine Version erstellt, die die For-mulare mit den wichtigsten Eingabedatenfeldern zur Erfassung und Listen für die Ausgabe enthielt. Im Krankenhaus wurde die Datenbank auf einem PC eingerichtet und die Daten

aus Krankenblättern übernommen. Dabei tauchten die ersten Probleme auf : die Auswahlmöglichkeiten für Eingabewerte bei einigen Feldern reichten nicht aus, Einheiten und Feldgröße bei Meßwertdaten stimmten nicht, Felder fehlten. Neue Formulare mußten ebenfalls erstellt werden, denn erst beim praktischen Einsatz wurde man sich schrittweise bewußt, welche Daten zur Dokumentation des Krankheitsverlaufs unbedingt notwendig waren.

Die Änderung der Einheiten sowie die Hinzunahme neuer Felder hat keine Auswirkung auf bereits bestehende Datensätze. Auf diese Weise ist es möglich, Änderungen durchzuführen, ohne daß der bereits eingegebene Datenbestand verloren geht.

Das Formular "Blutzuckerwerte" wurde nochmals umgestellt, da es dem Arzt wichtig erschien, die Insuline, die der Patient spritzt, und ihre Dosierung aufzunehmen (s. Abb. 5).

```
 Städt. Krankenhaus            D I A C O N S           MEDIS-Institut der GSF
 Bogenhausen     * B Z - W E R T E   S T A T I O N Ä R *   04/01/80 01:23:49

 Pat. Nr. : 00001 1 Is I                      Name : E. Patient

 Datum    : 30/05/86   Inswech. 9 RR1 : ___/___  RR2 : ___/___  Puls : ___

 Uhrzeit   | BZ-Wert  |Vela H(5)      |Vela H        |Insulatard H | Kohlen-
 (hh:mm)   | (mg/dl)  |Insulat.H(16)  |              |             |hydr.(BE)

   2:__       125                                                      __
   6:__(nü)   134
   7:30                   21            __            __               4
   9:30       139                                                      3
  11:30       103         __            __            __               4
  13:30
  16:__                                                                2
  17:__       212         __            6                              6
  22:__       178                                      7               2
   __:__          Anzahl der BZ-Werte : 6                              __
```

Abb. 5 Formular "Blutzuckerwerte" (3. Version)

Nach einer Gesamtzeit von ca. acht Wochen war die Entwicklung des Prototyps so gut wie abgeschlossen. Abb. 6 zeigt einen Ausschnitt aus der Menüstruktur.

Insgesamt umfaßt der Prototyp für die Diabetesanwendung

- 28 Menüs

- 20 Formulare mit insgesamt ca. 700 Datenfeldern

- 68 Listen

- 102 Verknüpfungen.

Mit Hilfe von DATAEASE läßt sich ein solch komplexer Prototyp sehr schnell entwickeln. Es ist zwar nicht möglich, alle Wünsche zu berücksichtigen, aber man erhält einen sehr guten Überblick und kann für die spätere Entwicklung eines Systems wertvolle Kenngrößen zum Informations- und Kommunikationsbedarf ermitteln. In einem sechsmonatigen Feldversuch werden bestehende Falldaten aus Krankengeschichten eingegeben und so der Informationsumfang pro Fall, die Vollständigkeit und die Benutzbarkeit des Systems getestet.

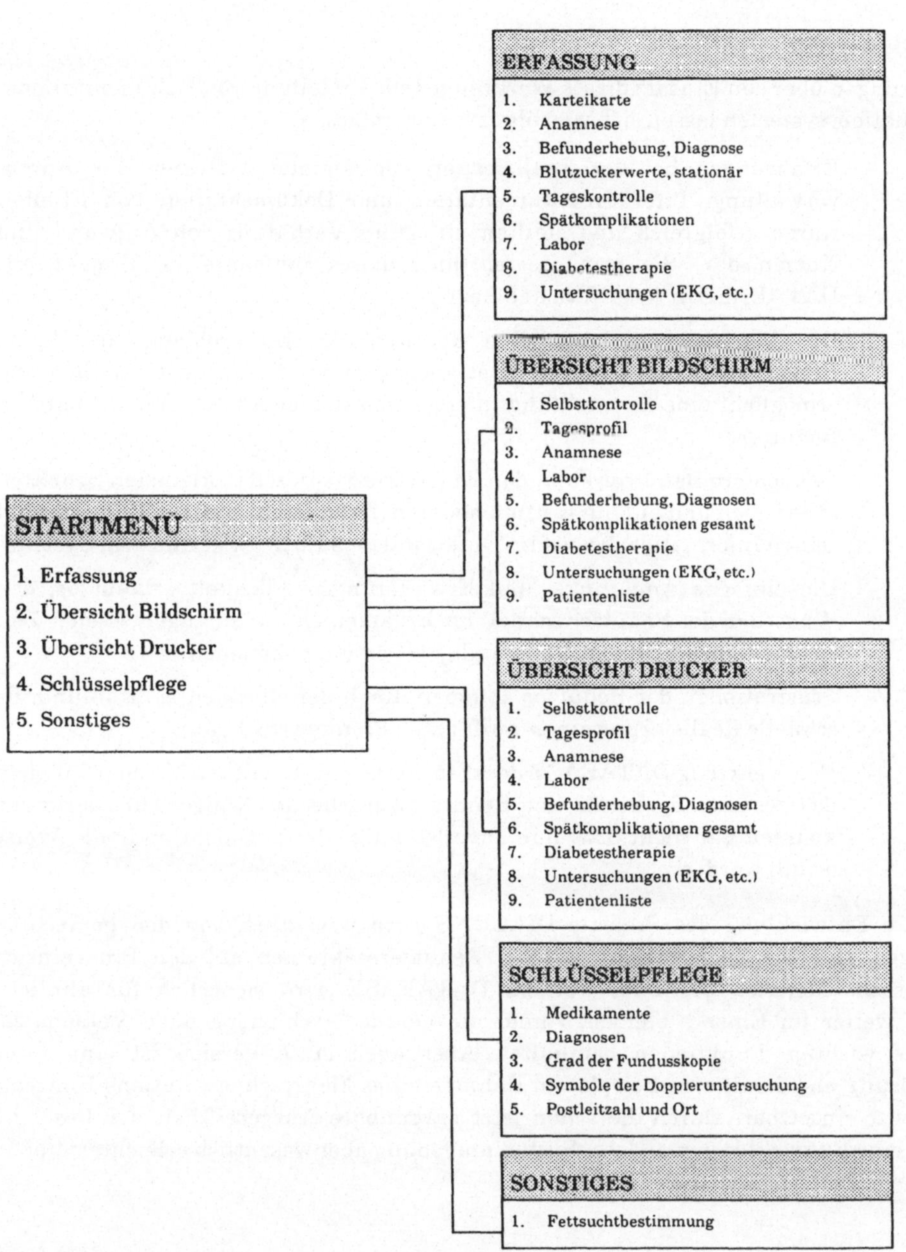

Abb. 6 DIACONS Menüstruktur (Ausschnitt)

Zusammenfassung

Die Erfahrungen über den Einsatz dieses Werkzeuges zur Erstellung von Dokumentations- und Informationssystemen lassen sich wie folgt zusammenfassen:

- Erfahrungen bei der Realisierung von kleinen Systemen zur Adreß- verwaltung, Literaturdokumentation und Dokumentation von Studien waren erfolgreich und stellten ein gutes Verhältnis von Aufwand und Nutzen dar. Sie ermunterten uns, dieses umfangreiche Projekt mit DATAEASE in Angriff zu nehmen.

- Das Werkzeug verlangt eine Spezifikation des Problems und keine Programmierung. Dadurch ist es ausgesprochen änderungsfreundlich und ermöglicht eine Entwicklung in enger Zusammenarbeit mit dem späteren Benutzer.

- Der spätere Benutzer kann den Entwicklungsprozeß in kleinsten Schritten miterleben und auf ihn Einfluß nehmen. Es ist "sein" System. Er beschreibt seinen Informationsbedarf im Dialog mit dem Entwickler und dem System.

- Die einfache Änderungs- und Erweiterungsmöglichkeit erlaubt es, den Wünschen der Benutzer schnell nachzukommen und in angemessener Zeit zu einer einsatzfähigen, vollständigen Version zu kommen.

- Frustrationen der Benutzer kommen durch den direkten Einfluß und die schnelle Realisierung eines lauffähigen Prototyps nicht auf.

- Das Werkzeug DATAEASE deckt in der augenblicklichen Version 2.0 nicht das gesamte Spektrum der Benutzerwünsche ab. Einige Anforderungen konnten gar nicht bzw. nur unvollständig oder auf nicht optimale Weise erfüllt werden.

Die weitere Entwicklung des Projekts DIACONS wird wesentlich von den gemachten Erfahrungen und den noch zu erwartenden Benutzerreaktionen auf den Probeeinsatz während sechs Monaten bestimmt werden. DATAEASE wird sicherlich für ähnliche Aufgaben weiter im Einsatz bleiben, zumal die gerade erschienene neue Version 2.5 zusätzliche wichtige Funktionen beinhaltet. Aber auch diese Version ist eine reine Einplatzlösung und damit zum Beispiel im Rahmen eines Mehrrechner-Stations-Konzepts nur begrenzt einsetzbar. Durch die schon jetzt erkennbare Ausgereiftheit der Problem- lösung ist eine Entwicklung in anderer Systemumgebung aber wesentlich erleichtert und in relativ kurzer Zeit möglich und sinnvoll.

Literatur

(1)   DATAEASE User Manual, M & T Software Verlag, 1984

(2)   Ellsässer, K.-H., Köhler, C. O., Wagner, G. : KRAZTUR - A Generator for Medical Documentation and Information Systems, Meth. Inform. Med. 20, 1981, p. 191 - 195

(3)   Engelbrecht, R. : Experiences in Designing Human Computer Interfaces for Doctors'
        Office Computers. In : Peterson, H. E., Schneider, W. (eds) : Human Computer
        Communications in Health Care, North Holland, Amsterdam, New York, Oxford,
        1986, p. 219 - 233

(4)   Engelbrecht, R. , Schlaefer, K. : Information und Kommunikation im Krankenhaus -
        Leitfaden zur Systemanalyse, ecomed, Landsberg/Lech, 1986

(5)   Giere, W. : BAIK Befunddokumentation und Arztbriefschreibung im Krankenhaus,
        Media, Köln, 1986

(6)   Hice, G. F. , Turner, W. S. , Cashwell, L. F. : System Development Methodology,
        North Holland / American Elsevier, Amsterdam, Oxford, New York, 1974

(7)   Immich, H., Wagner, G. : Basisdokumentation in der Klinik. In : Koller, S., Wagner,
        G.: Handbuch der medizinischen Dokumentation und Datenverarbeitung, F. K.
        Schattauer, Stuttgart New York, 1975

(8)   Köhler, Claus O. : Ziele, Aufgaben, Realisation eines Krankenhausinformations-
        systems, Springer, Berlin, Heidelberg, New York, 1982

(9)   Volke, M., Giere, W., Börner, M. : Rechnergestützte Erstellung, Dokumentation und
        Auswertung des Durchgangsarztberichtes mit BAIK : Diskussion zweijähriger Er-
        fahrung, 29. Jahrestagung der GMDS 1984, Springer, Berlin, Heidelberg, 1985, p.
        185 - 188

Band 98: Öffentliche Verwaltung und Informationstechnik. Neue Möglichkeiten, neue Probleme, neue Perspektiven. Proceedings, 1984. Herausgegeben von H. Reinermann, H. Fiedler, K. Grimmer, K. Lenk und R. Traunmüller. X, 396 Seiten. 1985.

Band 99: K. Küspert, Fehlererkennung und Fehlerbehandlung in Speicherungsstrukturen von Datenbanksystemen. IX, 294 Seiten. 1985.

Band 100: W. Lamersdorf, Semantische Repräsentation komplexer Objektstrukturen. IX, 187 Seiten. 1985.

Band 101: J. Koch, Relationale Anfragen VIII, 147 Seiten. 1985.

Band 102: H.-J. Appelrath, Von Datenbanken zu Expertensystemen. VI, 159 Seiten. 1985.

Band 103: GWAI-84. 8th German Workshop on Artificial Intelligence. Wingst/Stade, October 1984. Edited by J. Laubsch. VIII, 282 Seiten. 1985.

Band 104: G. Sagerer, Darstellung und Nutzung von Expertenwissen für ein Bildanalysesystem. XIII, 270 Seiten. 1985.

Band 105: G. E. Maier, Exceptionbehandlung und Synchronisation. IV, 359 Seiten. 1985.

Band 106: Österreichische Artificial Intelligence Tagung. Wien, September 1985. Herausgegeben von H. Trost und J. Retti. VIII, 211 Seiten. 1985.

Band 107: Mustererkennung 1985. Proceedings, 1985. Herausgegeben von H. Niemann. XIII, 338 Seiten. 1985.

Band 108: GI/OCG/ÖGJ-Jahrestagung 1985. Wien, September 1985. Herausgegeben von H. R. Hansen. XVII, 1086 Seiten. 1985.

Band 109: Simulationstechnik. Proceedings, 1985. Herausgegeben von D. P. F. Möller. XIV, 539 Seiten. 1985.

Band 110: Messung, Modellierung und Bewertung von Rechensystemen. 3. GI/NTG-Fachtagung, Dortmund, Oktober 1985. Herausgegeben von H. Beilner. X, 389 Seiten. 1985.

Band 111: Kommunikation in Verteilten Systemen II. GI/NTG-Fachtagung, Karlsruhe, März 1985. Herausgegeben von D. Heger, G. Krüger, O. Spaniol und W. Zorn. XII, 236 Seiten. 1985.

Band 112: Wissensbasierte Systeme. GI-Kongreß 1985. Herausgegeben von W. Brauer und B. Radig. XVI, 402 Seiten, 1985.

Band 113: Datenschutz und Datensicherung im Wandel der Informationstechnologien. 1. GI-Fachtagung, München, Oktober 1985. Proceedings, 1985. Herausgegeben von P. P. Spies. VIII, 257 Seiten. 1985.

Band 114: Sprachverarbeitung in Information und Dokumentation. Proceedings, 1985. Herausgegeben von B. Endres-Niggemeyer und J. Krause. VIII, 234 Seiten. 1985.

Band 115: A. Kobsa, Benutzermodellierung in Dialogsystemen. XV, 204 Seiten. 1985.

Band 116: Recent Trends in Data Type Specification. Edited by H.-J. Kreowski. VII, 253 pages. 1985.

Band 117: J. Röhrich, Parallele Systeme. XI, 152 Seiten. 1986.

Band 118: GWAI-85. 9th German Workshop on Artificial Intelligence. Dassel/Solling, September 1985. Edited by H. Stoyan. X, 471 pages. 1986.

Band 119: Graphik in Dokumenten. GI-Fachgespräch, Bremen, März 1986. Herausgegeben von F. Nake. X, 154 Seiten. 1986.

Band 120: Kognitive Aspekte der Mensch-Computer-Interaktion. Herausgegeben von G. Dirlich, C. Freksa, U. Schwatlo und K. Wimmer. VIII, 190 Seiten. 1986.

Band 121: K. Echtle, Fehlermaskierung durch verteilte Systeme. X, 232 Seiten. 1986.

Band 122: Ch. Habel, Prinzipien der Referentialität. Untersuchungen zur propositionalen Repräsentation von Wissen. X, 308 Seiten. 1986.

Band 123: Arbeit und Informationstechnik. GI-Fachtagung. Proceedings, 1986. Herausgegeben von K. T. Schröder. IX, 435 Seiten. 1986.

Band 124: GWAI-86 und 2. Österreichische Artificial-Intelligence-Tagung. Ottenstein/Niederösterreich, September 1986. Herausgegeben von C.-R. Rollinger und W. Horn. X, 360 Seiten. 1986.

Band 125: Mustererkennung 1986. 8. DAGM-Symposium, Paderborn, September/Oktober 1986. Herausgegeben von G. Hartmann. XII, 294 Seiten, 1986.

Band 126: GI-16. Jahrestagung. Informatik-Anwendungen – Trends und Perspektiven. Berlin, Oktober 1986. Herausgegeben von G. Hommel und S. Schindler. XVII, 703 Seiten. 1986.

Band 127: GI-17. Jahrestagung. Informatik-Anwendungen – Trends und Perspektiven. Berlin, Oktober 1986. Herausgegeben von G. Hommel und S. Schindler. XVII, 685 Seiten. 1986.

Band 128: W. Benn, Dynamische nicht-normalisierte Relationen und symbolische Bildbeschreibung. XIV, 153 Seiten. 1986.

Band 129: Informatik-Grundbildung in Schule und Beruf. GI-Fachtagung, Kaiserslautern, September/Oktober 1986. Herausgegeben von E. v. Puttkamer. XII, 486 Seiten. 1986.

Band 130: Kommunikation in Verteilten Systemen. GI/NTG-Fachtagung, Aachen, Februar 1987. Herausgegeben von N. Gerner und O. Spaniol. XII, 812 Seiten. 1987.

Band 131: W. Scherl, Bildanalyse allgemeiner Dokumente. XI, 205 Seiten. 1987.

Band 132: R. Studer, Konzepte für eine verteilte wissensbasierte Softwareproduktionsumgebung. XI, 272 Seiten. 1987.

Band 133: B. Freisleben, Mechanismen zur Synchronisation paralleler Prozesse. VIII, 357 Seiten. 1987.

Band 134: Organisation und Betrieb der verteilten Datenverarbeitung. 7. GI-Fachgespräch, München, März 1987. Herausgegeben von F. Peischl. VIII, 219 Seiten. 1987.

Band 135: A. Meier, Erweiterung relationaler Datenbanksysteme für technische Anwendungen. IV, 141 Seiten. 1987.

Band 136: Datenbanksysteme in Büro, Technik und Wissenschaft. GI-Fachtagung, Darmstadt, April 1987. Proceedings. Herausgegeben von H.-J. Schek und G. Schlageter. XII, 491 Seiten. 1987.

Band 137: D. Lienert, Die Konfigurierung modular aufgebauter Datenbanksysteme. IX, 214 Seiten. 1987.

Band 138: R. Männer, Entwurf und Realisierung eines Multiprozessors. Das System „Heidelberger POLYP". XI, 217 Seiten. 1987.

Band 139: M. Marhöfer, Fehlerdiagnose für Schaltnetze aus Modulen mit partiell injektiven Pfadfunktionen. XIII, 172 Seiten. 1987.

Band 141: E. G. Schukat-Talamazzini, Generierung von Worthypothesen in kontinuierlicher Sprache. XI, 142 Seiten. 1987.

Band 142: H.-J. Novak, Textgenerierung aus visuellen Daten: Beschreibungen von Straßenszenen. XII, 143 Seiten. 1987.

Band 143: R. R. Wagner, R. Traunmüller, H. C. Mayr (Hrsg.), Informationsbedarfsermittlung und -analyse für den Entwurf von Informationssystemen. Fachtagung EMISA, Linz, Juli 1987. Proceedings. VIII, 257 Seiten. 1987.